Contents

Note on Graphic Content ix

Introduction. The Paradox of Coal-Fired Democracy 1

PART I Forging (1880–1950)

I Civil War in the Coalfield State 17
II National Problem, National Obligation 46
III War and Peace 68

PART II Stasis (1950–1969)

First Interlude: Between Deep Time and the Future 95
IV Atomic Menace 117
V An Inherent Danger of Explosion 138

PART III Renegotiation (1969–1972)

Second Interlude: This Total-Energy Dream 173
VI Walk Out—Before They Carry You Out 186

VII If Letcher County Was a Pie ... 211
 VIII Jobs, Lives, and Land 237

PART IV Bounding (1973–1981)

Third Interlude: East and West 263
 IX Rights and Obligations 273
 X Revolution of Declining Expectations 296

Conclusion. Energy Citizenship In Transition 325

Acknowledgments 333
List of Abbreviations 335
Notes 339
Index 415

Note on Graphic Content

One of my core motivations in writing this book was to put the human toll of the U.S. energy system at the center of how we think about the politics of energy. As such, this book contains graphic descriptions of violence, maiming, and death. These horrific accidents and acts of violence tore lasting holes in families and communities. Most of the victims were not public figures. Because many of them still have living immediate relatives, I have not included any details of deaths that were not publicly available in newspapers or Bureau of Mines fatality reports. The names of those whose deaths are described explicitly in the text are included in the book's index.

ENERGY CITIZENSHIP

citizenship as flowing through the nation's energy system—what I call *energy citizenship*.

Coal miners never used the precise phrase *energy citizenship*, yet the term fits a persistent and dynamic thread of miners' own political thought. Following this thread, we can better understand how civil and social citizenship, which historians recognize as central to our understanding of modern U.S. politics, have been defined by their relationship to the energy system. The same coal that represented their power and through which miners pursued a wide range of democratic political aspirations—from civil and labor rights to workplace safety to environmental protection—also represented the democratic deficiencies of the energy system, which left energy citizenship's rights denied and obligations unfulfilled. Miners could see in the same seams of coal disregard for their lives, from both the coal company and the nation. They could see the risks of the nation's energy system, which they bore unequally: the threat of lifelong disablement and occupational disease; the loss of coworkers, friends, and loved ones; the destruction of the land they called home; and, always looming, the risk of their own deaths. As miners navigated the paradoxes of coal-fired democracy and forced them into the national political arena, they illuminated the intimate link between the country's coal-fired social contract and the violence of the mining workplace—violence that was not incidental to the larger energy system but constitutive of it.

That violence was concentrated along the coal beds that occur abundantly across the continental United States, from Texas to Alaska. While meaningfully comparable cross-industry statistics are difficult to come by for the early twentieth century, coal mines logged fatalities at more than twice the rate of the notoriously deadly steel industry, with its steam boilers, molten metal, and industrial machinery.[8] In the mines, explosions, collisions, machinery, and—most deadly of all—falling rock killed thousands of coal miners each year in the early twentieth century. That violence was especially concentrated in Appalachia, where the majority of the miners in the United States have worked some of the world's richest coal seams, stretching from central Alabama to northern Pennsylvania, and where the sources I used to write this book took me.

Labor unions and administrative reform did make mines safer across the twentieth century, but *safer* was a comparison against a horrendously dangerous baseline that left no mining community untouched.[9] Those safer mines continued to exact an extraordinary human toll, a fact captured by the persistent relative danger of the mines compared to other industries as the century progressed. By 1970, the two next most dangerous industries—meatpacking, well known for amputating injuries, and metal mining—registered accident severity rates at less than half of the coal industry, and the coal mines had accidents at nearly five times the national average for all industry.[10] And that was before factoring in the devastating effects of occupational disease, as the full scale of the black lung crisis had not yet come into national focus.[11] Miners carried the burdens of the nation's energy system even as increased electric intensity removed coal piles from everyday life and concentrated coal use in power plants, a shift that made the American dependency on coal harder and harder to see.

While the coal may have been physically out of sight, the questions Americans confronted about their energy system and the nation's political community emphasized coal's continued salience. How much risk—whether bodily, environmental, economic, or political—was acceptable in a democratic energy system? And, just as importantly, who should bear that risk? What did energy producers and energy consumers owe to each other, and how did they come to see these obligations as legitimate? Who constituted the proper community of interest in energy decision making? How should Americans evaluate the fairness of their energy system? And, perhaps the most troubling question of all, could an energy system powered by a dangerous and dirty fuel like coal ever *really* be democratic for all the people who were part of it? As Appalachian coal miners grappled with these questions between the New Deal and Ronald Reagan's inauguration in 1981, they effected their own transformation from a group living on the margins of the nation's political community into a uniquely powerful group of energy citizens, people who seemed to embody the aspirations and limits of the country's coal-fired democracy.

This is a book about the United States that unfolds in a particular place, Appalachia. It is not a regional history, yet the politics of region weighed heavily on the lives of the coal miners who lived, worked, organized, and died there. A combination of stereotypes and distortions have cast as distinct and apart a region that is deeply connected to the rest of the country through family ties, flows of energy and capital, the movement of people and ideas, and, of course, a shared system of federal government. It has obscured the wider country's understanding of the region's importance in processes of national political transformation. According to the historian

Ronald Eller, the idea of Appalachia has been marshaled in many attempts to ease national tensions over progress, modernity, and development.[12] Appalachia was a laboratory for development policies that were then exported elsewhere and a testing ground for Great Society programs, some of which resulted from coal miners' activism.[13] For decades, scholars of the region have also situated Appalachia within a global political economy, defying persistent provincial assumptions about the region's importance.[14] Particularly when viewed through the lens of energy, Appalachia belongs at the center of U.S. politics, not on the margins.

Appalachia is both a place and idea, invented rather than discovered. Its geography became visible only through a series of political, economic, and cultural processes of construction that created a single region out of a varied landscape of mountain ranges, plateaus, and valleys, each with their own geological, social, and political history.[15] That process intensified in the waning years of the nineteenth century. As the United States extended its continental empire to include overseas territories in the Caribbean and Pacific, a new generation of writers imbued with imperial sensibilities flocked to Appalachia. There, they found people they described as "contemporary ancestors" or emblems of the nation's "Irish problem," descriptions that revealed more about the author than about the people of Appalachia.[16] Behind their narratives proceeded a scramble for Appalachia's wealth of natural resources, one that tightly bound coal and Appalachia together.[17]

Coal has defined Appalachia in the wider American imagination, rivaled only by poverty—specifically, white poverty. Narratives of Appalachian poverty, present in scholarship, popular commentary, and political discourse, naturalized the extraction of the region's resources while casting its poverty as innate and pathological, as an inherent flaw of the people who lived there.[18] In making the Appalachian story one of white poverty, wider American narratives about the region also whitened and anglicized the way most people picture Appalachia, obscuring the long history of rooted Black, Indigenous, and immigrant communities who shaped the culture, politics, and social movements of Appalachia, including the movements in this book.[19]

Most Appalachian coal miners throughout the twentieth century were white men, but the development of the Appalachian coal industry and coalfield culture emerged from a diverse set of lifeways, work experiences, and organizing traditions—particularly those of Black miners, who negotiated coal-fired inequality's intersection with Jim Crow for most of the twentieth century. Two Black disabled miners, Charles Brooks and Robert Payne, were the first leaders of important reform groups in southern West Virginia. Bill Finley, a Black supporter of the Miners for Democracy reform movement, organized the Black vote to support the democracy movement in the 1972 election for the union's top leadership and ran for union office himself.[20] And Johnny Mendez, a Mexican American miner from West Virginia and a union organizer, signed his name to a federal suit in an attempt to force the Bureau of Mines to enforce mine safety regulations. Black, Chicano, Indigenous, and immigrant miners lived, worked, and organized in a world that usually imagined and represented coal miners as white, native-born, Anglo men.[21] Although examining the complex role of race and racism in shaping energy citizenship lies outside my scope here, I have read my sources attentive to this gap between how miners were represented and who they actually were. And drawing on the rich scholarship on Black life and work in the Appalachian coalfields, I consider the important interplay between coal miners' collective and individual political subjectivity as I examine how miners attempted to navigate the paradox of coal-fired democracy.

There are many histories of coal miners, but they have largely overlooked how miners, through their distinctive structural role and collective political action, have shaped the meaning of citizenship in the United States. Many scholars focused on individual communities, hollows, or coalfields in order to document their distinctive histories, cultures, and struggles. Mildred Beik and other scholars, often the children of coal miners, wrote about the communities in which they had grown up. Chuck Keeney, the great-grandson of the union organizer who led miners at the Battle of Blair Mountain, and historians like him are not just recovering history; they are also defending it from future destruction. This book is deeply indebted to their work of crafting narratives and identifying sources that do not merely reproduce outside assumptions about who coal communities were and that foreground the voices of coal miners, their families, and their communities in their own stories.[22]

A second thread of scholarship emerged from a different though often related intellectual project: understanding the character of modern class formation and relations through studies of industrial conflict and social transformation. Both in the United States and elsewhere, coal miners' efforts to organize unions, secure concessions from employers, and form sectoral bargaining structures shaped the contours of industrial democracy. Some of these studies focus on local or regional battles. Other times they examine wider questions of collective bargaining, labor organizing, and political economy. Scholars working on the later twentieth century often analyze these questions from a rank-and-file perspective, many of them having participated in movements to democratize the United Mine Workers or in efforts to secure occupational safety measures. Thomas Andrews insists that taking miners' agency seriously can help us rethink accepted narratives and received wisdom of modern American history. I similarly owe a great deal to these scholars who foreground the ability—and insistence—of miners to secure their lives and dignity and to imagine a better future in the face of daunting odds.[23]

These rich studies, however, mostly underestimate the importance of the nation and the politics of citizenship in the history of U.S. coal mining. Conversely, they also underestimate the importance of coal and coal miners in defining the nation's social contract. These studies have also given us a temporally uneven narrative, concentrated on the years between 1902 and 1939 and, to a lesser extent, the years between 1969 and 1978. Finally, they often consider coal in isolation from the wider energy system of which it was part and the political economy and practices of governance that it made possible. In the process, the significance of coalfield politics for broader questions of American political development has been obscured.

Lyndon Johnson's presentation of coal as the fuel of freedom and democracy would have seemed strange indeed at the turn of the twentieth century. In the Gilded Age and Progressive Era, coal was as much malady as remedy for a democratic country. Coal miners lived on the margins of the nation's political community. Politicians, commentators, and journalists often looked upon coal miners with suspicion or disdain. They doubted the capacity of miners for self-governance, portraying them as subversive radicals, unassimilated immigrants, racial and ethnic others, hillbillies. They believed miners lived in un-American spaces lacking most of the features of democratic civil society. And indeed, miners often found themselves subjected to the private despotism of coal operators, stripped of their most basic rights, and seemingly subjected to a different set of laws and governance practices than other Americans. Dependent as the country was on the coal these miners extracted, the growth of coalfield autocracy in a democratic nation presented a vexing problem for the era's reformers.

ENERGY CITIZENSHIP

Energy Citizenship

COAL AND DEMOCRACY
IN THE AMERICAN CENTURY

Trish Kahle

Columbia University Press
New York

Columbia University Press
Publishers Since 1893
New York   Chichester, West Sussex
cup.columbia.edu
Copyright © 2024 Trish Kahle
All rights reserved

Library of Congress Cataloging-in-Publication Data
Names: Kahle, Trish, author.
Title: Energy citizenship : coal and democracy in the American century / Trish Kahle.
Description: New York : Columbia University Press, [2024] |
Includes bibliographical references and index.
Identifiers: LCCN 2024012065 (print) | LCCN 2024012066 (ebook) | ISBN 9780231215442 (hardback) | ISBN 9780231215459 (trade paperback) | ISBN 9780231560795 (ebook)
Subjects: LCSH: Coal—United States—History. | Coal—United States—Social aspects.
Classification: LCC HD9540.5 .K34 2024 (print) | LCC HD9540.5 (ebook) | DDC 338.2/7240973—dc23/eng/20240503

Cover design: Elliott S. Cairns
Cover image: West Virginia and Regional History Center, WVU Libraries

For every worker killed by the quest for cheap energy

Introduction

The Paradox of Coal-Fired Democracy

The history of the modern United States is the history of coal. President Lyndon B. Johnson affirmed as much when he declared National Coal Week in 1967: "It is essential to our national well-being," he proclaimed, "that this great natural resource, which has meant much to our history, continue to play a significant role in the development of America's tomorrow." Coal, Johnson understood, represented a critical energy source for the United States. At different points in the nation's history, coal powered steam engines, smelted iron, warmed homes, and generated electricity. These examples, situated in the broader story of conquest and progress, reveal transformations of energy as a form of political power. Coal-fired steam engines "conquered our rivers and pushed our frontier westward." Coal-fired blast furnaces powered the American economy's rise to global dominance. Energy-intensive, all-electric living undergirded the United States' Cold War narrative of capitalist abundance. To Johnson, coal was the cornerstone of American democracy: "It fired—and is still firing—the furnaces of freedom."[1] This declaration stood in a decades-long tradition of similar remarks by American politicians and administrators, a form of political rhetoric familiar to Americans' ears. Johnson's proclamation was intended to convey strength, to make visible the importance of the country's most abundant fossil fuel in powering a particular brand of Cold War liberalism, and to infuse a longer story about the rise of U.S. global dominance with a vein of geological inevitability—manifest destiny reimagined for the American Century.

Yet that same statement inadvertently hinted at the fragility of a democracy powered by coal. Freedom's furnace could run cold should the coal run out. The coal-fired freedoms Johnson described were shot through with dependencies, not least dependency on the hundreds of thousands of miners who extracted that coal and who bore many of the burdens of coal production without reaping an equal share of the benefits of high-energy abundance. Johnson only alluded to coal miners in his statement, but his vision of coal-fired freedom rested on a paradox that he studiously avoided. The stable, democratic growth he imagined coal could provide was built on a series of spatial, temporal, and moral asymmetries. Coal-fired democracy was deadly. By 1967, more than a hundred thousand miners had been killed while working the nation's coal seams. Hundreds of thousands more had been disabled by workplace injuries or had died or were dying from occupational diseases, especially black lung, an umbrella term for respiratory ailments caused by inhaling coal dust. Surface mining and the dumping of mine waste had rendered vast stretches of the Appalachian landscape nearly uninhabitable. Although Johnson and other political leaders resisted publicly admitting it, the country's coal-fired democracy had also generated profound injustice and inequality.

Coal miners and their communities disproportionately bore the costs of the country's energy system, but they were neither bystanders to the country's coal-fired democracy nor solely its victims. Instead—and paradoxically—they had created it with their labor, with their political and industrial mobilization, with their deeply held commitment to democracy, and with their insistence on the value of their lives. As coal miners defined their place in the country with the fuel they mined, they also reshaped the meaning of U.S. citizenship, weaving energy relationships into the rights American citizens might claim—and the obligations they had to one another.

American democracy has been marked profoundly by its entanglement with coal. Between the overthrow of Reconstruction and the end of the twentieth century, coal touched almost every aspect of American life and politics, from home heating to assembly lines to military logistics.[2] The United States relied on coal to power its rise as a global empire and industrial power, to fuel the "arsenal of democracy." Even when coal vanished from most American homes, when railroads and ships converted to diesel,

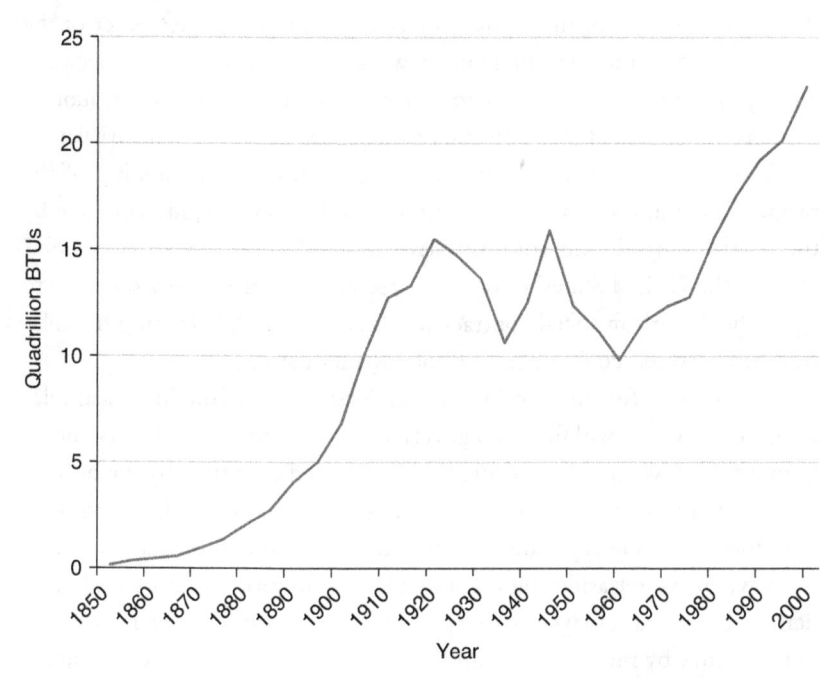

Figure 0.1 U.S. Coal Consumption, 1850–2000.
Source: EIA, *Annual Energy Review, 2009*, DOE/EIA-0384 (2009), August 2010.

and when the broader U.S. energy system shifted to a complex, multifuel system after World War II, coal remained foundational to the country's energy system.[3]

In the postwar decades, nearly every American continued to depend on coal, even if they didn't know it. Utilities burned it to generate the electric power that had become ubiquitous. American steel companies used vast quantities of coal to fire blast furnaces. The alloys they forged circulated throughout the country and the world as tools and machinery, as building materials and home appliances, and through the movement of railroad cars, ships, airplanes, and automobiles. And as the country's most abundant fossil fuel, coal underwrote the nation's energy system, which faced substantial global challenges: concerns about peak oil, Third World oil producers' efforts to shape international markets and sometimes to nationalize their reserves, and the painstakingly slow pace of commercial nuclear power development.[4] But coal could not exist as a fuel without workers mining it.

To say that the history of the United States is the history of coal, then, is also to say that the history of the United States is the history of coal miners.

That is the project of this book: to place coal miners at the center of the history of U.S. democracy. In doing so, we see anew the relationship between energy and politics by recognizing energy systems as sets of continuously contested and renegotiated political relationships. Energy systems are part of the U.S. social contract—the implicit, ever-shifting understanding of the proper distribution of a society's burdens and benefits, made concrete by the legal, political, and administrative order that expresses that vision.[5] During the United States' most coal-fired century, the years from 1880 to 1980, the American social contract was fueled by coal, balancing the relationship between coal miners and the broader nation.

This account further develops our understanding of the historical relationship between fossil fuels and governance by emphasizing that its underlying fragility was not something slowly revealed over time by the heating planet but a problem that coal energy regimes have contended with since the nineteenth century. The history of the modern United States changes form when we set aside the commonplace assumption that its coal-fired democracy was a relatively stable political form undone in the later twentieth century by increased recognition of coal's destructive environmental effects and the country's increased dependence on foreign oil.[6] As coal fueled the United States' energy intensification in the post–Civil War years, a distinctive form of coalfield autocracy emerged which many saw as a direct challenge to the country's democratic future. This autocracy was only dismantled after decades of armed conflict, labor organizing, and, finally, hard-won government support for the rights of miners. Alongside commodity flows and chokepoints, miners laid claim to political standing—not just political-economic leverage.

The United States' coal-fired democracy was fragile, unstable, and contradictory. The coal-fired social contract made possible its continued existence. The coal miners who forged, negotiated, and renegotiated that coal-fired social contract laid bare the contradictions of the country's democracy even as they attempted to resolve them. This is a book about how coal miners fueled American democracy and how they grappled with the fundamental tension at its heart: as coal fueled both democratic imaginations and administrations, the violence of the coal-mining workplace simultaneously eroded it from within.

Coal miners left indelible marks on the United States' laws, practices of governance, and political imagination as they fueled the nation's energy system and navigated working at its deadly fulcrum.[7] Some of these marks, like the 1933 National Industrial Recovery Act or the 1969 Federal Coal Mine Health and Safety Act, are well known. Others, like the Bituminous Coal Conservation Acts of 1935 and 1937 and the Black Lung Benefits Act of 1972, have been largely overlooked. By showing how coal miners shaped these laws and their implementation, we can see how they participated in a larger pattern of lawmaking, statecraft, and regulatory administration. The United States governed its energy system largely by attending to the relationship between coal miners and the broader American polity. This history shows us that American democracy was not made against a stable backdrop of energy inputs. Instead, the struggle over what fuel would power the country and on what terms entailed a century-long struggle to define what citizenship would mean in an energy-intensive democracy.

Coal miners understood the paradox of the United States' coal-fired democracy better than anyone. They lived and worked with it each day. In working seams of coal, miners could envision the worlds of steel and light and power that coal would fuel. By the mid-twentieth century, they earned paychecks that allowed them to participate in the mass consumption economy. They could feel a sense of pride in the skill and strength, camaraderie and courage their work required. Most of all, miners occupied a distinctive place in the nation's energy system as the producers of the energy source that undergirded U.S. political and economic power and that made possible for many Americans a standard of living that would have been unthinkable a century earlier. Over the course of the twentieth century, miners came to recognize how this position made them politically powerful as well as industrially powerful. The coal they mined represented an economic relationship with the coal operators but a political relationship with the country that relied on it for fuel.

Across the twentieth century, miners embraced their leverage over the political bonds that sustained and traveled through the country's coal energy system. The coal they mined forged political and moral relationships with other Americans. The relationship between miners and the rest of the country was negotiated and renegotiated through iterations of the coal-fired social contract, first during the New Deal, then again in the postwar years, and finally in the years after 1968. In these years of negotiation, coal miners and their union, the United Mine Workers of America (UMW), defined their relationship with the rest of the country. In the process, they also developed a distinctive understanding of the rights and obligations of

Many observers commented on this reality, though perhaps none with more clarity than Heber Blankenhorn, a labor activist, journalist, and occasional military propagandist. Writing in the mid-1920s, Blankenhorn believed coal's labor problems threatened the nation's future. "Coalbeds are simply the liveliest battlegrounds in the struggle for power in American life," he wrote.[24] That was an astonishing statement to write in the winter of 1924, as the country reeled from years of postwar violence; rising xenophobia, racist massacres from Tulsa, Oklahoma, to Rosewood, Florida; and the death of President Harding and the posthumous exposure of the depths of his administration's corruption.

But as Blankenhorn saw it, the country stood at a historical crossroads, not unlike the one it had found itself in a century earlier as the growth of the U.S. continental empire and plantation economy thrust the nation into sectional crisis. In response, Congress had enacted the 1820 Missouri Compromise, meant to balance power between free and slave states. Drawing on this history in 1924, Blankenhorn observed how the coalfields seemed intractably divided between democracy and autocracy and wondered whether it was "possible to legislate a 'Missouri compromise' in the coal industry."[25] His evocation of the Missouri Compromise conveyed how serious he considered the coal problem to be. Yet the Missouri Compromise, as Blankenhorn certainly knew, did not avert civil war. At most it delayed it, leaving unaddressed the moral rot that ate away at the country's political life.

Blankenhorn's next sentence seemed to recognize this fact, deliberately evoking Abraham Lincoln's famous 1858 speech to the Illinois Republican Convention, where he had affirmed, "I believe this government cannot endure permanently half slave and half free." Blankenhorn seemed equally skeptical that the American coalfields could power the nation if they remained two-thirds union and one-third nonunion. On one side, the pro-union miners demonstrated "democratic forces and habits that can hardly be prohibited," but on the other, autocratic coal operators violently repressed the miners' democracy with the support of the laws of a "proclaimedly democratic nation."[26] In Blankenhorn's words lay a palpable anxiety over the future of the United States' energy-intensive social, political, and economic order. The fate of the workers who mined coal was bound up with the fate of the country that depended on the energy and steel that coal produced. Blankenhorn concluded that for this very reason, "You can't keep a book on coal from turning into a book on democracy."[27]

Blankenhorn's somber observation stated plainly a truth that historians of the United States have too often left unspoken: the country's energy system is the key to understanding its political history. To make sense of how coal has shaped the United States and its democracy, we need a new history of coal and coal miners that does not take this national context for granted and that examines a period broad enough to see a fuller arc of political and energy system transformation. I have chosen to place miners at the center of that story and to extend my field of view across the United States' most coal-fired century, from 1880 to 1980. During this time, millions of people worked in the country's coal mines. Hundreds of thousands of them died from it. Coal may have been the energy foundation that gave rise to the American Century, but the specific legislation, jurisprudence, regulations, and administrations of state power that defined the relationship between the United States and its energy system had as much to do with managing the rest of the country's relationship with the workers who mined that coal as it did with the fuel itself. This insight reveals the administration of the country's energy system as a democratic society's effort to negotiate and sustain a social contract between those citizens who mined coal and those who depended on the electricity and steel that coal produced.

In particular, *Energy Citizenship* shows how the transformation that political historians understand as the rise and fall of the New Deal order was shaped by the miners who powered American liberalism. Miners shaped the practices of energy administration, regulations on environmental protection and occupational health and safety, and labor law and the structure of U.S. industrial relations, just to name a few. They secured a landmark union-controlled healthcare system and pension fund. And, critically, as they left these marks on the country's practices of governance, they also shaped the country's political imagination of energy as miners and their union made their case to the public with both words and deeds. They ran for office, testified in government hearings and court proceedings, traveled to cities to engage the public, and gave television interviews. In these critical decades, as miners forged and renegotiated the coal-fired social contract, they also made the case to the public that the prosperity of the postwar decades, the mass consumption economy, and key elements of liberal social policy all depended on the coal they mined. As a result, Americans had incurred a political obligation to meaningfully redress the inequalities produced in the process of powering the country. By the late 1970s, this obligation would be recognized by the Supreme Court, a decision that demonstrated how miners, in forging and renegotiating the coal-fired social contract, had created energy citizenship.

By the early 1980s, miners came to accept new limits on the idea of energy citizenship which they had themselves created. Faced with a hostile political climate and a westward shift in coal production, the UMW, which had been historically strongest in the east, lost some of its capacity to shape politics. During these same years, the emerging environmental justice movement drew attention to how frontline communities had also borne the burdens of the country's energy system, with its toxic emissions and runoff released by coal combustion and storage. In the decades that followed, the U.S. public came to understand coal's role in creating our present climate emergency and to recognize that burning coal is incompatible with a habitable planet.[28] Yet the persistence of coal and coal miners in national political discourse, especially around the elections during which Americans vote on the country's future, suggests the hold that the coal-fired social contract retains on the American political imagination. The idea that coal and American democracy are intimately linked but possibly fundamentally incompatible has a long history. That is the very paradox of coal-fired democracy with which miners contended throughout the American century.

PART ONE

Forging
(1880–1950)

CHAPTER I

Civil War in the Coalfield State

By 1921, some observers thought civil war had already arrived in the Appalachian coalfields. As the spring thaw set in, the social worker–turned-journalist Winthrop Lane warned that the "deep seated and continuous" struggle over power in West Virginia represented nothing less than a civil war that had been underway for three decades.[1] The most recent escalation in the simmering conflict between miners and operators began in the fall of 1919 when the United Mine Workers launched a nationwide strike.[2] Soon after, the UMW's new president, John L. Lewis, convened a mass meeting in Bluefield, a bustling coal city on West Virginia's southern border. As he addressed the gathered crowd on a mild January day, he declared the UMW's intention to organize the southern part of the state once and for all—an announcement that could not have escaped the attention of the Baldwin-Felts private detectives, who had regional headquarters in town.[3]

With the operators firmly entrenched in their opposition to the union, escalation seemed inevitable. The conflict burst back onto the national stage in May, when a group of Baldwin-Felts arrived in Matewan to evict miners from company housing. Within six hours of their arrival, a dramatic shootout ensued. Twelve people died in the hail of bullets: the town's mayor, two miners, seven Baldwin-Felts agents, and two bystanders. The gun battle captured the nation's attention.[4] Violence continued in fits and starts for the following year, reaching its zenith in September 1921 when miners assembled an army in the hills of Logan County, just north over the ridge from Matewan.

Armed coalfield conflict was a fact of life in the Progressive Era. The shootout in Matewan was neither the first nor the last such incident. To be sure, that conflict was not confined to West Virginia or Appalachia or even to the eastern coalfields—the Colorado Coalfield War and its 1914 Ludlow Massacre made that clear. Coalfield warfare also took place against a nationwide backdrop of violent class conflict and racist terror.[5] But the conflict in Appalachia was a protracted, multidecade event that could be traced from the Coal Creek War that erupted in Tennessee in 1891 to the Harlan County War in Eastern Kentucky forty years later and that ranged from the Alabama fields in the south to Pennsylvania in the north. As coalfield violence captured national attention in the years following the Great War, however, Lane cautioned readers not to miss the true conflict that underlay the gun battles. The real conflict, he warned, was "more fundamental than occasional strikes and more sensational, even, than the murder of mine guards and miners."[6]

Like most observers at the time and since, Lane understood the conflict as representing the larger social struggle between labor and capital.[7] As a Progressive, steeped in the emerging world of social work, he was deeply concerned with social justice and sympathetic to the miners' plight.[8] Lane's account also echoed longstanding concerns about how industrialization and wage labor might circumscribe Americans' capacity for self-ownership and, by extension, self-governance.[9] As he wrestled with the meaning of West Virginia's civil war for the wider nation, he provided valuable insight into how the country's energy systems transmuted coalfield violence into democratic anxieties far beyond the coal regions. As the Progressives wrestled with how best to reform the organization of state power to meet the demands of modern governance and the moral imperatives of a transformed economy, the questions Lane raised could not have been more salient.[10]

The drama of open class warfare shrouded deeper questions that, in some ways, would prove more difficult to resolve: could a coal-fired society govern "producing" and "consuming" regions with the same set of laws? Could a democratic society powered by coal distribute the burdens and benefits of an energy-intensive society equitably among all its citizens? Or would coal-producing communities be citizens of a different kind: subjected to particular kinds of risks, unique obligations, and the regular and structural curtailment of their rights? In other words, could a coal-fired energy system be democratic for everyone who was part of it?

Winthrop Lane insisted these deeper political questions about the relationship between the coalfields and the larger country raised "a fundamental question of democracy" that concerned all Americans.[11] Americans depended on the coal produced in Appalachia, but Lane insisted that coal was produced in distinctly un-American conditions. The Appalachian coalfields had its own "coal-mining civilization," which functioned as an "alien order imbedded in a democracy."[12] In Lane's telling, political life in the coal regions was feudal and paternalistic. It lacked all distinctive components of democratic society that Americans took to be constitutive of their way of life. There were no "independent citizens" or voluntary associations. Home- and landownership were virtually nonexistent. People did not live in towns "where people lead an inter-related, many-sided, and mutually dependent existence." Commerce was stunted rather than free, and perhaps, most shockingly, "the ordinary citizen has no property rights and can secure none."[13] The danger of coal extraction both resulted from and exacerbated these antidemocratic characteristics, which, taken together, cast the coalfields as a unique space of governance, one that was fundamentally unfree, as its residents had lost the ability to self-govern.

This "alien order" seemed un-American to Lane, but it was in fact a form of energy governance foundational to modern U.S. statecraft, economic growth, and everyday life: the coalfield state. As a pattern of governance, the coalfield state manifested unequally across Appalachia, more like an archipelago than a large, contiguous territory. Between the coal towns, small farmers eked out a living on the sides of the mountains and atop their distinctive plateaus.[14] Yet reports by much of the popular press allowed these pockets of autocracy to define the whole region. Resource extraction defined the coalfield state rather than geological features or state boundary lines.[15] Still, the coalfield state was a distinctive kind of place, organized by coal seams and coal camp social relations, governed through violence, identifiable by miners and outside observers alike as politically isolated from the rest of the country.

The same coalfield state that Lane identified as alienating miners from the American political community and that had prompted the American Federation of Labor leader Samuel Gompers to label the coalfields "Russianized" in fact formed the basis for the country's coal-fired energy system.[16] Coal production in the United States grew exponentially in the decades after the Civil War as commerce, industry, and empire increased the country's energy demands. Through coal stockpiles that appeared in every American city, through the global system of steam engines overland and on the sea, and through a form of domestic life that made coal a constant companion in the household labors of many, the coalfield state was part and parcel of the Progressive Era and its troubles never far from the public mind.

The energy intensification of U.S. industry and transportation in the final decades of the nineteenth century drew coal operators and miners deeper into the nation's richest and most rugged coalfields: southern West Virginia. Small mining operations had appeared across the region in previous decades, but industrial coal production in the area began in earnest around 1880 as the growing market for coal justified the difficult journey to reach the region's thick, high-quality coal seams.[17]

Southern West Virginia is a stunning landscape, defined by steep, ancient slopes dating back five hundred million years. The mountains appear soft and blue from a distance, but on closer inspection prove difficult to navigate. While the slopes of the state's coalfields had been spared carrying the weight of glaciers during the Ice Age, as water ran off the ice, it cut through the stone, carving the gorges, ravines, and other narrow water runs that define the landscape. In the colder Pleistocene temperatures, water lodged between layers of sediment, freezing and thawing repeatedly, fracturing the earth and sending stones tumbling down the hillsides, where they still rest today, clustered in groups like tombstones. Anyone making their way through the dense forests, complete with a thick green undergrowth that helps make the region one of the most biodiverse in North America, soon realizes that the land beneath them had been folded like cloth.[18] This geological legacy slowed the railroad's entry into the region. As a result, southern West Virginia's coalfields were the last in the East to industrialize.

The same terrain that had made the region so difficult to access conversely made the coal seams easier to mine—at least initially. Coal seams coursed up to the surface of the steep hillsides, requiring little preliminary excavation. The seams' elevations above the valley floors eased drainage problems without the expensive pumping systems required in other coalfields. Relatively small injections of outside capital quickly resulted in coal camps throughout the region. The new West Virginia coal, rich in energy, captured markets across industrializing cities in the eastern part of the country.[19] The population of the coalfields boomed as thousands migrated to the region from both within the United States and around the world to work in the mines. The collapse of Reconstruction, the white violence that swept across the South in its wake, and the myriad oppressions of the sharecropping system on the old plantations led many Black workers to leave for the Appalachian coalfields.[20] On the other side of the globe, in Italy and the Austro-Hungarian Empire, economic hardship and political tensions made the promises of U.S. coal company recruiters more appealing, and many more migrants made their way to the coalfields on their own.[21] It was a resource frontier in the interior.[22]

Although often depicted as an isolated hinterland, Appalachia's integration into the world economy had been underway for the better part of a century, a process fostered primarily by the export of raw materials. The very series of commercial exchanges that moved those resources out from the mountains to the nation's cities also extended the perceived distance between producers and the final consumer, making Appalachia appear more remote than it was.[23] The hinterland image was further reinscribed by journalists who flocked to the region as the popular press grew. These writers arrived with the frontier mindset that permeated American thought at the end of the nineteenth century, from the well-known Frederick Jackson Turner to Berea College's president William Goodell Frost, who described Appalachia as a place where the "pioneer spirit" had survived the closing of the frontier.[24] The coalfield state often looked more imperial than feudal or republican—a product of both the conditions in the coalfields and the changing political economy and energy dependencies of the United States and its empire in the same period.

The coalfield state's connections to the wider country and global economy were forged by people, commodities, ideology, energy, and violence. To see those connections, you just had to follow the coal: in the railroads it powered across the West, in the coking ovens and steel factories of Pennsylvania, in coal-fired military vessels that connected the mainland United States with its overseas colonies, the refrigerated commercial shippers that eased corporate imperialism for fruit companies, the steamers that brought coal-company recruits to the United States from Italy, the Austro-Hungarian Empire, and elsewhere. Coal-fired steam power was most closely associated with the "annihilation of space by time," allowing new modes and heights of domination and market integration.[25] The expansion of railroads across the West consolidated American control across the continent in the second half of the nineteenth century, while the use of coal-fired steamers increased U.S. military power outside of North America.[26]

Coal drove the transformation and growth of the U.S. economy as well. By the early twentieth century, the U.S. steel industry, sustained by captive coal mines, rose to global dominance.[27] American corporations like United Fruit deepened their economic and political entanglements with Central America as American capitalists used coal in new ways. They commissioned "purpose-built" coal-fired steam ships that refrigerated bananas as they journeyed from Honduras, Guatemala, and Costa Rica to the United States.[28] Together, speed of transport and temperature control transformed the banana from a luxury item into a harbinger of the mass-consumption economy, a process that deepened economic and political interventions in Central America by fruit company executives and U.S. politicians alike.[29] These political-economic changes marked the long and ongoing shift from an energy system radiating from plantations and farms to an archipelago of factories and mineral-extractive zones linked by rail and steam.

In the central Appalachian coalfields, the world that most new arrivals encountered looked much more like an imperial periphery than a part of the American democratic state. In fact, the coal town was rarely anything resembling a democracy. Most miners—and in some regions, like the new fields of southern West Virginia, an overwhelming majority of them—lived in company towns.[30] Company towns were a feature of nineteenth-century industrialization in the United States, its formally claimed empire, and the overseas outposts of its corporations. They could be everything from a conscious effort at social engineering to haphazard and hastily constructed boomtowns.[31] For most of the coal miners who lived in them, the defining feature of the coal company towns was that they were unincorporated areas under private company law, often policed by private guards or nominally public sheriffs and police who had built their résumés in the country's colonies and borderlands.

Company governance existed to extract coal and transform it into profits. And if the company towns were the heart of the coalfield state, the miner's pay slip was the fulcrum of this private government.[32] They featured deductions for everything from rent to funeral costs. The sociologist John Gaventa documented how the pay slip "symbolically fused" miners' identities "as worker, tenant, consumer, and citizen" and routed them

Figure 1.1 A miner picks coal out of a narrow seam.
Source: Photograph by Lewis Hine, Library of Congress, Prints & Photographs Division, National Child Labor Committee Collection, nclc 01077.

through company institutions, like the company store.[33] These institutions facilitated miners' often hand-to-mouth survival through the issuance of company scrip.[34] Company towns helped operators maximize their returns and extend company control. Unlike the nation's factories, which were increasingly the target of industrial science, miners retained a fair amount of autonomy over their work practices at the coalface. To make up for limited managerial control underground, operators paid miners by the ton—piece rate. Piece rate production placed many operational risks onto miners. While the companies ultimately translated everything into dollar amounts that could be balanced in ledgers, from the perspective of miners, those risks were both economic and physical.[35]

Miners' encounter with the nation's energy system began with a dangerous and embodied act: entering the earth's crust and cutting at the seam, blasting away walls of rock, often hearing the mountain groan around them from the strain. Sometimes they worked in spaces so cramped their joints locked up. Other times, their working places filled with cold water, and in winter, miners recalled sometimes their clothes would freeze once they emerged above the surface. They squeezed in between mule and rock, pounded wooden posts into place to hold up the roof. Around them, the coal exuded methane, which could explode if ignited at a high enough concentration, and the coal dust created in the mining process was as explosive as it was dangerous to breathe in. The ever-present, latent potential for explosions built danger into the work process, since miners often relied on illumination from open flames, and machinery and tools regularly sent off sparks while working. Both could be deadly in a gassy or dusty environment.

Above ground in the breaker rooms, young boys picked slate out of the coal. Legally, they had to be twelve, but they were often younger, sometimes abused by supervisors, even more often becoming disabled from their work as they lost fingers and arms and inhaled copious amounts of coal dust. The Pennsylvania Department of Mines lamented that the boys "frequently fall on or into the machinery, and are injured or killed."[36] Miners, from the coalface to the breaker rooms, took coal from seams compressed in layers of rock and dissected it to transform it into usable fuel. Labor relations, home life, and community organization all cascaded from that process of commodifying coal.

To make mining more profitable and keep miners in subjugation, operators often turned to coercion. The exercise of power often fell to the companies even in places where government offices existed to enforce national, state, or county authority. Winthrop Lane decried the deputy-sheriffs of the coalfield state—nominally "public officials" whose salaries were often funded by the operators.[37] Pennsylvania's Coal and Iron Police, established through acts of the Commonwealth's General Assembly in 1866, received state commissions but were paid for and controlled by the coal operators. They quickly gained infamy for their crimes: beatings, intimidation, murder, and rape.[38]

In Logan County, West Virginia the operators officially supplied $32,700 a year to fund the salaries of a group of deputy-sheriffs led by Don Chafin, perhaps the most notorious company-paid sheriff in the country. Behind the funding the operators openly admitted, even larger sums changed hands as bribes. In return, Chafin kept a "secret service" to monitor the county's miners and railways.[39] His deputy-sheriffs performed duties as requested by the operators, including "clubbing men who talked unionism." They "ran union organizers out of the county."[40] Just as often, miners and their family members faced private guards like the Baldwin-Felts, who brandished guns, made death threats, and evicted families without even the false veneer of state legitimacy.

The intensification of private autocracy in the coalfields stood in sharp contrast to narratives of electricity as a source of "wonder" and "progress."[41] But the development of the coalfield state and the electrification of the United States were linked processes, which only emphasized a fact that many in the United States who lived and worked on the margins of democratic governance already knew: political systems that appeared democratic in some contexts could be profoundly undemocratic in others.[42] In the United States, the relationship between the democratic and authoritarian aspects of its political system was in part organized and sustained through the organization of energy production, transportation, and consumption.

The coalfield system of private government emerged from and was enforced by interlinking forms of violence. Alongside the authoritarian power of company rule—which, ironically, was often enacted in moments of crisis by public officials—the structural violence of the coal-fired energy system could also be measured in roof collapses, dust and gas explosions, and other banally horrific "accidents" that killed thousands on the job each year. Slow violence was harder to measure, because it often went deliberately dismissed for years as aches, coughs, and being a little out of breath. The interpersonal violence featured in coalfield newspapers could be difficult to link directly to the coal seam, but upon close examination, it too revealed the organization of coalfield power.[43] And in the southernmost reaches of the Appalachian coalfields—Tennessee, Georgia, and Alabama—white politicians and administrators funneled men, overwhelmingly Black men, into convict leasing schemes. The convict leasing system aimed to develop the states' industrial economies through forced labor that was as deadly as it was dehumanizing.[44] This violence unfolded on the periphery of what most Americans conceived of as their everyday energy practices, increasingly concerned with adapting to electric power at home and work. Once the coal was on the train, headed away from the mine and the coal camp, that coal's ability to represent the social relations of extraction diffused over a geographical area that ebbed and flowed with the nation's imperial and commercial ambitions.

Winthrop Lane was onto something when he insisted that the shootouts and standoffs of the mine wars threatened to obscure a deeper and more fundamental story. Observers from outside the region may have cast these conflicts as spectacles that confirmed their belief that the miners who engaged in these uprisings were not fit to be part of the American demos, but the mine wars were a symptom of the coalfield state's authoritarianism, not its cause. Miners, for their part, understood these conflicts differently, as flashpoints that highlighted their political agency in an energy system defined by the dehumanizing violence of coal mining. Because although gun battles in the coalfields might have signaled a crisis for the American dream of coal-fired progress and empire, the violence of these episodes paled in comparison to the everyday violence of the coalfield state.

In terms of sheer human cost, nothing could compete with the mining process itself, which claimed thousands of lives each year. Bureaucrats and operators alike often blamed the victims of mining accidents, claiming that victims were either careless or ignorant of the danger. Immigrant miners found they were doubly blamed, charged not only with causing their own deaths but also with making the mines more dangerous for others.[45] This view of the mines' dangers was eminently self-serving for the operators and administrators who levied it. In suggesting danger emanated from the volatility of geological formations—weak roofs, gassy seams—they concealed how the violence of the coal seam reflected a regime of risk governance and commodity valuation in which miners' lives mattered little.

The intensification of the country's coal-fired political economy was built on a structural devaluation of miners' lives. Wages might have been relatively high while a miner lived (and when there was work to be had), but the cost of a miner's death to the companies was minimal; indeed, it barely registered. Instead, the costs—economic, social, and emotional—were offloaded onto workers, their families, and the communities in which they lived. They were absorbed through networks of national and global migration and justified by energy-hungry cities that quivered when the coal stockpiles ran too low.

One coalfield story depicted how miners understood this process. "I had the boss man say one time," Nimrod Workman recalled: " 'Don't get that mule in no place where the rock will fall in on him,' . . . I said, 'Well what about me? . . . What if the rock fall in on me?' and he said, 'We can always hire another man. We have to buy that mule.' They think more of a mule than they do a man." Workman's story appears in nearly identical fashion so often, and in so many contexts, as to become a parable about the trauma of that dehumanization.[46] The interpretation of miners' deaths often became a point of conflict not only because operators proceeded with such callousness for the lives of their employees but also because not everyone conceptualized the dangers of the mine in the same way. Miners like Workman, and the many others who shared stories with similar lessons, cast the mine as a site of dehumanization and devaluation. Operators, with much incentive to do so, tended to focus on the violence of the space as fundamentally geological: deaths from a methane explosion expressed chemical volatility rather than asymmetries of power. While these two explanations might appear, at first glance, counterposed, that very incongruity lay bare, for miners, a deeper unity.

The mine was not a hole in the ground but a nexus of the nation's political system, its energy system, and its economy, a site that made possible and helped organize wider systems of energy practices. The gases, dust, and strata of the mine could unleash violence only in tandem with an energy system that sent miners venturing below ground for a few cents per ton in the first place. The coal mines, workers insisted, were not inherently deadly. The operators—and the energy system they represented—were killing them. This core insight would remain central in miners' organizing across the twentieth century.

The coal carried this violence, constitutive of its existence as fuel, everywhere it went. When traced through kinship networks, coal shipments, and processes of financial accumulation, this violence had national and even international reach. As isolated as even the most remote Appalachian hollows might have seemed, coal linked each mining community in multiple ways to a wider, increasingly energy-intensive world. The story of coal-fired energy intensification could be told through the experiences of the everyday violence that defined coalfield life, experiences that had global reach but remained startlingly intimate.

Antonio Triolo, originally from the Mediterranean island of Corsica, found work in the newly opened mines of McDowell County at the end of the nineteenth century. Eventually, he was able to send enough money home for his brother, Giovanni, to make the journey to the United States as well. Giovanni did not initially follow his brother to the coalfields. At the encouragement of an immigration officer, he went to Buffalo instead, where he found work laying rails for the city's newly electrified streetcar system. Not lured by the high wages of the coalfields, Giovanni stayed in Buffalo even after witnessing the assassination of President McKinley. But then, in 1902, he received a telegram that his brother had been seriously injured in a mine accident. Giovanni quit his job on the spot and boarded the next train south, but Antonio had already died from his injuries by the time he arrived.[47]

The emergency trip turned into a permanent relocation. Without the funds to return north, Giovanni walked through the hills to nearby Logan and took a job laying track once again, this time not for a municipal streetcar system but for a railroad cutting its way deeper into the hills until it reached the site for a new mine. Then he began working in the mines themselves—which must have presented daily reminders of the accident that killed his brother. He retired after World War II, age seventy-three, and by then, Giovanni Triolo had worked in the mines for nearly half a century. Triolo made the best he could of a hard life. Persistently in danger and regularly underemployed, he nonetheless took pride in his work and skill, and he imparted to his children a sense of dignity about their coalmining "heritage."[48]

Most miners killed in these early years of the coal industry died like Antonio Triolo. In 1902, the year he was killed, he was one of more than 1,700 miners who would meet a similar fate. The scale and regularity of death in the mines, combined with the fact they appeared to occur in a "natural" geological formation, made a truly staggering death toll nearly invisible to an American public more inclined to focus on the spectacle of open class warfare. However, this death toll prompted miners to regard the coalfield as a conflict zone, one that made armed struggle seem not only necessary but perfectly reasonable and, perhaps, even a safer alternative.[49]

Between 1880 and 1922, as hundreds were killed in shootouts, ambushes, and massacres, more than sixty-five thousand miners had been killed on the job.[50] Uncounted numbers of miners who managed to survive their journeys underground would still pay with their lives when they died of long-term occupational diseases, especially silicosis and black lung. These linked forms of violence accompanied the maturation of the coal-fired energy system in the United States. The "mine wars," as a series of discrete armed conflicts, would taper off by the 1930s, but the deadly toll of the mining workplace and coal mining–related occupational diseases continued to climb. Even once the gun battles ended, the annual death toll of mine accidents climbed past one thousand every year.

As devastating as that death toll was, especially in regions with a relatively small population compared to major urban centers, the violence of the extractive process was not easily contained at the mine face. It filtered out from the mine to the coal camp, through the hollows, and across the region. Workplace death and company authoritarianism operated together, particularly in areas where the company town was the dominant form of political organization. In southern West Virginia at the height of the early-twentieth-century coal boom, company towns outnumbered independent municipalities five to one.[51] Operators exercised total control over these towns. They owned the houses and the land, ran the company store and cinema, financed the schools, and controlled the church and the police.[52]

The dictatorial power of the company system manipulated miners' political participation far beyond the boundaries of the coal camp. In county and state elections, the stakes were high for the operators—taxation schemes, sheriff's offices—but miners realized the outcome was likely to have little impact on life in the coal towns themselves. The sociologist John Gaventa contended that because the "county rarely intervened in the coal camp . . . the vote was like a franchise in a foreign election," and miners sometimes sold their votes for their local cash value.[53] The infamous Logan County sheriff, Don Chafin, employed men to ensure enough people voted the "right way." One of those men was Dewey Browning—until he lost his job when Chafin learned Browning voted the *wrong way*, Republican.[54]

Companies often denied the right to assembly except for religious purposes and, as in many workplaces, confronted union organizers with violence for speech and the distribution of pamphlets.[55] Lana Blizzard Harlow recalled how the company would "post guards up at the church, tell you if you could go in or not. They'd tell you if you could catch a train."[56] Miners who lived in the more mature coalfields of Pennsylvania and Ohio or who lived in proximity to larger cities like Pittsburgh or Birmingham, where other forms of employment might be found, often fared better, though they still found their rights curtailed the moment conflict arose. But with the opening of the West Virginia coalfields, more and more miners found themselves subjects of the coal companies rather than citizens of a nation. Even for those miners who were not denied full citizenship because of race or country of their birth, coalfield citizenship in the Progressive Era was, for many, partial citizenship.

The coalfield state's private power faced resistance. Black miners in McDowell County were part of a voting bloc that held the balance of power in the county. Although they only made up around 35 percent of the male, voting-age population, very little of the foreign-born white population was naturalized, and the native-born whites were split along party lines. Black migrants to the coalfields would have quickly recognized the similarities between the company town and the postemancipation South—although, unlike in the agricultural South, Black men in West Virginia continued to be able to exercise the franchise.[57] The majority of Black voters organized themselves as part of the McDowell County Colored Republican Organization and used the Black-run paper *McDowell Times* to facilitate political engagement.[58] For the growing number of Black miners in the state, most of whom had come from the agricultural South, engagement with Republican Party politics figured centrally in their day-to-day political lives.[59] Amid the increasing statutory codification of Jim Crow segregation and the systematic disenfranchisement of Black voters across the South, the McDowell County Colored Republican Organization took pride in describing itself as the most organized group of Black voters south of New York.[60]

But the same organ that reflected the richness of political organization and civic life among Black voters in McDowell County still managed to capture how the company shaped the exercise of power in local disputes, including those inflamed by growing ethnic tensions. In 1913, an Italian miner was beaten by a white man in a bar after an argument; he then fled to the house of another Italian friend. He was followed home by a group of ten to fifteen native-born whites, who fired into the house with a revolver and threw bricks through a window, injuring a woman in the home so badly she could not nurse her infant. The mob, led by none other than the chief of police, broke down the door and destroyed furniture before arresting the unnamed Italian and taking him to jail. After a group of Black community leaders intervened to examine the man and catalogue his extensive injuries, the Italian's mine superintendent arrived, asking that the man be released because "he was one of the best workers and most peaceable men employed on his job." The chief of police agreed, and the man was sent home, a "near riot" averted.[61]

Black readers of the *McDowell Times* would have quickly noticed the terrifyingly familiar elements of a barely averted lynching and likely placed the story in a national context. This form of extrajudicial violence was inflected by its coalfield context but not unique to it. The paper was careful to note that everyone involved in the affair was white except for the Black community leaders who catalogued the man's injuries. Black leaders would almost certainly have seen their actions in the context of escalating national protests against lynchings. Lynchings, including of Black people, were less common in West Virginia than in other areas of the South, but, as noted by the historian Joe William Trotter Jr., the "lynching sentiment seethed just below the surface," a fact the coal companies were happy to use to their advantage in thwarting attempts at building interracial solidarity.[62]

Earl Whitney and Ed Whitfield, Black miners who worked for the Island Creek Colliery Company in Logan County, West Virginia, would not be as lucky as the unnamed Italian. The coalfields, like the rest of the country, were in turmoil in the aftermath of the Great War, with sharpened political conflict among civilians and soldiers alike.[63] By December 1919, tensions were on edge because of nationwide and local conflicts. For nearly a month and a half, the United Mine Workers had been on strike in defiance of a federal injunction. Nearly fifty thousand West Virginia miners had joined the strike, which finally ended on December 10. As the nation's cities stared down a serious fuel shortage, miners secured a 14 percent wage increase and a promised federal investigation into the coal industry.[64] African Americans faced a wave of white supremacist violence sweeping through the nation's cities.[65] Earl Whitney had been injured at work in the mines and denied just compensation. Then, a few days later on December 14, Jesse Meek, a white foreman, was murdered.[66]

Whitney and Whitfield were blamed for Meek's death and arrested. Then a white mob seized them, tied them to freight cars, and shot them dozens of times before dumping their bodies in the Guyandotte River. No one from the coal company intervened, as they had in the attempted lynching of the Italian.[67] Although Joe William Trotter Jr. suggests the lynching of Whitfield and Whitney was one of the last such instances in the West Virginia coalfields, coal operators continued to organize their workforces in ways that deliberately exacerbated ethnic and racial tensions. Their antiunion violence dovetailed with racist terror. Elsewhere in Logan, John Wilburn recalled, a sheriff's deputy attacked a Black organizer for giving a speech. The deputy "tore the clothes" off the organizer and "smashed him in the face with his gun" before hauling him to jail.[68] Further south, in the majority-Black Alabama fields around Birmingham, the Ku Klux Klan worked alongside company guards to intimidate and terrorize miners out of political activity.[69] For Black miners, the violence of the coalfield state was inseparable from the racist violence that organized political and social life in the United States.

The mine wars thus emerged in a political landscape organized by multiple, intersecting forms of violence, all inflected by the organization of power in the coalfield state. Company power had so malformed coalfield governance that miners often found themselves with few avenues for recourse that a citizen of a democratic state might expect. With little promise of justice and practices of governance that miners perceived as designating the spaces that produced coal as politically distinct from the spaces that consumed it, it is unsurprising that violence broke out with such regularity in these early decades.

Beginning with the Coal Creek War of 1891, where free miners took up arms to prevent mine owners from replacing them with leased convict labor, the unrelenting violence of the coalfield state was punctuated by two-sided battles over the next four decades.[70] Each conflict had a unique spark and was kindled by different local conditions. Nonetheless, miners' grievances and demands demonstrated remarkable consistency throughout this period. Miners demanded both the state and the operators respect their civil rights, and they sought the end of the private guard system. By the time ten thousand armed miners marched through Logan County in 1921 to confront the operators, their private guards, the county sheriffs, and the state police, the coalfields were indeed in a protracted state of "civil war." Observers referred to it as such even when it was, as Winthrop Lane had written, "fought through many of the ordinary channels of civilization," and even though these "wars" and the kinds of violence they created paled in comparison to the everyday violence of the coalfield state. Where observers saw spectacles, miners saw moments of parity with the coalfield state run by and for the companies.[71]

Coalfield violence in the years after the Great War highlighted the relationship between the federal government and company dominance, as the role of the state in buttressing antidemocratic and illiberal repression reached a fever pitch. For coal miners, this period demonstrated that their national citizenship was intimately linked to the coal they mined. The war, the historian David Alan Corbin argues, also instilled in miners a "highly ideological insistence on their democratic rights."[72] State and federal governments demonstrated their willingness to intervene on the side of company rule, so long as the coal kept flowing to vital industries and urban centers, which, unless they had access to hydropower, depended on coal's energy for power, light, and heat.

Figure 1.2 Armed miners pose with an American flag.
Source: Van Amberg Bittner Papers, West Virginia and Regional History Center.

In southern West Virginia, the end of the Great War looked more like a military occupation. The U.S. Army stationed hundreds of troops in southern West Virginia, with smaller outfits dispatched or placed on alert from Alabama to Pennsylvania in anticipation of the 1919 national coal strike. Sixteen hundred more troops arrived when Logan County miners organized a march attempting to unseat the notorious and unpopular sheriff, Don Chafin. In the months after the shootout in Matewan, West Virginia's governor, John Cornwell requested the assistance of federal troops four times. The repeated appeals, made under a wartime arrangement that allowed governors to request troops directly from military leaders, were eventually escalated to the War Department. Although federal troops had regularly aided states in the "restoration of order"—the resumption of production—during wartime labor disputes, the Wilson administration had begun to scale back this practice. Ultimately, Wilson's secretary of war ordered federal troops to leave the coalfields by the end of 1920—but the removal proved only temporary. Indeed, by the spring of 1921, as Winthrop Lane's depiction of the coalfield civil war went to press, West Virginia's new governor, Ephraim Morgan, placed Mingo County under martial law. President Warren Harding signed an even more expansive proclamation at the federal level for the secretary of war to promulgate as he saw fit. The U.S. Army's presence in the West Virginia coalfields peaked months later, in September 1921, with more than two thousand soldiers and fourteen army aircraft.[73]

Federal troops continually deployed to West Virginia because it lacked an organized national guard or state police, the forces that other states were instructed to deploy before calling for federal assistance. This underdevelopment of West Virginia's police forces, however, was intimately tied to the development of the coalfield state. Company governance had foreclosed the development of a mature state policing system. The dominance of company towns meant that the private guard system dominated state policing practices. And although miners, better than anyone, knew the abuses of the private guards, they also opposed replacing the guards with a state police force, which miners believed would use taxpayer money to "serve only one class, the wealthy capitalists."[74] At least one union local promised armed resistance to any state police force. The state labor commissioner seemed to affirm miners' fears when he maintained that the only reason to form a state constabulary was to intervene in the coalfields.[75]

When West Virginia finally established a state police force in 1919, it attracted men like Harvey Rexrode, who commanded the first unit of state police deployed to Mingo County after the Matewan shootout. The *New York Times* referred to Rexrode obliquely as a former army captain.[76] Indeed, Rexrode *had* been a captain in France during the Great War, but his record extended much further. He had no less than sixteen years' experience as a soldier on the imperial periphery: in the U.S. colonies of the Philippines and Hawai'i, as well as the U.S.-Mexico borderlands. He concluded his career shaping the development of the West Virginia State Police.[77] Rexrode's biography was hardly unique. Those who enlisted, for example, included James Brockus, whose military résumé read like a map of the nation's imperial expansion during his lifetime. He was first posted at Montana's Fort Keough on the borders of the Crow Reservation in 1893. He was discharged a few years later but quickly reenlisted; Brockus had developed a taste for imperial soldiering. Before arriving in West Virginia, he completed stints in Alaska and the Philippines, deployed to China during the 1900 Boxer Rebellion, and then was posted to the U.S.-Mexico borderlands in Texas and Arizona.[78]

The colonial careers of the West Virginia state police were paralleled by those of the army officers sent to West Virginia, who drew on their experiences in the nation's colonies to restore "order" and coal production.

Tensions in southern West Virginia flared in the summer of 1921, after Governor Morgan's declaration of martial law. Baldwin-Felts detectives murdered Matewan's pro-union police chief in broad daylight on the steps of the McDowell County courthouse.[79] Newly inaugurated President Warren Harding—no friend of labor—sent five hundred troops under the order of Colonel Samuel Burkhardt to patrol around the mines. Previously, Burkhardt, as captain of the 19th Infantry Regiment in the Philippines, had led "strikes [against] insurgents near Calindres, Panay," burning "quarters" as he went.[80] Colonel Herman Hall and, later, Brigadier General Harry Bandholtz were also dispatched to southern West Virginia. Both Bandholtz and Hall were seasoned veterans of the colonial constabulary in the Philippines.[81]

By the time Bandholtz arrived in Charleston, West Virginia, on August 26, 1921, the situation had deteriorated still further. The governor had once again rejected miners' demands, and in response, miners had assembled an army in the hills of Logan County, led by the miners' own "general," Bill Blizzard. The Battle of Blair Mountain had begun. Bandholtz drew on his experience in the Philippines deploying psyops against anticolonial radicals when he met with the UMW leaders upon his arrival in West Virginia. He warned that if the miners' army was not dispersed, "we are going to snuff them out like that," snapping his fingers in front of Frank Keeney, a union leader.[82] Fighting continued for days until more federal troops arrived on September 2. Ultimately, according to the historian Alfred McCoy, Bandholtz averted a much bloodier conflict, securing a victory for the operators by "employing the same subtle strategies he had practiced in the Philippines."[83] But the impact of these tactics was amplified, no doubt, by a coincidence of empire. An insurgent miner, Harvey Dillon from Boone County, had served as an orderly under Bandholtz back in the Philippines. Amid swirling misinformation and uncertainty, Bandholtz's threat gained credibility. Dillon helped convince the other union leaders that fighting the federal troops was the wrong decision.[84]

The coalfield war in West Virginia was the largest insurrection in the United States since the Civil War. Even in an era where labor conflict often turned violent, coalfield warfare stood in a category of its own. It lay bare, according to Samuel Gompers, that the "mines of West Virginia constitute the last refuge of autocracy . . . upheld by a private army of killers."[85] The *New York Times* worried that even though a truce had taken hold in early September, a "future outbreak of warfare is only a matter of time," as miners had almost certainly hidden their munitions in the mountains, which they knew much better than the federal troops.[86] A reader of the *Times* that day, September 8, 1921, would also have been warned that the problem was not confined to southern West Virginia. The adjacent column described another conflict underway in Illinois, more than four hundred miles away, where hundreds of miners camped out awaiting "reinforcements" as they battled sheriff's deputies and private guards. The miners had armed themselves because they heard rumors of a massacre. A battle was averted only, according to the *Times* correspondent, by a heavy rainstorm that gave tempers time to cool off.[87]

The Senate had been monitoring the situation in West Virginia since the summer, holding its first hearing on the conflict in July. After the Battle of Blair Mountain, they reconvened. Clearly, the situation had not been resolved. In October, the Senate Committee on Education and Labor offered the union and the operators two days each to explain their side of the story.[88] But it didn't take that long to cut to the heart of the matter. The UMW representatives laid out the stakes of the conflict in their opening statement. The committee had to determine if the coalfield state, in which coal towns under private government powered an industrializing core, was a sustainable energy system.

On this question, the UMW issued a stark warning: "Unless this committee sees . . . the justice of taking such action as will absolutely assure every man in West Virginia . . . his constitutional rights, the right of free speech, the right of peaceable assembly, the right of intercourse with his fellows . . . guaranteeing them the right of collective bargaining, guaranteeing them the right of American citizenship," any plan for arbitrated labor settlements would fail, as they had in the past.[89] The operators countered with a typical business argument of the day: their representative implored the committee to "tell these people that we have a right to run these mines ourselves . . . a right guaranteed by the Constitution."[90] Both parties seemed to recognize that regardless of whether one believed that the conditions in the coalfields were moral, to accede the rights that miners demanded would require a complete reorganization of coalfield governance—in other words, dismantling the coalfield state.

Miners were eager to claim and exercise the rights they believed were theirs, and the first UMW witness to come before the Senate committee put the problem of citizenship at the core of his statement. That witness was Phillip Murray, the UMW's young vice president, better remembered for his leadership of the steelworkers' union. Murray was a naturalized citizen who had arrived in the United States from Scotland in 1902. He was sixteen then but had already been working in the British mines for years, since he was ten years old, and he carried his union card with him to the United States. In 1905, only nineteen, he was elected president of his local in western Pennsylvania, and he quickly made his way up through the union's leadership.[91]

Now in his mid-thirties, he sat in the halls of government, appealing to Progressive ideals by casting the coalfield state as a "festering, cantankerous sore" upon a body politic that had proclaimed itself "the healthiest, sanest, richest, and most civilized self-governing nation in the world." The coalfields were "the worst indictment that can be brought to-day against our free Government, its institutions, and the processes by which it functions" because it showed that "this very Government of ours is founded upon a fallacy." Murray insisted that it was precisely "in the hope that we may demonstrate ourselves to be good citizens . . . that we shall make our presentation to the committee."[92]

Murray condemned coalfield violence and authoritarianism as a mockery of the United States' system of government. In doing so, he suggested that the denial of citizenship to the residents of the coalfield state was not simple hypocrisy but in fact revealed the way coal-fired Progressivism produced disparities in government, in accordance with the flows and distributions of energy. The advance of "civilization" was driven by "autocracy" on the periphery. The "constant breakdown in civil government" in the coalfields revealed violence as a feature of the nation's coal-fired progress. Failure to rectify these inequalities and secure justice for citizens in the coalfields called into question the entire premise of the nation's political project. Murray called on the committee to institute immediate safeguards, which included the guarantee of basic rights and the "assurance that democratic institutions will not be subordinated to industrial control." If the federal government could guarantee miners' rights, Murray claimed, the UMW could help ensure a stable supply of bituminous coal.[93]

In making his case for federal intervention in the unorganized coalfields of southern West Virginia, Kentucky, and Alabama, Murray overstated the living conditions and civic freedoms enjoyed by the organized miners further north in the central competitive field (CCF), the anthracite fields, and the West. Still, the UMW's organization remained strongest in the CCF, which comprised Western Pennsylvania, Ohio, Indiana, and Illinois. When there was work, a miner might make more money in this region, but work could be hard to come by, and conditions deteriorated quickly when work evaporated. Industry overdevelopment meant that by the spring of 1922, only 10 percent of the nation's mines operated full time, and the living conditions of underemployed miners in those regions declined. Miners demanded a thirty-hour work week to help institute a wage floor.[94]

In the spring of 1922, as the employment situation in the CCF worsened and as the CCF contract's expiration date approached, the war in West Virginia was still fresh in everyone's minds. The Senate understood the importance of reaching an agreement. Without one, the violence in West Virginia might spread into the CCF. They called a new set of hearings to investigate conditions in the region. But the operators in Ohio and western Pennsylvania saw the opportunity to break apart the fieldwide agreement for local ones that would allow for greater wage variation—and greater profits. They refused to bargain. On April 1, the contract expired, and UMW president John L. Lewis called the miners out on strike during the third day of hearings. The miners in the CCF were joined in the strike by the anthracite miners, whose contract expired the same day, as well as some 75,000 unorganized miners looking to join the union.[95]

By the time the Senate committee convened on April 24 for a seventh day of hearings, the strike was entering its fourth week, and a group of miners from western Pennsylvania arrived to address the committee. Although the CCF was highly organized and had a framework for bargaining, the miners' testimony revealed that, once again, miners' basic rights had been curtailed. They faced systematic violence, and immigrant miners in the process of naturalizing had their citizenship papers withheld—all to pressure them to return to work. These efforts were especially directed at miners who had joined the strike hoping to join the union and work under a UMW agreement. J. P. Luterancik, an interpreter and union official from the UMW's District 5 in southwestern Pennsylvania, described the attacks by the state police that began in the strike's first week. The state police, he testified, drove through groups of men walking on a public road, injuring thirty. Two days later, mounted state police broke up a meeting held on a farm with no links to the coal companies. They beat attendees with clubs as they tried to flee. At another meeting, the state police arrested a union official while he was speaking with two other organizers—again, on private property the union had rented for the meeting. Luterancik recounted men being "put on the train and shipped out" and "proclamations" being posted around the coal towns limiting the right to assembly to three men or fewer.[96]

Union-organizing materials for the strike emphasized that the union was not simply fighting over wages. A card printed to help build the strike stated it clearly: miners were striking to "end fear." Without the union, miners "lived in fear" of the boss and his spies and gunmen and of being blacklisted and evicted. They could not "meet and discuss their problems as Free Americans." As if to prove the miners' point, men found distributing this strike invitation card were arrested within hours. The sheriff justified the blatantly illegal arrests "on the ground that the mining population was mostly 'a bunch of ignorant foreigners.'"[97] It was difficult not to hear in such xenophobic remarks echoes of similar comments by the Pennsylvania Department of Mines blaming the dangers of mining on immigrant workers.[98] In both cases, anti-immigrant sentiments externalized a deeply American form of unequal citizenship built into the country's coal-fired energy system.

Luterancik's testimony highlighted how blatant the practice was. Judge Charles Prentiss Orr, a federal district court judge in Pittsburgh, withheld the citizenship papers of striking miners until they agreed to return to work. Judge Orr's actions leveraged the power of the state on the side of the companies amid a labor dispute and demonstrated how miners' citizenship was increasingly articulated through and attenuated by their relationship to their work mining coal. Luterancik testified that Judge Orr offered to ease the naturalization process for any miner who would cross a picket line by waiving the requirement to bring witnesses to their hearings: "Here are the words he uses as a rule: 'I will not grant your papers now. When you go to work you can come back and get your papers, and you don't even need to bring your witnesses with you.'"[99] Withholding citizenship papers until a miner agreed to return to work underscored how citizenship for these men was intimately bound to their daily labors. Luterancik insisted the case was not an isolated incident, and, indeed, members of the Senate committee were able to corroborate his story, because it had been reported as far away as Washington, DC.[100]

The targeting of immigrant workers was unsurprising, given the national context.[101] The rising tide of nativist sentiment led to vigilante attacks on organizing workers elsewhere when their status as "American" was called into question.[102] Similar tensions emerged in the eastern coalfields, where the workforce had expanded rapidly in the previous decades, largely through migration from southern and eastern Europe. As xenophobic sentiment grew across the country, the UMW tried to play immigration politics both ways. They organized new migrants in the coalfields rather than excluding them, as some unions had, and promoted assimilation programs. At the same time, they supported immigration restrictions and engaged in xenophobia in national politics.[103] These duplicitous positions perhaps left their union vulnerable to political targeting, especially in Pennsylvania, where nearly 60 percent of miners were immigrants and where Judge Orr was withholding miners' naturalization papers.[104]

The UMW's leadership was in many ways ill-prepared to meet the antilabor and antidemocratic challenges of the xenophobic years after the Great War. The UMW promoted citizenship among its members and even cast itself as a citizen-making institution. However, the union wielded citizenship as a tool to discipline its members to a particular practice of labor politics: "You can see the necessity of becoming citizens of this, your adopted land, and the United Mine Workers of America have made and still are making every effort to make good, law-abiding citizens of you right here."[105] As elsewhere in the labor movement, the UMW sought to distinguish between an "American-style" unionism, which they cast as patriotic, voluntarist, and suitable for a liberal democracy, and other radical forms of labor politics that were popularly associated with immigrant communities: Bolshevism, anarchism, and socialism.

Lewis reserved special ire for communists and syndicalists, who maintained a foothold in coalfield organizing through the 1930s. Lewis, a lifelong Republican, purged radicals from the union and was more than happy to suggest that "disloyalty" to the UMW was un-American.[106] That claim obscured how in the early decades of the twentieth century, many miners and their families came to associate citizenship with mining coal. For many, the struggle to unionize had inculcated a particular definition of what it meant to be democratic or American.[107] But UMW demands for miners to act in a manner befitting "good citizenship" was also shaped by the fact that, in West Virginia, the miners' leaders were standing trial for treason.

The leaders of the UMW's District 17 had been charged with treason and murder for their role in the Battle of Blair Mountain. It was a naked attempt to prove that miners were not "patriotic freedom fighters" as they had claimed but instead "enemies of the state . . . as dangerously subversive as Bolsheviks."[108] The first union leader to face the court was Bill

Blizzard, the leader of the miners' armed forces. He was prosecuted not by a state's attorney but by lawyers hired by the coal operators. The trial drew national attention but ultimately had the opposite of the intended effect, which had been to vindicate the government's actions at Blair Mountain. Not only was Blizzard—somewhat miraculously—acquitted, but the national press reported to readers what miners had long known: they did not have the rights of citizens. The *New York Times* stopped short of defending miners' actions but admitted that the miners could not be "trying to subvert the Government of West Virginia" because the coalfields had no "rule of law" and lacked "a republican form of government."[109]

Armed violence in the years after the Great War focused national attention on the coalfield state, but ultimately, this authoritarian form of coalfield governance survived the scrutiny it received between 1919 and 1922. The miners in southern West Virginia faced a legal onslaught after taking up arms in 1920–1921. The UMW's District 17 in southern West Virginia claimed fifty thousand members during the Battle of Blair Mountain. By 1929, they had only six hundred. Across the country, UMW membership plummeted. At the beginning of the 1920s, the UMW boasted half a million members. By the end of the decade, fewer than eighty thousand remained.[110]

Making matters worse, the UMW faced serious internal divisions. In his first decade as president, John L. Lewis had substantially curtailed democratic practice within the union. He expelled the UMW's socialist, communist, and syndicalist members, who then went on to form alternative unions that consciously embraced leftwing political traditions, like the Communist-affiliated National Miners Union.[111] At Lewis's direction, the UMW invested significant time and effort attempting to discredit these challengers. Then, Lewis, the lifelong Republican, made another, at best, misguided decision. He turned to Herbert Hoover for help.

Hoover's victory in the 1928 presidential election came in part from the coalfields and Lewis's efforts, whose campaign speech to the miners was reprinted by Republicans and distributed around the nation.[112] Lewis painted Hoover as a harbinger of prosperity, whose opposition to antitrust laws would benefit the coal industry, which would finally be able "to introduce coordinated industrial planning and work toward the elimination of unemployment."[113] But his gamble came to nothing. What followed was one of the darkest periods in the UMW's history. This nadir was the result of broader economic and energy-use trends as much as Lewis's political miscalculations. Internal division and a weak market for coal dovetailed with state persecution and industry backlash.[114]

In the Central Competitive Field, conditions continued their rapid backslide.[115] Railroads and mine owners, the UMW charged, conspired to destroy the union because it was "the one and only restraining influence . . . from hammering coal miners' wages down to the poverty and starvation level." Mine owners reneged on contracts, evicted miners from housing en masse, and reemployed private guards.[116] They also took advantage of a national rise in reactionary populism, exacerbating racial tensions by recruiting largely Black workers from across the South and from the nation's major industrial cities to break the strike.[117] Lewis argued that reactionary coal operators had sent miners back into "serfdom." In the process, "American government and law over great stretches of territory" had been "destroyed"—even in places where, for a time, miners had eked out better wages and living conditions.[118] The coalfield state had not been broken by the warfare of the early 1920s. It was intensifying.

In 1925, the largest coal producer in the country, the Pittsburgh Coal Company, reneged on its agreement with the UMW. The company contended that it was impossible to meet the previously agreed-to wage scales under worsening economic conditions.[119] The dispute dragged on for years as miners clung to concessions that had been won through bloodshed. More than eight thousand families were evicted from their homes in the winter of 1927–1928. The evictions were a clear demonstration to miners of the arbitrary power of the coalfield state, even in the regions that had typically fared better than the remote hills of southern West Virginia. In addition, the union collected 218 graphic affidavits detailing "atrocities and brutal conduct practiced by coal-company gunmen and thugs" against striking miners who refused further pay cuts and demanded the company abide by their agreements with the union. "These companies," the UMW contended, "have obtained from courts injunctions of the most amazing character, curtailing and destroying every right that is guaranteed to American citizens by the Constitution."[120]

The Coal and Iron Police, Pennsylvania's state-sanctioned private police force, committed many of the atrocities. By the late 1920s, it was a uniformed army, four thousand strong, which still received state commissions despite their growing list of crimes. This army carried guns and nightsticks, Phillip Murray, the UMW vice president, told a Senate committee. He also charged they "even [had] machine guns and tear gas bombs, and all the equipment known to modern warfare." The commissioned army was supplemented by irregular guards who were "just running wild, creating a condition of terrorism and oppression." With a force larger than the state's National Guard answering to the operators, Murray concluded that "the police powers of the State . . . have been usurped."[121]

Further south, in Harlan County, Kentucky, open war had broken out. The conflict began over a 10 percent wage reduction in February 1931 and by June had escalated to armed conflict. The Harlan County War—or "Bloody Harlan," as it would come to be known—once again brought to national attention the fact that the coalfields were a company state. The county sheriff, J. H. Blair, "freely deputized company officials," who then roamed the county with near impunity.[122] After one of the guards shot into a crowd, killing four people, the American Civil Liberties Union (ACLU) telegrammed the Kentucky governor in protest. The violence, the ACLU warned, threatened a return to "civil war."[123]

This political and industrial violence sustained the deadly working arrangements that continued to define the U.S. coal industry. During the 1920s, the coal industry's "sick" decade, death in the coal seam continued apace. Even though coal production declined in the late 1920s and early 1930s, as did the estimated number of working miners, death rates remained horrifyingly high. In the deadliest year of the slump, one of every 296 miners died on the job.[124] This experience of multiple overlapping forms of violence echoed decades of earlier experiences. Coalfield authoritarianism was rooted in the regular and systematic denial of miners' basic rights and freedoms: curtailed freedoms of speech, movement, and assembly; denial of basic bodily security and property rights; and the cooption and appropriation of legislative, executive, and judicial powers of the state. By the late 1920s, however, company authoritarianism failed to achieve even its stated goal of company profitability. Operators despised the union on ideological as much as business grounds. But even after reducing the union to a fraction of its former membership, profitability flagged.

The UMW grew more insistent on the tight link between coalfield authoritarianism and the broader U.S. energy system. John L. Lewis castigated the operators for their mix of "fundamental evils and economic maladjustments," which had not only deprived miners of their rights but also turned the question of coalfield governance into a crisis for the whole industrial system.[125] Wrote Lewis: "Life as Americans live it, is two-thirds dependent on coal. . . . Behind every prophecy of super-power and vista of electrified civilization we find coal and yet more coal, the condition precedent." Lewis, for all his shortcomings of political imagination, recognized the nub of the problem: "American civilization must rest upon American foundations . . . no industrial superstructure can remain American in its characteristics if it depends upon an un-Americanized mining industry."[126] The paradox of the coalfield state lay in that foundational relationship between democratic and undemocratic nodes of the energy system, increasingly seen as "a blight upon a society that calls itself civilized."[127] It would, in many ways, be the fundamental question miners contended with over the coming decades. Even when they spoke in the language of wages, hours, and working conditions, the fundamental problem of democracy that Winthrop Lane had identified was still there, always lurking.

Commentators around the country struggled to find the right words to describe the regular armed conflicts of these decades. The *New York Times*, in its repudiation of treason charges against the miners, called it private war; others claimed it represented the degeneration of the American government into lawlessness.[128] Winthrop Lane and others who described the conflict as civil war probably came closest. The coalfield state that emerged in the process of industrialization lacked the robust political and legal institutions that might have prevented recurrent violence.[129] It was a system of governance premised on the curtailment of miners' rights and freedoms. It relied on terror and coercion. Unless something changed, wrote the journalist Heber Blankenhorn, "the destiny of the Great Republic" would proceed in the same way, "with a bellyache in its coalbeds."[130] The coalfield state as a mode of energy governance—one inextricably bound up with both U.S. national and imperial politics—would shape the course of energy politics for decades to come.

So too would the legacy of its civil wars. The miners' justification for their participation in the warfare of these decades was survival, but that warfare, even when it was unsuccessful in achieving short-term aims, also raised deeply political questions about how the country's energy system would be governed. Miners fought the coalfield state not only for higher wages and union recognition. They struck and, when necessary, took up arms for the rights they believed were guaranteed to all Americans: free speech and assembly, freedom from unreasonable surveillance and searches, freedom from arbitrary and indefinite imprisonment, and freedom of movement.

They also insisted on living in a democratic society, one with independent religious institutions, schools, and social life. They wanted housing security and sanitary living conditions. They demanded laws that represented them and officials who were accountable to them to execute those laws rather than the private guard system under which many lived. In other words, they wanted to be full citizens. By the end of the 1920s, many miners recognized that although the country's dependence on coal had been used as leverage against them, it was also a source of political standing. That lesson would shape their organizing and political imaginations for decades to come.

CHAPTER II

National Problem, National Obligation

In 1925, John L. Lewis warned that "ever widening pits of industrial and political degradation" threatened to engulf the United States.[1] To protect the nation's economy, its democracy, and its energy system, he called on Americans to lend moral and political support to the United Mine Workers' "endeavor to restore the status of citizenship to many thousands who are now deprived of the elemental rights and privileges of American manhood and womanhood."[2] But by the early 1930s, miners continued to face company repression that denied them the most basic of constitutional rights, and the country had careened over the precipice into economic freefall. Both challenges called into question the future viability of the country's energy system.

Economic depression plunged into crisis the very idea of energy-intensive modernity, on which elites of the liberal capitalist democracies had pinned their hopes.[3] The violence in the coalfield state across the preceding decades emphasized that energy-intensive modernity and democracy had, at best, a tense and often contradictory relationship. Energy-intensive societies like the United States had yet to find a meaningful resolution to these tensions. The fact that "democratic" societies depended on undemocratic spaces for their resources was nothing less than a fundamental challenge to countries that claimed to be democratic while pushing the violence of energy appropriation into hinterlands, peripheries, and colonies. Increasing a citizen's energy consumption tended to improve their standard of living. Producing energy had far more ambiguous effects.

Regardless, the United States needed coal energy for its economy to recover and for its political system to remain intact. Without dismantling the coalfield state and more fully integrating the coal regions into the country's democratic and administrative systems, the United States would face the prospect of periodic guerilla warfare in the coalfields and industrial instability driven by cycles of speculation and overdevelopment. The United States arrived at this crossroads at the very moment the federal government's willingness to experiment with policy, statecraft, and institutional reorganization made it possible to explore new modes of governing energy—the New Deal. During the New Deal years, federal support for miners' rights democratized coal regions previously under authoritarian company control. To ensure the country's political, economic, and energy security, New Deal energy politics explicitly yoked the labor rights of miners to a broader right of the American public to affordable and accessible coal energy. The New Deal tied the country's social contract to coal—and to coal miners.

Miners sensed a new moment of political opportunity when Franklin D. Roosevelt was sworn in as president in March 1933. Almost immediately, they took their political futures into their own hands. Miners resolved to rebuild their union, decimated by a decade-long employers' offensive. This process, as the legal scholar James Gray Pope has demonstrated, was bottom-up. By April, miners from Pennsylvania to West Virginia were organizing mass meetings, striking, and joining—sometimes rejoining—the United Mine Workers in droves. At the end of May, John L. Lewis threw the UMW's entire treasury behind the organizing. Congress passed the National Industrial Recovery Act, or NIRA, before breaking for summer recess.[4]

The NIRA created the National Recovery Administration (NRA), with the stated goal of stabilizing the nation's basic industries—including and especially coal, the country's energy foundation. Roosevelt recognized that the coalfields would be the energy foundation of any recovery in heavy industry, a key pillar of the "nationwide attack on unemployment."[5] Industrial sites had little coal stored, amplifying miners' leverage. Roosevelt conceded the immediate stabilization of the coal industry was necessary to avert "threatened disaster."[6]

Roosevelt recognized NIRA's "far-reaching" scope for the coalfields, but it was miners who gave it content. They struck by the tens of thousands and rioted at mines into the fall. The United Mine Workers made quick use of the organizing opportunity offered by the new legislation. Signs at the mines declared "The President wants you to join the union," marking the decline of voluntarism and a wider acceptance of the state's role in the normalization of labor relations.[7] The act lent new political legitimacy to miners' efforts to counter private capital's dictatorial power in the coalfields by giving state sanction to miners' unions and a path to incorporate unions into coalfield governance on a permanent basis. As miners embraced the NIRA from below, it did not mean they unquestioningly accepted Roosevelt's program and new kinds of federal authority. Instead, miners used the relatively narrow openings offered by these programs to insist that their democratic freedoms would not be deferred again in the name of economic recovery.

As the UMW, the coal industry, and the federal government worked out the details of both a contract between the UMW and the Appalachian operators and the NRA bituminous coal code, everything that "happened in Washington was conditioned at all times by conflict in the field."[8] The operators seethed at the new arrangement, but they, like the federal government and the UMW, recognized that without a coal agreement, armed conflict with miners would likely result.[9] In September 1933, Lewis finally signed a historic contract with the Appalachian coal operators, covering 90 percent of the region's mines.[10] The agreement signaled that collective bargaining had returned to the coalfields, this time with state backing. It legitimized the miners' decades of struggle even as it sought to foreclose future armed conflict—mostly successfully, despite "dynamite outrages" in the Pennsylvania anthracite district and the lingering conflict in Harlan County, Kentucky.[11]

The NRA undercut the authoritarian power of the operators by fashioning mechanisms for tripartite industrial governance that included labor, industry, and the state. The NRA coal codes, signed the same month as the Appalachian agreement, set minimum prices for coal, abolished company scrip, set maximum working hours, and ended child labor in the mines.[12] The agreements secured by the UMW under the NRA regime more than doubled wages and established mine committees to represent workers. These changes were democratizing not simply for raising the standard of living among coal miners but also because they lessened the arbitrary financial and bodily precarity that had defined coalfield life for decades. There would be no more private guards. Miners also secured greater access to judicial redress, a seat at the policy table, and the ability to exercise workplace decision making with greater political and legal legitimacy. Howard B. Lee, West Virginia's attorney general, called it a "peace treaty."[13]

The change was so drastic that miners compared it to emancipation from slavery. One Virginia miner, Charles Jessee, "thank[ed] God and President Roosevelt for the time which is here when our people have free privilege to do as they choose." Although he was still on strike when he wrote, since the company he worked for continued to resist signing the Appalachian agreement, Jessee's words rang with optimism that the end of company authoritarianism was in sight. "While it hasn't done me any good yet," he continued, "I hope to see the time when I can get a job and be free and not have to be a company skate."[14] Another miner, John Vanusek, wrote that the post-NIRA organizing wave had "freed from slavery" the miners of West Virginia. He pointed to the newly expanded role of the federal government in the coalfields to explain why. Before, he had "loaded coal by the acre," but, he explained, "today coal is loaded by the New Deal."[15] Luther Keen later reflected that had the New Deal legislation not passed, "We'd probably still be living under slavery today."[16] In Fairmont, West Virginia, the miner Gus Joiner reworked a traditional spiritual to say the union "gave me mo' freedom dan I ever had . . . It moved de fences from round' de camps . . . An' did away wid de bulls-eye lamps"—the bright lights used by the companies to surveil the coal camps.[17] John L. Lewis echoed these sentiments when he proclaimed, "There has been no legal instrument comparable with [the NIRA] since President Lincoln's Emancipation Proclamation of seventy years ago." It wasn't utopia. In the next breath, Lewis criticized what he saw as half-hearted implementation.[18] Within a decade, miners would bristle against state demand for coal production. But in the wake of the new legislation, they felt freer than ever before—even though they had entered into new kinds of constraints on what constituted legitimate action.[19] The difference was their new relationship to the federal government and the opening of real mechanisms through which they might participate in policy making. For miners, this change signified that they had the rights of citizens and that the rest of the country recognized their claim to those rights.[20] To Charles Jessee, Luther

Keen, John Vanusek, and many other miners, the normalization of coalfield relations meant freedom and citizenship.

Miners' labor militancy continued into the new era, but the NIRA regime signaled the end, for the most part, of the armed conflict that had so powerfully shaped coalfield politics for nearly half a century. It normalized a new framework for the extraction of coal and legitimized exercises of collective power by workers that had been extralegal under the coalfield state. Miners successfully organized 90 percent of the country's coal mines. The wave of unionization after the passage of the NIRA undermined private systems of coalfield governance and brought miners into a new relationship with the federal government and the rest of the country.[21] But miners also extended their influence beyond the energy system. Starting in 1935, the UMW supported the wave of industrial organizing that swept the country when John L. Lewis bucked the American Federation of Labor's leadership to found the Congress of Industrial Organizations, or CIO. The CIO, backed by the UMW's organizers and treasury, quickly set its sights on the steel industry. Lewis understood that organizing the steel mills would also make it possible to win closed shops in the steel companies' captive coal mines, the biggest obstacle to the UMW's plan to bargain truly national agreements.[22]

The transformed political relationship between coal miners and the state was even visible in Harlan County, Kentucky, where armed conflict continued. The National Guard was called in to defend miners like Howard Williams, a Black miner who had been beaten by deputy sheriffs before being taken "to the Virginia line and told . . . to stay out of the county."[23] Such intervention would have been unimaginable a decade before. Further emphasizing the sea change in coalfield governance, the Justice Department opened a case against the Harlan operators in 1938. The attorney general's office spent eleven weeks and more than $300,000 to prosecute operators for a "terrorist-style campaign against union organizers and sympathizers," a campaign that had been pursued in violation not only of the Wagner Act but also of a "Reconstruction-era civil rights statute."[24] The case ended in a mistrial, but the journalist I. F. Stone dubbed it a "Roosevelt Revolution" in the *Nation*. Company autocracy in the coalfields, he argued, was at an end.[25] Revolution was an overstatement. Nonetheless, a corner had been turned in coalfield governance. The Harlan operators finally relented and signed the UMW contract later that year.[26] The bounds of that newly protected collective action and the right to participate in coalfield governance would, in the coming decades, be tested, circumscribed, and resented—but never fully revoked.

Miners' imagination of New Deal citizenship drew on their own organizing to dismantle the coalfield state, but that struggle also dovetailed with state efforts to promote electrification. The UMW's ability to quickly organize under the NRA as other New Deal programs promoted electrification together represented the foundation of a new kind of social contract—a coal-fired social contract. Electricity had remade the political fabric of American life by creating new sites in which the mechanisms and scope of political authority might be contested. As the historian David Nye explains, electrification unleashed "an open-ended set of problems and possibilities."[27] The New Deal expanded and accelerated this process with electrification programs like the Rural Electrification Administration and the Tennessee Valley Authority (TVA) by explicitly conceiving of electrification as social policy.

President Roosevelt saw electrical modernization as central to the project of national revitalization and the creation of modern citizens.[28] Modern citizens must live, Roosevelt contended, in modern, electrified homes. Housing programs meant to curb evictions and electrical modernization programs were mutually reinforcing. Electric refrigerators, electric cooking stoves, and more were necessities of modern democratic life. In this way, the historian Ronald Tobey has demonstrated, even programs that were not explicitly electrification programs ultimately supported the integration of electricity into the promises of social citizenship.[29] New Deal programs like the TVA's "Electricity for All" program operated on the assumption that a country could remake its citizenry by getting them to use electricity. In this sense, miners' efforts to underscore the connection between the coal they mined and the country's social contract mirrored other efforts to make visible, regulate, and improve the energy foundation that made democracy possible.

The TVA looked to regional watershed planning as the core of their program rather than coal mining, but their policy interventions had the potential to extend far beyond hydropower systems. TVA planners recognized that alongside big infrastructure projects, they needed to change the way people lived with electricity on a day-to-day basis. Available hydropower was meaningless if it was not being put to work. Using NIRA funds, David E. Lilienthal, one of the TVA's first directors, established the

Electric Home and Farm Authority, which worked both to make appliances more affordable and to make sure ordinary people could purchase them.[30]

The TVA's "Electricity for All" program placed the electricity consumption of ordinary people at the center of energy system democratization. Increasing their use of electricity at home, power users would do more than reduce the drudgery of housework: the TVA insisted the impact of home electricity use went further.[31] By consuming power "with refrigerators, ranges and water heaters which bear the [TVA] emblem, families of average income may enjoy the full benefits of electricity," but they would also be supporting the expansion of that same energy system to those who did not yet have access to it by helping drive down power rates for everyone.[32] Although the program's success was limited in terms of the number of appliances it placed in homes, it successfully made the case that the government could intervene in everyday energy practices, even those governed by the market, to achieve its goals of electrical modernization.[33]

While New Deal interventions into coal and river energy systems appeared to operate as though they existed in different worlds, their overlaps were clear to Appalachian residents who had been deeply affected by economic crisis. Even by the standards of the era's hard times, people in Appalachia had been particularly hard hit by the Depression—in part, because for so many of them, it had started many years before, during coal's sick decade. During 1933, 49.5 percent of the region's families received federal relief.[34] The severity of the crisis perhaps made regional residents more willing to accept this status as a laboratory for New Deal policy. The *Charleston Daily Mail* opined in late 1934 that "so long as there is a disposition at Washington to make West Virginia the laboratory for costly and elaborate social experimentation, there will be no objection from the residents of this state, either among the beneficiaries or mere onlookers. . . . The more Utopias we have and the more government spends in this particular state creating them . . . the better we like it." But this paper, published in the heart of the coalfields, did not count the TVA as one of these "utopias," no matter the promise of democratic development and cheap electric power.[35]

The TVA aroused anxiety because some residents saw it as a threat to a regional economy so heavily dependent on coal production to sustain regional incomes, tax bases, and working lives.[36] For the UMW, "cheaper than rainwater" hydropower electricity threatened to displace coal and undermine recent gains in coalfield democratization. John L. Lewis stood to lose his newfound status as the face of industrial unionism in the United States, a position that afforded him a great deal of power and influence. The TVA, he said, "can only mean vast increases in unemployment."[37] On this, Lewis and the operators found common ground. From the industry perspective, cheap electric power introduced new forms of economic instability by undercutting systems of private investment. The TVA, in the coal industry's view, was instability masquerading as social welfare.[38] According to the *Bluefield Daily Telegraph*, the welfare and freshly won political rights of miners were, counterintuitively, at odds with the TVA's regional development plans. This perspective revealed how tightly bound were the newly won miners' political rights and coal extraction in the Appalachian public imagination.[39]

Although many miners and the UMW leadership thought the TVA imperiled the still-fragile system of democratic coalfield governance, few doubted the benefits of increased access to electricity. The question was how to achieve both. The United Mine Workers would suggest that the TVA represented just a fraction of new electrification projects that were remaking the everyday experience of energy for rural communities across the country—and that coal powered many of those projects. While the Rural Electrification Administration had been designed "for the good of the farmer," it was also creating "work for miners."[40] Campaigning for Congress in Virginia's Ninth District—the state's coal-rich southwestern panhandle surrounded by West Virginia, Kentucky, North Carolina, and Tennessee—Republican candidate Luther E. Fuller attempted to outline a strategy that would preserve the bargaining power of the United Mine Workers. "There is no question," he said, "but that the development of cheap electricity marks a step in the program of civilization. But ... there is a place for coal, for electricity, and for fuel oil. Their uses should be coordinated and they should be conserved through a program of preservation of our natural resources."[41] Even in arguing about the dangers posed by the TVA, Fuller had adopted many of the New Deal's assumptions about planning, conservation, and employment—and the role of the federal government in carrying out that vision.[42]

And while the UMW opposed the TVA when the subject arose, it ultimately arose very little, rarely mentioned in the *United Mine Workers Journal*, infrequently commented on by UMW officials.[43] The union and the TVA had common enemies in the New Deal's opponents. During the La Follette

Committee's investigation into the Bloody Harlan conflict, the operators retained lawyers from the Liberty League. One of those lawyers, Forney Johnston, had made his name opposing both the National Industrial Recovery Act and the Tennessee Valley Authority.[44] The UMW also had little reason to campaign against a single New Deal program when it had benefited so much from other New Deal policies. The presence of the TVA alongside the democratizing coalfields ensured that "reform" and "development" were not singular ideas but contested terms directly linked to efforts to democratize the nation's energy systems.

By the spring of 1935, New Deal efforts to stabilize the country's coal energy system would be put to the test at the very moment when the New Deal's opponents succeeded in rolling back several major reforms. As the country stared down the expiration of agreements that had brought relative peace to the coalfields, Roosevelt convinced both the UMW and the operators to accept short extensions to the agreement to avert catastrophe. But the Supreme Court dealt negotiations a devastating blow. In May, it declared the NIRA unconstitutional in *Schechter v. United States*. Although the federal government remained committed to miners' collective bargaining rights, it was not clear if the coal operators would continue to bargain without the minimum price for their coal guaranteed by the NRA codes. Equally, no one doubted that the miners would go to great lengths to hold on to what they had won, even if it meant open conflict. The House Ways and Means Committee argued that only a legislative remedy addressing industry problems writ large would be enough "to bring order out of chaos."[45]

New Deal Democrats believed that the federal government should play a central role in stabilizing the country's energy system, but it was not clear exactly what kind of remedy might be both politically tenable and held as constitutional before the courts as New Deal legislation came increasingly under judicial fire.[46] Three months after the *Schechter* decision, Congress passed a "little NRA" intended exclusively for coal: the Guffey-Snyder Bituminous Coal Act of 1935. The act contained the clearest distillation of the New Deal's coal-fired social contract to appear yet, reflective of the Pennsylvania senator Joseph Guffey's insistence that "to foster and safeguard the industry is a national problem and a national obligation."[47]

The act declared that mining and distribution of bituminous coal fell squarely in the public interest, thus rendering legitimate a system of federal regulation that could ensure "the maintenance of just and rational relations between the public, owners, producers, and employees; the right of the public to constant and ample supplies of coal at reasonable prices."[48] The act, in setting minimum prices for coal, also inscribed special protection for miners' right to organize and their right to public assembly. It compelled operators to bargain with the union—or have steep taxes levied on their coal. And it undercut the power of operators by legislating the miners' right to choose who would weigh the coal they mined. Company-selected checkweighmen for decades had been central to the exercise of company power over miners' lives. Under this legislation, the rights of coal miners went hand in hand with a right to coal that belonged to the much wider consuming public. The federal government had a responsibility to stabilize the industry so the rights of all parties could be met without undue burden falling to any one group.

This wide-ranging reform became the next focus of the Supreme Court's efforts to further circumscribe the New Deal expansion of federal authority. As a hostile Supreme Court bench continued its assault on the New Deal through 1936, the coal operators saw an opening to squarely defeat this new mode of energy governance once and for all. James Walter Carter, president of the Carter Coal Company, sued his own company to prevent payment of the new taxes for noncompliance with the coal codes imposed by the Guffey-Snyder "little NRA."[49]

The coal operators' longstanding efforts to avoid regulatory incursion in their operations found a ready ally in Carter's counsel, Frederick Wood, the attorney who had argued *Schechter* and became known as the "lawyer who helped kill the NRA."[50] He was part of a cohort of corporate attorneys emboldened in their opposition to the New Deal by the *Schechter* victory.[51] The Guffey-Snyder Act riled him up so much that during oral arguments, he paced around the courtroom while recounting the debates of the Constitutional Convention, "gesticulated . . . forcefully," and spoke so loudly that Chief Justice Hughes told him to tone it down.[52] His efforts to curb federal authority and the New Deal's regulatory powers far exceeded his concern with coal. So too did the concerns of Justice George Sutherland, the conservative opponent of the New Deal who penned the opinion in *Carter v. Carter Coal Co.*, the decision that declared the Guffey-Snyder Act unconstitutional. His opinion in *Carter* was a lengthy defense of his views on federalism, where he drew a sharp line between interstate commerce and local conditions of production.

Wood and Sutherland's concerns were situated outside the particulars of the case. Neither had the framework or interest to consider how the Guffey-Snyder Act had constituted something new by singling out coal as uniquely worthy of NRA-style governance. But as Wood's argument shaped Sutherland's opinion, and Sutherland's opinion shaped the dissents of his colleagues, and the dissents shaped Congress's future attempts to define federal authority over coal production, their arguments would have longstanding consequences in the way energy was governed in the United States.

The *Carter* decision that ruled the Guffey-Snyder Act unconstitutional was 5–4: much narrower than the unanimous ruling in *Schechter*. Chief Justice Hughes castigated the majority for too narrowly defining the commerce power. But Justice Cardozo offered a more robust dissent, one that not only offered a critique of his colleagues' reasoning but also affirmed the constitutionality of the act's intent and offered a blueprint for Congress to revise the legislation. Cardozo argued at length that while the *means* of the labor provisions were indeed unconstitutional, the *ends* were legitimate. Stabilizing the coal industry represented a matter of acute public interest: labor unrest "was not merely a menace to owners and to mine workers," which would be a matter of private contract. Coal industry instability, replete with "violence and bloodshed and misery and bitter feeling," he wrote, "had long been a menace to the public, deeply concerned in a steady and uniform supply of a fuel so vital to the national economy."[53]

He also argued that these ends were achievable through the regulation of prices. "To regulate the price for [sales of coal] is to regulate commerce itself, and not alone its antecedent conditions or ultimate consequences"— even if such regulation could be ensured to have a wider effect.[54] By organizing intervention in the coal industry to clearly fall under the purview of the commerce clause, revised legislation could have the same impact *in effect* without substantially broadening federal authority over industry. Congress took up this challenge and passed a revised version of the Bituminous Coal Conservation Act, known this time as Guffey-Vinson, in 1937. This act relied on the same taxation mechanism as the 1935 act but eliminated the lengthy labor section. With the passage of the National Labor Relations Act, the section of the 1935 act outlining collective bargaining rights seemed unnecessary, and, following Cardozo's logic, Congress looked to the taxation mechanism to take care of the rest of the labor issues addressed in the 1935 version of the law. Unsurprisingly, the operators challenged its constitutionality again, in *Sunshine Anthracite Coal Co. v. Adkins*, charging that the tax was not a tax at all but a penalty for legal business practices unjustly levied under dubious authority.

This time, however, the Supreme Court ruled in favor of the federal government, in part because Congress had so closely adhered to Cardozo's recommendations but also because the balance of the court had shifted. In the interim between *Carter* and *Sunshine v. Adkins*, Roosevelt had appointed four new justices to the court, all of whom affirmed Cardozo's dissent: the ability to regulate interstate commerce fell clearly within federal authority. They also affirmed his reasoning about the use of pricing mechanisms to serve other ends. The federal government, wrote the court, had great and legitimate interest in the regulation of coal prices as a means of improving the wages and working conditions of miners *and* protecting the needs of consumers. Justice William O. Douglas, a New Dealer and Roosevelt nominee still in his first year on the court, wrote in the opinion that "if we undertook to narrow the scope of federal intervention in this field . . . we would be blind to at least thirty years of history. For a generation there have been various manifestations of incessant demand for federal intervention in the coal industry. . . . The history of the bituminous coal industry is written in blood as well as in ink."[55] Douglas argued that if the bituminous coal industry's strategic importance to the nation's political economy—combined with the "chaotic" conditions under which it had operated for decades—could not stand as justification for federal legislation, it was "difficult to imagine what would."[56]

These efforts to stabilize the nation's coal energy system ultimately left a contradictory mark on American energy politics. New Deal experiments both from the top down and bottom up legitimized new sites for federal intervention in energy policy. Conversely and simultaneously, however, efforts to inscribe these changes in the nation's laws profoundly narrowed the mechanisms for renegotiating the terms of that intervention and the kinds of claims that would have a place at the bargaining table. That narrowed scope of intervention meant that political aims would have to be introduced by the proxy of prices.

Roosevelt appeared to recognize the policy challenges presented by that narrowing, with stakes that extended far beyond the coalfields. His administration understood that coal was not only a "basic industry" but part of an increasingly integrated, nationwide, multifuel energy system that included coal, hydropower, oil, and natural gas. It was time, Roosevelt suggested, for a national energy policy that could "recognize—more fully than has been possible or perhaps needful in the past—that each of our great natural resources of energy affects the others."[57] Careful management of the country's energy resources was an absolute necessity and so too was federal authority to coordinate and regulate the production of energy. The National Resources Committee (NRC) rebuked the court for its shortsightedness in *Carter*, concluding that "no amount of confusing legalistic discussion of limitation of powers can obscure the reality of the choices before us."

By narrowing the possible scope of federal intervention in the country's energy system, the Supreme Court had missed what the NRC felt was a basic truth: "The paramount responsibility of Government is to protect the general welfare. That way lies safety and a progressive evolution of our economy and our political institutions. . . . To protect the general welfare in our time—in an industrialized and urban economy—means, above all else, to build and maintain in good order a sound economic structure. In an industrial civilization the energy resources constitute the foundation of that structure."[58] The statement echoed John L. Lewis's argument from fifteen years earlier: energy, including coal, was the foundation of the country's political institutions. Understanding and defining the relationship between the country's energy system and its political structure represented a fundamental and urgent challenge for the modern American state.

That urgency became even more apparent as the country's coal-dependent energy system and steel industries came under strain with the shift to defense production. The coal-fired social contract, still weakly defined, relatively untested, and constrained by the courts, rested uneasily on three pillars: the National Labor Relations Act, which replaced the labor provisions of the NIRA; the Guffey-Vinson Coal Act, intended to stabilize coal production and thus make collective bargaining possible; and a weak, patchwork administrative apparatus dedicated to mine safety spread across the federal Bureau of Mines and the states' departments of mines.

This system was unstable if for no other reason than it introduced separate, overlapping arenas of authority over the coal energy system at the federal level, in addition to a growing mosaic of state laws. The frictions produced by overlapping authority threatened the success of the gains that had been made, particularly in tripartite efforts among union, state, and industry to stabilize the coal industry.⁵⁹ Nonetheless, coal output rose substantially. From a 1938 low of 394.5 million tons, miners dug out 570.5 million tons in 1941.⁶⁰ This system also had an expiration date. Both the Guffey-Vinson Coal Act and the national bituminous coal agreement were set to expire in the spring of 1941, and mine inspection legislation remained stalled in Congress.⁶¹ By 1941, strikes, legal challenges, and legislative stalling imbued the coal energy system's future with a sense of uncertainty.

Workplace danger formed the strata on which the other issues were debated. Powering the U.S. economy out of an economic depression and into a defense powerhouse incurred a substantial human cost. In 1941 alone, 1,266 miners were killed at work. Another 2,181 suffered injuries that left them permanently disabled. And 61,284 miners suffered serious injuries that may have left them with permanent pain but did not prevent them from returning to work after recuperating. The severity of these "nondisabling" injuries was captured by the fact that, on average, these 61,284 miners missed forty-one days of work after their accident. But these numbers, however stark, could not capture the reality of danger as miners actually experienced it: pervasive, unrelenting, capricious.

The roof fell without warning. Twenty-three-year-old Leland Stuchell, father of two, had been loading coal on the night shift at the Rochester & Pittsburgh Coal Company's Kent No. 2 mine on December 30, 1940. Now he was trapped underground behind seventy feet of collapsed rock along with four other miners, the oldest among them only twenty-eight. Terrified that rescuers would not find them in time, they wrote letters to their families by the light of their lamps. But soon they heard voices on the other side of the rock and shouted back. Rescuers dug through the stone for eighteen hours until they reached Stuchell and his fellow miners, who were hungry and exhausted but otherwise unharmed. The men were reunited with their families in time to ring in the New Year. Despite his terrifying ordeal, Stuchell's experience did not appear in the catalogues of accidents, since no one was physically injured.⁶² But six months later, to the day, Stuchell was on day shift when disaster struck again.

James Kinter, the fire boss responsible for checking the mines for dangerous conditions before work began, found two gassy areas in the Kent No. 2 mine that morning, June 30, 1941. He put up danger signs warning miners to stay out of the section. Foreman Charles Ramsell and assistant foreman Elmer McGee entered the restricted section to retest the active working areas for gas, but they did not test the areas that had already been mined out—the very areas where Kinter found gas. Ramsell and McGee removed the warning sign and sent miners into the section to work.

With mining underway in the active sections, three men went into the gassy, idle section to remove equipment, unaware of the danger. Their test lights ignited the methane, setting off an explosion that tore through two miles of tunnel. The explosion killed all three, throwing their bodies eighty feet backward down the tunnel. Elmer McGee, who had removed the warning signs at Ramsell's direction, was also killed, along with three others elsewhere in the section. Once again, Leland Stuchell was lucky. He survived the massive explosion, spending only a few days in the hospital with burns. These burns represented just one of the 61,284 such "temporary injuries" catalogued by the Bureau of Mines statistics, a classification that obscured the context of that injury, where death, maiming, and pain—or the threat of them—were a constant.[63]

The inability or unwillingness—and sometimes both—of the nation's legal and administrative systems to hold operators accountable for dangerous working conditions further normalized this violence. After one Pennsylvania mine explosion in July 1940, a judge found the mine superintendents had been grossly negligent, leading to the preventable deaths of sixty-three workers. But the judge only fined the three men $100 each and suspended all further sentence.[64] At the Kent No. 2, even with two serious incidents in six months, mine management was spared legal consequences. Ramsell was tried for seven counts of involuntary manslaughter and acquitted, and at the Pennsylvania Department of Mines' request, the state dropped charges against Lawrence Redding, the mine superintendent.[65] These failures to secure accountability for disasters were particularly egregious as a series of major explosions in 1940 and early 1941 killed hundreds of miners.

Congress finally passed a bill that made coal mine inspections a federal prerogative in May 1941. In this bill, Congress attempted to reconcile two basic facts: first, that preventing mine explosions was relatively simple and inexpensive and, second, that despite the first fact, explosions continued unabated.[66]

Federal mine inspection power would exist alongside state inspection mechanisms, which were weak and unavailable to miners or the public in most cases. The 1941 version of the bill allowed federal inspectors to enter mines, conduct investigations, gather data, publish their findings, and recommend safety practices. To ensure its constitutionality, Congress replicated the interstate commerce language of the recently affirmed 1937 Guffey-Vinson Coal Act on its first page.[67]

Like the Guffey-Vinson Coal Act, the mine inspection bill came under scrutiny for expanding federal authority, even though the bill contained no mechanism for enforcing the inspectors' recommendations. The bill's critics worried that inspections might become "a weapon to completely stifle production"—an intolerable possibility when "90 percent of our defense industry is energized by coal."[68] Under what legitimate terms might a federal inspector gain access to a mine? The bill's strongest supporters believed inspectors needed wide latitude. Death rates in the nation's coal mines were an "indictment" of federal administration and threatened to undermine regulatory legitimacy. "There should be no limitations" on when an inspector could enter a mine, insisted one congressman. Others suggested that a miner's death or injury should trigger an inspection.[69]

Criticisms of these proposals revealed the normalization of miners' injuries and deaths in national politics. One Kentucky Republican scoffed, "Before we go any further . . . there will be a death or accident practically every day in the large mines."[70] An Ohio Democrat added that it would be unreasonable to inspect a mine "every time a fellow cuts a finger off, or some little accident, that happens every day."[71] Behind each injury or fatality statistic were stories as horrifying as Leland Stuchell's, but from these critics' perspective, those accidents did not necessarily require federal investigation. Even in designing legislation to help prevent death in the mines, deaths and injuries were nonetheless seen as a normal part of their operation.

Questions lingered about overlapping authority with the Guffey-Vinson Coal Act. The boundary between "improvement in the safe operation of the mines" and "regulat[ion] and supervis[ion] of the industry" was a narrow one.[72] On the House floor, the Michigan Republican Roy Woodruff queried whether the bill did not simply mirror the Guffey Coal Act's constitutional justification but in fact replicated its legislative mandate. "Is it not true," he asked, "that under the provisions of the Guffey Coal Act the [Bituminous Coal Division] . . . already has the power to do everything this proposed bill would permit anyone to do?" Tennessee's John Jennings agreed but pointed out that if the Bituminous Coal Division indeed had the power to inspect mines, they had not acted on this authority.[73] The shadow of the Guffey-Vinson Coal Act was all the more present as, down the hall, the Ways and Means Committee entered its third day of hearings on whether to extend the act beyond its expiration date.[74]

Continued disagreement about the purpose and proper scope of the Guffey-Vinson Coal Act made it harder to accurately assess its potential overlaps with the mine safety bill. Across a week and a half of testimony, few disputed that the act should be extended. After extensive study, the prices set by the Bituminous Coal Division at the Department of the Interior had only been in place for five months. More time was needed to understand how to make these price floors work properly. Moreover, coal, as the nation's basic fuel, was too important to the defense program to risk any industrial chaos that would upset relationships among workers, producers, and consumers. Minimum prices for coal, the act's defenders claimed, allowed the government to ensure that these relationships were fair—even if they remained precarious and experimental.

But what exactly were the prices regulating and stabilizing? Some, like the coal company president John Brunot, saw the act as "primarily a stabilization of wage bill" that also helped ease pressure to "skimp and save at the cost of safety measures."[75] Another perspective looked to the act to assert scientific administration over the nation's coal-fired energy system. "For the first time," testified Abe Fortas, counsel for the Bituminous Coal Division, the nation had "a picture of what actually goes on, what kind of coal is produced, what sizes, what grades, where coal is shipped."[76] Secretary of the Interior Harold Ickes, with the benefit of a wider view than most involved in the industry or administration, saw the act's purpose most expansively, noting "the possibility that a new era of peace, order, and stability has emerged which will benefit the millions of people who depend on this industry for a livelihood, the thousands whose money is invested in it, and the Nation as a whole," particularly the people who relied on coal to heat their homes but could store little of it, making them exceptionally vulnerable to supply disruptions. In other words, the issue for Ickes was not only the price the consumer paid but also whether ordinary people across the country could reliably find the energy to heat their homes. This same notion of "fair supply" had animated the act from its inception.[77]

Clarifying the role of consumers represented the thorniest issue before the committee. Where some saw in the act's extension an opportunity to give consumers more voice, others charged that the implementation of the act had not considered consumers as a full partner in the way the act had intended. Still others saw an opportunity to privilege farmers and consumer cooperatives as a special class of consumer.[78] The extent of consumer representation provided for by the act, Ickes suggested, was a promising experiment in governing a new kind of economy. But in the five months since the price schedules had gone into effect, the challenges of actively including consumers in energy governance became clear. More than seven hundred eager consumers wrote each month to their representative in the Bituminous Coal Division, the Consumers' Counsel, who filed one hundred petitions per month on their behalf. The counsel's office found consumers were "often . . . unable to couch legitimate complaints in formal language with supporting factual information."[79] But the Bituminous Coal Division was hampered by limited knowledge, too. In hearings, the division admitted that it could only infer the delivered prices of coal to consumers. They simply did not have the statistics.[80] The committee chairman insisted that working the issues out was a matter of some urgency, for consumers formed the base of the whole market. "What use would you have for a mine," he asked, "if you didn't have the consumer? You would have no market at all. . . . They are all backed up by the consumer."[81]

Energy consumers mattered for mine safety too, since mine safety issues ultimately translated into questions about fair price. Operators passed on the expenses incurred through the everyday disasters of mining to consumers, to the tune of ninety million a year. However, "costs" to the consumer were also energetic. Accidents and labor unrest disrupted the steady flows of coal to consuming centers. Even before serious coal shortages existed, these disruptions could disturb the everyday energy use of cities, businesses, and homes. Coal stoves and furnaces were designed to burn particular kinds of coal. The users who operated them had to learn both to use the technology and how to use the grade of coal they could buy to fuel it—how fast it burned, how easily it lit, how dirty it was. Coal from different sources burned differently, making it harder to use in domestic and commercial contexts. Sometimes the differences in coal composition might result in needing to burn more coal, an economic cost. But other kinds of disruptions might affect users' lives in ways that were difficult to track economically, for example, the extra time a housewife spent cleaning soot and ash or getting a new coal to burn.[82]

Operators argued that making mines safer would cost less than the annual cost of disasters, in aggregate, but that the risk of investing in safety could only be borne if prices were guaranteed. Minimum prices, in this schema, could make mines safer and coal cheaper by shifting the arrangement of risk in energy production. Making mines safer would also ensure that consumers could reliably access a coal they could burn and know how to use efficiently. It would erode, as John Brunot suggested, the standard operators' refrain that dangerous mine safety violations resulted from market pressures rather than management choices. C. J. Potter, a coal industry witness, echoed Brunot: "Common practice in the coal industry is to be only as safe as you have to be; take chances; go along, keep your costs as low as possible." Extending the act, he insisted, would allow the operators "to rehabilitate our mines, in such a manner that could have a safe operation" and save the consumer money. Workplace explosions, according to the operator argument, made for volatile prices and unstable supply. Committee members rebuked him for such an "inhuman statement," since as "citizens of this country," coal operators had a "duty" to protect miners' lives.[83] The exchange exposed the limits of the Guffey price mechanisms for regulating the nation's energy system. Most people easily recognized that the mortal risk borne by coal miners and the financial risk borne by operators were different, but the Guffey system thrust both into the logic of economic mediation. More regulation was needed even if the boundaries of the different regulatory authorities appeared to overlap.

The labor contract mechanisms for enforcing safety practices also overlapped with these other forms of authority. Working conditions were subjected to negotiation in collective bargaining, which was underway at the wage conference in New York City. As Congress debated the inspection bill, the United Mine Workers crafted their own inspection clause to be inserted in their contract with the operators, which would thus fall under a separate chain of authority. John L. Lewis portrayed the clause as needed because of national failure. "No civilized country in the world," he excoriated, "exposes its miners to the same degree of hazard as exists in our own country."[84] The policy committee of the UMW proposed giving a miners' safety committee the right "to inspect any mining operation." If the committee found "dangerous and menacing conditions," they would have the authority to stop work until "conclusive inspection and finding are made by the State and Federal authorities." Miners understood that they were usually the best situated to assess the safety of their working conditions, provided they were granted the authority to make those assessments without the threat of employer retribution.[85] The UMW's leadership would also have the authority to declare "mourning periods." The mourning periods would honor miners who had been killed at work by halting coal production.[86] In other words, if Congress or the Bureau of Mines would not fine the operators for safety violations, the UMW would.

Although these debates unfolded in separate rooms, everyone interested in the issue recognized that mine inspections, the stabilization of the coal prices, and the collective bargaining process went hand in hand. Members of Congress walked between hearings on the Guffey-Vinson Coal Act's renewal and floor debate on the coal mine inspection bill. The UMW tied its new proposed contract language on safety to the expanded power of federal inspectors, and despite being involved in a contentious wage conference, John L. Lewis dispatched Secretary-Treasurer Thomas Kennedy to Washington to represent the union before the Ways and Means Committee. Most witnesses who testified about the extension of the Guffey-Vinson Coal Act asserted that the extension of the act and a successful outcome at the wage conference were linked, but Secretary of the Interior Harold Ickes stated it most plainly in his testimony. He painted the Guffey-Vinson Coal Act as preventing a return to an earlier "bloodier and more violent" period. Since the act had come into effect, "labor relations in this industry have been excellent . . . in marked contrast to the situation existing in years gone by . . . Congress should not prejudice this situation by failing to extend the Coal Act."[87] Similarly, the *New York Times* suggested that the Guffey-Vinson Coal Act had made the government a "partner" in the union's wage negotiations.[88]

Congress concluded that the federal inspection system would allow the nation to meet its obligations to miners, who were "patriotic people": "We could not live in this country without their work," affirmed one member, "and they are entitled to everything we can offer them." John Jennings, the Tennessee Republican, agreed that miners' patriotism secured the case for the legislation. Recognizing the extent to which miners had shaped the terms of coalfield governance, another member credited the miners for the legislation's existence, adding that the bill represented "a mandate" from coal miners as "patriotic American citizen[s]."[89]

But in the end, neither the inspection bill nor the Guffey-Vinson Act's extension had been finalized by the time the miners' contract expired at midnight on March 30, 1941. Because defense production had increased industrial coal demand, coal stockpiles were low. Only the utilities had the normal two-month coal supply on hand—as Ickes had warned Congress only three weeks earlier.[90] Steel mills, small industry, domestic retailers, and most municipalities had at most two to three weeks of coal left. The *New York Times* editorial board, decidedly opposed to the Guffey Coal Act in principle, nonetheless conceded that the strike was unlikely to be resolved by a new wage agreement alone. The strike was a "hint that Congress had better hurry up and give Mr. Lewis the new Guffey Act he wants."[91] This bitter comment concealed a relative consensus among workers, operators, administrators, retailers, and consumers that the Guffey-Vinson Coal Act should be extended, while wage increases for miners were far more contentious. As the historians Melvyn Dubofsky and Warren Van Tine show in their biography of Lewis, the operators refused to negotiate seriously over wage increases until the Guffey-Vinson Coal Act's extension was assured.[92]

Ickes's testimony that the act was the barrier between war and peace in the coalfields seemed prescient when violence erupted once again in eastern Kentucky, only two years after the violence of "Bloody Harlan" appeared to have come to an end. A mine guard died in a shootout on April 1. By mid-April, at least eight were dead and thirty more wounded. Children were warned to stay off the streets, and the county judge issued warrants charging seven members of the coal company with murder.[93] Eastern Kentucky remained an outlier, as it had been since the signing of the first Appalachian agreement in 1933, but it nonetheless reminded the nation of what could happen if the coal-fired social contract held together with wage agreements, the Guffey-Vinson Coal Act, and federal administrative support crumbled altogether. Renewed domestic violence would have been disastrous for the nation's defense economy. Roosevelt finally signed a two-year extension of the Guffey-Vinson Coal Act into law on April 12.[94] The UMW and northern coal operators reached a tentative agreement by April 16, but the recalcitrance of the southern operators ultimately led Secretary of Labor Frances Perkins to refer the dispute to the National Defense Mediation Board, the precursor of the National War Labor Board (WLB), on April 24. Meanwhile, the nation's coal was running out. While mediation of the dispute would continue throughout the summer, temporary agreements reopened the fields by May 1.[95]

Critically, the 1941 agreement ultimately included both the dollar-a-day raise *and* the union safety committee. The safety committee was a major victory, though it got far less attention in the national press. Coal miners were the first workers in U.S. industry to secure this right. A contractual right to a safety committee composed of rank-and-file workers ensured that when Congress did finally pass the inspection act, miners would have an active role and voice in the process.[96] The Coal Mine Inspection Act, signed into law on May 7, allowed federal inspectors to enter mines, conduct investigations, gather data, publish their findings, and recommend safety practices. It also denied any authority of enforcement and did not mandate union representation.[97] Federal inspectors investigated the Kent No. 2 after Leland Stuchell's second lucky escape that summer. As they entered mines around the country, Bureau of Mines officials unsurprisingly found enormous gaps between their recommended standards and everyday practices. Any gains made during that summer and autumn, however, were quickly "counteracted" by the energy demands of the warfare state.[98] The new mine safety committees were left to do the work of enforcement. Under the new wartime regime, the UMW enjoined the miners' safety committees "to prevail upon management to comply with federal recommendations . . . to insist upon the state mining department's backing to the fullest extent the Federal inspection recommendations." Miners who tried to implement that authority found that it fell far short of what was needed. Their warnings were ignored, and the human costs of mining coal continued to accumulate.[99]

The problems exposed in the spring and summer of 1941, as the country reoriented to a defense economy, were left unresolved. All the solutions merely secured an extension of a system of energy governance that was, doubtless, better than what had preceded it but nonetheless riddled with serious flaws. Not the least of these were lingering questions over who had the right to make which decisions about energy in a democratic system and how the fairness and equity of those decisions would be adjudicated. Because of the history of the Guffey Coal Acts and their concomitance with the wage conference schedule, these larger questions were often expressed in concerns about wages and prices.

Everyone involved, however, understood that the process of setting wages and prices was also an attempt to reckon whether the risk a miner took in venturing underground for work was fair and that setting prices was also a way of balancing the relationship between miners and the rest of the country. The same agreements that had extended this system thus virtually ensured that it would be renegotiated by aligning the date for the next extension of the Guffey-Vinson Coal Act with the expiration of the UMW's contract: spring 1943. Expanding authority, it would soon become clear, was not the same thing as unifying it.

CHAPTER III

War and Peace

For the United Mine Workers, World War II began with victory. Riding the momentum of their triumph in the 1941 bituminous wage conference, the UMW struck the steel companies' captive coal mines on November 17, 1941. In addition to the 53,000 workers in the captive mines, 150,000 bituminous miners walked out in sympathy strikes. Clashes erupted on picket lines in West Virginia. Eleven strikers were shot in Pennsylvania. By November 22, John L. Lewis had accepted an arbitration offer from the White House.[1]

A little more than two weeks later, on December 7, 1941, the arbitration board ruled two-to-one in favor of the UMW, with John R. Steelman representing the Roosevelt administration, functionally acting as the deciding vote on a three-man board, given that the other members were Lewis and the president of U.S. Steel. The arbitration decision affirmed, yet again, that miners had the right to participate in the governance of their workplaces and that the federal government would help ensure that right. Soon after the board reached its decision, news of Japanese attacks reached Washington. As the miners declared victory, the United States entered the war.[2]

But on the morning of December 8, armed guards appeared at the mines around Canonsburg, Pennsylvania, a coal town midway between Pittsburgh, Pennsylvania, and Wheeling, West Virginia. Canonsburg's chief of police reorganized his forces so the mines would be under careful watch twenty-four hours a day. He charged the sentries with "the most careful vigilance" but also gave them wide latitude to question "strange or suspicious persons at all times, at all places." Preventing sabotage that might disrupt bituminous coal output was a top priority. Such surveillance was familiar to mining communities and widely despised.[3] On any other day, the deployment would probably have merited more than a few sentences below the fold in the Canonsburg *Daily Notes*.

The return of the guards complicated the miners' victory by suggesting that saboteurs might be lingering in the area and by subjecting "suspicious" miners to interrogation. That nearly half of the miners in this region were immigrants could only have exacerbated the tension between these two realities.[4] In the end, fear of Axis saboteurs in the mines proved to be paranoia, but the test of the New Deal relationship between miners and the federal government was decidedly real. Could the coalfield governance system, narrowed from the early National Recovery Administration model to a combination of collective bargaining and price-fixing, sustain the production levels necessary to fuel the warfare state?

Government officials had real reason to worry about the sustainability of the monumental increases in coal production achieved between 1939 and 1941 as war mobilization entered a newly frenetic phase. From its early days in 1939, the transformation of the U.S. economy into a war machine resuscitated the coal industry. Miners, ready to claim what they saw as their due, struck accordingly. In 1941, one in twelve American workers went on strike—more than any other year since 1919.[5] Coal miners accounted for one-third of lost time and one-third of large strikes involving more than ten thousand workers.[6] Getting miners underground regularly and reliably presented a substantial challenge, evidence of both the successes and limits of New Deal efforts to bring democracy to the coalfields and for miners to secure their rights as citizens. Formal entry into the war rearranged the conditions under which coal would be produced, distributed, and consumed. These changes threatened to upend the recently rebalanced relationships between workers, industry, consumers, and the state, jeopardizing what had so recently been secured.

Miners, federal officials, politicians, operators, and an array of other Americans used debates over coal prices and miners' wages to question the fairness of the nation's energy system. In evaluating that economic balance, miners assessed whether they were getting a square deal, and the Bituminous Coal Division at the Department of the Interior gauged the health of the country's coal energy system. But entry into the war fundamentally altered the institutions through which the federal government managed the nation's energy system—in particular, the administrations for setting prices, resolving labor disputes, and distributing fuel—and the terms on which they would negotiate with miners.

Wartime disputes over prices and wages, taken in their full legal, administrative, and social context, show how the warfare state governed the energy system. The Guffey-Vinson system was soon trumped by much larger mechanisms for economic planning and price controls: the Office of Price Administration (OPA). The *United Mine Workers Journal* blamed the Coal Division for "meekly surrender[ing] its authority" over prices to the new administration.[7] Wartime inflation didn't help. As inflation creeped upward in the summer of 1942, the War Labor Board pegged wage increases to January 1941 levels plus 15 percent, a policy widely known as the Little Steel formula.[8] Lewis, long skeptical of the WLB and its predecessor, the National Defense Mediation Board, charged that the Little Steel formula turned a "court of equity into an anti-inflation instrument."[9] Both these changes undermined the complex set of mechanisms governing the coal industry and curbed workers' ability to negotiate as equals, as wages were set by formula. And while for workers generally, this formula meant wages rose faster than inflation, for miners, real income fell.[10] "The WLB doesn't understand miners' problems," one Kentucky miner concluded.[11] There was no disentangling the control of prices and wages from the larger energy system they were used to manage. Disputes over wartime fairness reflected deeper unresolved issues inherent in the recent democratization of the U.S. coal energy system. Thus, at the very moment that the U.S. war economy reached a fever pitch, it was at its most energetically vulnerable.

The demands of war production underscored the inadequacies of the price and wage mechanisms for coalfield governance, particularly when they ran up against embodied limits. An energy governance system that often operated by adjusting prices and wages had a difficult time accounting for the workplace death and disablement that defined mining life. Perhaps administrators could look at a production schedule without focusing on the human cost behind it, and when death tolls were too large to overlook, they were always faced with the unrelenting rise in casualties in the war's active theaters. Miners could not.

As miners wrestled with the value of their lives and labor in the context of wartime, they also had to reevaluate what it meant to be a good citizen, an identity that, for them, had been dearly won and remained intimately bound to coal. Miners' understanding of the war's meaning was yoked to their distinctive experience of energy citizenship. Their understanding of what war was and where and how it was fought emerged from three dynamic, intersecting, and often contradictory threads: the long context of autocratic rule in the coalfields, the dangers of the coal mining workplace, and the contested character of the energy relationships called upon to power total war in the United States, a set of relationships in which the boundaries between warfront and home front often blurred and redefined each other.

What it meant to be a *good* energy citizen figured into coalfield conflict during the war and emphasized how much remained unsettled about the rights and obligations of national belonging as they flowed through the energy system and about what it meant for miners to be "good citizens" in a country so dependent on coal, particularly when it went to war. A coal miner, the journalist McAlister Coleman argued, embodied the paradox of the energy citizenship that coal miners had created. A miner was, he wrote, "a sober, God-fearing, patriotic, hard-working citizen, [even] though he swears allegiance to the most militant, most hated, and most

Figure 3.1 Miners end their shift in Bishop, West Virginia.
Source: West Virginia and Regional History Center.

feared of all American trade unions, the United Mine Workers of America."[12] The country felt that tension acutely during military conflict. As one administration official noted, without coal, "the arsenal of democracy is an empty shell."[13] But the horizon of the problem extended still further. According to Coleman, this question was at the heart of the nation's future. "Since we became a world power," he wrote in 1943, "in every crisis in our national life, sooner or later, it seems, we have to reckon with coal and the men who mine it."[14] Coalfield labor conflict during the war both deepened and complicated the bond between the nation and coal miners, a bond forged through both changing patterns of energy use and the political turmoil that put the seemingly remote coalfields in the middle of yet another political crisis.

Right before Christmas in 1942, Harold Ickes, Roosevelt's stalwart secretary of the interior, now also the acting solid fuels coordinator, pleaded with anthracite miners to "work every day possible," including the traditionally observed holiday of "second Christmas," December 26. By asking the miners to work through the holidays, Ickes hoped to relieve an acute fuel shortage across the Northeast.[15]

These fuel shortages arose because of wider wartime shifts in the nation's energy use patterns. While bituminous coal fueled the arsenal of democracy by forging steel and generating electricity, anthracite coal was used mostly for heating. It burned more cleanly than bituminous coal and was thus more suitable for everyday use in heating schools, workplaces, and homes. For that very reason, anthracite had been a staple fuel for heating in the Northeast and Mid-Atlantic regions' frigid winters for much of the nineteenth century.[16] In recent decades, many users had converted their coal stoves to fuel oil boilers, but the wartime administration looked to reinvigorate anthracite use to help conserve that oil for defense use.[17] Gasoline rationing had been in place for months, but Americans entered the winter of 1942–1943 with rationed fuel oil for the first time.[18] Converting to coal-fired heating systems was portrayed as a patriotic act, whether undertaken by individuals in their home or by larger institutions. One suburban defense plant worker helped a neighbor take out a gas stove from the kitchen, replacing it with an old coal stove that had been stored in the cellar "so he might be warm these cold days."[19] At the New Year, newspapers announced that Madison Square Garden was converting its oil heating system to anthracite.[20] While anthracite miners had increased production more than 30 percent from a 1938 low, a combination of increased demand and logistics challenges made that coal feel scarce.[21]

December 26 came, but the miners, for the most part, did not. The cause was not immediately apparent, nor was a general pattern immediately visible. Around Hazelton, only five out of twenty-six mines operated that day. A reporter visited the local union office and found it locked, but that was normal on any Saturday, and December 26 was both a Saturday and a bank holiday. In some instances, company officials had declined Ickes's request to open the mines. In other places, the mines "opened," but not enough miners showed up to operate them.[22] Twelve hundred miners at the Ewen Colliery, who had been on strike since early December, *returned* to work.[23] Some mines remained closed because of winter flooding from the nearby Susquehanna River.[24] In one pit, seven hundred miners stopped working when a foreman struck a miner with a safety lamp.[25] On December 30, the *Wilkes-Barre Times Leader* announced that John Konopko had been killed overnight in a rock fall at the Westmoreland Colliery. Konopko was the 225th anthracite miner to die on the job in the small hard-coal region that year.[26] A few columns over, a separate report announced that 1,300 miners had walked out at the South Wilkes-Barre mine that morning, payday.[27]

Within a few days, the situation became clearer: miners' simmering anger over rising prices and frozen wages had boiled over when the union announced a fifty-cent hike in union dues, setting off a wildcat strike. By January 4, miners also demanded a pay increase of $2 per day.[28] Dissatisfaction with the UMW's treatment of the region and other local disputes amplified the sense of injustice and violation represented by the dues hike and frozen wages.[29]

The fifty-cent monthly dues hike hit an economic nerve but also revealed how the wartime price administrations threatened the recent, hard-won democratization of the country's coal-fired energy system. With miners shut out of meaningful participation in setting their wages, operators and coal consumers reaped the benefits, violating miners' expectations about what the nation owed them for their role in energy provision.[30] One local president said that miners had borne a 38 percent increase in the price of food but that the dues increase "was carrying it too far."[31] Another characterized the violation represented by an out-of-balance price-wage ratio even more plainly: "[We] have shown no brazenness. We have shown our indignation. We don't want to let the country down but we don't want the country to let us down."[32]

The wildcat strike did not result in a significant loss of tonnage. Although it lasted three weeks, anthracite production that month reached 97.8 percent of its January 1942 total.[33] Aggregate losses were less than the anthracite stored at the mines already prepared for shipment.[34] Only about a quarter of the anthracite workforce joined the strike, and the miners who continued to work were working faster than ever before, six days per week.[35] Nonetheless, Roosevelt telegrammed the presidents of striking locals on January 19 with a threat: if miners did not return to work within forty-eight hours, "your government will take the necessary steps to protect the security of the nation against a strike which is doing serious injury to the war effort."[36] The nature of the injury and its severity are less obvious than they might appear, since anthracite, unlike bituminous coal, was not used heavily in industrial production. It was, however, used as a substitute for recently rationed fuel oil, a fact that exacerbated the impact of the relatively small contraction in tonnage.

As the strike ended its first week, anthracite demand spiked.[37] Cities and towns across the East Coast received notice from the OPA that their fuel oil allotment was being slashed even further. The OPA expected the decision "to give great stimulus to OPA's program to compel conversion of commercial oil-burning equipment to coal or other non-critical fuel."[38] Increased regional demand dovetailed with localized shortages. Closer to the mines, anthracite was already in short immediate supply for families that traditionally used the fuel to heat their homes, since households often lacked the ability to build substantial stockpiles. Local truckers claimed that they were limiting delivered amounts "to prevent some families from being without heat."[39] By week two, the *Philadelphia Inquirer* had labeled John L. Lewis "Enemy No. 1 on the Home Front!"—regardless of the fact that the strike had been undertaken to Lewis's surprise and without his approval.[40] Energy anxiety gripped the nation.

Even a relatively small disruption to the wartime energy system could have a widespread effect because of the way the OPA and the fuels coordinators at the Department of the Interior had tried to balance rapidly expanding defense and domestic energy needs. Ickes suspended all anthracite exports to Canada and any shipments heading farther west than Erie, Pennsylvania. He also ordered that bituminous coal be shipped to the shivering in New England and the Mid-Atlantic regions. Bituminous coal miners had continually exceeded their production estimates, and supplies were so substantial that one assessment suggested that "the East could receive large quantities without strain on the rest of the country."[41] By January 23, the War Production Board hinted at the possibility of nationwide "dimouts" to conserve coal—not because bituminous coal was in short supply but because fuels in general were.[42]

The strike dragged into a third week as the nation "shivered and wondered" about the miners' patriotism. Johnston Kerkhoft, a reporter from Philadelphia, made the hundred-mile trek to understand the miners' position. As he spoke to striker Oscar Servaczgo in his kitchen, the phone rang. Servaczgo learned that his son had been killed in action in the Pacific. It was rare indeed to have a reporter close by to capture the raw reaction as the miners' fight collided with human cost of combat. Overcome with grief, Servaczgo cried out, "I ain't a traitor, damn'em, I ain't a traitor. I'll stay out till hell freezes over.... Dickie was fighting for one thing. I'm fighting for another. And they ain't so far apart."[43] *Time* used the outburst to lead a story about the strike but could not make sense of what Servaczgo meant by comparing the strike with the war.

Servaczgo's sentiment was not isolated. Another miner wrote to President Roosevelt that "miners are fighting for their freedom at home while American armies fight the same battle on foreign soil."[44] One miner's wife wrote, "We don't want strikes, but we are not slaves.... We are supposed to be free."[45] Perhaps Servaczgo's statement would have been easier to interpret if the public had recalled the testimony of Congressman Ivor Fenton from two years earlier, during congressional debates over the mine inspections bill. Fenton, a physician who had served in both combat and coalfield, had somberly remarked, "Only war itself produces injuries that approximate those of the mines."[46] But if the country had been unwilling to really grapple with what Oscar Servaczgo meant by comparing a fight for a $2-a-day wage increase to combat, it would soon have no choice.

The strike fizzled amid threats from Roosevelt and Lewis's promise to pursue a $2-a-day wage hike in open defiance of the Little Steel formula. But McAlister Coleman keenly observed that the "issues raised by the stoppage were not settled by its ending."[47] Indeed, with both the wage agreement and the Guffey-Vinson Coal Act due to expire later that spring, confrontation loomed. When commentators questioned "the ethics of using the strike weapon in the midst of a coal consuming war," they implicitly articulated the tensions that had been built into the coal-fired social contract during the New Deal. What happened when the mechanisms for labor, energy, and economic administration overlapped with or contradicted one another? Which institutions could credibly assert legitimate authority over which aspects of the nation's energy system? What were the boundaries of that authority in a complex, multifuel system? In the first two years of the war, since the 1941 wage agreement and extension of the Guffey-Vinson Coal Act, these questions had only become more pointed. The federal government had become substantially more complex, reorganizing and extending its authority. A reckoning was only a matter of time.

The showdown came that spring with the opening of the 1943 Appalachian negotiations. John L. Lewis arrived with a robust list of demands that echoed those of the anthracite strikers: a $2-a-day increase and double-time on Sundays, vacation pay, no more "check offs" that passed the cost of miners' work tools and safety equipment from operators to workers, and "portal-to-portal pay," which ensured that miners were paid for their long and dangerous trips from the mine mouth to their working places. McAlister Coleman reported that the "sheer audacity of the demands left the operators and the public breathless."[48] The UMW policy committee made its demands in open defiance of the "arbitrary and miserably stupid" Little Steel formula, yes, but also the National War Labor Board and the Office of Price Administration.[49] Miners proclaimed that their contract demands were "a matter of justice."[50]

Despite all the calls for equality of sacrifice, miners believed they were bearing a disproportionate burden of the war effort in dollar costs, in danger, and in deprivation. To have their patriotism questioned on top of it all was too much. Miners argued that to willingly enter a coal mine to extract fuel for the war economy took more patriotism than most Americans understood. "We know we could go to war plants and get a lot more money for easier work. We also know that somebody has to mine coal—the prime mover of American industry . . . we know we are serving our country best by remaining there . . . *we are only asking for simple justice.*"[51] John L. Lewis, presenting the miners' position to the Senate, contended that miners were making the sacrifices expected of patriotic citizens without being given the fair consideration or redress that a citizen might see as their due.[52]

Portal-to-portal pay became a flashpoint, braiding the interlocking issues of workplace danger, out-of-kilter mechanisms for governing wages and prices, the persistence of arbitrary company power despite the gains made over the previous decade, and the vexed, unresolved problems of authority. When miners spent up to an hour each way traveling to and from their working places, they encountered dangerous conditions, a risk for which they were not compensated. "We . . . ask that we be paid for the most *dangerous part of our day's work*," the UMW argued to the American public.[53] Miners contended that in refusing to pay miners for this time, the nation expected them to bear unequal sacrifice for the war effort, distinguishing them from workers who were not asked to carry the same unpaid risk.

To underscore their argument, miners pointed to a recent decision in the Fifth Circuit Court of Appeals that ruled in favor of portal-to-portal pay for iron ore miners, while the operators and NWLB rejected an identical demand from the coal miners out of hand.[54] Lewis highlighted the crux of the problem before a Senate investigatory panel. If the decision regarding the iron ore miners did not also apply to coal miners, that meant that coal miners were singled out for a separate set of rights more circumscribed than those afforded other Americans. If it did apply to coal miners, then there were competing claims from competing chains of authority. Testified Lewis: "The court says that we cannot . . . contract away the rights conveyed by the statute. The coal operators and the War Labor Board say they won't pay for it. . . . What do you think we should do?" Maine Republican Ralph Brewster, who only moments before had reprimanded Lewis for allowing a wintertime strike to break out in the anthracite fields, threatening the fuel supplies of his constituents, concurred. "I agree with you completely about integrating our administrative authority so we can really have one final authority to deal with these questions," Brewster conceded. "I think that is the only practical answer."[55]

The problem of authority became even more pointed as the nation stared down the April 30 deadline for a new agreement between the UMW and the operators, when the Guffey-Vinson Coal Act, already sidelined by the WLB and the OPA, ultimately "died of neglect."[56] In its stead, Roosevelt appointed Harold Ickes, the solid fuels coordinator, to head the new Solid Fuels Administration for the War (SFAW). The SFAW was directly modeled on the Petroleum Administration for the War established the previous winter, but unlike its petroleum counterpart, SFAW made explicit references to labor issues. This labor provision, tucked deep in the middle of an executive order otherwise mostly copied from its petroleum precedent, centralized energy decision making into the SFAW, where previously the union had participated directly. First, the executive order gave direct authority for the SFAW to confer with the War Manpower Commission to secure workers in the event of a "labor shortage"—the looming bituminous strike. Second, it based this authority on the perceived energy needs of the nation, giving Ickes substantial leeway to determine when a labor shortage interfered with military, industrial, and domestic energy requirements. Roosevelt's order stopped short, however, of granting Ickes direct authority over the two biggest challenges facing the wartime energy system that spring: the labor negotiations themselves and the transportation of fuel. Consequently, the SFAW would be dependent on at least seven other agencies to make major decisions.[57] The broad scope of the SFAW, alongside the limits on its authority where it overlapped with other administrative agencies, would prove a massive headache for Ickes and his deputy Harold Gray as they struggled later that fall to get the right coals to the right places in time for cold weather.[58] But for the time, Ickes had bigger problems on his hands.

By the last week of April, miners began walking off the job. Twenty-six thousand failed to report to work on April 27 and double that number the following day. By May 1, the nation's mines were shut down. The WLB insisted that miners settle their grievances through the established administrative authority rather than on the picket line. The miners, by walking out in defiance of the WLB, had clearly refused.[59] Roosevelt seized the mines for the federal government and charged Ickes with their operation, and the miners were back at work by May 4, working under a tenuous truce. Miners favored government operation of the mines but also made clear there were limits to their flexibility. "I will work for the President but not [under] no guards," insisted one miner from Logan County, West Virginia, where only two decades earlier, armed guards had terrorized mining communities. The Logan County miners also drew another hard line: they would strike without hesitation "to get our rights."[60]

And indeed, the miners would walk out once more on June 1, when operators again refused the portal-to-portal pay demand. The walkout ended with an eleven-million-ton production shortfall. The tonnage loss infuriated Ickes, who lashed out at miners and tried to fine them each a dollar a day for the strike. Miners met Ickes's order with equal fury, though they generally regarded Ickes favorably. Ickes quickly rescinded the fines. But the unrest spurred Congress forward on antistrike legislation in the form of the Smith-Connally Act, emboldening the WLB to reject the miners' demand for a wage increase once again. The UMW pointed to the overlapping authority of the WLB and the SFAW as the fundamental cause of the conflict. By rejecting a wage increase for miners, the *United Mine Workers Journal* suggested, it was the WLB, not the miners, who were undermining the effort to secure energy supplies for the prosecution of the war.[61] The miners struck again June 20 and were back in by June 24. The next day, Congress passed the Smith-Connally Act over Roosevelt's veto. With anti-union sentiment raging in Congress, Lewis bought himself more time and assured the nation the miners would stay at work until October 31.[62]

The mines were empty again on November 1, despite a threat from Roosevelt that coal would be mined with or without the miners. With winter arriving and concern about the wider impact of miners' militancy on rank-and-file workers across the country, Roosevelt handed the mines to Ickes once more. But unlike the spring, this time he authorized Ickes to negotiate directly with Lewis. The men reached a contract in two days. Ickes conceded miners' demand for portal-to-portal pay. Although some small disputes persisted through winter, the months-long standoff was finally over.[63]

Throughout, most reporting focused on Lewis's outsized personality and irrefutable thirst for power. But the real problem ran much deeper: the country's system for energy governance was not simply strained. It had completely broken down. The prices and wages mechanisms had fractured. Mining communities reviled the OPA, believing it was discriminating against coal communities. The mine inspection legislation had not made mines safer. Miners saw the WLB as illegitimate.[64] And critically, coal strikes were not only a labor problem. They had the potential to throw the nation's entire energy system into crisis, a possibility amplified because consumer demand for coal had outpaced advances in production, despite miners' sacrifices to get coal out of the ground.

In fact, miners dug out nearly 7.5 million tons *more* bituminous coal in 1943 than in the previous year, despite the repeated strikes.[65] But aggregate tonnage could be deceptive; coal didn't move through the energy system in a uniform way, and the process by which available coal became available energy depended on many other factors. The strikes exposed the complexity and interdependencies of the wartime energy system as several other factors compounded their impact. There were not enough workers to run the mines at full capacity, even if they went to work, because so many men had been drafted. The mechanized mines of North America could produce more tonnage per day than the mines of the other Allies, but training a miner to use that equipment both safely and efficiently took time. A cold spring had left coal yards bare at the very moment miners went on strike and delayed shipments into the north country of the Midwest, which relied on Great Lakes shipping routes, postponing the rebuilding of stockpiles.[66]

At the same time, the wartime transformation of the workforce had increased domestic coal demand. People migrating to work in defense industries had increased coal demand in particular localities, often without a corresponding drop in demand in the place from which they had migrated. Defense industry employment also altered workers' sense of what was owed to them for their contribution to the war effort. According to Harold Gray, defense plant workers simply were not willing to shiver through the winter and double up in beds when their wages were high enough to afford more coal. Wood was also in short supply in regions like New England and the Pacific Northwest, which had typically relied more heavily on it for home heating. Finally—and vexingly, to anyone interested in the equitable distribution of whatever coal *was* available—the American energy system had developed in highly specialized ways. Households desperate for heating coal in Massachusetts simply could not burn leftover coal from a stockpile at an idled Ohio factory.[67]

Continued coal supply problems throughout 1943 undermined the Solid Fuels Administration's efforts to expand coal use to save oil for the war effort.[68] This plan hinged on consumers' buying coal steadily over the year, building their own stockpiles where they could, or at least placing orders so the SFAW could plan coal distribution well in advance. Coal retailers in the nation's cities echoed the SFAW when they placed threatening ads—"Don't say we didn't warn you"—encouraging customers to buy coal while they could.[69] However, while consumers felt coal shortages most acutely in the winter, concern about the strikes' impact on the energy system was visible from the summer as users curtailed nonessential use. The Office of War Utilities prepared extensive recommendations for civilians to help them conserve electric power, reorganizing their use of light, asking women to attend to their cooking and cleaning efficiently.[70] Plants shut down, usually smaller facilities without the large stockpiles of the big steel companies.[71] Notably, these announcements of shortages circulated nationally, well beyond their area of impact, making them feel more intense than they likely were. But by winter, shortages were more serious.

Figure 3.2 A poster created by the Solid Fuels Administration for the War encouraging consumers to stockpile coal.
Source: National Archives, NAID 515864.

Residents of Nassau County, New York, shared their limited coal supplies to prevent families from freezing.[72]

After the first bituminous walkouts in the spring of 1943, Secretary Ickes sent Office of War Information (OWI) investigators to the coalfields of Pennsylvania and southern West Virginia, trying to grasp miners' motivations and perspectives. Richard Deverall, reporting from southern West Virginia, found no evidence of Lewis's iron fist in miners' decision making. Instead, he chronicled miners deeply invested in their democratic obligations to both nation and union. Local union leaders, according to Deverall, carefully read the papers to evaluate the positions of the War Labor Board and the Office of Price Administration, which were then

Figure 3.3 Miners gather in a Kentucky schoolhouse for a union meeting.
Source: National Archives, NAID 541440.

discussed by miners, who "seem to know as much about the entire proceedings as any person in the government concerned directly with the problem . . . they know their facts cold."[73] Miners emphasized the importance of "majority rule," and even miners who did not want to strike recognized the importance of a "meeting to discuss [the decision to strike] rightly."[74] Deverall concluded that whatever Lewis might tell the miners, "they make up their own minds. It is thrilling to watch the democratic process at work on this level—and it is also a warning to the Administration that there must be a just settlement on the issues."[75] Miners had made it clear that they would have a say in what constituted a fair settlement and that their support for Lewis as their representative in bargaining remained strong as ever.

The strikes of 1943 amplified longstanding perceptions that miners' citizenship was intimately tied to coal. As the conflict proceeded, a wide group of Americans subjected miners' political rights, practices, and belonging to amplified scrutiny. The journalist McAlister Coleman argued that this public vitriol toward the miners fit into a larger pattern of belligerence across the country toward groups of Americans "struggling for recognition": attacks on Mexican American zoot suiters in Los Angeles, racist attacks in shipyards and other industrial workplaces, increasing paranoia about immigrants.[76] For miners, "good citizenship" was not enough, Coleman concluded. "It is only in combination with his fellows that he achieves status."[77] Coleman's choice to compare a multiethnic, multiracial mining workforce of mixed citizenship status to groups of ethnic and racial minorities was revealing if imprecise: it hinted at the continued precarity of miners' political belonging.

Public responses to the 1943 strikes demonstrated the extent to which Americans beyond mining communities had anchored their understanding of good citizenship for coal miners not only to their work but also to working in a particular way during wartime. The officers of one Pennsylvania Lions Club contrasted their own Americanness to that of anthracite miners striking only a couple of hours away. "As loyal Pennsylvanians and true Americans," they wrote in a short missive to President Roosevelt, "we feel that severe measures should be taken with these unpatriotic people who call themselves American citizens." With miners' national belonging being called into question, the club officers felt "whatever measures you may take, however drastic, will be justified."[78] As the unrest in the anthracite fields turned into the threat of a nationwide bituminous strike, Frank McCoy of Massachusetts telegrammed the president to express his anger and disbelief at the actions of John L. Lewis—whom McCoy referred to as "problem number one . . . a Benedict Arnold"—the UMW, and the nation's coal miners: "Why should miners delay for a second the war effort and don't they want future security, life, health, and pursuit of happiness for themselves and their children?"[79] More than 16,000 miners had walked out by the time Helen Assad wrote to the president from her home in Fort Thomas, Kentucky, just across the river from Cincinnati. "If those strikers were drafted and realized something of this war," she scolded, "they wouldn't be doing what they are."[80] Even those who did not outright question miners' citizenship and loyalty nonetheless suggested there was something un-American about refusing to mine coal. One Kansas man telegrammed the president because he "believe[d] ninety percent of Lewis's followers are Americans at heart and are willing to continue work for the sake of their liberty."[81] Other writers, however, were more suspicious. W. J. Carpenter from Tampa, Florida, claimed "three fourths of those miners are of foreign extraction and love their foreign ideals of government. THEY ARE

NOT LOYAL AMERICANS." With little sense of irony, he identified himself as "an ex-coal miner" to add weight to his words.[82]

By the middle of the war, coal miners were mostly U.S. citizens, by birth or naturalization. More importantly, they considered themselves as patriotic, good citizens contributing to the war effort and a broader fight for freedom and democracy. The Office of War Information reported that "there is a deep personal identification of these people with the war. . . . The men see no conflict between striking and their patriotism and the struggles of their boys and brothers and fathers in the front lines. They are intensely proud of their patriotism and will fight any person who even questions it."[83] Even if John L. Lewis was sharply castigated by *Stars and Stripes*, servicemembers from the coalfields, the OWI found, "are writing home letters telling them to strike and fight for their rights." McAlister Coleman observed that the same miner who walked out on strike "against the express orders of the President of the United States and [to] the universal condemnation of the nation's opinion" also "then goes home to tend his Victory Garden or stand in line at the local post office to buy War Savings stamps out of his meager earnings."[84] One miner's wife told the OWI investigator, "Our men folks don't get enough [meat and greens] to eat . . . but us colored folk will not say anything because we think these sacrifices are needed to win the war."[85] Far from traitors, striking miners saw themselves fighting for something akin to what their sons and brothers were fighting for overseas.[86] How did miners and nonminers come to perceive the meaning of good citizenship so differently?

The federal mine inspectors who visited the Jamison No. 9 mine in April 1943 might have been able to offer some insight. The inspectors had been dispatched to conduct a security inspection of the mine near Farmington, West Virginia—one of hundreds of such inspections at the country's coal and strategic minerals mines. The Jamison No. 9 was one of the nation's largest and richest mines and had produced 619,449 tons of coal for the war effort in 1942. Despite this enormously high output, the mine's production still fell below expectations because of persistent labor problems, particularly high turnover and absenteeism.[87] While both high turnover and absenteeism were regular features of coal mining employment in the United States, in wartime these practices were recategorized as a security threat. As the inspectors assessed the mine's vulnerability to wartime disruption and sabotage, they found the miners' aspirations for the basic rights of American citizenship unmet: in place of shared sacrifice, borne equally by all, was a burden that could be measured in rock falls, dust exposure, explosions, and machine accidents.

The violations at the Jamison No. 9 mine demonstrated blatant disregard for miners' lives in pursuit of war production. The mine operated in flagrant violation of the industry's most basic safety practices. Electric wires ran without conduits in the dusty, gassy mine. Flammable kerosene was used to clean, and the mine's explosives were stored next to the ventilation fans. The working areas had no hoses to fight fires; indeed, no plan for fighting mine fires even existed. There was no rescue equipment, even though the three Jamison mines in the area had experienced two major disasters since opening in 1910. The disregard for miners' lives underground extended to their living quarters. In the camp, the inspectors found 124 shoddy company-owned houses inadequate for human habitation.[88] The Jamison miners were denied the very things that Frank McCoy, writing from Massachusetts, had implied they should be defending: their personal security, life, and health.

Americans who telegrammed their anger with the miners to Washington, claiming that miners "work[ed] for their country under much better conditions than is enjoyed by any soldier anywhere," were countered by Ickes, who issued a statement on mine safety soon after taking control of the mines. From Ickes's perspective, the mines were as dangerous as combat. The Bureau of Mines called for quick action "to avoid stigma of a national, even worldwide scandal because of the callousness with which the lives of its workers are being sacrificed."[89] The maiming, however, continued, and the UMW encouraged miners to think of the coal mine as a front in the war. When an explosion ripped through the Sayreton Mine in Alabama, the *United Mine Workers Journal* shared photographs of survivors with "burned, charred flesh" being rescued from the "Coal Mining Front."[90]

The OWI investigator Richard Deverall placed the conditions in the coalfields in a wider context that went back to the mine wars of decades past. His reports to Secretary Ickes suggested that the conditions the inspectors found in and around the Jamison mine were representative. Miners, Deverall wrote, felt "that the aims of the war were phony, especially when their conditions have become worse and worse." The frequency of accidents in the mines left "scores of mine widows in this area—women who have seen their sons and boys go down into the pits, to return lifeless masses of flesh ground under the coal." Since the beginning of the war, more men from the region had died in the mines than on the battlefield. As for the coal camp itself, Deverall suggested that conditions were so bad that they had to be seen—and smelled—to be believed. "Living under such conditions as they do," Deverall warned, "I am quite sure a lot of them would rather bring home the Army and set it to work on the coal operators."[91] Miners certainly placed the situation in the longer history of coalfield wars. The *United Mine Workers Journal* equated the WLB recommendations with the hated yellow-dog contracts that had forbidden miners from joining a union as a condition of employment.[92] The war might be an exceptional context for others, but the opinions of the public mattered little to miners who had "fought for so many years" against these very conditions of coalfield life. "The present situation," Deverall concluded, "is merely one more incident in a long fight."[93] And indeed, the miners' fight would continue after the Allies declared victory.

Ringing in the first New Year after the war's end, *Stars and Stripes* looked ahead to the United States' "first year of full peacetime production" in many years. Across the country, workers struck in incredible numbers, particularly in heavy industry, as they sought to recoup the wages and morale lost amid the postwar reconversion of the economy. But as readers scanned down the page, they came across a grisly discovery: the recovery of "four more bodies of . . . miners entombed by an unexplained explosion" in eastern Kentucky. The bodies were so "burned and mashed" that rescue workers despaired of finding any more survivors, even as fourteen workers remained missing.[94] The war had ended in Europe and Japan, but the coal mining front remained active.

Only two weeks later, disaster struck again, this time in West Virginia. A coal dust explosion tore through the Havaco No. 9 mine near Welch. Fifteen miners were killed. Dozens of people, both workers and bystanders, were injured. As horrific as that death toll was, observers recognized that it could easily have been much worse. More than 270 miners had been underground at the time in the mine, which emitted more than 11,000 cubic meters of methane each day. The dry winter weather exacerbated the danger from the gas; miners sometimes referred to winter as "explosion season." The first area residents to arrive on the scene initially thought no one could have possibly survived such a powerful blast. They had good reason to worry. A school for Black children, only five hundred feet away from the mine entrance, was severely damaged, and several children were

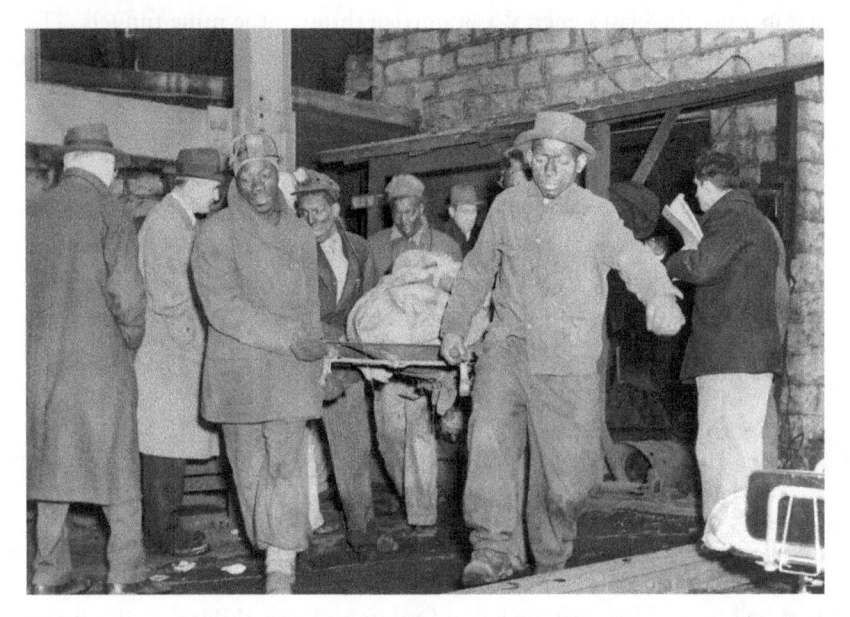

Figure 3.4 Rescue teams recover victims of the Havaco disaster.
Source: West Virginia and Regional History Center.

injured badly enough to require hospitalization. Miners' homes around the area lost windows and doors in the middle of winter. The mine had exploded before, too, thirty-four years prior, killing eighty miners.[95]

As it turned out, the explosion had ripped outward through the coal camp rather than through the narrow underground tunnels. Had the explosion originated in a different spot in the mine, the death toll would almost certainly have reached into the hundreds, a scale of disaster the state had not seen since the Monongah disaster killed more than three hundred in 1907. A company official, doubtlessly relieved he would not be associated with a disaster of that scale, proclaimed it the "most miraculous escape from death in the history of West Virginia coal mining."[96] Regional newspapers echoed the miracle narrative even as they recounted in grim detail a heavy casualty toll that overwhelmed local hospitals. The outcome, however, was only part miracle. Mine inspectors credited two key safety practices the UMW and other reformers had advocated for decades with mitigating the underground impact and saving hundreds of lives. The first was ventilating tunnels and working areas with fresh air. The second, known as rock dusting, entailed spraying surfaces and entryways with pulverized limestone. In the event of an explosion, the limestone absorbed the heat, dampening the blast's energy as it hurtled through the mine tunnels. The chief of the West Virginia Department of Mines praised mine management after touring the site with federal inspectors.[97]

Elmer Mitchell, a miner recently returned from the European theater, saw things differently. He had survived the front only to become a "near casualty" in a mine explosion less than six months after arriving home. On the day of the explosion, he was working on the tipple outside the mine but had stepped away for a smoke break when the earth began to rumble. Mitchell instinctively began running and soon found himself under a hail of debris. When he could focus again, he saw the tipple had been destroyed. He rushed back to the mine entrance to help those underground evacuate, many with serious injuries.[98]

Mitchell was not the only recently returned veteran at the mine that day. Not all were as fortunate. The heat of the explosion left recently discharged Ernest Wagner, only twenty-three, with second-degree burns around his eyes. Ab Ambern had been home less than two months and perished in the blast, leaving behind a wife and two children.[99] But it was Mitchell's attempt to grapple with his experience that was captured in the public record. As a member of the 28th Division, Elmer Mitchell survived the Battle of Normandy, but "artillery barrages," he recounted, "were nothing compared to this." Mitchell's account evoked a strong response. His story spread around the coalfields and across the country, in papers from Maine to Arizona, Idaho to Louisiana, all of which printed the horrifying story of a "mine blast worse than guns in war."[100]

Miners who read this story in the paper almost certainly interpreted its meaning differently than the wider public. The tone of the story as it was reprinted around the country was clearly meant to elicit shock. It is hard to imagine, however, that anyone with experience in the mines could have been shocked by Mitchell's comparison. The mine's perils were too familiar. Even though the war had ended in Europe and Japan, the nation's miners remained embattled with the same system of energy production they had been at war with for more than half a century. The upheavals of war had transformed the nation in many ways. Individuals became accustomed to new ways of living, working, and consuming. The American state had vastly expanded its capacity to administer domestic affairs and shape the international order. But so much of the day-to-day experience of work in the mines remained unchanged.

If "peace" fell unevenly across the world in 1945, what would peacetime mean for the miners of the United States? The Guffey-Vinson system had failed. Some hoped it might be revived after the war, but the warfare state's reorganization of federal authority made such an effort appear untenable. The experience of the mining workplace in wartime also reshaped the UMW's postwar demands. Harold Ickes, who had spent substantial time in control of the nation's mines, knew the UMW would only support a new system that offered greater union representation and independence from the Department of the Interior.[101] It would take four years of conflict and negotiation between miners, operators, and the government to reach and implement the agreement that would form the basis for the postwar coal-fired social contract.

Miners struck when their contract expired on April 1, 1946, issues of health and safety heavy on their minds. John Lewis put the issue at the center of bargaining. The operators clung to the more limited frame of negotiation over wages.[102] The nation had only a month's worth of coal stockpiled—supplies that were unevenly distributed. When miners cut off the nation's coal supply, the Supreme Court saw such measures as "a serious threat to orderly constitutional government and to the social and economic welfare of the nation."[103] The strike continued into late May, and President Harry Truman ordered Ickes's replacement at Interior, Julius Krug, to seize the mines and negotiate a contract with the UMW. Krug had extensive experience in the utility sector, ultimately directing the Office of War Utilities during the coal shortages of 1943. Attuned to the importance of coal in everyday American life and receptive to miners' concerns about health and safety, Krug reached a deal with Lewis that conceded union-administered medical funds and a welfare fund run jointly by the union and federal government. He also conceded to the operators' demand that the welfare fund be financed with a per-ton royalty rather than a payroll tax. Krug then extended the agreement to cover mine safety, promising that a federal mine safety code would be formulated and applied while the U.S. government ran the mines.[104] These concessions ultimately provided the framework for the 1950 agreement that established the postwar coal-fired social contract.

In the interim, strikes erupted regularly over a range of issues: broken promises, contract expiration, outrage at the rising tide of antiunion politics, and mine safety. The Krug-Lewis agreement sounded better on paper than the reality miners experienced, particularly on safety issues. Lewis blamed Krug for insufficient attention to and slow implementation of the promised safety standards. The antiunion climate also curbed miners' safety committees' efforts to enforce safety practices on the job. The president of UMW District 12, which covered the Illinois coalfields, explained how antiunion legislation undermined mine safety committees in day-to-day operations: "The mine workers determined that there was an immediate imminent danger in that mine, and they refused to enter it. [The coal administrator] wrote me a letter that his report showed there was no immediate or imminent danger in there and to immediately get those men back into the mines. Well, he did not say the Smith-Connally Act would be applied, but he went all around it . . . they were just put back into the mines under a court injunction, with a very severe penalty."[105]

In southern Illinois, 111 miners paid for the gaps between code, contract, and everyday practice with their lives. On March 25, 1947, 142 miners, working for the federal government under the Lewis-Krug agreement, were underground on the day shift at the Centralia No. 5 mine when the mine exploded. Sixty-five miners died from the force of the explosion or burned to death. Forty-six more succumbed to carbon monoxide poisoning as they tried to escape. Only thirty-one miners survived.

Conditions in the mine were "exceedingly dry and dusty," with explosive coal dust gathered in heavy deposits throughout the mine. "Very little effort," accident inspectors assessed, had been made to remove the dust. Rock dusting practices, which could have tamped the impact of the blast, were inadequate. Mine management supplied improper fuses for blasting and detonated explosions while miners remained underground, in direct violation of the recently implemented safety code.[106] Inspectors knew the mine was dangerous. They had inspected the mine twice in the previous six months. Both inspections revealed dozens of safety violations—sixty and fifty-two, respectively. Additionally, the miners' safety committee had complained about the safety conditions to the government. In a long list of unsafe conditions, they noted that their "biggest grievance is dust"—the same dust that had amplified the power of the explosion. Of the three-man safety committee, Paul Compers and Gus Hohman died in the explosion. Stephen Maloney was spared only because he was home sick that day.[107]

Lewis called miners out of the mines for a week of mourning. He laid the blame on Krug for dragging his feet on the implementation of safety standards despite an obvious need to do so. The mass death at Centralia, particularly with the government operating the mine, "pricked the public's conscience."[108] But if Centralia was a particularly egregious example of the systemic disregard for miners' safety, it also exemplified a trend that held across the coalfields. Safety officials inspected 3,345 mines in 1946. Only two complied with federal safety standards. Government-operated mines ran with an average of twenty-seven violations each.[109] As the Senate convened for their fourth day of hearings to investigate the Centralia disaster, mine rescuers raced to find survivors from another explosion in a smaller mine in Exeter, Pennsylvania. Seventeen men were on shift that morning. The explosion killed ten of them.[110]

The Wyoming senator Joseph Mahoney heard about the Exeter explosion over the radio before Krug began his testimony about the Centralia disaster and asked him for more information. Krug demurred, saying the mine was an anthracite mine and thus not under his direct control. But as questioning continued, Krug failed to provide a convincing explanation for the persistence of atrocious safety conditions, which he attributed to longstanding industry practices, even after more than ten months of government control. He went as far as to suggest that the mines were safer than ever, "notwithstanding the Centralia disaster."[111] According to Melvyn Dubofsky and Warren Van Tine, Krug opted not to fully enforce the safety agreements because to "do so would have meant at least the temporary shutdown of much of the industry."[112] Krug argued that violations were a regular part of operations. Indeed, he said, "nothing could be more unrealistic than to assume that a mine is dangerously unsafe so long as there is a single 'violation' of the code."[113] Krug's interest in the coal was the stability of the country's energy system and economy, not his own profit or the war effort. His testimony revealed how even in the postwar years, the country's normalization of the mine's dangers continued. Federal mine safety legislation with enforcement power would not be on the books until 1952, finally pushed over the finish line by another mass casualty explosion in West Frankfort that killed 119 miners, only forty miles from Centralia.[114]

Despite the operators' continued intransigence, there was no going back from the concessions Krug had granted the miners during the seizure. However, on the main issues the union had raised in 1946, particularly safety issues and the health and welfare funds, the operators remained intransigent. Despite an increasingly hostile political environment, successful prosecution of Lewis for contempt in the courts, and signs of decline in coal markets, miners held fast to their demand. Over the next two years, a combination of official and unofficial strikes finally encoded this new system, the United Mine Workers Welfare and Retirement Fund, into the 1950 agreement between the UMW and the mine operators.

The 1950 agreement reestablished a coal-fired social contract for the nation, replacing the New Deal system, which had broken under the strain of war, and it represented a major victory for the nation's coal miners. This updated coal-fired social contract enshrined a wider set of mechanisms for ensuring stability that traversed the economic and the energetic, the miners' body with the body politic. It created a coalfield health care system and a pension fund for miners, controlled by the union and funded through an operator-paid royalty on each ton of coal mined under union contract, the United Mine Workers Welfare and Retirement Fund. The Fund established hospitals throughout the coalfields, undercutting the power of the operators by offering a medical alternative to company doctors. The UMW hoped that the Fund's medical program could serve as a model for a future national health care system.[115] The Fund's impact was life changing for many miners, pensioners, and their families. Longtime reformer and UMW ally Josephine Roche headed the Fund, seeing an opportunity to "build new values, new realities" in the mining regions.[116]

This victory did not come without concessions. The UMW agreed to a financing system that tied miners' health care system and pensions to the economic welfare of the coal industry, and the union also agreed to increased mechanization to help secure industry profitability—a choice that would decimate employment numbers in the coalfields over the coming decade. Union support for mechanization would have unintended consequences for occupational health and safety; these would become clear during the 1960s.[117] The role of the consumer, who had in theory been equal to producers and workers under the Guffey Acts, now functioned as a background logic justifying the pursuit of stability, the political relationship between miner and coal consumer left implicit and obscured.

This new coal-fired social contract would sit at the heart of the postwar political order. Lasting for two decades, it would prove the most durable version of the coal-fired social contract yet. But the very health and welfare components that transformed miners' lives also funded the coalfield welfare regime by digging more coal. The mines, safer than they had once been, remained deadly. That violence would ultimately be the postwar coal-fired social contract's undoing.

PART TWO

Stasis
(1950–1969)

First Interlude

Between Deep Time and the Future

Across the first half of the twentieth century, the coalfield state became more fully integrated into the structures of national governance, a process that incompletely and imperfectly democratized the coalfields. But the drama of renegotiating the coal-fired social contract after World War II also regionalized a much larger story. A global energy transformation unfolded in the wake of total war, driven by the reorganization of international trade in fuels, the fracturing of the European and Japanese empires, the anchoring of the world's monetary system to the U.S. dollar, and the dawn of the nuclear age and Cold War. In the five postwar years it took the United Mine Workers, coal operators, and the American state to refashion the coal-fired social contract, this changing international order had altered the energy system that contract was meant to stabilize. The UMW thus entered the postwar period with a coal-fired social contract negotiated to stabilize an energy system that was fast disappearing.

The enormous wartime increases in coal production gave way to precipitous decline. By the mid-1950s, production reached only 60 percent of its wartime highs, around the same levels as during the Great Depression. The impact of those declines went further than production numbers alone suggested, because John L. Lewis had agreed to increased underground mechanization to help coal remain "competitive" with other

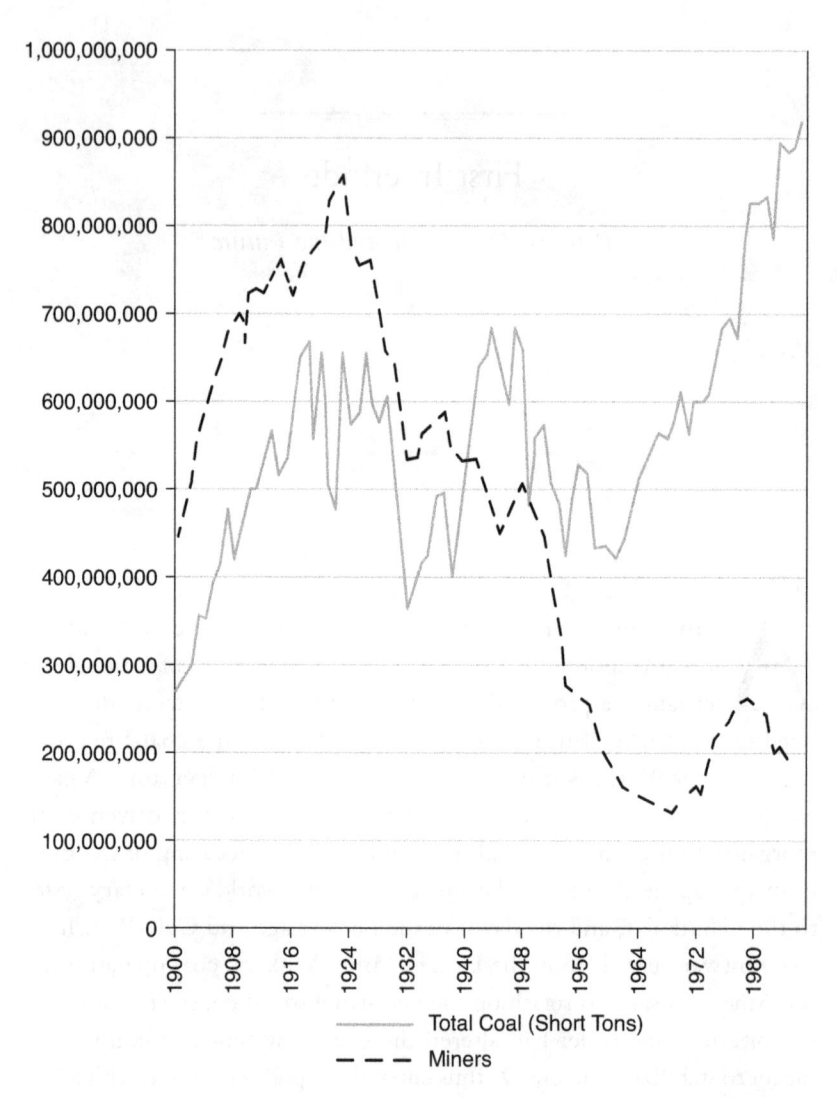

Figure Int.1 Increased Productivity in U.S. Coal Mines, 1900–1985.
Source: BM and National Mining Association, Bituminous Coal Data (1972); Commonwealth of Pennsylvania, Department of Mines, Anthracite Annual Report (1953), 3–4; DOL, MSHA, "Coal Fatalities, 1900 Through 2020"; EIA, Annual Energy Review, September 2012, table 7.2.

fuels—especially the residual fuel oil making quick inroads in East Coast utility markets. The resulting community-level devastation was nothing short of apocalyptic. Forty percent of the mining jobs that existed in 1945 vanished within a decade. By the time employment numbers bottomed out in the late 1960s, nearly 75 percent of the nation's mining jobs had evaporated, even though coal production had recovered. The moment meant to signify a new era in coalfield governance also ushered in an existential threat to the union's future. The UMW leadership's tone quickly shifted from the brash assuredness of the high-production war years to increasingly anxious accommodation.[1]

At the same time, observers within and beyond the coalfields increasingly recognized that the different fuel industries constituted a single national energy system. The illusion of separate fuels and separate markets had been dispelled. Coal's problems would have to be negotiated in a broader, multifuel arena of energy politics. To survive this transformation of the country's energy system and political economy, the coal industry, and the UMW with it, needed to adapt. To secure coal's place in the nation's energy mix both ideologically and materially, the UMW sought to make clear what had been undeniable during the war: coal was the baseload fuel of American democracy.

UMW leaders aligned with the operators as they sought to position coal as the nation's basic fuel for electric power, a booming industry. They hoped expanded use of coal for electric power would help prevent social and economic collapse across the coalfields and sustain the UMW's nascent healthcare and pension system. They justified their collaboration with industry by arguing that coal—and coal miners—faced a new kind of foe: "foreign oil," a framing that obscured that much of the oil was being produced by American companies in "frontier" spaces reminiscent of the coalfield state.[2] Amid the escalating Cold War, their argument went, economic threats to the coal industry and coal miners represented an ideological challenge to the nation and threatened national security by weakening its energy undergirding. In the first decade of the national security state, they connected miners' demands for economic and bodily security to wider national discourses of energy policy and national security. But the UMW's conscious situation of energy politics as the fulcrum on which miners' economic security and the country's national security might be balanced was a choice, born of perceived necessity, which would have longer-term consequences as the UMW entered a new era, particularly after John L. Lewis stepped down from the UMW presidency in 1960.

As the nation's most widely available domestic fuel, the postwar outlook for coal should have been bright, with the rapid acceleration of energy consumption during these years sometimes termed capitalism's "golden age." But by the mid-1950s, the coal industry confronted a strange paradox: energy consumption writ large was rising rapidly, and the use of coal was declining with equal speed.[3] The roots of this change were complex and multicausal.

Converging technological, social, diplomatic, and political-economic changes collapsed and reshaped coal markets in the 1950s. The railroads, traditionally one of coal's largest markets, dieselized their fleets. By the mid-1950s, railroad use of coal was so insignificant no one bothered to count it. Retail coal deliveries continued to decline as more people electrified their heating systems or converted to oil and gas. Coal even faced challenges in its growth sectors. The small but growing export market also portended long-range decline in the U.S. steel industry, another major coal market.[4] Steam generating stations rapidly increased their megawatt rating during the postwar period, and these larger stations deployed new technology that burned coal more efficiently.[5] The growing amount of electric power produced by utilities thus outpaced the growing amount of coal burned in generating stations. Still, in the postwar years, coal's future was yoked to electric power.

Scholars have typically ascribed the changes in this period as an energy transition from a coal-fired regime to an oil-powered one, but the transition narrative is not as tidy as it first appears. Coal did indeed recover by the end of the following decade. More accurately, the American energy system became a mature, interdependent, multifuel system. In the early decades of the twentieth century, coal had accounted for three-quarters of all primary energy in the United States, but in the second half of the twentieth century, no single energy source would ever achieve that kind of dominance again. At the same time, the country lacked a unifying energy policy that could manage the relationships among fuels, even though the federal government had been aware of the need for such a policy since the late 1930s. The impact of that shift destabilized not just the coal industry but the entire energy system, leading to power disruptions, gasoline shortages, and unemployment not just in the coalfields but the oilfields as well.[6]

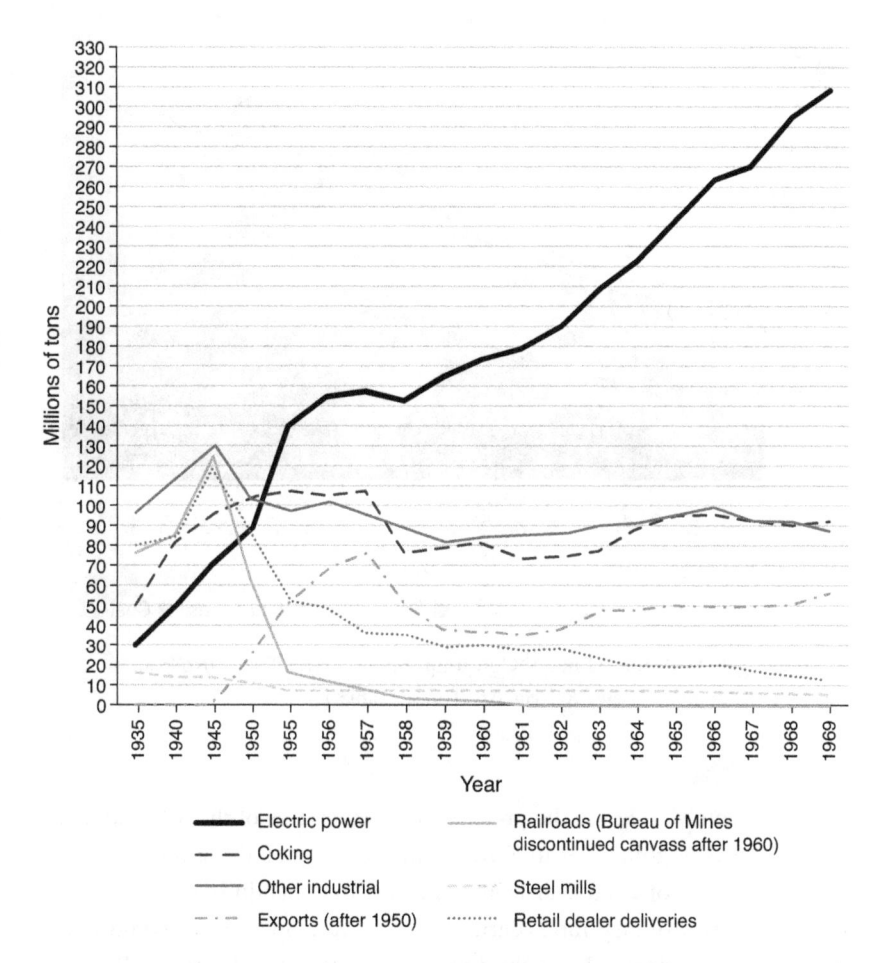

Figure Int. 2 Bituminous Coal Consumption by Consumer Class, 1945–1969.
Source: Charles River Associates, *The Economic Impact of Public Policy on the Appalachian Coal Industry and the Regional Economy* (Cambridge, MA: n.p., 1973), 11–12; 183. BM, Minerals Yearbook, 1969.

This reorganization of the nation's energy production and use patterns would have been challenging enough to navigate in peacetime, but as quickly became apparent in the 1950s, "postwar" was not the same thing as peace.

War, preparation for wars, and the intensifying American-Soviet standoff figured centrally in energy decision making. Politicians looked to the nation's energy system to affirm the superiority of American lifestyles over Soviet ones *and* to provide an energy stockpile for new national security

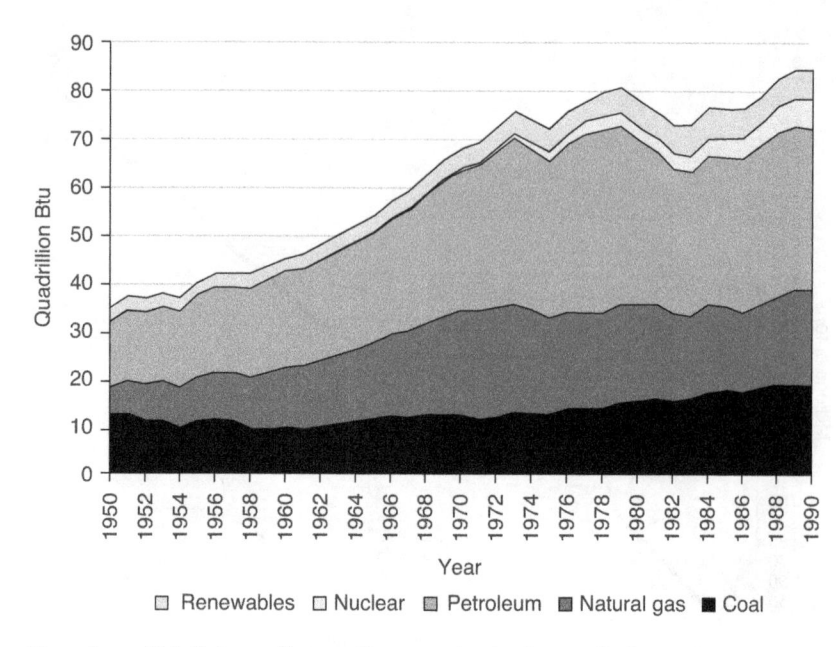

Figure Int. 3 U.S. Primary Energy Consumption by Source Fuel, 1950–1990.
Source: EIA, *Monthly Energy Review*, April 2021, Table 1.3.

commitments. Alongside the preparedness imperative of the national security state was ongoing war in Korea—and Korea would not be an isolated conflict. A mix of Cold War militarization, an expanding global network of U.S. bases, military interventions, and covert operations would make warlike energy demands on the U.S. state in the decades that followed.[7] Politicians debated not the fuels themselves but rather how to manage their interconnectedness, how to decide between competing interests, and how to demonstrate the United States was indeed an energy-intensive democracy, one that could serve as a model for "the progress and freedom of man."[8]

Americans' vision of liberal prosperity in the Cold War rested on rapidly growing energy consumption, suggesting that the increased use of fuels refined from petroleum did not pose the long-range threat to coal markets that many assumed. The more oil-dependent the country became, the more appealing the nation's coal appeared as a means of slowing the depletion of oil reserves. In the short term, that might mean using coal in electricity generation and other industrial applications. In the long term, policy makers and industry leaders hoped that the mass production of synthetic liquid fuels derived from coal, or synfuels, would become economically viable.[9] Domestic oil reserves recoverable with available methods were limited, and despite efforts to ensure American control of oil concessions in Latin America and the Middle East, rising economic nationalism in oil-producing countries threatened U.S. access to those reserves. The growth of American economic and cultural dominance deepened global energy interdependence—and the potential for supply disruptions. Even as American capital investment in global energy development increased drastically, reaching more than $18 billion by 1964, energy flows faced political obstacles and uncertainties as they passed through contested spaces: tribal lands, decolonizing and postcolonial states, disputed sea routes.[10] The eruption of war in Korea amplified fears of supply disruptions, and Egyptian president Gamal Abdel Nasser's nationalization of the Suez Canal Corporation in 1956 rekindled them once again.[11] Moreover, decades of American oil diplomacy had largely been carried out by private firms even if those firms had state support. Oil produced under an American flag—whether in the country or in overseas concessions—was not, ultimately, controlled by the state.[12]

The expansion of U.S. international power in the early Cold War could be traced in flows of coal as well as flows of oil. In the nineteenth century, coal's close relationship to U.S. imperial power had been most closely tied to the infrastructures necessary to power coal-fired steamers.[13] By the 1950s, however, coal-fired ships were mostly a thing of the past.[14] In the postwar years, the international future of American coal lay at the intersection of the emerging coal export market and American attempts to reshape the international order. Although the foreign market for American coal remained relatively small, it shaped the politics of coal during the 1950s because of the Cold War context and because it was one of the few markets for coal that was growing. In earlier years, coal exports from the United States had been almost entirely hemispheric. Canada, the largest importer of American coal, had such close ties with both heavy industry and electrical generation in the United States that Canadian markets were more like an extension of the U.S. market than an export market. The United States also exported comparatively smaller amounts to Latin America. The war reorganized global coal markets. While Canada continued to be the largest market for American coal, the war's destruction opened new markets for U.S. coal in Western Europe and Japan.[15] The fracturing of the

French and British empires opened small but growing markets for American coal in Africa and Asia. As the United States cornered these new markets, it became the world's largest net exporter of coal, followed by the Soviet Union and China, though in true Cold War fashion, U.S. analysts considered China and the Soviet Union a single bloc rather than separate exporters. By 1960, the world energy market was bifurcated into "free" and "Communist" coal.[16]

"Free" American coal made for good rhetorical flourish but offered little consolation for communities devastated by the industry's postwar collapse. Even the most optimistic outlook for coal's growing export market could not hope to salvage the situation. Only domestic, coal-fired electric power generation could do that. As a result, in coal's darkest decade, from 1953 to 1963, UMW leaders allied with industry officials to secure coal's dominance in electric power generation in ways that were profoundly shaped by the global Cold War. The debate over how to power the growing domestic appetite for electricity presented an opportunity to reassert coal's importance in the story of American freedom—or, depending on one's vantage point, the American way of empire.

The UMW called for major investments in coal research—perhaps even at the scale of federal investments in the development of atomic power. To advocate for coal research, UMW leaders deepened relationships with industry leaders, ultimately forming the National Coal Policy Conference (NCPC) in 1959.[17] They presented this institution as the future of industry-labor relations, demonstrating collaboration rather than conflict. Fuels of the future needed new models of industrial relations. Lewis took a leading role in this outreach, aided by a cadre of hand-selected deputies—most consequentially, Lewis's special assistant, W. A. "Tony" Boyle. Through policy-based coalitions and coal-centered institutions, this group of "coal men" composed of industry and union leaders cultivated political and business alliances across trade policy, research and development initiatives, and efforts to protect coal's share of domestic markets.

The coal men made two primary interventions in defense of coal. First, they advocated for mandatory oil import quotas, a venture in which they were joined by the domestic oil producers known as the "independents." They suggested the fortunes of the coal industry were foundational to newly salient ideas of national security, a relationship that entitled coal to special economic protections. Second, they lobbied for government investment in coal research, particularly toward projects that would make synfuels from coal technologically and economically viable. In a country that used energy intensity as a measure of living standards, they claimed coal offered a reliable power source for energetic statecraft—if only, the argument went, the state would not subject coal to unequal treatment in the marketplace.

The UMW communicated both interventions in two directions—to the union's rank-and-file membership and to the broader American public, especially national politicians. They shaped the way that miners saw their place in the nation and the way the nation saw the plight of the coalfields. And inadvertently, they opened a space for coal miners to contest what "security" would mean and who would get to define it. As a result, the coal-fired social contract became intertwined with the discursive politics of security at the height of the Cold War.

Coal men used the language of national security to suggest that the "free enterprise system of this American republic" and "the precious heritage of political liberty" were at stake in determining which fuel would power the postwar future.[18] To present oil as a threat to the coal-fired story of freedom, they bound renewed concerns about the availability of future oil reserves to a legal tradition stretching back to the oil antitrust cases in the early part of the twentieth century. Coal men portrayed oil as geologically scarce, naturally predisposed to monopoly, and subject to undue foreign influence, especially from countries in the Third World.[19] Coal advocates warned that interdependence could endanger "the national security of the nation and the future of Americans as a people."[20]

Because this debate centered on the utility markets, the focus of these policy debates was not gasoline, diesel, or jet fuel but the residual fuel oil created as a byproduct in the refining process. "Dumping" of residual fuel oil on the eastern seaboard, mostly from Venezuela, led some utilities to convert their generating facilities to burn it.[21] Coal men joined the independents in advocating for import quotas to support national security goals and to facilitate fair competition between domestic fuels in the utility markets. Together, coal men and the independents formed the Foreign Oil Policy Committee (FOPC) in 1953. The "flood of foreign fuel," the coal members of the FOPC argued, posed "a critical threat to . . . the military and domestic economy." They further argued that the national security state required multifuel domestic development to keep the country in "a state of constant readiness."[22]

Although coal men joined with the independents to campaign for oil import quotas, they strongly disputed the independents' claim that stateside oil reserves were substantial. Too much dependence on domestic oil, they argued, exposed a paradox. Where exhaustible fuels were concerned, improved productive capacity in the name of war preparedness also drew down those same domestic reserves that might become even more politically precious were a war to break out.[23] This depletion problem tilted the scales heavily in favor of coal, which occurred abundantly across the North American continent. In 1953, the U.S. Geological Survey conservatively estimated that of the 1.9 trillion tons of coal spread across the continent's winding coal seams, more than 950 billion tons could be recovered with contemporary mining methods.[24] Coal men were quick to point out that at 1953 usage levels, those reserves would last more than two thousand years. No other fuel, they argued, could offer such long-term stability.[25]

This argument located coalfield instability in oilfields thousands of miles away, rather than in the industry's own bloody and tumultuous history. The coal members of the FOPC argued that their industry had been "relentlessly attacked" in the years after the war "by a competitor willing to sell its product at severe losses . . . to establish markets at the expense of coal." In particular, coal men never missed a chance to suggest that Venezuela was sending tankers carrying unemployment. By 1954, Venezuelan residual fuel oil deliveries to East Coast markets had reached 445,000 barrels daily. Coal's advocates in the FOPC argued that this oil was keeping twenty-two thousand American miners out of work. They argued that while coal competed fairly, making "every effort to keep itself competitive with other fuels, in the best tradition of the American economic system," the Venezuelans flooded markets, flagrantly disregarding the laws of supply and demand. "Although world markets are demanding increasingly more motor fuel, kerosene, and distillates, Venezuelan oil is being literally downgraded into coal to compete . . . in coal's rightful markets." This misuse of oil resources had thus deprived American coal of its "rightful future."[26]

The remark revealed their understanding of the relationship between energy and the United States' political economy and national security, an understanding that assumed each fuel had a proper role to play in the nation's energy system. The FOPC's coal members argued that coal, because it generated domestic employment and was less subject to foreign influence, was more compatible with American political culture and thus a better choice for generating electric power. Considering such remarks, the alliance between coal men and domestic oil producers in the effort to secure oil import quotas seems paradoxical. In working with domestic oil producers to secure a place for coal in the national security state, coal's advocates hedged that in the long run coal could outperform and outlast domestic oil in key markets.

The first wave of industrial lobbying did not secure the import quota the FOPC wanted, but President Eisenhower formed a Cabinet Committee on Energy Supplies and Resources—one of many such attempts to reorganize the administration of energy policy in the second half of the twentieth century. Eisenhower tasked the new committee with establishing a national fuels policy to govern the proper production and use of each energy source. The FOPC's lobbying also resulted in a long-range foreign aid program that would require the production and export of ten million tons of coal. Coal advocates hoped to expand U.S. exports to as much as 200 million tons, all to help build the American century.[27]

Eisenhower's Cabinet Committee ultimately rejected the idea of an imposed quota on oil imports, calling instead for voluntary action. They concluded that "every effort should be made and will be made to avoid the necessity of government intervention." Coal, they said, could be stabilized by increasing exports and requiring all government agencies to purchase their coal on a contract basis at least 75 percent of the time.[28] Here, union leaders and industry executives diverged. While the National Coal Association called the report "a step in the right direction," the UMW insisted the report failed "to meet squarely the realities facing the coal industry."[29] Instead of providing a long-term path to coalfield stability, the UMW charged, the Eisenhower administration's response provided new avenues by which residual oil imports could continue. The voluntary system was ineffective and short-lived. In March 1959, Eisenhower admitted its failure and established the Mandatory Oil Import Quota Program. During the first six years of the quota program, coal orders for utilities increased dramatically.[30] Still, thanks to mechanization, coal employment lagged recovery in coal production.

Even after the institution of the mandatory import quotas, the UMW remained concerned over growing trade liberalization. The union believed that the U.S. government was not doing enough to ensure "fair" energy markets. Coal could compete for utility markets *and* bolster national security, they insisted, if only the oil companies weren't allowed to dump their waste oil into the coastal markets, "threaten[ing] the life of the free and destroy[ing] freedom in the interests of revolution."[31] Further, the UMW insisted that domestic energy security was central to the national security state. Without domestic development promoted by protective quotas, the union argued, "the armed forces of this nation will be forced to fight to protect not American liberty, but international oil companies."[32] Coal men asserted the fundamental incompatibility of national security governance rooted in foreign oil dependence. Their criticisms built on a longstanding popular portrayal of the oil industry as antithetical to the practice of free enterprise and democracy.[33]

As they ascribed the political tensions of midcentury energy policy to the inherent qualities of individual source fuels, coal men made powerful claims about what they believed industrial society should look like and how it should be governed. Coal was a known quantity, embedded in the nation's already existing energy infrastructures. And given its wide geological occurrence, many in industry and government hoped it would become a source for synthetic versions of fuels traditionally derived from petroleum.[34] In so doing, then, they participated in a kind of political geology that reinterpreted the meaning of various fuels based on a new historical context and changing and contested visions of modernity.

The arguments about the character of different fuels and their suitability for electric power generation in the United States ironically obscured the labors of extraction. Despite the heavy involvement of the UMW in these efforts, and although the "Americanness" of coal had been profoundly shaped by the struggles of coal miners over the preceding decades, miners themselves only figured tangentially in these high-level discussions. Usually, they appeared as unemployment numbers to buttress support for the import quotas. By contrast, their own lived experiences of insecurity appeared to matter little. But as national security increasingly framed the politics of fuel choice, miners developed their own vision of what security might mean.

Security discourse among miners foregrounded representations of miners as citizens: soldiers reporting for duty, homes under attack, participants in Cold War preparedness. Through these depictions, miners strengthened the idea of energy citizenship, asserting the coal they extracted represented their political bonds with other Americans while also highlighting how the coal-fired social contract entailed unequal burdens, overwhelmingly borne by the coalfields.

The coalfield politics of security were deeply rooted in working-class vernaculars of stable employment central to New Deal conceptions of security.[35] But security simultaneously conjured Cold War national security discourse and a new language of security tied to the politics of productivity. For miners, there was no separating these politics of security from the persistent bodily insecurity they experienced at work. Between these slippery meanings of "security," coal miners came to understand their place in a changing energy system that nonetheless continued to depend on coal mined from deep within the earth, under extraordinarily dangerous conditions.[36] Certainly, danger in the mines was not new, but a new historical context reshaped the justifications presented for why miners should bear this risk and, in turn, how miners represented their citizenship claims.

Coal's shift from primarily serving as an industrial and transport fuel to primarily a source of electric power redefined how coal figured as a guarantor of the American way of life. If during World War II miners had been fulfilling an obligation to soldiers on the front line, in the postwar period, they ensured domestic abundance. But as many Americans consumed greater amounts of electric energy in their daily lives, mining communities remained poor and less connected to the energy-intensive lifestyle that

Figure Int. 4 Ray Zell, "This Is War," 1962.
Source: UMWJR 60/6.

increasingly signified consumer citizenship.[37] According to the UMW, the great degree of "human suffering and misery" in coal communities made "a mockery of the overly advertised well-being and wealth of our society."[38]

In its pages, the *United Mine Workers Journal* tied together coal's new markets with miners' changing understanding of citizenship. Ray Zell, the *Journal*'s cartoonist, melded markets and citizenship in his cartoons, encouraging miners to see energy policy as lived experience and to see these workplace experiences as linked to the fate of the nation. For Zell, miners were the nation's front-line defenders of the nation's energy system, a role that entailed obligations not unlike those borne by soldiers. In one of his cartoons, Uncle Sam inspects a union miner, standing at soldier's attention with his shovel held at his side, evocative of a gun, and deems him to be "passing inspection" by meeting his obligation to the nation's energy needs.[39]

Zell linked lived experience to the energy system by mixing images of energy workplaces, infrastructure, and coalfield landscapes with the visual culture of empire and militarism. In one cartoon titled "This Is War," Zell represented Venezuelan residual fuel oil imported to coastal utility markets as oil-barrel bombs raining down on the coalfields, sending the aspirations for postwar economic stability in the region, quite literally, up in smoke.[40] Miners suffered from this warfare both as producers and consumers. "Coal producing areas," the FOPC wrote, "are themselves huge consumers but if paychecks grow smaller or disappear entirely, the whole economy suffers."[41] If coalfield instability had once been seen as tightly linked to raucous—and often armed—struggles, in the postwar coalfields, instability meant something different: a threat to Keynesian models of growth.

The specific perils of the mining workplace also featured prominently, both contrasting energy and bodily security while also emphasizing how the nation expected sacrifice of miners. Zell linked the economic health of coal miners and the dangers of the mining workplace to the security of the entire nation. He suggested the deadly outcomes of common underground accidents, like roof collapses, were felt above ground as well. One cartoon depicted a congressman walking nonchalantly through a coal seam, unaware of the fracturing roof threatening to crush him if Congress failed to strengthen mine safety laws. The implication: danger and instability in the mines threatened Congress's ability to govern from Washington.[42]

But the roof fall metaphor could be deployed in even more complex ways, as the metaphor for a price collapse that nonetheless evoked the

Figure Int. 5 Ray Zell, "'Roof Fall' . . . Hurts the Nation, Too!" 1962.
Source: UMWJR, 60/6.

dangers of mining. In 1962, as concern over the future of the mandatory oil import program mounted, Zell titled one cartoon "'Roof Fall' . . . Hurts the Nation, Too!" Conjuring the common and deadly accident that crushed workers under thousands of pounds of rock, Zell depicted a miner being crushed beneath an oil barrel. With the miner lying in mortal peril, the nation is injured as the barrel lands on Uncle Sam's right foot. To miners, the implication of these visual stories would have been clear: the costs of national security were borne unequally. The metaphors of workplace danger situated miners in the national security imagination even as they revealed the ambiguities of security politics in the mining workplace. Competing definitions of bodily, economic, and national security overlapped and often contradicted one another.

The visual arguments in Zell's cartoons both shaped and reflected other statements by UMW leaders in public forums. A typical example came from the Pennsylvania anthracite field, the region most devastated by the changing energy system as anthracite markets in home heating collapsed.[43] District President August Lippi contended that the region's dire economic conditions endangered national security in a letter to the region's congressman. In only a decade, an 89 percent decline in the mining workforce pushed

10 percent of the population out of Pennsylvania's principal anthracite counties. The resulting loss of royalty payments into the anthracite Welfare and Retirement Fund, funded separately from the bituminous program, threatened the pensions of 9,500 retired miners and an annual flow of $3,420,000 into the local economy. Lippi blamed oil imports. The wide-ranging impact of lost mining jobs, he wrote, "could lead to the sapping of our Nation's strength in case of war." National defense and economic growth were two sides of the same coin, and the development of the coalfields may "tip the scales in our favor" were a national security emergency to arise. This claim drew on previous efforts by the Solid Fuels Administration for the War to encourage domestic coal conversion as a way of saving liquid fuels for direct military applications. The "peril to our Nation's security," he suggested, compelled public interest in the coalfields.[44]

UMW members across the eastern bituminous coalfields, who supplied most of the coal for utility and industrial applications, also presented themselves as energy soldiers and reliable partners in the national security state. A UMW officer in Virginia wrote to President John F. Kennedy that miners "have never failed our government when they have called upon them in time of crisis to produce the fuel that was so vitally needed to carry on our economy and our wars."[45] The officers of Local 5741 warned in their letter to the president that increased oil imports would "cause the Mine Workers of this Nation to lose their jobs. . . . Not only this, but should this nation be attacked, the coal mines would be insufficient to furnish the necessary fuel for the safety of this Nation."[46] The communications were the product of a letter-writing campaign organized from the national office, but the internal instructions for this campaign asked letter writers to focus on unemployment and economic devastation without mentioning national security.[47] Writers appear to have added these observations on their own, having imbibed both Zell's imagery spread across the pages of the *Journal* and the public statements of union officials and coal industry leaders. By arguing that coal's place in the national security state was intimately tied to the economic fortunes of the workers who mined it, the UMW, from its international officers down to its local leadership, presented its own vision of national security through economic development. As went the coalfields, they argued, so did the nation.

To secure coal as the fuel of American aspirations, the UMW and the coal industry looked to federal investment in research and development to strengthen the links between national security statecraft and coal-fired economic growth. The coal men presented themselves as dependable partners willing to undertake new obligations and ethics of service to provide a nation increasingly reliant on electricity as its "lifeblood" with a stable supply of coal.[48] The fact that coal men believed Americans could be convinced to accept such claims given decades of bloody history in the coalfields suggests the depth of change effected by the negotiation of the coal-fired social contract. In this new narrative, domestic coal powered the tremendous increase in per capita domestic energy consumption that cultivated citizen buy-in to Cold War policies.

For coal to maintain its position, Americans had to see more than a past laden with violence and conflict. Americans had to look at the coalfields and see a vision of the future that emerged from a different kind of historical narrative. Coal's advocates suggested coal was geological evidence of the United States' manifest destiny. "Many years before the first one of our ancestors crawled out of his cave, nature had started producing the future fuel for American industry," explained the Appalachian Electric Power Company's G. South Dunn during a promotional television program. The program's host, future West Virginia congressman Jim Kee, concurred. To make his point, he lifted a shiny piece of coal from the presenter's table. "Without coal, without this product here, our progress in America could not have been possible . . . no manufacturing centers, no railroads to conquer the west, no great foundries to turn out our weapons."[49]

Although Kee took care to note how that shiny piece of coal had been mined from the Sycamore Coal Company's Cinderella mine, he carefully avoided giving any history of that particular mine even as he used its coal to symbolize coal's place in American history in general. He neglected to mention that in 1914, a fire in the Cinderella mine killed five men who suffocated as the flames that trapped them underground also consumed their oxygen. Or that in 1918, an officer of the Sycamore Coal Company murdered the local chief of police in a "crime of passion." Or that the mine was in Mingo County, West Virginia—the site of the 1920 Matewan Massacre.[50] In pursuit of what they believed was their rightful place in the American century, coal's advocates in industry and government were content to replace energy's history with geological mysticism. For Kee, a cleaner version of history made for a brighter future, where the fact that "every American is dependent on coal every hour of every day" was a promise of shared prosperity rather than precarious dependence.[51]

To achieve this coal-fired vision of the American century, coal's advocates asked for support from the federal government. A Congressional Special Subcommittee on Coal Research determined in 1956 to find out "whether or not there is a possibility that an effective research program for coal might be developed in the same magnitude and on the same general organizational basis, as those which have been and are now currently conducted by the Atomic Energy Commission." The heavy investment of the U.S. government in developing civilian nuclear power over the preceding decade had opened the door to greater claims on research and development for energy resources.[52] Moreover, coal miners' supporters in Congress insisted that "coal miners . . . have some rights to ask . . . this attention and consideration."[53] Congress backed a bill that would have established a Coal Research and Development Commission, but the bill was pocket-vetoed by President Eisenhower in the fall of 1959—just months after he had implemented the MOIP. Eisenhower noted that this function already fell under the scope of the Interior Department and suggested Congress come back with a narrower bill that would grant Interior the ability to contract coal research funding, rather than trying to, once again, duplicate state authority by creating a new agency.[54]

Supporters of an independent coal research office pointed to the Atomic Energy Commission as an example of the possibilities presented by a standalone office, and some, like Kentucky congressperson Carl Perkins, suggested that keeping coal research in Interior would result in discrimination against coal because of the power of the other fuels, which, like oil, had more sway with department leadership.[55] But Congress ultimately acceded to Eisenhower's request, housing the new Office of Coal Research (OCR) in the Department of the Interior. The new office devised a logo meant to bring coal into the future: a flaming piece of coal in front of a test tube and electric bolt.[56]

The OCR worked to develop a research program that would boost coal recovery rates and utilization both in the short term and longer range, but the core of the program revolved around a few key technologies. Booz-Allen Hamilton completed the first OCR contract in 1962, a study of the shorter-range possibilities for expanded coal use. Their recommendations concerned a more conventional use of coal in electric power generation; they focused on reducing transportation costs by turning coal into a liquid slurry and moving it by pipeline and by extending the nation's infrastructure for long-distance, high-voltage electricity transmission. Operating costs at generation plants could be decreased by automating the generating process and by improving boilers and furnaces.[57] But many of the OCR's contracts revolved around the enticing possibility of converting coal into synfuels, both liquid and gaseous, that would allow users to substitute coal products for petroleum or natural gas ones. Ambitiously, the OCR predicted that new "coal refineries" could be opened at mine sites where coal "would be used and reused until every possible value has been wrung out of it," providing substantial employment in the process.[58]

The UMW was not a bystander to this process. They actively promoted the possibilities latent in these new technologies to their membership, testified before congressional committees, and directed substantial resources to the National Coal Policy Conference. The UMW eagerly portrayed the union and its miners as modernizers. As evidence, they presented the union's support for underground mechanization where other unions had opposed automation or, at least, sought to manage its implementation more directly. The *Atlantic*'s A. H. Raskin credited the UMW's vigorous support for mechanization with "assuring continuity of supply for the electric utilities and other big burners of coal, and expanding markets for coal in

Figure Int. 6 Ray Zell, "The Road Back," 1962.
Source: UMWJR 60/6.

its war of survival against the competitive onsurge of oil and natural gas."[59] Above ground, new technologies made strip mining coal an increasingly economically viable method of recovery, as new contouring technologies allowed the massive machines required by the process to navigate the rough Appalachian terrain.

The UMW was deeply invested in developing better ways of *using* coal. The Booz-Allen Hamilton study credited the UMW with advocating for expanded electric space heating as early as 1959, before it became a mainstream idea.[60] The UMW also hoped federal research investment could address growing issues with coal transportation—especially railcar shortages exacerbated by railroad dieselization. Could coal slurry pipelines replace traditional rail and trucking methods? What about mine mouth generation, which would eliminate the need for substantial transport away from the mine? Perhaps most seductively of all, could new technology convert coal into a liquid fuel? If coal could meaningfully compete with oil and natural gas, coal's status as "king" would be virtually assured—and miners' energy citizenship with it.

Ray Zell communicated these possibilities to miners in visual terms. In "The Road Back," Zell drew on the settler colonial tropes of westward

Figure Int. 7 Ray Zell, "Seeded/Sown with Hope," 1961.
Source: UMWJR 60/2.

expansion to suggest a new kind of coal-fired manifest destiny. Playing on the ubiquitous visual culture of nineteenth-century settler colonialism, a miner stands next to a pipeline meant to carry coal to new markets, crying "Eastward Ho!" In drawing on this well-known—and whitewashed—historical narrative, the cartoon yoked together a "new dawn" for coal with a future of national prosperity. Coal miners, in reopening coal's "frontiers" in the east, would make possible a future of energy abundance.

More subtle in its suggestion of expansionism was a cartoon promoting coal by wire that Zell drew around the same time, where a miner—pick in hand—stands beside a bucket of coal that has "sprouted" an electric pole, with wires stretching off into the distance. In suggesting that the electric grid grew from coal like a plant from the soil—a "coal burning plant," Zell termed it—the cartoon further emphasized how the technology made coal power "clean," an increasingly pressing issue as concern about air pollution grew across the country. Read alongside Zell's suggested captions, which included possibilities like "flowering power" and "fertile growth," the cartoon centered coal-fired electricity into the story of American economic

Figure Int. 8. Tony Boyle.
Source: UMWJR 35/2.

expansion, carefully husbanded by the coal miner.[61] In Zell's depiction, coal was a fertile soil indeed, especially in the miners' hands. Another cartoon depicted a miner carefully tending buckets of coal arranged like flowerpots. Behind "more coal research" waited a host of other coal-fired plants waiting to grow: mine safety, jobs, energy security through domestic production, and aid for distressed areas.

The UMW's vision of coal modernization was not limited to technological innovation but to the larger energy system of which it was part—and as the previous decades had made clear, that included industrial relations. In that arena, change loomed too. John L. Lewis was aging, and an inevitable change in leadership at the UMW loomed. Increasingly, Lewis directed his attention toward the National Coal Policy Conference, and his carefully cultivated group of deputies in the international office began to take on larger roles in the union. Replacing Lewis, a towering figure in the U.S. labor movement who had been at the UMW's helm for four decades, seemed impossible. In his shadow, however, a core of loyal officials had gained decades of experience. Most consequential among them was Lewis's special assistant, Tony Boyle, who, thanks to a combination of bureaucratic proceduralism and the death of Lewis's well-liked successor, Thomas Kennedy, found himself at the union's helm in January 1963.[62]

Boyle was the product of the old energy system from which the coal-fired social contract had emerged. He would also figure centrally in its disintegration. Born into a family of Irish miners in Montana in 1904, Boyle entered the mines in the early 1920s and by 1940 was the president of UMW District 27, the last Montana district president to be elected rather than appointed for decades.[63] The core of his political experience came not from union organizing but from his participation on the Montana State Unemployment Compensation Commission and the war production boards.[64] Lewis appointed Boyle as his special assistant in 1948. When Boyle finally stepped into the presidency, the world he knew so well was rapidly unraveling.

CHAPTER IV

Atomic Menace

The postwar coal-fired social contract, epitomized by the 1950 bituminous coal agreement, demarcated distinct periods of coalfield politics, a bifurcation only reinforced throughout the wider energy system by the advent of the atomic age. The effort to develop a commercial nuclear power program in the shadow of the mushroom cloud and a growing nuclear weapons arsenal wound together images of looming total destruction with those of cheap, even free, energy abundance.[1] The atom's advocates contended that the development of nuclear technology represented a civilizational advance, "a stimulant to a new moral maturity," as much as a "deterrent to immoral aggression."[2] Critics pointed to the devastating social, political, and ecological consequences of the nuclear bomb, the expanding popular understanding of radiation's impact on the body, the psychological tolls of nuclear fear, and the threat from nuclear accidents and disasters.[3] Still, people across the United States considered the detonation of the nuclear bomb a bifurcating event in world history, one that would fundamentally alter the way humans lived, worked, and interacted with the world around them.[4] Atomic power, concluded both boosters and critics, was a tool that could remake the world.

The U.S. Department of Labor's recognition of the atom's importance led the agency to form an Atomic Energy Study Group. The group echoed nuclear optimists' predictions of unprecedented abundance but also warned that an atomic society would face challenging labor problems. They felt nuclear technology required strict and disciplined operation. The strikes, lockouts, and other disputes that were a regular feature of U.S. industrial relations simply could not be tolerated in a nuclear context. Further, they predicted that whatever mechanisms were worked out for dealing with nuclear-sector labor issues would inevitably spill out to the broader realm of industrial relations, remaking the way the United States governed the relationship between employers and employees and the role that collective bargaining played in that process.[5] Thomas E. Murray, a nuclear booster who replaced David E. Lilienthal at the Atomic Energy Commission, suggested that nuclear power had radically shifted the energy foundation of American political economy and that it fell to the postwar generation to work out a new way of powering a "specifically American version of capitalism."[6]

Perhaps no U.S. labor leader took these claims more seriously than Tony Boyle, who ascended to power as the country's nuclear frenzies and perils reached their zenith. Boyle's tenure as UMW president is better remembered for events that, in 1963, were still years away: the 1969 order to murder his rival, the union reformer Jock Yablonski, and his departure from the union's top office in disgrace three years later, in 1972. In 1985, he would die in prison.[7] Boyle's rise and fall, nothing short of a coal-fired rendering of *Macbeth*, has typically been framed as a story of corruption in organized labor. But that framing has obscured a second important story: how Boyle's obsession with nuclear power encouraged miners to incorporate the growing understanding of environmental harms produced by the nation's energy system into the way they talked about the workplace dangers that had long animated their organizing and political activity.

Boyle closely tracked developments in the nuclear industry during the late 1950s and early 1960s. The "vision of a brave new world powered with nuclear energy" emerging from gatherings of leading international scientists stirred anxiety over the impact nuclear power would have not only on the coal industry but on American society more broadly.[8] Still, atomic power was not the only—or even principal—threat that the coal industry faced as it attempted to secure its place in the postwar energy system. Most of the attention of the UMW's national office remained focused on residual fuel oil. UMW Counsel Willard Owens dismissed the threat posed by the domestic development of commercial atomic power. The primary U.S. interest, he believed, lay not in domestic development but in international programs to "fulfill its obligation to the rest of the world, particularly in the underdeveloped areas." By his measure, the United States and the Soviet Union had little need to invest in domestic civilian nuclear power, since they possessed more than half the world's known coal reserves. It was the "have-not" nations more generally that Owens viewed as "seriously deficient in the supplies of energy."[9] The project of the American century, then, need not interfere with the development of domestic coal markets at home. U.S. support for nuclear development abroad might even *increase* domestic reliance on coal.[10] But by the early 1960s, Tony Boyle, unlike his counterparts, had become obsessed with the specter of nuclear power.

Boyle latched onto the atom quickly in part because it provided a new, seemingly modern outlet for an older cultural narrative of the "passage through destruction to rebirth"—a narrative that had great purchase in the wake of total war and the decimation of the coalfield economy.[11] In the years that followed, he wove a narrative in which the atom threatened the jobs of all miners and the lives of all Americans. For Boyle, that threat would justify a perpetual survival mentality, even as coal's market outlook improved. But Boyle's antinuclear crusade ultimately unleashed a series of unintended consequences. Antinuclear politics in the UMW, although they came from the top down, sharpened miners' understanding of the connection between environmental harm and workplace danger. Further, top-down discussions of the dangers of nuclear power implied that miners, by bearing the dangers of the coal energy system, kept the rest of the country safe from nuclear disaster. Boyle's antinuclear campaign suggested the persistence of unequal energy citizenship and thus eroded the perceived legitimacy of the coal-fired social contract.

The most potent aspect of Boyle's veritable crusade against nuclear power remained his effective connection of the atom's promise of energy abundance with its penchant for destruction. Both his own rhetoric and the union's official communications depicted nuclear power as an energy source that portended mortal danger not only to miners but to the entire country. The UMW argued that the Price-Anderson Act, originally passed in 1957 and renewed in 1966, by capping the liabilities assumed by commercial nuclear power plants, also limited the value of human life.[12] Boyle's antinuclear campaign warned of mass death and the poisoning of water, land, and air should a nuclear catastrophe occur. These warnings spoke to real concerns spurred by attempts to expand the use of nuclear power, but they also echoed the problems miners already faced in the coal industry: persistent workplace safety issues, increased incidence of occupational disease, and the pollution of air, water, and land. The resonances between the harms of nuclear power and coal revealed to miners that despite the major gains achieved by the 1950 agreement, the postwar energy system remained fueled by workers' deaths.

Miners latched onto Boyle's rhetoric but used that ambivalence toward the atomic age to express the tensions of the coal-fired social contract. Boyle almost certainly intended the focus on the atomic menace to jobs, lives, and land to deflect from the problems caused by coal. His antinuclear crusade, however, helped coalesce rank-and-file miners' understanding of environmental and safety issues as fundamentally linked, all while emphasizing how inadequate Boyle's brand of unionism was to address them. It made coal-fired harms, like occupational disease, legible in new registers that would shape miners' political agenda over the coming decade. The atomic age in the coalfields brought to the fore of public and union discourse many unresolved antagonisms in the nation's energy politics: questions of private ownership and public interest, occupational health and safety, environmental degradation, and the relationship between energy and the United States' exercise of international power during the Cold War. At the core of the debate was the reality that amid the age of abundance and the years of the Great Society, substantial disagreement remained over the acceptable amount of risk in an energy system, who could legitimately be asked to shoulder that risk, and on what terms.

Drawing attention away from the ideological conflict, industrial disputes, and democratic anxieties that defined coalfield politics, and thoroughly imbibing the Cold War political climate, Tony Boyle made the Atomic Energy Commission into a villain. Before nuclear energy had even made real inroads into electric power generation, the UMW charged the AEC with threatening to poison the nation both physically and politically.[13] If the UMW presented oil as a symbol of foreign autocracy incompatible with the promises of economic freedom to which coal miners were entitled, nuclear power quickly came to represent a different kind of possible energy future: state control and the encroachment of technocracy on democratic politics. Boyle contended that the ideological danger of atomic power was evidenced by the mortal harm it portended and that the best way to preserve energy abundance and protect American democracy was UMW coal. But if Boyle found his rhetorical stride in castigating the Atomic Energy Commission, he seemed completely unable to grasp the implications of the way that his denunciations of nuclear power intersected with the experiences of miners' day-to-day lives. Boyle's antiatomic crusade also catalyzed a chain of events within the UMW that ultimately led to his downfall.

In March 1963, unaware he was the harbinger of his own tragedy, Boyle turned his attention to David E. Lilienthal's recent lecture "Whatever Happened to the Peaceful Atom?"[14] By 1963, Lilienthal, the one-time TVA director and AEC chair, was running a private consulting company focused on international and domestic development projects.[15] On the face of it, Lilienthal seemed an unlikely source of inspiration for the UMW's new president, but over time, Lilienthal had become more critical of nuclear power. He felt the atom had not revolutionized the whole world order as promised. In fact, Lilienthal described not revolution but resurrection, nothing less than coal's "second coming."[16] Utilities across the country adopted explicitly growth-oriented programs to develop their service areas, which promised to improve their customers' lives with all-electric living. The utilities generated much of that electricity by burning coal. As Americans consumed greater amounts of electricity at home, at work, and in public life, coal use began to recover, promising an era of coal-fired opportunity for all.

Later that month, Boyle quoted Lilienthal's lecture to the House Subcommittee on Mines and Mining as he argued for increased coal research funding. Given that Lilienthal, the one-time nuclear advocate, insisted that the "glamour, the excitement of the boundless possibilities of power from the peaceful atom is gone," Boyle hoped to secure research and development commitments to ensure the nation's coal-fired future.[17] However, despite Lilienthal's critique, the civilian nuclear power program's budget continued to increase. Those increases incensed Boyle, who pointed out to the committee that the increase alone in the civilian nuclear power appropriation was seven times the total budget of the Office of Coal Research.[18] If Lilienthal believed the promise of the atom had faded away from the previous decade's ambitions, Boyle would shift focus to the long-term threat that nuclear development continued to pose to coal miners.

Although Boyle adopted Lilienthal's words for his own purposes, the perceived threat from the development of atomic power could be traced back to the different visions of energy-intensive democracy offered by the UMW and the Tennessee Valley Authority in the New Deal era, when

Lilienthal played a foundational role in shaping the TVA. The postwar nuclear sector owed much to the intellectual experience and the physical and administrative infrastructure of the TVA.[19] Plans for commercial nuclear power applications formed a key avenue for the international projection of American power even as nuclear weapons helmed the nation's national defense plan.[20] Nuclear advocates saw the development of industrial-scale civilian atomic power applications as critically important, but civilian development proved equally fraught with tensions between state interest and private investment, particularly on the multivalent question of risk: the risks entailed in investing in an unproven industry that wasn't immediately in demand, the liabilities of a possible disaster.[21] Anticipating that Americans' electricity use would continue to accelerate, the Federal Power Commission hoped that government expenditure could stimulate the nuclear sector's development and "play an important part in setting ceilings for prices of power in an increasing number of locations," as the TVA had done on a regional basis. As the price ceilings came down, the FPC projected service areas would grow and that prices to consumers would drop even further.[22] The UMW worried this vision of the nation's energy future, so evocative of earlier TVA rhetoric, would dim the future of the coal-fired social contract and the recently revived prospects for coalfield recovery with it.

The UMW leveraged the near-mythic power of "free enterprise" rhetoric, as they had in the dispute over residual oil imports, to insist that government subsidy of nuclear power when the nation had more than enough coal violated the nation's social contract and the principles of its energy system and political economy.[23] In a truly competitive domestic market, they argued, coal would not only continue to claw its way back, as if from the dead, but would secure the nation's increasingly electrified energy system and thrive there, perhaps for centuries. The UMW further adapted the language deployed in the fight against residual oil imports to argue that government subsidy of atomic power left unemployed miners who "wish to work and would have an opportunity to do so" if atomic plants were not built that "simply cannot be justified from a competitive standpoint."[24] Boyle promised he would "swear eternal hostility against any force which would unfairly and willfully . . . contrive to build an industry based upon perpetual recourse to public funds at the expense of free enterprise" and, by extension, coal.[25] Using the language of free enterprise, Boyle presented coal as the middle way between the threat of heavy-handed government intervention in the economy through the "unfair" subsidy of nuclear power, on the one hand, and heavily consolidated industrial power from the international oil companies, on the other. Coal, Boyle insisted, was an energy source ideologically compatible with the United States' liberal capitalist democracy.

While the UMW's rhetoric cast the differences between coal and nuclear power in civilizational terms, years of history between the UMW and the AEC suggested that coal was not as antithetical to nuclear power as Boyle liked to suggest. Nuclear sites from Ohio to Washington State often came with large coal contracts, as much as 3.5 million tons per year.[26] Boyle knew that better than anyone. Indeed, his connection with nuclear power went back further than most people not directly engaged in the industry. In the late 1950s, as John L. Lewis's special assistant, Boyle had handled the coal contracts for the Hanford nuclear site run by the AEC in Washington State. In a decade marked by mine closures and relentless unemployment, the Hanford coal contracts were highly sought after. One Montana town appealed to the UMW for help after losing a Hanford contract—a loss that dealt "a severe blow to our community," a community of which coal miners were "our most substantial citizens."[27] In the decade before Boyle assumed the UMW presidency, the union's relationship with the AEC and the Hanford site demonstrated the surprisingly close ties between the coal and nuclear industries.

Boyle's time working to secure coal production contracts from the Hanford nuclear site eerily foreshadowed many of the issues that would lead to his own downfall. Around the Hanford contracts, Boyle and his brothers built a small patronage system that stretched across the bargaining table and was sustained by nepotism, corruption, and coverups.[28] One brother, Jack J. Boyle, was president of the Mountain States Mining Company, which supplied coal for the Hanford contracts. His other brother, Richard J. Boyle, was president of UMW District 27, which represented the miners who extracted the coal for those contracts.[29] The scattered correspondence retained by the UMW national office illustrates how Jack Boyle and other coal companies in the West relied on Boyle as they navigated the federal bidding process.

Jack Boyle contacted the UMW Washington office regarding Hanford when they lost the bid to supply coal to the site by a mere penny per ton. The result, according to Jack Boyle, was that "all our miners are now unemployed and mine closed."[30] Later that month, Tony Boyle sent his brother R. J., the District 27 president, two copies of a memorandum on the Hanford contracts along with copies of materials from competing firms. One was for the district's use, the other for Jack, "with the distinct understanding that this material is confidential and must be used with extreme discretion."[31] A later investigation into the Boyle family by the *Billings Gazette*'s Roger Hawthorne strongly implied that the brothers manipulated the federal mine inspection system to close down competing mines while covering up safety issues in Jack Boyle's mines, firing safety committeemen who dissented. Definitive evidence, Hawthorne found, proved elusive, since no minutes existed for the meetings surrounding key events.[32] As a result, miners were soon back at work in Jack Boyle's mine after the 1957 closure. Less than a year later, a roof fall killed four of them.[33]

If Boyle's handling of the contracts illustrated his own fatal flaws, the contracts themselves suggested nuclear power and coal could, in fact, coexist. Given the enormous growth of energy consumption across the United States and the projection that such expansion would continue, such a vision of collaborative growth could not have seemed outlandish. But the potential went still further. In 1961, Glenn Seaborg, AEC's chairman, gripped with atomic optimism, imagined a deeply entangled future for coal and nuclear power—one that perhaps could mutually constitute new markets for both. Seaborg insisted that "nuclear energy holds promise of being of great assistance to the coal industry." He saw potential to deploy nuclear science and technology throughout the industry, "from the actual mining operation through the development of new uses and new markets for coal and coal products." Such applications included the possibility of using the heat produced in nuclear reactions in the process of coal gasification, or in the extraction process itself, helping release the coal from the surrounding rock.[34]

With the possibility of such wide-ranging applications, Seaborg unsurprisingly saw nuclear technology's potential to transform the work of mining as well. Reimagining the relationship between coal and the atom could transform the labor process in coal mines, "showing the way to improvements in mining and processing operations themselves." Atomic technology, Seaborg felt, could be used to "improve efficiency of operation" in the nation's coal mines. Radioisotope gauges could help map coal reserves, assist in scientifically managing coal-fired power plants for efficiency, and perhaps help calibrate control of mining equipment. Seaborg went as far as to claim that the "radioactive isotopes produced by nuclear processes may well be instrumental in improving health and safety conditions in mining operations."[35]

These suggestions cut to the heart of key problems facing the midcentury mining workplace: mine explosions, pollution, the dangers worsened by mechanization, and the concern for profitability in an industry still working to reverse a sharp decline in production. Radioisotopes, Seaborg argued, could be used to "lessen the chances of mine explosions" by reducing the risks posed by static electricity discharge. A radioactive tagging system might allow new tracking of "the flow of noxious gaseous and liquid mine effluent," which would aid in pollution control and assist in assessing the "integrity of roof support structures, hoisting equipment, and other critical equipment."[36] His suggestions pointed to a broader vision of how atomic power, once developed, might not be bound into a single industry but would broadly remake the fabric of work in the United States. Seaborg's research program for coal, notably, did not consider the development of coal and the atom as needing to be balanced, or of the atom as ultimately replacing coal, but instead that the atom would remake the coal mining workplace just as mechanization had, offering new forms of management and measurement that ostensibly would allow for increased safety in the mines while also expanding managerial control underground.

Despite Seaborg's gestures, the debate over nuclear power continued in the UMW, and the Hanford site became the focal point of an early confrontation between the UMW and nuclear power's supporters over the nation's energy future.[37] Even after the AEC announced its intention to begin a coal research program with $5 million in government funding, tensions escalated. For coal's supporters, the $5 million was a paltry sum compared to the overall AEC budget of more than $2.6 billion.[38] The AEC hoped to launch a program at Hanford that would contribute to the "study, development, and design for nuclear processes which have application for improving and utilizing coal and coal products."[39] The UMW vigorously opposed the research program. They believed that the public would come to see coal's future as tied to the construction of new atomic facilities and that the program constituted an "unwarranted intrusion" by the federal government into the utility sector.[40] Boyle went as far as to say the UMW would rather scrap the coal research program entirely than have it tied to the Hanford site.[41] The UMW leadership felt it could not "countenance trading research appropriations for coal in return for the construction of an atomic power plant," since the growth of nuclear power represented "a grave danger to the future well-being of the coal industry and the members of the United Mine Workers of America."[42]

Furious, Senator Jennings Randolph of West Virginia demanded an explanation from the UMW: "How can anyone rationalize destruction of our country's whole atomic energy program, including its vital military preparedness elements, to defeat a single project which the individual and his organization oppose?"[43] Yet this incident only marked the beginning of Boyle's antiatomic crusade. Indeed, under Boyle's leadership, the UMW's critique of nuclear power extended its focus beyond nuclear power's potential to undermine coal in the fierce competition to fuel the growing utilities market. Increasingly, UMW antinuclear rhetoric emphasized the mortal dangers posed by nuclear power.

The shift from concern over market competitiveness to a wider nuclear antipathy was clear by March 1963, when Boyle leaned on David Lilienthal's growing nuclear ambivalence to lobby for increased coal research funding. Boyle faced critical questioning from the members of the House Mines and Mining Subcommittee in response to that statement. When faced with members' skepticism about whether nuclear power was *really* competitive with coal or would be in the foreseeable future, Boyle redirected them away from the competition issue entirely: "Yes, I think there is a great threat from atomic energy. I am not so concerned about the immediate problem of atomic energy taking over the coal markets. . . . But I don't think anyone has given enough thought and concern to the radioactive waste materials of this atomic energy and what is going to happen to the future generations."[44]

By summer of 1963, Boyle planned to expand the antiatomic crusade that he seemed to believe would make his mark upon history. He increasingly focused on the safety aspects of nuclear power, from extracting uranium to operating power plants near major cities: uranium miners dying of occupationally contracted cancer, plants blowing up, toxic waste polluting the oceans. As "the union delved into [the study of nuclear power], it was found that such plants are hazardous and dangerous for this generation and future generations."[45] With Boyle's attention drawn to the workplace and environmental dangers of atomic energy, his argument became increasingly detached from the question of whether the atom could compete with coal.

Instead, the use of coal was a moral imperative to save American citizens from the atom.

In July 1963, Boyle directed Rex Lauck at the *United Mine Workers Journal* to begin writing articles on the dangers of the atom.[46] Antiatomic articles appeared in nearly every issue between late 1963 and 1969. These articles drew power from the way they portrayed the federal government as responsible for arbitrating the risks of an energy system—and as having failed that responsibility by renewing the Price-Anderson Act, which severely curbed liability for nuclear accidents for utilities and industry, while shifting the financial burden of this liability onto taxpayers.[47] Not only did UMW leadership see Price-Anderson as socializing unnecessary risk, it also capped liability at $560 million—a mere 8 percent of estimated potential damages.[48]

Yet moving away from the longstanding practice of translating questions of energy fairness into dollar values, the *Journal* also directly addressed the environmental politics of nuclear power, particularly the idea of irreversible contamination. The articles "Pandora's Box of Poison," published in March 1968, warned against the threat posed by radiation. Ray Zell drew an accompanying cartoon that showed a hand representing the nation's nuclear energy program opening Pandora's box and unleashing "radioactive evils" on the world.[49] Other articles mourned the preventable deaths of uranium miners from lung cancer caused by exposure to radon gas.[50] These dangers uncannily mirrored the dangers of the mining workplace that miners knew so viscerally.

These articles encouraged the coal miners who read them to connect workplace and environmental harms in new ways, to think about the everyday danger they knew so well as extending from the mining workplace into the broader nation through the impact on the landscape and through exposure to dangerous contaminants like radon gas and coal dust. As miners discussed the dangers of radiation, they forged an environmental imagination that they would eventually apply to their own longstanding struggles: to articulate how mining practices had poisoned their water supply, to describe occupational disease as a moral question for the entire nation, and to organize opposition to strip mining, slag heaps, and gob ponds, which destroyed the land and their ability to live on it.

Such arguments powerfully captured the imagination of miners like Joseph Grego, who wrote to President Lyndon B. Johnson in October 1967 that he and the members of his local were "alarmed . . . about the threat to the health and safety of the public from proven harm of radioactive wastes from atomic plants subsidized by our tax money."[51] Edward Stearns wrote to urge Boyle to "stop the free flo of our tax money to private power companies," and the members of Local 7365 petitioned Congress "to stop all appropriation for the development of nuclear energy, excepting for national defense," adding they would join Boyle's call to boycott "Westinghouse Electric, General Electric, or any other manufacturer of atomic reactors."[52] Convinced that nuclear reactors would "pollute the already polluted atmosphere with radiation that would cause an increase in Leucemia and cancer a thousand fold and the death of millions," they wrote that they were "against the Government, any Company, or any person building Atomic Energy Plants at any time, any place, and for any reason."[53] Kerman Lovelace reported that "our men fear atomic plants may cause national disaster," in addition to the "ruin of coal miners' jobs and welfare fund."[54]

Miners' concerns about nuclear power also reflected growing national concern with the environmental debts the nation had accumulated through industrial development and exploitation of the nation's landscapes and natural resources. Jess Ballard hoped Boyle's efforts would "awake[n] Congress to its responsibility and duty to stop the development of civilian atomic power affecting the health and safety of the public, radioactive air and water pollution."[55] Some miners' wives wrote in, concerned about the claims made by the *United Mine Workers Journal*. Mrs. Clarence Kirkendoll wrote that "as a rule, I usually leaved the reading of the *Journal* to my husband, tho I glance at the jokes, recipes." However, the "Pandora's Box of Poisons" article had captured her attention. She was "so amazed" that she insisted "everyone in the United States who has the ability to read should read it," and she thanked Boyle for "seeking an explanation and solution" to the problem.[56] Boyle appealed to her to "contribute to this humanitarian effort by bringing these articles to the attention of your many friends and neighbors."[57] Mrs. Kirkendoll's encounter with Tony Boyle's antinuclear crusade left her fearful of the dangers of nuclear power.

Miners' antinuclear sentiment was not confined to letters and telegrams. On a brisk fall day in November 1967, a small group of miners drove into Denver, Colorado, to protest the nearby Fort St. Vrain nuclear generating station, under construction and scheduled to come on line in five years. Some brought their wives and children.[58] The miners' signs warned that "atomic energy poisons the air, the land, the water" and could turn Colorado into a "poisonous atomic wasteland." Worried that an accident at Fort

Figure 4.1 Miners protest in Denver, Colorado, against the Fort St. Vrain nuclear plant, November 15, 1967.
Source: UMWJR 52/12.

St. Vrain "could create another Hiroshima catastrophe in the city of Denver and surrounding area of over two million inhabitants," the local unions of UMW District 15 dedicated a substantial amount of time to protesting the planned facility, located about thirty-five miles outside of Denver, including filing legal action to halt construction of the plant.[59]

The efforts expended by District 15 took place amid a regional explosion of "energy activism" led by members of the Navajo nation, who had borne much of the toll of the United States' nuclear power development in their bodies and on their lands—and who also represented an important segment of UMW membership in the region.[60] As Peter Eichstaedt has written, uranium mining had left a "shadow of death" across Navajo mining communities in the Four Corners region of the Southwest, where after "the biggest uranium boom the world had ever known was largely over . . . miners had been sent home, many to die slow, painful deaths."[61] Only a few hours southwest of Denver, the landscape was a veritable "poisoned atomic wasteland" of polluted water and unreclaimed mines. As miners picketed in front of the State Service Building, they must have seemed an oddity to a nation in the throes of a pitched debate over air pollution, particularly the air pollution caused by the coal-fired generating stations that ringed urban areas and were sometimes sited directly in their working-class, Black, and immigrant neighborhoods.[62] But the Fort St. Vrain project made plausible the apocalyptic future Boyle's crusade portended.

As the efforts against the new nuclear generating plant continued, Boyle moved the union's constitutional convention across the country to Denver so the full weight of the union could be brought to bear to support the efforts of District 15. The bulk of the legal department report centered on the effort to halt the station's construction. Given that the UMW faced unrelated and serious challenges from cases filed under the auspices of the Labor Management Reporting and Disclosure Act, a 1959 law targeting corruption within unions, the emphasis was striking.[63] The legal department, along with the UMW's research and marketing department, detailed their work producing "specialized witnesses in the field of nuclear energy," culling "economic data," and making a presentation to the Colorado Public Utilities Commission. When they failed to stop construction at the initial hearing, they filed an appeal and registered a separate challenge with the board that was supposed to grant the construction permits. The UMW, however, felt they were unlikely to get a fair hearing, since the Atomic Safety and Licensing Board, which would hear the challenge, was "a three-man committee, all appointed by the Atomic Energy Commission."[64] Although its efforts in Colorado had achieved nothing, the legal department vowed to the gathered delegates of the 1968 convention that it would continue its opposition.

The campaign against the Fort St. Vrain station was meant to be a model that could be applied elsewhere as nuclear reactors were planned closer and closer to large cities. Political support for the UMW's efforts against Fort St. Vrain and other antinuclear legislative tactics came not from local Colorado politicians but instead from politicians from the eastern coalfields: Virginia's William C. Wampler, West Virginia's James Kee, Pennsylvania's John P. Saylor, and Wayne L. Hays of Ohio. However, these wider political efforts also failed despite repeated attempts to increase legislative oversight of atomic development, slow ongoing AEC projects, and introduce other antinuclear legislation. By 1968, the UMW had failed to effectively prevent or halt the building of a single nuclear generating station. The legal department had only one victory to trumpet at the convention. The UMW, they announced, had helped stop experimental underground atomic blasting aimed at increasing underground natural gas storage in Pennsylvania. This small victory, Boyle promised, was "only the beginning of our program."[65]

Boyle directed locals to boycott corporations involved with the construction of nuclear reactors, inculcating concern about nuclear power while building an industrial coalition that might, through collaboration, influence policy through intense lobbying. The effort to boycott these companies drove a wedge between the UMW and its affiliated nonmining locals in District 50. Some District 50 members were in fact employed by the boycotted firms. But Boyle continued his antinuclear crusade, for he had come see in nuclear power evidence of the country violating the coal-fired social contract.[66] He insisted that the development of nuclear power was politically irresponsible and morally questionable when "God gave this great land an almost unlimited supply of coal."[67]

Miners were not bystanders to the union's antinuclear politics but engaged them in ways that reflected their own experience—and that Boyle seemed unable to anticipate. Boyle's war against the atom, whether it was being fought in congressional hearing rooms or the pages of the *United Mine Workers Journal*, relied on narrative and visual tropes that resonated deeply with miners. Sometimes the adaption of these images was so obvious that the artists and editors could simply superimpose new meaning over a nearly identical image. Two of Ray Zell's cartoons capture the way visual meanings could be reappropriated in the pursuit of the antiatomic crusade. In "Hours of Peril," drawn by Ray Zell in 1962, a miner prevaricates at the beginning of his shift, weighing whether he should descend into the "unsafe mine" for work. Five years later, Zell produced a nearly identical cartoon. Even the title, "Graveyard Shift!," appeared to connect it to the earlier portrayal. Yet the images were placed into separate narratives. Zell replaced "unsafe mines" with "uranium," he brightened the darkness of the coal mine, and drew lines extending from the mine mouth suggestive of the perils of radiation.

Boyle's crusade against the atom might have been self-serving, but it tapped into real fears percolating across the coalfields about dangers that miners—coal or uranium—would be asked to shoulder in an energy-intensive society. At the height of the Cold War, and subjected to the U.S. government's frenzied demands for maximum weapons production, uranium miners were exposed to exceptional amounts of radiation. At least

Figure 4.2 Ray Zell, "Hours of Peril" (1962).
Source: UMWJR 60/6.

one thousand uranium miners, disproportionately Navajo, died from that exposure.[68] The dangers of the uranium mining workplace were ones with which coal miners could identify—the spike in lung cancer among the uranium miners could not have more closely mirrored a deepening occupational health crisis across the Appalachian coalfields driven by black lung, a set of respiratory diseases caused by inhaling coal dust. In the coal mines, wrote the journalist Jeanne Rasmussen, mechanization had "pushed health and safety to the edge of an abyss."[69]

Yet through this very connection, this common experience that made legible for coal miners the "invisible deaths" caused by radiation, Boyle's antinuclear campaign also demonstrated the extent to which he seemed incapable of observing the changes in his own industry. The *United Mine Workers Journal* reported on a speech by Leo Goodman, at the time the director of the Atomic Energy Technical Committee at the AFL-CIO. Uranium miners, he said, "must rise up and insist on the priority to which their role in society entitles them." Instead of being revered for their role in national defense and energy production, he claimed that their "widows cannot even get a measly workmen's compensation," while "the AEC's funds are used instead to create a national psychology that they have the safest industry in the country and besides no single person has ever been hurt."[70] A comparison with the dangers of the mines and difficulties miners disabled with black lung faced in their struggle to receive compensation would have been apt indeed.

Boyle, however, seemed unable to connect his antinuclear rhetoric back to the coalfields. In 1969, as coal miners shut down the West Virginia coalfields to demand black lung compensation, Boyle issued press releases that devoted two sentences to coal dust before turning to spend four paragraphs detailing the UMW position on safe levels of radon gas in uranium mines, where "failure to require ventilation ... had resulted in hundreds of cases of lung cancer." Boyle decried the "neglect ... by the government" of the dying uranium miners' widows.[71] Only days later, he would caution skepticism against "modern day prophets of doom"—referring to the public advocate Ralph Nader, Congressman Ken Hechler, and activists in the UMW—who made nearly identical claims about coal.[72] Although Boyle proclaimed a bright future for coal would follow his antiatomic crusade, the coal-fired social contract was coming apart, and with it Boyle's belief he could manage and collaborate his way to industrial peace, higher wages, and political stability. As would soon become apparent, this unraveling was driven by the very changes in the energy sector that had brought coal back to life: the transformation of coal production to serve utility markets. By the end of the decade, the limits of the coal-fired social contract would be clearer than ever, aided by Boyle's own megalomania.

Tensions over the threats posed by atomic power came to a head in the early months of 1968. The UMW's affiliated locals, organized under the auspices of the supposedly independent District 50, which had been chartered by the UMW in 1936, voted to support the development of nuclear power, as well as the participation of Dow Chemical in the atomic field. Boyle lashed out at his "thankless child"—a phrase that underscored the paternalistic nature of the UMW's relationship with these affiliated locals. In a fit of rage, he expelled them from the union.[73]

District 50, a formally independent district of affiliated locals, organized workers in a range of industries, many of them coal adjacent: clerical positions, chemical production, construction, coking facilities, and chemical plants. Under the AEC contracting system, however, many of them also worked in atomic-adjacent firms, like Dow Chemical.[74] Although appearing to fall outside the purview of the day-to-day coalfield politics, District

50 "acted as a buffer . . . against the raiding tactics of craft unions" and had "brought employment opportunities to many thousands of mine workers" idled by mechanization, "employ[ing] them on road building and mine construction jobs." In many coal-mining states, District 50 workers built state highways and federal interstates. Moreover, during a period of substantial contraction in the UMW's working membership because of high unemployment, District 50 brought millions in revenue to the UMW treasury and funded organizing campaigns. It organized thousands of new members in Atomic Age industries. John L. Lewis warned his successors to take care when addressing conflicts with District 50, since it was "of great importance" to the UMW.[75]

Despite its importance and relative success, by the early 1960s District 50 represented a constant source of financial tension among the UMW leadership. The district fell into debt and required loans from the UMW, which then went unpaid.[76] District 50 officers countered this claim by alleging that "many millions" in membership dues had been collected by the UMW and that neither those members nor District 50 had ever received "any accounting whatsoever of the use of the funds." The leaders of District 50 claimed that the real source of the tension that had been building since the early 1960s was its refusal to submit to Boyle's "dictates."[77] This refusal to submit extended to Boyle's crusade against the atom, resulting in what Boyle described as a "basic and ethical conflict."[78] At stake, Boyle suggested, was nothing less than the safety of the nation:

> The United Mine Workers has taken a strong, aggressive, and positive position on the dangers and hazards of atomic energy for domestic uses . . . ."District 50"—this thankless child that we created—is willing to risk the lives of every citizen in the country for the sake of a few members they have in atomic plants. . . . For the sake of a few members in this organization or any other labor organization, I'm not going to jeopardize the lives of children and future generations nor will I be party to jeopardizing the lives of those who work in uranium. I will not jeopardize them for this pittance of dues that may be collected. I'm not that hungry for dues.[79]

Beginning in early February 1968, following the publication of an article in *District 50 News* supporting nuclear development, Boyle began to receive letters and telegrams in which locals and districts weighed in on the decision to discipline and ultimately expel District 50 and offered their own explanations of why the miners in a particular area supported the move.[80] The messages poured in for months, eventually numbering in the hundreds. Some, like Local 2026 in Westland, Pennsylvania, focused on District 50's debt and demanded "that all debts owed to the United Mine Workers of America be paid promptly."[81] Others voiced boilerplate support for Boyle or worried that District 50's "propaganda for Dow Chemical" was equivalent to "helping companies put us miners out of a job."[82]

But these letters were overwhelmed by those that speculated on the danger atomic power represented. Some, like Local 1243, equated membership in the UMW with an antinuclear stance: "If they don't support . . . your fight against nuclear energy, they should not be permitted to use the name of the United Mine Workers."[83] Lee Roy Foltz from Bulger, Pennsylvania, said that District 50 "should have been dealt with severely," since they had endangered "their own fellow workers and the welfare of millions of other HUMAN beings and the natural resources of the nation."[84] The members of Local 1284 wrote to "request an aggressive opposition to the destroyer of our way of life—nuclear energy power plants," because they "hold in contempt District 50, Betrayer . . . for its unwise attitude favoring nuclear energy power plants."[85] Elmer Hall, the recording secretary of Local 1513, noted that nuclear power, in undermining the coal-fired social contract, might also place miners' future benefits in peril. He worried their "welfare benefits are being jeopardized by nuclear energy . . . our members are both alarmed and worried."[86] James Balsamelle agreed: "We foresee what [nuclear energy] will do to our welfare and pension plan."[87]

The host of telegrams and letters also demonstrated what appeared to be a genuine intertwining of concern for miners' jobs with the safety of the broader community. "Don't they know," asked Local 1346, "that you and the United Mine Workers are fighting the building of the nuclear plants and are fighting to protect the American people from the fallout of such plants, are fighting to protect the security of mining industry and the United Mine Workers?"[88] Marshall Martin urged Boyle to "inform [the AEC] and the public that these plants may cause an atomic explosion," while Erne Bigham of Local 5134 worried that District 50 was a "Frankenstein" and begged Boyle to tell the Atomic Energy Commission "of the fears of the local miner concerning the increasing use of atomic reactors to generate electricity. These fears are not only for ourselves but for the multitudes living in the immediate zones that surround these plants.

Our lives and our livelihood are being seriously threatened by the utter disregard for the safety and welfare of the population of this country."[89]

By 1965, coal industry observers felt that the coal industry had met "the challenge of the nuclear age."[90] Boyle remained undeterred. He continued his antinuclear crusade through and beyond the expulsion of District 50, suggesting the depth of the atomic menace he saw in the world around him. Boyle's mistake was to imagine that so long as the coal market grew, both the coal-fired social contract and his regime would remain intact—even if he overstepped his bounds as union president to counter dissent in and around District 50. In the end, Boyle's treatment of District 50 would come to signify the dangers of his leadership rather than the menace of the atom. Boyle insisted "this is no time for the demagogue."[91] He seemed unaware he prophesized his own fate.

Boyle's multiyear crusade against the atom and the Atomic Energy Commission only slowed when open rebellion in the coalfields over a safety and occupational health crisis forced his attention elsewhere. The UMW's role in antinuclear politics at the height of Boyle's power shows how Boyle was motivated by a particular understanding of how coalfield power operated, one that was shaped by having risen through the union's ranks during the New Deal, then World War II, and finally during the postwar iteration of the coal-fired social contract. At the core of his philosophy lay a commitment to stabilizing the relations between coal miners, coal operators, and coal and electricity consumers. That vision sought to marry growth in productivity with an industrial welfare regime that allowed the nation's energy system to operate as smoothly as an assembly line, with minimal class conflict.[92] The decision to devote extensive resources to arguing that atomic power was the greatest threat to that system—rather than, say, oil or natural gas—was not inevitable, and it was Boyle's decision.

Coal and nuclear power never meaningfully competed for market share in the 1960s. Many of the promises of postwar mass consumption rested on expanded electricity use both at home and work: brightly illuminated suburban homes filled with a growing range of electric appliances, climate-controlled office buildings, electrified factories. Improved transmission technology allowed electricity to appear cleaner than ever, removing coal from the everyday lives of many.[93] The future of electric power and the fuels that generated it appeared so bright that in 1964 the Federal Power Commission estimated national electricity use would double, maybe even triple, by

1980. Yet the arrival of the atomic age ultimately set the coalfields and the United Mine Workers down a new path of destabilization just as the coal sector appeared poised to recover.

This destabilization had a structural basis and almost nothing directly to do with atomic power, as Boyle had suggested. Instead, the destabilization of the coalfields was rooted in how midcentury liberalism reorganized American inequality. The suburbanization of the United States, modeled on free-standing, low-density housing, "was dangerously dependent upon cheap fuel," writes the historian Kenneth Jackson.[94] Coal provided most of the nation's electric power, and an overwhelming majority in coal-rich regions, but the delivery of coal "by wire" obscured electricity's tight relationship with coal. Power lines turned dirty, volatile coal into "clean" and "gentle" electric power.[95] Coal thus powered tremendous growth in residential, commercial, and industrial electricity consumption.[96]

This everyday energy intensification, powered by coal and spurred by suburbanization, cemented the relationship between coal and postwar liberalism as flowing through currents of electric power. These energy relationships underlay new patterns of inequality at the "high tide" of American liberalism: in housing, access to public programs, municipal finance, workplace safety, and occupational health.[97] The coal-fired social contract quickly began to unravel, a process accelerated when yet another disaster raised new questions about the relationship between coal miners and the rest of the nation, when a massive explosion ripped through the Consol No. 9 mine near Farmington, West Virginia, on November 20, 1968.

CHAPTER V

An Inherent Danger of Explosion

Motormen Lester Willard and Walter Slovekosky liked to joke with each other over the radio to pass the time during their shift in the Consol No. 9 mine near Farmington, West Virginia. Hauling coal was dangerous: cars could become uncoupled and run away, trips could derail and crush miners against the wall, sparks from metal hitting rock could trigger an explosion if enough methane or coal dust was in the air. Bureau of Mines fatality reports catalogued the horrors haulage accidents had caused and the lives they had claimed. But the work was also monotonous, and Lester and Walter were on the overnight shift—in other contexts called the "graveyard shift." Several hours in, Walter drove a load of coal up the west side of the mine with his partner Smokey Stevens. Lester passed them, heading deeper into the mine with empty cars, and he teased Walter over the radio, like usual. A few minutes later, Walter and Smokey heard Lester's partner Charlie Hardman report their location to the dispatcher. Then the power went out briefly before the lights flickered back on. It was the first sign that something had gone horribly wrong.[1]

Elsewhere in the mine, George Wilson was cutting coal when the power went out. "I taken, I expect, two or three steps when this thing came in on us," he recalled. "Just like that through the air and there was flying debris, rock dust, coal dust, and everything so intense you couldn't see." Lewis Lake recalled "mining coal as usual and all at once the power went off . . . and then I knew it was something I had never seen in the mines before." Electrician Alex Kovarbasich had been dealing with power issues in the mine all night, but he was outside when he felt the ground shake and saw the lights dim momentarily.[2] The loss of power took on the quality of an omen, given the broader context in which mining was a "way of death."[3] Ninety-nine miners went underground that night, but only twenty-one returned alive: Walter Slovekosky, Smokey Stevens, George Wilson, and Lewis Lake among them. Lester Willard and Charlie Hardman did not.

On November 20, 1968, the Consol No. 9 explosion became the worst American coal mine disaster in more than fifteen years. The *New York Times*' Ben Franklin described an apocalyptic scene: fire "burst up 600 feet through the portals and ventilation shafts, blowing the internal works of the mine to atoms. . . . For days, a boiling plume of poisonous black smoke alternatively belched from the shaft and then unaccountably reversed its flow and inhaled, bursting forth with renewed detonations below."[4] Ten days after the explosion, distraught families learned the mine would be sealed with concrete to deprive the "underground holocaust" of oxygen. But still, the mine continued to burn.[5] An observer might be forgiven for thinking the mine was alive and vengeful. The truth was far worse.

November 20 was a frigid, dry night—perfect conditions for a methane explosion. The coal in the No. 9 was known to be "gassy," meaning that millions of years earlier, as intense pressure and heat converted plant matter into coal, the large quantities of methane generated in the process also became trapped. When miners cut into the coal, it released the methane. The methane exuded even faster when miners cut into the coal with massive continuous miners—machines with a large, rotating cylinder lined with metal "teeth" that chewed coal from the seam more than a hundred times faster than a miner could by hand.[6] Intensified mechanization more than doubled the Consol No. 9's methane emissions. In 1968, the mine emitted around eight million cubic feet of methane each day.[7] Winter weather only increased the danger. When the atmospheric pressure dropped—for example, when a cold front came through—the coal released even more methane. Explosion season, as winter months were known, was especially treacherous for the miners who entered the No. 9.

Representative Ken Hechler of West Virginia quickly noted that coal men and politicians were concerned less with methane gas than with the 9,600 tons of high-quality bituminous coal that the No. 9 mine produced each day.[8] The mine's location in one of the highest-quality bituminous coal seams in the world had secured the mine's continued existence in the face of repeated methane explosions. Eleven dead in October 1916. Nineteen killed in January 1926. An October 1951 explosion miraculously killed no one, but a November 1954 explosion entombed fifteen miners, including Alex Kovarbasich's brother Nick, in a "flaming pit." A November 1965 blast triggered by a stray spark killed four.[9] Previously operating as the Jamison No. 9, this same mine had been inspected during World War II to identify security risks—only to find horrendous working conditions.[10] In between the newsworthy disasters, the mine's deadly record was stacked with safety violations. Consolidation Coal management failed to report gassy conditions during the dangerous winter months. Poor ventilation, noted in earlier inspections, contributed to methane buildup in mine tunnels in advance of the November 1968 explosion.[11] Working conditions in the mine, always perilous, had deteriorated. In the days leading up to the explosion, Emilio Megna told his family "they're gonna blow the mine up . . . they're not taking care of it."[12] That night was supposed to be the last time Megna, forty-eight years old, married, with two children, went underground. After thirty years underground, he was leaving the mines to open a gas station. Instead, the Consol No. 9 became his tomb, his body one of nineteen never recovered.[13]

Despite the mine's atrocious record, industry, state, and union officials rushed to the defense of Consolidation Coal and the coal industry in general. Hulett Smith, governor of West Virginia, naturalized the disaster, saying that "what has occurred here is one of the hazards of being a miner." Undersecretary of the Interior J. Cordell Moore stated that despite decades of mine safety research, "we don't understand why these things happen, but they do happen."[14] UMW President Tony Boyle defended the company for being "one of the better companies as far as cooperation and safety are concerned."[15] Consol, to Boyle, represented the future of the coal industry—a coal firm that supplied electric utilities and heavily invested in efforts like the National Coal Policy Conference, which sought to maintain labor peace while boosting production and seeking new markets for coal.[16]

The UMW's response to the Consol No. 9 explosion stood in stark contrast to Boyle's antinuclear crusade, where Boyle had warned miners— and, he imagined, the whole nation—about the dangers nuclear power represented to the nation's cities and argued that coal was safer by comparison. The year before the Consol disaster, the *United Mine Workers Journal* promoted coal-fired power plants with the caption: "This one won't blow up."[17] The argument that coal represented the safe alternative to nuclear power in a world where mine disasters were inevitable tragedies suggested that mine explosions were merely the price of public safety from nuclear power.[18] But we have to wonder how the fifty-nine miners who had been "blown up" in smaller explosions during the preceding year would have felt about that logic, where the risks borne by miners helped avoid a high-profile nuclear accident.[19] Fifteen of those men could give no answer; they were dead. But no one bothered to ask those who had survived the ordeal. In the wake of the Consol No. 9 disaster, Boyle's obsession with nuclear danger as the coal-fired energy system concentrated the risks of explosion in the coal mining workplace appeared even more out of touch.[20]

These efforts to circumvent responsibility for the disaster at the No. 9 mine away from Consolidation Coal represented more than an attempt to diffuse coalfield anger. It is hard to imagine that anyone in the coal industry could have believed such statements would mollify the rage felt by miners, the family members of the entombed men, and the wider community. Instead, these statements were clearly directed elsewhere, and perhaps as a salve for the unease of those who issued them, crafting a self-serving narrative where miners sacrificed their lives in the face of unknowable and inevitable danger. Beneath the long track record of neglectful oversights, regulatory violations, and geological dangers, the basic problem as they framed it was not that an explosion had occurred but that too many miners had been killed by it—more than was acceptable in the pursuit of electricity, in any case. This assumption belied the moral economy of the coal-fired social contract, premised upon a certain level of acceptable mining deaths. The sudden exposure of this transgression and the wide net of complicity it suggested prompted disquiet. Miners, however, understood their access to the promises of liberal social citizenship rested on their participation in an energy system that routinized their deaths, whether at work or from occupational disease.

During the postwar years, electricity laundered the human costs of coal. After all, utilities proclaimed, electricity was "the cleanest form of energy and is safe to use anywhere."[21] For years before the Consol No. 9 explosion, miners protested the human suffering obscured by this process, both at the mine face and when the UMW Welfare and Retirement Fund slashed healthcare benefits in 1960 and pension benefits in 1961.[22] The desperation of disabled pensioners and the miners dying in explosions could be difficult to see in the brightly lit homes and offices they powered, sometimes hundreds of miles away.[23] But they were tightly bound together. Coal produced more than half of all kilowatt-hours nationwide, more than double any other source. The link between coal and electricity grew even tighter east of the Mississippi River. The West tended to rely much more heavily on natural gas and hydropower, but in eastern utilities, coal dominated.[24] This reality had just become harder to see for most Americans. Coal piles mostly disappeared from daily life as most Americans encountered coal by wire, but they were often much more dependent on coal than they realized. The human impact of coal-fired electricity had been pushed out of the sight of suburban populations increasingly concerned with problems of air and water pollution.[25]

Embedded in this new form of reliance lay a moral conundrum: how many miners could acceptably die to power the country's homes, suburbs, and offices, which were increasingly designed to rely almost entirely on electric power?[26] The displacement and concentration of coal's impacts amplified the moral stakes of energy production as it made more pronounced the disparities between the benefits of electricity consumption and the human costs of coal production. The coal-fired social contract rested upon an appearance of stability that concealed a percolating conflict held latent in accumulating coal dust, mine accidents, and methane explosions.[27]

The relationship between electricity, coal production, and miners' bodies appeared differently depending on one's position in the energy system: in one cartoon, the *United Mine Workers Journal* declared "Well Balanced" a miner walking an electric wire like a tightrope, with buckets of coal on each end of his pole, one representing "high production," the other "low cost." From the union leadership's perspective, the spectacle represented the triumph of industrial collaboration, union and industry pulled back from the brink of obsolescence. This balance, however, came at a dangerous price, for alternatively one might see a miner teetering on a shaking high-wire to deliver coal to the cityscape below, the precarity depicted by the movement implied by the lines drawn around his shoulders and the wire supporting him. As he chases the idea of "coal by wire," the potential savior of the coal industry in the eyes of Boyle and his ilk, the miner moves forward well balanced, perhaps, but his bodily well-being at the whim of prices and production quotas.[28] The cartoon distilled the fragility of the coal-fired social contract.

The extent to which coal mine dangers had been naturalized in an era marked by growing energy affluence could be seen in the warnings printed in the *United Mine Workers Journal* each fall cautioning miners to take care in the impending "explosion season."[29] The *Journal* warned "no magic solution" to mine explosions existed, advising instead "complete and realistic cooperation" with industry.[30] Naturalizing explosions as a geological feature of coal mines obscured the way disasters were embedded in the logic of the coal-fired social contract and entangled with the social relationships, industrial planning, and structural dependencies that gave the mining workplace salience in national politics. Miners who worked in the coal seam every day saw the geological explanation for the obfuscation it was. They charged that the state, their union, and the companies—the very parties who had forged the coal-fired social contract and who held responsibility for its day-to-day implementation—did little more than oversee an energy system that killed them so other Americans might have more and cheaper electricity.

Electric power had corresponding human currents, which the nation's coal miners increasingly leveraged to reshape national energy politics. In the wake of the Consol No. 9 disaster, miners increasingly took their health and safety into their own hands, in open defiance of Tony Boyle. They situated the coal mining workplace as the site of displaced energy risk and as the fulcrum between the nation's energy producers and its consumers. The same forces that drove coal's resurgence also led miners to rebel in defense of their lives. Reform-minded miners cast the real cause of the disasters not as methane or explosive coal dust—natural parts of the coal mining workplace that many felt could be adequately managed under the right conditions—but instead as a moral rot within the nation's energy system that had hollowed out the promises of democracy and citizenship in the name of production. This insistence on the moral problem of coal production allowed them to connect the Consol No. 9 disaster with the other major occupational health crisis in the coalfields, black lung.

The coal-fired social contract as it had been negotiated in the postwar years proved incapable of responding to mine disasters or the scourge of black lung because it tied miners' social citizenship to high levels of mining productivity, which always worked at odds with safety. Working safely

Figure 5.1 Herb Block satirizes the coal operators, 1968.
Source: © The Herb Block Foundation.

required more miners, and it required those miners to work more slowly. But abandoning the parameters of the postwar agreement was unthinkable to Boyle, not least because it would have threatened his own power. As a result, he prevaricated on issues that for miners were matters of life and death. He sided with the companies on questions of mine safety and insisted black lung activists and union reformers were more concerned with fighting his leadership than they were with miners' lives.

With the channels of coalfield power cut off to them, working and disabled miners alike joined with welfare activists, doctors, allied politicians, journalists, and public advocates to demand change through demonstrations, wildcat strikes, and the formation of new organizations, most notably the Black Lung Association (BLA). Eventually, they launched a direct challenge to Boyle's leadership of the union. Through it all, Boyle's administration attempted to enforce a vision of energy politics that subordinated miners' democratic rights to what Boyle perceived as their economic right to a job.

This perceived tension between the "life" of the industry and the lives of miners was also reflected in the public sphere and exposed a pitched debate over what the right to life meant for coal miners in an energy-intensive economy. Miners felt that the epidemic of black lung and the persistence of deadly workplace accidents in the only industry that could provide decent wages through much of Appalachia had deprived them of the freedom, in any meaningful sense, that was their right as U.S. citizens. The cover of the *United Mine Workers Journal* had declared in 1968, "Old King Coal returns!" but miners quickly made it clear they had no intention of sacrificing their rights and their lives for coal's recovery.[31] The 1969 coalfield revolt and Boyle's response to it revealed radically different visions for the future of the coal-fired social contract. Miners' belief that their most basic human and political rights were once again at stake led them to act. In the process, they forced a national reckoning with an energy system that tied growing affluence among many Americans to high death rates in the coalfields.

After the Consol No. 9 explosion, Tony Boyle had commented that "as long as we mine coal, there is always this inherent danger of explosion."[32] But the explosion that followed, rocking both the coalfields and the wider country, wasn't only caused by methane and coal dust. The "violence boiling" in the Appalachian coalfields, the accumulated anger at the injustices of coal-fired liberalism, finally erupted.[33]

People who weren't miners tended to focus on large disasters like the Consol No. 9 explosion when talking about the dangers of coal mining, but that perspective inadequately reflected how miners themselves thought about questions of health and safety. Miners instead focused on what the *New Republic* distilled into the phrase "mining as a way of death," less a story of individual deaths and disasters and more a structure of power which devalued miners' lives.[34]

The coalfield safety crisis came from two directions. Mine disasters could strike without warning: a sudden buildup of methane, a slip next to a machine, a collapsing roof. Danger persisted despite the safety laws, both state and federal, which were already on the books. After the legislation allowing for federal mine inspections first came into force in 1941, a second federal law providing mechanisms for enforcement of safety standards passed in 1952, and in 1966 Congress expanded the law's authority to include small mines that employed fewer than fifteen workers—and which were much more likely to be nonunion.[35] In part, these laws proved ineffective because mine inspectors were either unwilling or unable to enforce them. One reformer charged that the inefficacy of the already existing laws had to be understood as a vestige of the coalfield state, from a time when coal miners lived on the nation's periphery in an age of empire building. Addressing a rally, he insisted, "There are colonies within the United States; West Virginia is such a colony. That means, not a free state."[36] Democracy, and particularly equal protection of the law, had once again been usurped by the coal industry, which governed the state with the law of low-cost production, all for the benefit of the wider nation, which used the electricity and steel products that coal produced. In 1967, around 80 percent of the nation's underground coal mines had operated in violation of already existing federal safety standards.[37]

At the same time, mechanization had reshaped the landscape and technoscape of underground danger—the way that accidents happened and how coal dust was produced in the process of mining. Safety legislation lagged industrial change, and old ways of "knowing" the mine and its dangers did not always provide safety in the automated mining landscape. Loud machines disrupted the aural traditions of work among miners and the aural ecologies of the mining workscape—the sound of a sturdy versus dangerous roof might be masked by the sounds of other equipment, and roof bolters who worked with new machines had to relearn how to feel the roof.[38] The same machines produced greater and finer amounts of coal dust, which might explode or which miners might breathe in, and automation allowed for new kinds of access to coal seams, changing the traditional patterns of mine construction.[39] The result, an observer noted, was that miners had "watch[ed] the grandeurs of science and technology bring a new life to millions of Americans, and gouge out more coal per minute . . . while [bringing] greater threats to the health and safety of the coal miner."[40]

But coal mining also killed slowly, through black lung. It made itself known to the victim by slowly taking away their breath, a death sentence as soon as the disease had progressed enough to be noticed. Moreover, black lung had been excluded from many workers' compensation laws, meaning miners who developed it and their surviving family often had no legally defined right to compensation.[41]

By the late 1960s, black lung had been known to miners for more than a century, even if it was by different names, like miner's asthma. Still, exact numbers are difficult to discern, since coal companies had engaged in denialism around the disease for decades, contending the condition did not exist, making diagnoses difficult to obtain, and the federal government had no program to keep track. State-level black lung compensation and testing programs, where they existed, had mixed records shaped by longer histories of collusion between companies and the state. But we know the number is high. The bigger picture emerged from the records of the UMW Welfare and Retirement Fund. In 1966, 40 percent of all the death certificates filed with the fund registered respiratory conditions associated with black lung as the cause of death, but even that was likely an undercount, because black lung often killed through heart failure.[42] In the previous seventy-five years, more than one hundred thousand coal miners had been killed in mine accidents. Conservatively, probably twice that number died from black lung.[43] Incidence of the condition appears to have increased alongside the mechanization of coal mining that began in the 1920s but rapidly accelerated after the 1950 bituminous coal agreement and the creation of a coalfield welfare regime. Dr. Lorin Kerr, the UMW Welfare and Retirement Fund's assistant medical director, used Fund records to show that the rate of black lung had doubled between 1950 and 1969.[44] Indeed, by the late 1960s, black lung was the most prevalent occupational disease in the United States, and John L. Lewis's dream of a union-run coalfield welfare system was in tatters.[45]

Both black lung and explosions represented how "modern" coal mining seemed to miners little more than a modern death sentence. The fact that the two movements occurred together, tying together the interests of disabled miners with those still working underground, represented that miners' understanding of the crisis was not about the type of disablement or disaster but rather about a relationship between work and death that could be traced across different arcs of time—the lifetime of a miner who might narrowly escape death one day but over the next ten years contract the black lung that would ultimately kill him; the generations of miners through whose stories other miners came to interpret their own; the accumulated geological time, compressed into seams of coal, they cut from the earth each day to fuel the nation's acceleration through the American Century; even a future-oriented timeline that looked forward to the ultimate moment of their own death, a death that seemed inevitably tied to coal.

The Consol No. 9 disaster represented a turning point in how Americans like Ken Hechler, congressman for West Virginia's Fourth District, evaluated whether the coal-fired social contract was fair or just. Although Marion County, where the Consol No. 9 mine was located, was not in his district, Hechler later recalled the disaster "galvanized me into action and really changed my entire life."[46]

Ken Hechler was a West Virginian by choice. Born to an estate superintendent and a former schoolteacher on Long Island, New York, Hechler attended Swarthmore College at the height of the Great Depression. At Swarthmore, in the green, wooded outskirts of Philadelphia, Hechler read accounts from Bloody Harlan published in the *Nation* and the *New Republic*. The violations of miners' basic rights shocked him, and he would later point to those years as the origin of his interest in the rights of coal miners. But after leaving Swarthmore, Hechler went to New York rather than Appalachia.[47] He completed a PhD in history and government at Columbia University.[48] In 1942, he was drafted into the army as a combat historian; after the war, Hechler joined the Truman White House and became involved in Democratic Party politics. By the late 1950s, Hechler had the urge "to get out in the grass roots," and he accepted a faculty position (and a substantial pay cut) at West Virginia's Marshall College.[49] On January 22, 1957, he boarded the train to Huntington, a city of around 85,000 people on West Virginia's western border, with a large port that transferred coal into river barges to be sent up or down the Ohio River. Two years later, he was sworn in as Huntington's congressional representative, quickly gaining a reputation as a liberal maverick and staunch defender of civil and labor rights.[50] In September 1968, as he neared the completion of his first decade in Congress, Hechler introduced a bill to improve coal mine health and safety. But Congress's focus had shifted to the coming election, and according to Hechler, "it was obvious . . . no action would be taken" that year, a delay that would haunt him two months later, when he learned of the horrific explosion in his adopted home state.[51]

Hechler phoned an official "high up in the Department of the Interior" to demand answers about what had happened in the Consol No. 9 mine, but the official chided him: "Don't let an accident like this excite you. After all, nobody did this on purpose."[52] Perhaps Hechler's reputation preceded him. When Hechler visited the mine site, Assistant Secretary of the Interior J. Cordell Moore insisted Hechler not "go blaming anybody or looking for scapegoats."[53] The attitude of futility expressed by administrators, industry men, and union leaders enraged him. His rage was spurred into action when the widows of the men entombed in the mine confronted him, demanding he "do something about all this coal dust which coal miners breathe and gives them black lung, as well as contributes to explosions."[54]

From that encounter began the legislative fight that would consume most of his remaining eight years in Congress: a struggle to protect what he described as the miners' "divine right to live, to breathe."[55] Hechler insisted that if the United States was to make claims on modernity and civilization, it had to address the "criminal" conditions in the nation's coal mines, and the responsibility he felt clearly fell to the nation as a whole, which must "rise up and demand that strong and effective mine-safety legislation be passed by Congress."[56] He told Interior Secretary Stuart Udall that "we must move beyond being mere determinists. . . . we can fuel the world's lamps without snuffing out lives in the process."[57] By that point, Hechler had been in Congress for a decade and engaged in politics for much longer. He settled in for the drawn-out legislative fight he knew was coming.

Miners felt unable to wait for legislatures to reckon the moral problems of energy production. The Black Lung Association first targeted the West Virginia state legislature as it considered a black lung bill. A six-hour committee hearing in Charleston made clear to miners the bill was unlikely to pass without grassroots pressure. Members of the BLA threatened to close down fields if the law was not passed. Hundreds carried placards reading "No Law, No Work," a slogan meant to echo the UMW maxim "no contract, no work."[58] A week later, on February 18, 1969, 282 miners from the East Gulf Mine in Raleigh County in southern West Virginia walked off the job because, as one striker explained, "the legislature is not bearing down. They're letting it cool off too much."[59] The next day, most of the county's mines were idle, and within a week, twenty thousand miners, mostly in the state's southern counties, were on strike. Thousands marched on the state capitol in Charleston.[60]

Ken Hechler initially hesitated to support the wildcat strike, believing working through the legislative process offered the miners the best chance of success. But after meeting with the miners in Charleston, he donated a

Figure 5.2 Miners demand black lung legislation.
Source: Photo by Earl Dotter, www.earldotter.com.

thousand dollars of his own money to the Black Lung Association and threw his full support behind the miners.[61] As the walkout gathered momentum, it spread into the northern part of the state and to neighboring states including Pennsylvania and Kentucky.[62] Soon, forty thousand miners had idled every coal mine in West Virginia, and a federal judge concluded he had "no authority to order striking coal miners back to work."[63] From the UMW headquarters in Washington, Boyle was finally forced to respond to the crisis. His administration drafted proposed legislation that miners immediately rejected as too weak. Boyle's proposals for dealing with the problem revealed his failure to grasp the political impact that a widespread strike might have in an electrified society so reliant on coal. He claimed he didn't believe that Congress would pass legislation "because I have shut down every coal mine in the United States and have a *little blackout here and there*."⁶⁴ What Boyle could not see, miners had acted on themselves.

Addressing the dust problem in the mines threatened the mechanized coal production practices that undergirded the coal-fired social contract, specifically the use of continuous mining machines. Continuous miners created a lot of fine coal dust, which increased both the risk of explosion and the likelihood of acquiring black lung; they also allowed fewer miners to extract greater quantities of coal, lowering per-ton recovery costs. Boyle's proposal to decrease dust levels in the mines "would have the effect of prohibiting the use of continuous miners," effectively undoing the mechanization that the UMW had long supported.⁶⁵ Pushing back on his proposal, Boyle's own administration argued that continuous miners accounted for 50 percent of underground production in 1968 and represented a vital part of the industry's market competitiveness.

Boyle and his administration seemed to recognize how efforts to assuage industry leaders were likely to appear to most rank-and-file miners. They went to great lengths to avoid the seemingly inevitable perception that by meeting with industry leaders they were "fraternizing with the enemy."⁶⁶ Boyle convened a special meeting of "district officers and very selective rank and file representatives carefully chosen by the International leadership."⁶⁷ At this meeting, he arranged for a delegate from the floor to propose a resolution securing collaboration with operators and machinery manufacturers, while also creating a select committee that would work to redirect black lung activism in the districts away from the kinds of direct confrontation unfolding in West Virginia.⁶⁸ This last-minute attempt to grab hold of the increasingly restless situation in the coalfields proved in vain. It reflected Boyle's inability to see the black lung crisis as anything but an indictment of his leadership, bargaining, and policy approaches.

The tone of the debate among Boyle and his administration suggested more concern for black lung legislation's effect on coal's market position than for the miners dying of black lung after a lifetime of work in the industry. The head of the UMW Research Department suggested that Boyle go to great lengths to assuage the fears of the "coal industry and the mining equipment manufacturers."⁶⁹ These remarks echoed a company doctor who reportedly told one miner to "not mention" his black lung because "you'll die faster from not eating than from coal dust in your lungs."⁷⁰

Such thinking highlighted the tension between the UMW leadership's focus on bread-and-butter unionism and miners' right to life.

Bread-and-butter unionism in the postwar period accepted a limited idea of unions' purpose in American life: securing higher wages and stronger benefits packages for its members via collective bargaining. That mode of unionism also shared the core belief of the "consumers' republic": the promises of social citizenship would be deepened by participation in the mass consumption economy. Miners were in theory also consumer-citizens, but the vision of an egalitarian world of rising consumption could not have seemed more distant to those dying in mine accidents or from black lung. How could miners fully claim the rights of citizenship in the mass consumption economy when the energy system fueling that economy structurally compromised one of their most basic, fundamental rights?[71]

Miners recognized how the ability to purchase cars, home appliances, and more came at the cost of their lives. One miner interviewed by Robert Coles and Harry Huge for the *New Republic* powerfully captured that tension. They left the miner unnamed, as if to underscore that his experience was not unique but representative. Only thirty-one, this miner had lost his brother in a mining accident, and he was himself already disabled from black lung after fifteen years underground. Black lung left him with all the telltale symptoms: a persistent cough, wheezing and shortness of breath, coughing up black phlegm. It was going to kill him. The way that he narrated his situation demonstrated how, for coal miners, life and death, future and past, security and insecurity all intermingled.

> I've had it. I'm an old man at 31. . . . Some of our kinfolk, they never went to the mines, and they near starve to death and freeze to death, come every winter. But you know, as bad as it is for them, I'm beginning to think they're better off than me and my brother. They don't see the money we do—if we live and don't get sick—and they can't have the things we buy. But I'd rather have it real, real terrible up in the hollows than end up like my brother. He got killed, in a second, just like that. The roof fell in on him down in the mine. And me, well you can hear me trying to catch enough air to stay alive. I never know when my lungs will just stop working altogether, and that will be the end. It's no way to die, let me tell you. It's no kind of reward for those years down in the mine. I wonder if a lot of people, they know that the coal they use to run the factories, it's all done at the expense of our

lives. We get killed down there, or our lungs go and get killed. And then a lot of us, we don't hardly get nothing to live on.[72]

This was the embodied reality of the coal-fired social contract as it had been negotiated in the postwar years. For miners, it represented two contradictory yet simultaneous futures: first, as a potential source of long-term political and economic security, their ticket of entry to consumer society, and second, as a "way of death," a mode of living in which instantaneous death loomed constantly at work and slow death accrued in their lung tissue for each day they survived. The contradictions, Coles and Huge argued, were enough to make anyone "a little sociological."[73] The article unsettled the very claims of American liberalism that the *New Republic* had been central in forging. Progressive disease substituted for promises of progress, a disease that was not an accident but a feature of the nation's energy system.[74]

The West Virginia black lung strike that began on February 18, 1969, shook the stalemate that had characterized the political battles over pending health and safety legislation. By February 25, public opinion on the strike had shifted from earlier calls for "sober thought and study" to address the black lung problem to the *New York Times*' assessment that "action on mine health and safety cannot wait. . . . It is time for the miners to stop losing. Their record of defeat is written in blood."[75] On March 12, West Virginia's Governor Arch Moore finally signed a landmark black lung bill that contained enough provisions for compensation to be accepted by the striking miners, and the dramatic three-week strike finally ended. Tens of thousands of miners returned to work the next day.[76]

The law broadened the definition of occupational lung disease, ending what the historian Alan Derickson termed "the long tyranny of radiology" by allowing clinical and physiological diagnosis for the majority of miners whose black lung didn't show up on X-rays. It also met the miners halfway on the question of presumption of disease. While the Black Lung Association had demanded presumption of black lung after five years underground, the West Virginia state law presumed disease progression in miners who had worked at least ten of the previous fifteen years in dust-exposure jobs.[77] Most keen observers could see that the issue of mine safety was far from resolved, however. Different elements of the law appeared to contradict one another, presenting potential obstacles for miners seeking compensation, particularly if they were afflicted by other lung diseases, like emphysema, as well.[78] A meaningful resolution seemed impossible without federal mine legislation.

The struggle to renegotiate the coal-fired social contract had begun in earnest. Miners rooted their activism in a conception of modern energy citizenship, a fact that many outside the coalfields recognized. The power of the black lung strike derived from the fact that the "Black Lungers"—as the national media described them—had "a claim on the conscience of a nation in which coal remains a vital fuel."[79] In a moment of rapidly increasing coal-fired electricity consumption, the ability of miners to make political claims based on their role in the country's energy system appeared unlikely to dissipate anytime soon. Far from resolving the moral and political crisis facing the nation's energy system, the black lung strike would open it to full throttle. It catalyzed efforts to expand the role of the federal government in the regulation of occupational health and initiated the effort to remove Boyle from power and bring democracy back to the United Mine Workers.

In the meantime, the problem of federal legislation remained. Liberals, determined to pass an updated form of mine safety legislation and create some kind of federal black lung program, confronted an increasingly uncomfortable truth: the standard of living that was meant to provide evidence of American superiority over communism—and that many Americans saw as forming a basic part of their citizenship in a mass consumption society—was premised on a system of energy extraction that resulted in mass death among a subset of its citizens.[80] Miners, for their part, were increasingly making clear with growing numbers of wildcat strikes that they would no longer accept such blatant disregard for their lives, even if it meant threatening electricity shortages. What kind of safety law could possibly meet both challenges? If even the most modern and regulated coal mining industry would still result in some number of injuries and death, Americans would have to explain why a certain number of deaths could be tolerated while a higher number could not be. While everyone agreed that the seventy-eight miners killed in the Consol No. 9 was too many, many such tragedies unfolded on a smaller scale in the coalfields each week.

Think back to Lester Willard, the motorman who joked with Walter Slovekosky over the radio before perishing in the Consol No. 9 mine. Had Willard died in a haulage accident instead of a methane explosion so large it was felt seven miles away, it might have been reported in a few local papers. Though the tragedy his loss represented would have been the same for those who knew him, it would likely have slipped past national notice in a country accustomed to such costs for cheap energy. This scenario was far from hypothetical: it happened 233 other times in 1968 alone. The day before the explosion at the Consol No. 9, fifty-two-year-old John Caserta died in a coal mine in Washington County, Pennsylvania, crushed to death by a slab of rock five feet thick.[81] Even if politicians were reluctant to admit it on record, the nation's energy system functioned with an implicit threshold of acceptable death and injury in the mines. Such thinking was evidenced in a March 1968 letter that Boyle wrote to Department of the Interior Secretary Stuart Udall: the "217 men who were killed in coal mines in 1967 is too high a price to pay for the production of coal. On the other hand . . . it is a far smaller price, for instance, than the 1,388 men who died in coal mine accidents in 1940, the year before the passage of the original Federal Coal Mine Safety Act."[82] Like many legislators, regulators, and industry men, Boyle appeared to accept that there was a tolerable number of dead coal miners, a level at which the personal cost of their lives would equal the benefits remunerated to the nation by electricity.

The linked processes of workplace deaths may have been longstanding, but the energy system around them had changed. While mining certainly had remained a deadly occupation, by all accounts and measures, the death rate in American coal mines *had* declined substantially since the earlier part of the century. Indeed, as the UMW, operators, and federal government hammered out the 1950 bituminous agreement, the rate of coal mine deaths per 100,000 miners had fallen below two hundred for the first time—and then remained there. Both fatal and nonfatal accident rates had dropped more than 40 percent since the 1930s.[83] But by the late 1960s, the gains in mine safety had not only stagnated but appeared to be reversing as several transformations in the American energy system came full circle.

In 1966, for the first time, the United States had burned more coal to generate electric power than it did for all other purposes *combined*—a trend only intensified in the following years. In energy policy, the federal government foregrounded access to cheap energy as a key component of social policy: a perspective that miners increasingly felt not only came at the expense of their lives but violated the longstanding basis of the coal-fired social contract that recognized the rights both of coal miners and coal consumers. Miners drew on this changed context to tie illuminated cities,

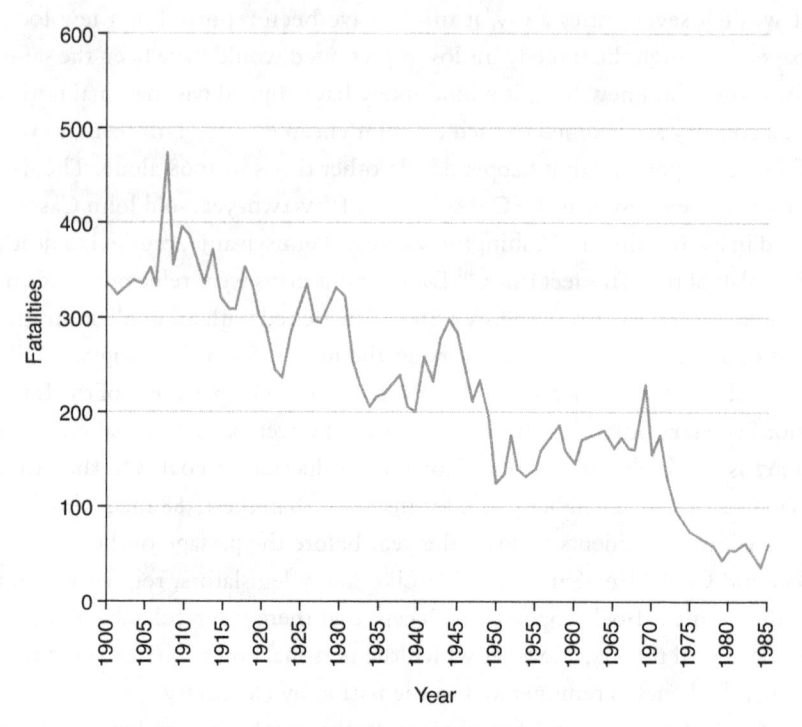

Figure 5.3 Workplace Fatalities per 100,000 Miners, 1900–1985.
Source: MSHA-DL.

all-electric homes, and increasingly automated factories to individual death narratives that might otherwise have been explained by a particular geological location or industrial context—the weakness of a particular roof in a mine with a lot of slate, for example, or a certain company's shooting practices. Now these deaths would signify the moral failures of the nation's social contract. What kind of citizenship was a death sentence?

Coal miners were not the only Americans grappling with this question, which made the claim on a "right to breathe" legible to the broader public. By the late 1960s, a notion of the right to a clean and healthful environment had entered the country's politics. In January 1970, President Richard Nixon, responding to public pressure, had declared that "clean air, clean water, [and] open spaces" were natural rights, "the birthright of every American."[84] This framework rooted both the occupational health demands of miners and the environmental health demands of the broader nation in the fundamental democratic claims of American politics. Miners, in claiming the right to breathe, drew on a theory of American democracy as a set of moral connections between people—one that reimagined the form of association as a national community bound by the energy that flowed between them.[85] This energy community was formed of people who primarily interacted with the American energy regime as producers and those who overwhelmingly interacted with it as consumers.

Miners believed recognition of these bonds opened new democratic possibilities that had intensified along one form of connection—electricity. In other words, it was not simply that miners had a right to breathe, which certainly they did, but also that the rest of the country, cast as consumers in the coal-fired social contract, owed it to them. Miners and their allies forced a federal reckoning with mine safety legislation that would write the right to breathe and the right to survive the workday into the nation's social contract and that would funnel significant federal monies to the administrative institutions charged with protecting those rights and compensating miners for past violations.

The West Virginia black lung strike had demonstrated miners' moral claim on the United States based on their role in electricity production, but Congress struggled to codify these claims into law at the federal level. Legislators grappled with the high-energy moral calculus, which in the end came down to the amount of coal dust permissible in a working mine and the number of dollars a miner disabled by black lung might receive. These decisions only appeared technical and economic; each decision delineated the energy consuming public's moral culpability. Mine safety was a matter of political urgency as well as technocratic adjustment. The importance of such decisions was evidenced by the fact that things like dust levels were legislated in the text of the law itself, rather than waiting until the regulatory agencies promulgated new rules three to six months later.[86] Debates over the milligrams per cubic meter of allowable coal dust, over the processes for injunctive relief on safety violations, or over the dollar amount of penalties were heated not only because of their potential dollar value or company intransigence. They revealed with uneasy clarity the extent to which liberal social policy had been premised on mass death and disablement.

Senator Harrison Williams felt that the challenge was to create a legislative framework that would make the costs of coal-fired energy more visible. The "legal" definition and the "human" definitions of the nation's obligations to its coal miners were out of sync. Nixon's new secretary of the interior, Walter Hickel, summarized the stakes of that challenge to Congress: "Coal must continue to play a significant role if the country's future energy requirements are to be satisfied. At the same time, it is clear that our society can no longer tolerate the cost in human life and misery that is exacted in the mining of this essential fuel." The choice for the nation was stark and unambiguous: "Unless we find ways to eliminate that *intolerable* cost, we must inevitably limit our mining of coal, which has almost inexhaustible potential for industrial, economic, and social good."[87]

The deep dependency of the U.S. energy system on coal allowed for little moral purity among politicians who felt they had to balance the rights of miners with the rights of Americans who depended on the energy that coal provided. According to Jennings Randolph, the Democratic senator from West Virginia who introduced one version of the mine health and safety legislation, everyone knew "the 'safest' coal mine and the 'healthiest' mine [was] the closed one."[88] Closing down mines, however, would not satisfy demands for increased production. Closed mines paid no wages and powered no generating stations. The challenge, Randolph argued, was "to achieve the feasible and the 'proper balance'" that would also be effective in keeping miners healthy and safe. Reducing electricity consumption was not an option.

By the late 1960s, energy consumption had, in the minds of American politicians, become both a measure of quality of life and evidence of American moral authority in international politics. If the moral costs of coal were high, so, it seemed, were the benefits of the energy it provided. Coal was, according to Randolph, "indispensable to our economy and our country."[89] But how many miners could acceptably die each year providing the rest of the country with light and power? How many cases of black lung could be tolerated to keep utility rates down? What benefits did the public owe disabled miners and the widows of miners killed on the job? At what point would the shame of the slaughter in the mines outweigh the exuberance of electrical abundance? "Just what is a human being worth?" Ken Hechler asked as the General Subcommittee on Labor debated one version of the bill. "I hope this committee and the Congress ponder that issue seriously. And if we go back and sharpen our pencils, I am convinced we will do it."[90]

The legislation looked to balance the burdens and benefits of the nation's energy system in two ways. One would determine what kinds of fines the

Bureau of Mines could impose for mine safety violations and who would pay them. The other would decide how past inequities, scarred into miners' lungs, would be redressed. By the early months of 1969, as the black lung rebellion erupted across the West Virginia coalfields, four different bills had been introduced in the U.S. Senate, all with varying approaches to worksite safety violation fines and black lung compensation schemes. While the length of time it ultimately took the 1969 act to pass has typically been assumed to reflect the coal industry's efficacy in stalling negotiations, the many days of hearings conducted on the matter, and the many different versions of what eventually became the Federal Coal Mine Health and Safety Act of 1969, it also offers a glimpse into a fraught debate about how to assess the moral costs of a coal-fired energy system and how to remedy the harms that system caused.[91]

The difficulties in crafting regulation that could seamlessly shift between miners' bodies and dollar amounts quickly became apparent when Tony Boyle challenged Senator Jennings Randolph and Senator Harrison Williams on their plans to fine miners substantially for mine safety violations—between $25 and $1,000 per infraction. Senator Randolph advocated such penalties to incentivize miners' compliance with new federal regulations. Boyle contended that not only did miners who violated safety regulations risk losing their jobs but that miners indeed already made payments for violations with their health, bodies, and lives: "the supreme sacrifice." Asked Boyle: "Would you want me to fine a dead man?"[92]

Boyle's sharp words were undercut by his own complicity in the unbalancing of the nation's moral ledgers—siding with the companies over miners, putting the industry ahead of the workers who made it profitable—a fact that miners had raised consistently in the aftermath of the Consol No. 9 disaster. Moreover, beyond the dispute over fines, substantial agreement existed on the need for modernized mine safety regulations. In that political moment, even some coal companies provided lip service to support for regulations, even if they continued to nitpick at the specifics to try and minimize the impact on their operations. A far more heated debate unfolded over what kind of compensation was owed to miners who had contracted black lung disease and who would pay for it. Estimates of disease prevalence ranged widely in policy debates, in part because of different ways of evaluating evidence of disease but also because of different levels of competency in simply interpreting the same data.[93] Whether the program would cover forty thousand claimants or more than 125,000, the concern over the cost of such a program, hundreds of millions of dollars each year, offered implicit recognition of the unequal burdens of the country's energy system—a burden carried by the nation's coal miners.[94]

Debate on the bill continued into the autumn. The anniversary of the Consol No. 9 disaster came and went. Nixon threatened to veto the bill over the sticking point of black lung compensation, raising the specter of inflation and spuriously invoking "state's rights." The delays irritated miners, who considered what options they had to increase pressure on the president. Widows of the miners killed in the No. 9, formidable organizers in their own right, threw their support behind a walkout like the black lung strike and committed to persuading miners to join. Sara Kaznoski, whose husband, Pete, died in the No. 9, understood that "as long as they're ... wanting production before lives, there'll always be tragedies." But she was also committed to ensuring what happened to her husband never happened again.[95] Hechler publicly warned Nixon there would be a national coal strike if he followed through on the veto threat. Coal stockpiles were already low after a year of unrest. If a strike became necessary to ensure Nixon signed the legislation, the real costs of failing to secure compensation and future protection through legislation would quickly become apparent if a wildcat strike drained those stockpiles even further.[96]

As the safety crisis recentered the importance of the coal-fired social contract in the nation's systems of energy provision, a power struggle erupted within the United Mine Workers. On May 29, Joseph A. "Jock" Yablonski announced he would run against Boyle in the 1969 election for the union's top office, the first contested election since 1926.[97]

On first glance, Yablonski appeared an unlikely candidate for such a challenge. He had been part of the union's leadership for more than three decades: as a committeeman, a local president, and, by age twenty-four, a member of his district executive board. His loyalty to John L. Lewis had earned him a seat on the International Executive Board and, later, appointment as president of western Pennsylvania's District 5. Despite an ill-advised run for the union's vice presidency in 1966 without Boyle's support—a move that resulted in his being fired from his position as the District 5 president—he remained part of Boyle's inner circle as late as 1968 and was selected to open the UMW Constitutional Convention that September.[98]

Figure 5.4 Jock Yablonski.
Source: Photo by Jeanne Rasmussen, JRP 4/19.

Still, the same participation at the convention that confirmed his place in the union's leadership also foreshadowed the coming parting of ways. At the 1968 convention—which had been moved to Colorado to highlight the union's fight against nuclear power—Yablonski's opening speech diverted attention from the tight focus on the atom. His focus landed on a concerning trend of horizontal integration by oil companies. Starting in 1963, the oil majors had begun acquiring coal companies; by 1968, the trend had accelerated.[99] The UMW's focus, he thought, should shift from the targeting of the AEC to the oil and gas companies. Believing the oil companies were on the verge of scientific breakthroughs that would allow them to turn coal into gasoline, petrochemicals, and pipeline gas, Yablonski warned that if the UMW was caught unprepared, workers would be shut out from "their rightful share" of the profits that these new energy production processes could yield.[100] He also noted that the oil and gas companies were as complicit in the creation of dangerous environmental conditions as the AEC.[101] Boyle, however, trained his attention on the Atomic Energy Commission throughout the convention, and Yablonski, despite his shift in focus, otherwise remained publicly loyal to Boyle, though the men disliked each other.[102]

Yablonski declared his candidacy the following spring, the situation in the coalfields having reached a "breaking point." Boyle's response to the Consol No. 9 disaster, the black lung strike, and the ongoing effort to secure updated mine safety legislation convinced Yablonski that Boyle was unfit to run the union in a new era. It echoed in many ways the events that had drawn Yablonski into the union's leadership in the first place. While he had been working in the mines since the age of fifteen, Yablonski got involved in the union in 1933, after a mine explosion killed his father, a Polish immigrant, and as miners around the country organized and went on strike to set the terms of the New Deal social contract.[103] A lifelong loyalist suddenly found it impossible to continue his thirty-five-year association with a union leadership that had "bred neglect of miners' needs and aspirations." Declared Yablonski: "The coal miners in this country are damn sick and tired of having a national president of [their] organization that's in bed with the coal operators."[104] The escalating safety crisis made clear that far from only being a problem of backdoor deals and sweetheart contracts, being "in bed" with the coal operators entailed cosigning the death certificates of miners who had been killed in explosions or roof falls or who had withered and died of black lung.

Boyle's autocratic hold on the union was tied to his outdated vision of the energy system, and miners increasingly perceived it as undemocratic not only because it dispensed with democratic procedure but because it violated a broader conception of democracy with which miners felt they might meet the challenges of the future. Yablonski's campaign knit a single narrative of democratic crisis from a wide set of issues plaguing miners because of energy system transformation: debates about the dangers of atomic power, competition for utility industry market share, and the externalities of energy production including mine disasters, occupational disease, and, increasingly, environmental degradation. As a result, Yablonski's campaign became a key point of convergence for several challenges to

Boyle's administration and, by extension, the outdated coal-fired social contract that Boyle worked tirelessly to prop up for his own benefit. Yablonski's campaign initiated a multiyear struggle for union democracy in the UMW, playing a formative role in setting the terms on which the coal-fired social contract would be renegotiated. Yablonski would outline a "vision of the future" for the UMW's role in American society, one that differed sharply from Boyle's.

The basic premise of Yablonski's campaign was that the coal-fired social contract had failed to live up to its promise. The energy system transformation that had driven massive increases in national energy consumption had also resulted in a spike in workplace deaths and occupational diseases. Yablonski could not just present a potential new leadership of the union, one free of Boyle's corruption. He had to project his own vision of the future, a new version of the coal-fired social contract. In this he was successful. His declared mission was bold; it confronted the crisis of coal-fired social contract with an eight-point reform plan built on a "broader vision" of the union's role in society.[105] It included a safety platform to confront Boyle's "profuse mouthfuls of fatalism" and sought to expand the UMW safety division's research program, ensure broader public investment in mine safety through new state and federal regulations, and enshrine "all possible safety and health protections" in the miners' contract, including "a special coal operator safety fund for advanced safety improvements beyond the law."[106]

Yablonski's campaign would likely have enjoyed substantial support from miners on its safety platform alone. His campaign foregrounded miners' knowledge and experience as the most important form of mine safety expertise. The right to life stood at the heart of what miners thought should constitute the coal-fired social contract, and the success of the black lung strike in February had demonstrated that miners' safety concerns could translate directly into political power with the ability to affect national energy policy. The link between workplace safety and the nation's energy future went far beyond Boyle's rather dubious contention that coal mines presented a safe alternative to the uranium mines that supplied nuclear plants. It called into question the nature of democratic decision making: who decided what made a workplace unsafe? Yablonski and his supporters' answer was clear: miners knew best when to make that call, so safety had to remain a strikable issue. At U.S. Steel's Robena mine, where thirty-seven miners had been killed in a 1962 explosion, miners turned out more than seven hundred strong to "overwhelmingly roar" their support for reform.[107]

As the campaign progressed through the summer and fall of 1969, the link between workplace safety and energy production continued to be a programmatic weakness for Boyle, who had suggested in the wake of the Consol No. 9 explosion that as long as the American energy economy used coal, there would always be workers who died mining it.[108] Miners like Stanley Kaczmarczyk lashed out at Boyle. Kaczmarczyk considered Boyle equally responsible as Consolidation Coal for the explosion that killed seventy-eight workers, and he pointed to the Boyle administration's failure to even recover the men's bodies to call his leadership into question. "If Boyle was any kind of leader," he wrote, "he should get after Pitts Consol and the U.S. Bureau of Mines to get those human beings out of that tomb."[109] The link between mine safety and the energy economy also became a personal liability for Boyle as his antinuclear crusade came under new scrutiny. In Montana, the *Billings Gazette* reporter Roger Hawthorne broke the story of the Boyle brothers' collusion in minimizing the deaths of four miners as Jack Boyle's company supplied the Hanford contracts.[110] The recently expelled membership of District 50 also pointed out how the scandal certainly put "Boyle's fanatic opposition to atomic energy" in "a new light."[111]

Yablonski's safety platform opened up a range of other demands: in order for the safety platform to be enforceable and effective, local unions needed the autonomy to respond to safety problems as they arose while maintaining the consolidated national power that gave the UMW the ability to set industry-wide working conditions with a national contract, and they needed an updated grievance procedure that met the needs of the changing mining workplace. A strong grievance procedure, Yablonski argued, could help minimize the wildcat strikes that by the end of 1969 had substantially drained the nation's coal stockpiles and that, commentators warned, would take months to recover if the miners stayed at work.[112] Reformers felt that bottom-up democracy rooted in the mines themselves was a key element of industry stability and would ultimately serve them better than the iron grip that Boyle had kept over the union.

The attempted rebalancing of power also extended beyond the workplace to the question of the UMW's proper role in society. Yablonski's social responsibility platform, like his safety platform, drew on some of the arguments Boyle had made during his antiatomic crusade. It framed the UMW as not only a union concerned with workplace issues but a broader defender of all working people and their interests. The persistence of coal company power in state and local politics represented the undemocratic vestiges of the coalfield state. Yablonski insisted that under his leadership, the union wouldn't tolerate the coal industry's manipulation of state and local politics.[113] Guided by a vision of union-directed regulation, welfare, and management, Yablonski declared that "every union should have a vision of the future." His vision entailed a renegotiated coal-fired social contract.

Such a contract would include its already existing, if unfulfilled, components: "adequate payment for work done, adequate compensation for injuries, adequate corporate investment in healthful and safe working environments, and adequate retirement benefits." But Yablonski's vision of the future would also expand it substantially because "unions represent men and women who are part of communities, are citizens of states and a nation. The public environment affects the well-being of miners and their families."[114] The UMW, in this argument, had an obligation to miners, the communities they lived in, and the broader country to help make the promises of energy citizenship real. Otherwise, the UMW, and the coal-fired social contract it had helped forge, would stand in between miners and the rights Americans had come to expect. Argued Yablonski: "What good is a union that reduces coal dust in the mines only to have miners and their families breathe pollutants in the air, drink pollutants in the water, and eat contaminated commodities? What good is a union that achieves an acceptable wage rate and then condones the reduction of that wage by frauds and abuses in the marketplace and waste or corruption in government?"[115]

Yablonski's "vision of the future" centered the political leadership of coal miners through a reformed UMW. This vision emphasized miners' political agency in ways that mirrored and extended grassroots War on Poverty efforts around the region and across the country.[116] It inevitably raised questions about who was most capable to determine the needs of production and the conditions of the coalfields. Moreover, it also linked these debates over workplace power and political regulation to a growing set of concerns around pollution and environmental quality before the passage of the major environmental legislation for which the era is remembered—the National Environmental Policy Act (1970), the Clean Air Act (1970), the Clean Water Act (1972), and the Safe Drinking Water Act (1974), as well as the creation of the Environmental Protection Agency (1970).[117]

The true outcome of the 1969 election, however, will never be known. Rumors of interference by Boyle and his supporters in the election began as early as the nomination process. Boyle illegally redirected union funds to his renomination campaign. Union staffers tried to bribe Yablonski supporters to change their votes. Boyle loyalists held unlawful nomination meetings and sometimes illegally adjourned meetings where Yablonski supporters outnumbered them. Boyle's men assaulted Yablonski himself.[118] Chip Yablonski, Jock's son and a labor lawyer, submitted a formal list of at least eighty-six polling violations, including the levying of death threats against his father's polling observers.[119] Despite it all, the race was narrower than the last contested election in the UMW forty-three years earlier, in 1926.[120] On December 11, 1969, Boyle declared victory with 75,680 votes in the official tally—63.4 percent of the total.[121]

Boyle's infractions against the democratic process sharpened the reformers' critique of the broader problem of democracy in the coalfields. Yablonski's running mate, H. Elmer Brown, a disabled miner with advanced black lung from southern West Virginia, was probably better poised than most to see what was at stake in this democratic failure. Brown had "risked his own life many times" in the struggle to unionize the mines of Mingo County, West Virginia, in the 1930s.[122] Now, Brown demanded that Congress use $250,000 to investigate the election and its results.[123] "One can only conclude that the Government is working with Tony Boyle and the coal operators, and against the interests of coal miners," an exasperated Brown wrote to Senator Harrison Williams, one of the miners' strongest allies in the Senate. Brown then cast democratic deficiencies as intimately tied to the problems of mine safety and occupational health: "Why is it," he asked, that "the health, safety, and lives of working people are always put second to the profits of coal operators? . . . We want our rights and we are prepared to fight, even if it means closing the coal fields this summer."[124] From a union election stolen by Boyle and his ilk to a representative government that failed to protect them, miners often saw the strike as their best choice to have a say over their lives and to give democracy substance. It was, after all, how they, their parents, and grandparents had turned coal-fired citizenship into a reality once before: fighting the coalfield state, giving the New Deal meaning from below.

On December 29, 1969, two weeks after the election, two widows of the Consol No. 9 disaster picketed in front of the entrance to Consolidation

Coal's Loveridge mine, less than ten miles from the mine that had killed their husbands. They were not picketing over the UMW election but because Nixon had yet to sign the mine safety bill into law. The miners who encountered the widows on their way to work turned back; union miners never crossed a picket line.[125] In southern West Virginia, around a thousand miners refused to work.[126] Seven more of the No. 9 widows, including Sara Kaznoski, flew to Washington with Ken Hechler, in hopes of meeting personally with President Nixon. Mid-morning, they phoned the White House and were told to come by early that afternoon—just two hours later. But by the time the widows and Hechler arrived, Nixon had changed his mind. They were told they would meet a member of the White House counsel office instead, and not in the White House. So the women and Hechler crossed the street to the Executive Office Building, where they met with Deputy Counsel Richard Burress, who laid the case *against* the bill.[127]

Then the phone rang. President Nixon had relented and would sign the bill. "It was a glorious coincidence," Hechler recalled sardonically, "after the miners' walkout the night before and after the visit of the widows."[128] Nixon, facing an imminent and credible threat of a national coal strike, signed the Federal Coal Mine Health and Safety Act into law on December 30, 1969. The signing took place in private, with no photographers, no ceremony, "almost surreptitiously," Ken Hechler observed. The move appeared to perfectly encapsulate the unease that required tempering the "basic fact" that "any human being is worth more than a ton of coal" with the knowledge that the nation did, in fact, need coal even if it was deadly.[129]

Ensuring the passage of the Federal Coal Mine Health and Safety Act had taken monumental organizing efforts by miners and their allies. The act formalized occupational safety reforms and introduced compensation for black lung as part of the coal-fired social contract. The law affirmed that miners were more precious than coal; outlined specific administrative and oversight roles where coal industry appointees could not be installed; proscribed penalties for violations; promulgated thirty-two pages of interim safety standards on everything from methane monitoring, to maximum dust levels, to mechanical and electrical standards, to mandatory federal inspections; and created a federal black lung compensation program that would pay benefits while state programs were created. Opponents of the bill, including the coal industry, had left their mark too, including a mechanism by which operators could apply for "noncompliance permits" that allowed them to operate mines that failed to meet respiratory dust standards. Miners were also skeptical of handing the federal black lung program to the Social Security Administration (SSA), since SSA seemed adept at finding many reasons to deny benefits under the nearly fifteen-year-old Social Security Disability Insurance program.[130] The act heralded a wave of new regulatory legislation that would remake Americans' relationship to their workplaces and their environment.

As monumental as the struggle to pass the bill had been, it also turned out to be less than half the battle. Less than twenty-four hours later after Nixon signed the act, three hit men, hired on Boyle's orders and paid with $20,000 of UMW money, entered the Yablonski house while Jock, his wife, Margaret, and their adult daughter Charlotte slept. While the men were there to kill Jock, Charlotte died first, still asleep, when Buddy Martin shot her twice in the head at point-blank range. The shots that killed Charlotte woke up her parents, but Jock never got hold of the shotgun he kept by his bed just for this very scenario. While the other two killers, Paul Gilley and Claude Edward Vealey, fumbled with their guns in the master bedroom, Martin walked into the room and shot Jock and Margaret too. Vealey heard Jock gurgling in his own blood and shot him a few more times to make sure he was dead. Only the family dog survived.[131] The grisly scene remained untouched for nearly a week. After days of missed calls and, most troubling of all, his father's absence from a public event he had been expected to attend, Jock's other son, Ken, drove to the house to check on his family on January 5.[132] Ken Yablonski had been concerned for his father's safety for months. Now his worst fears were confirmed.[133]

Boyle hoped his rival's death would send a warning to other would-be challengers, the rebellious miners, and their allies. That hope only underscored how little he understood the way the world around him had changed. The day after Ken Yablonski discovered the bodies of his parents and sister, twenty thousand West Virginia miners walked off the job in protest.[134] More than one thousand people—many of them miners—squeezed into the Immaculate Conception Church in Washington, Pennsylvania, for the Yablonskis' funeral. The family was eulogized by Father Charles Owen Rice, the same priest who had married Jock and Margaret more than three decades earlier.[135] As the funeral procession made its way to the graveyard, Chip and Ken Yablonski walked with the bodies of their mother and sister, but they "entrust[ed] our father to the coal miners he loved so much."[136]

Among the men who carried Yablonski to his grave were Mike Trbovich, a safety and democracy activist from Clarksville who had managed Yablonski's campaign, and Harry Patrick, a miner who lived only a few miles from the site of the Consol No. 9 explosion, whose father had lost his leg in a mining accident and whose brother had been killed in the mines only five years earlier.[137] Boyle couldn't have known it then, but carrying the casket of the man he'd ordered killed were some of the men who would ultimately bury his presidency.

After the funeral, in a nearby "school-house classroom," a gathering of reform-minded miners and some of their allies became the basis for a new reform group: the Miners for Democracy, widely referred to as the MFD.[138] To these miners, the 1969 campaign was less a power struggle between two men than a referendum on the crisis facing the coal-fired social contract. They had been presented a choice, between a way of death and Yablonski's "vision of the future." Yablonski was dead—and the miners knew Boyle was ultimately responsible, even if it would take years for prosecutors to prove it in court. The opposition movement, far from being quelled, only continued to grow, further drawing down coal stockpiles that were already low from a year of unrest.[139] If the central place of coal in the provision of electric power kept the nation at the figurative table upon which the coal-fired social contract would be renegotiated, the Yablonski murders solidified the increasingly prevalent belief that the miners themselves must have a seat at the table—not just the union officials. The only solution to the coal miners' problems, the reformers insisted, was real democracy. As Boyle's hold on the union crumbled, District Judge Edward Dumbauld compared him to Macbeth, quoting Shakespeare's Scottish play to him in court: "Now does he feel his title / Hang loose about him, like a giant's robe / Upon a dwarfish thief."[140]

PART THREE

Renegotiation (1969–1972)

Second Interlude

This Total-Energy Dream

Boyle's fall from power, just as his rise, was intertwined with the transformation of the U.S. energy system. Like Macbeth, unable to comprehend the real meaning of the witches' prophecy, Boyle failed to grasp how the changing energy system would remake the terrain of coalfield power and his ability to control it. Yet these changes had been underway from his first days in office. They had come into the open by the 1968 UMW convention in Denver, Colorado. As Boyle and the other UMW officers focused their attention on the Fort St. Vrain nuclear generating station, Jock Yablonski had focused attention on a deeper, structural shift in the nation's energy system: a series of acquisitions of coal producers by some of the world's biggest oil companies. In those disparate attentions lay a deeper unity, as well as a particular firm: Gulf Oil.

By 1968, Gulf wasn't really an "oil company"—though of course, it did produce, refine, and sell a lot of oil. The company traced its roots back to the early-twentieth-century opening of the Spindletop oilfield in Texas, but Gulf soon went global "before it was fashionable to be known as an international oil company," most notably securing a massive seventy-five-year concession in Kuwait in 1934.[1] By the mid-1950s, two-thirds of Gulf's net income came from its foreign operations—a percentage that seemed increasingly risky amid a growing global tide of resource nationalism.[2] Gulf's leadership decided to hedge their bets by increasing domestic investment in the United States, reducing their reliance on overseas income.[3] In

1963, Gulf purchased the Pittsburgh & Midway Coal Company, a firm which accounted for 1.66 percent of total U.S. bituminous coal production—or around 9,000,000 tons.[4] In the months before Gulf finalized the acquisition, Pittsburgh & Midway received a fifteen-year contract from the Tennessee Valley Authority to supply coal for the Shawnee Steam Plant near Paducah, Kentucky.[5] In 1967, Gulf also entered the nuclear power industry by acquiring General Dynamic's General Atomic Division, which they renamed Gulf General Atomic. The following year, Gulf organized another subsidiary, the Gulf Mineral Resources Company, to oversee its uranium mining operations in the United States and Canada.[6] Gulf optioned two other coal reserves in Montana the same year.[7]

By the end of the decade, the unease driving these decisions seemed to have been well founded.[8] Bolivia nationalized Gulf Oil's subsidiary in the country in 1969.[9] The Portuguese, looking to finance their decade-long war of repression against independence movements in Angola and Mozambique, began demanding greater prepayment of taxes and rents around the same time—even as Gulf faced serious security concerns in Cabinda, where their subsidiary operated in territory largely controlled by the People's Movement for the Liberation of Angola.[10]

Gulf, the same oil company that had led the trend of oil companies' acquisitions of coal firms noted by Yablonski, was also the principal nuclear contractor for the Fort St. Vrain generating station, the pilot project for Gulf's new nuclear investments.[11] When the United Mine Workers gathered in Denver in the fall of 1968, however, these topics were siloed. Convention speakers frequently mentioned both nuclear power and oil acquisitions, sometimes in the same speeches, but did not connect them as representing a unitary process—even though the UMW clearly knew about Gulf's involvement in the Fort St. Vrain project. The UMW had, after all, named Gulf General Atomic in the lawsuits filed to stop construction of the facility.[12] But in the months following Yablonski's murder, these changes and their significance for the country's coal miners would increasingly be laid bare.

Gulf was far from the only oil company to purchase a coal firm during the 1960s. Oil companies acquired coal companies in rapid sequence across the late 1960s, and in doing so, they attracted a great deal of attention in a nation that viewed oil companies and their industrial concentration with suspicion. In the labor movement, the acquisitions first caught the eye of the Oil, Chemical, and Atomic Workers Union (OCAW), who in turn shared the information with the UMW in the summer of 1968. The oil companies' actions also drew scrutiny from public interest lawyers, journalists in the coalfields and the nation's financial centers, Congress, and the Antitrust Division at the Justice Department.

Observers certainly saw this industrial concentration as part of a general trend of corporate diversification, which had increased the power of large conglomerates in the American economy. These acquisitions, however, had a distinct kind of significance, for they both reflected and deepened the impact of electric intensification on the country's energy system, which shifted how the relationships between different source fuels were governed, managed, and understood. The idea of a unified national fuels policy had been around since 1939, and as postwar attempts to regulate the relationship between coal, oil, and the atom demonstrated, politicians had attempted to bring such a policy into being.[13] But by 1970 it remained just that, an idea, difficult to achieve given the differing politics, geography, and interests surrounding each fuel. In the absence of significant government action, the oil companies had substantial leeway to manage corporate risk within the country's energy system. Diversification would have a long-range effect on firm identity.[14] Oil companies could no longer solely be identified as an "oil company" any more accurately than one might call them a "coal company." The choices these firms made created something new: the modern energy conglomerate.

Like Gulf, other multinational oil companies had plenty of reasons to diversify their resource holdings. Domestically, oil production began to stagnate at the end of the 1960s.[15] Internationally, the sovereign rights program of resource-rich states in the Third World had moved from margins to mainstream; nationalization—or the fear of it—threatened the overseas concessions of American oil firms. The Organization of Petroleum Exporting Countries (OPEC) exerted increasing influence over production decisions. The era of cheap oil appeared to be over.[16] These changes left American firms with new concerns about their ability to shape global flows of oil, to influence the prices paid for it, and to chart the industry's future.[17] Coal acquisitions not only offered a new revenue stream, as coal prices increased steadily in the background, but also provided a form of energy underwriting for a growing set of operational risks. These acquisitions also reduced the likelihood of an anti-oil campaign such as the one led by the National Coal Association and the National Coal Policy Conference in the

1950s, which had contributed to the short-lived Mandatory Oil Import Program. Additionally, oil executives, used to taking the long view, saw these investments as an opportunity to draw on coal industry experience in synthetic fuel research and development, as well as to secure a foothold in the utility markets.[18]

Gulf Oil's 1963 purchase of the Pittsburgh & Midway Coal Company was the first instance of an oil firm purchasing a top-fifteen coal producer, but Continental Oil became the trendsetter. In 1966, Continental Oil, the nation's tenth-largest oil producer, purchased Consolidation Coal, which mined 11 percent of the nation's bituminous coal. Afterward, the pace of acquisitions accelerated. Occidental Petroleum purchased both the Island Creek Coal Company and Maust Coal & Coke, Eastern Gas & Fuel took over Eastern Coal, and the Old Ben Coal Company came under the ownership of Standard Oil of Ohio. In 1967, Kerr-McGee began construction on a new mine scheduled to produce more than one million tons of coal each year. By 1968, Standard Oil of New Jersey had invested more than $20 million in coal reserves and dedicated $12 million annually to coal-related research and development. Shell and Atlantic Richfield also made bids to enter the industry.[19]

Before 1966, ten of the top fifteen coal companies had been independent—that is, only in the business of selling coal—and the captive companies were vertically integrated into the supply chains of the country's large steel firms, like Bethlehem or U.S. Steel, rather than horizontally integrated with competing fuels. By 1969, that picture had changed dramatically. Only three of the top fifteen coal producers remained independent by 1969, and together they produced only 5 percent of the nation's bituminous coal. In only six years, the oil companies had successfully gained control of nearly 27 percent of the nation's bituminous coal production through acquisitions that targeted the largest companies with already-established relationships with the electric utility markets.[20]

The emergence of the modern energy conglomerate coincided with and accelerated the legitimacy crisis facing the coal-fired social contract by undercutting the political economic structure on which it had been premised. In the old structure, the UMW had participated in bargaining with some measure of parity with the other parties involved, the companies and the state. Horizontal integration gave the companies more leverage at the same moment that a crisis erupted in the coalfields following the Consol

No. 9 explosion and Jock Yablonski's murder.[21] At the very moment of industrial reorganization, the UMW and the Bureau of Mines were wholly incapable of responding. Their attentions would be drawn elsewhere as deaths in the mines continued despite the new safety law, and the union proved incapable of meeting its obligations to protect miners or keep the coal coming out of the ground.

From the perspective of consumers, the legitimacy crisis facing the coal-fired social contract represented the early throes of what would come to be known as the energy crisis. The energy crisis was less a geological or technological problem than a political one, and more a question of choices than resources. Without a unified national energy policy to manage the relationships among the fuels, questions about the nation's energy choices were heavily influenced by market forces in an increasingly horizontally integrated sector. As increased asymmetry between firms, the union, and the state undermined the coal-fired social contract, the impact of industrial transformation would also be felt among a much larger group of Americans, who would have to contend with the way private firms had constrained the possibilities for democratic action on the nation's energy problems.

The companies made choices based on their own increasingly diversified interests in a range of fuels, but no similar mechanism existed for the country to make energy choices on a democratic basis that considered all fuels and aspects of the energy system together. Instead, workers' unions and regulatory structures remained siloed, which presented substantial challenges to the kinds of energy questions that would face the country in the following years: How should available energy be allocated? What constituted a "fair price" for energy given how centrally it figured in the meaning of citizenship in a mass consumption economy? What were the priorities for the nation's energy system? Who should have access to what energy, at what price, and for what purpose? These were questions that, by 1970, had a multidecade history in which miners were deeply entangled. As a result, unions in this newly identifiable "energy industry"—like the UMW and OCAW—offered some of the earliest and clearest insights on the political and organizational character of the problem, as the 1968 UMW convention demonstrated, even if they had not yet connected the changes in the oil and atomic sectors directly.

For those who anxiously watched the nation's fuel stockpiles, the political character of energy choices was sometimes obscured, manifesting instead as logistical constraints. The nation's logistics network, which relied primarily on railroads to transport coal, had not adapted to the new usage rates and patterns that accompanied dieselization of rail fleets, increased utility demand, and the growth of a coal export market. As a result, rail cars were in short supply and often in the wrong place at the wrong time. Some utilities invested in "unit trains"—connected rail cars dedicated to transporting fuel from contracted mines to generating stations—but the larger issue persisted.[22] Declining mine productivity exacerbated the transportation issues. In turn, coal prices increased, placing financial pressure on the many electric utilities that purchased their coal on "spot" markets.[23] Even long-term contract buyers felt the supply pinch. By the fall of 1970, the Tennessee Valley Authority cited increases in coal prices to explain system-wide supply problems. Usually, utilities aimed to hold about two months' worth of coal in their stockpiles, but the TVA had less than ten days' worth on hand. TVA chair A. J. Wagner warned that "an adverse turn in the coal situation could change our power supply from serious to critical within a few days."[24] The growing number of blackouts experienced in the United States increased the salience of utility leaders' claims, even though fuel shortages were not themselves the cause of the blackouts.[25]

The energy crisis emblematized by the long lines at gas stations in the 1970s extended back to this larger set of interrelated problems.[26] Industry men and federal administrators framed these problems as resulting from a painful shift from an era of energy abundance to an age of limits. According to Carl Bagge, who left the Federal Power Commission to head the National Coal Association in 1970, the crisis had snuck up on the nation, and especially "the American public," who "generally does not yet realize the pervasive effects a sharp and prolonged energy shortage would have on society." Even though much of the country appeared to be in denial, Bagge insisted "the only thing that is unreal about the energy crisis in the United States is the general public reaction to it."[27] As early as 1971, the Department of the Interior had admitted that "our mineral abundance *is* becoming illusory." But these warnings had not translated into political action.[28] That coal miners had set some of these limits by opposing the modern way of death in the nation's mines usually went unspoken.

As politicians evaluated the strained electric power situation, the political nature of the questions at its heart quickly reemerged. American electricity consumption grew much more quickly than did the population—three times as quickly, in fact. That growth, the White House Office of Science and Technology underscored, was the result of federal policy choices that had prioritized access to cheap electric power as a modernization strategy.[29] As politicians and a growing cadre of environmental activists drew attention to the havoc cheap electric power wreaked on the environment, they also recognized that electric power was the nation's "lifeblood."[30] Maine's Ed Muskie, a Senate leader on environmental policy, insisted that power reliability and environmental protection would have to be tied to increasing democratic decision making over the nation's energy infrastructure. Given the central importance of energy to the United States, its citizens, the country's economy, national security, and its military power, liberals like Muskie contended that energy decision making had to be pulled, at least partially, from the hands of private firms and subjected to public scrutiny and oversight.[31]

It is unsurprising that these critiques emerged as the legitimacy of the coal-fired social contract unraveled. Both reflected longstanding, unresolved questions about the relationship between coal and democracy. Muskie recognized that "no one wants to abandon the high energy production which supports the society most of us enjoy." That *most of us* carried much weight. The age of energy abundance had also accumulated debts, from black lung to air pollution, that could not be resolved by greater inclusion or increasing the size of the nation's pie. Coal-fired inequalities festered within the midcentury liberal order.[32] Reform-minded miners, who also had their eyes on the nation's coal stockpiles, said that if the nation's lights went out in the summer of 1970, it would be for a whole host of reasons, including "because the United States Government has flagrantly neglected its coal miners."[33]

By early 1970, coal had become energy. From the perspective of the energy conglomerates, coal was a form of their basic commodity, energy, which might also come from gas, oil, uranium, or tar sands. For the U.S. government and consuming public, coal was but an early stage in the energy lifecycle. Coal stockpiles were but caterpillars going through a process of metamorphosis into electric butterflies. These changes would have real implications for coal miners, now better described as energy workers.

From the perspective of coal miners, the transformation in ownership structure concentrated too much power in company hands and thus limited miners' ability to exercise power at work. However difficult it might have been to cut into Consolidation Coal's bottom line to exert leverage, doing the same to Continental Oil would be even harder. This change, in coming years, further encouraged miners to call on their political bonds with other Americans and with the federal government in their efforts to renegotiate the coal-fired social contract. Equally, miners would have to grapple with the reality that the coal-fired social contract was really part of a larger total-energy social contract, one that was imbalanced but where miners still exercised substantial leverage thanks to the amount of coal in the nation's energy reserves. Drawing on Yablonski's and Grospiron's addresses to the 1968 UMW convention, *Miner's Voice*, a reform movement newspaper, published an editorial outlining the situation: "Energy Workers Must Organize!" As much manifesto as editorial, it recognized that industry reorganization threatened miners' power over the nation's energy system, and the authors called for a new organizing vision for the coalfields, sneaking in a jab at Boyle in the process: "When it becomes clear, as it is in the companies' eyes, that you mine energy, not coal, just as the oil workers drill energy, and that you both work for the same people who own and control these companies, it's time to ask what the union leadership is doing to bring energy workers together to have sufficient bargaining power to obtain better contracts from the companies."[34]

The editorial challenged the common contention by UMW leadership that oil and coal were competing forms of energy: "If all the sources of energy . . . are owned by the same company then they are not competitive, but if the workers are organized into separate unions . . . then the company will be able to play one union off the other."[35] The form of this argument would have been familiar to miners even if the concept of an "energy worker" was not. The UMW, as a cornerstone of industrial unionism in the United States, had driven the spirit of industry-wide solidarity deeply into the way coal miners saw themselves. The task for reformers who spearheaded this vision of an energy workplace that could be an oil well or uranium mine as easily as a coal mine was to rearticulate the boundaries of what constituted "the industry" across which solidarity and organization must be built. The editorial's ambition of an energy workers' union went unfulfilled, but thinking about a wide range of energy flows remained core to reformers' strategic thinking about how miners could exert leverage over the nation's politics.

The key to that leverage lay in the utilities market, where coal miners' power was increasingly concentrated. For the companies to increase their profits in this sector and secure desirable long-term contracts, they would have to provide fuel reliably. Confronting the problem of fuel supply for electric power ultimately meant confronting the problem of production—regardless of the energy source. What appeared initially to be a problem of utilities' meeting consumer demand could be traced back to the problems of the workplace.

Coal in this moment became a particular target both because of its increasing potential for profitability but also because its problems were most visible.[36] Because of its enormous domestic reserves, the relative accessibility of coal seams, the already-existing infrastructure to move coal from mine toward the metropolitan centers, and—most critically—its spiking profitability without substantial price increases following mechanization in the 1950s, coal presented a massive opportunity for the industry. So large did its promise loom that the emerging energy companies could set aside the concerns about labor unrest that had panicked the utilities and coal operators alike.[37]

Spiking profitability and consolidating control provided an opening to make what George Love, president of Consolidation Coal, called a "total-energy complex," a new way of organizing the production of various fuels to create an energy safety net that would, in his mind, benefit both the industry and the nation.[38] The different fuels essentially produced the same thing, and if they were all knitted together, they could, in theory, stabilize a new kind of industry and ensure profit for years to come. This model was markedly different than the vertical integration of supply chains practiced by major steel companies, like Bethlehem and U.S. Steel, which maintained coal operations to supply their own factories. Instead, the new energy companies envisioned "energy" as a new commodity. With enough research and development, industry leaders believed that coal and oil might become essentially interchangeable—as though a shirt company bought a trouser company and instead of producing both shirts and trousers began producing jumpsuits in different colors. "This total-energy complex," Love described, "is a dream we've had for a long time."[39]

Heavy investment in coal signaled the industry's vision for the future of American energy production. The acquisitions had breathed new life into coal firms like the Island Creek Coal Company. "Once we were purchased by Occidental, our plans changed virtually overnight," Island Creek's president explained. Within a year, Occidental invested $175 million in its new subsidiary—more than double Island Creek's value at the time of purchase—and laid plans to triple the company's tonnage by 1975.[40] Other oil companies held billions of tons of coal in their reserves, even if it wasn't in active production, banking on long-term markets in electric power generation. Consolidation Coal, as a subdivision of Continental Oil, acquired seven billion tons of reserves by the end of the 1960s and was actively seeking to expand them.[41]

Coal was central to the intentional project of making energy companies. Kennecott Copper, which through a series of legal maneuvers aimed at evading antitrust law transformed their subsidiary Peabody Coal into Peabody Energy, described the process: "Thus a new pattern has begun to emerge in the fuel industry, consisting of companies committed to the highest utilization of all energy sources—oil, gas, uranium, and of course, *the basic fuel of all, coal.*"[42] The emerging energy conglomerates also looked to longstanding but unfulfilled dreams of synthetic fuels and coal gasification. Consolidation Coal sank more than $10 million into research on converting coal into synfuels and received more than $16 million in government grants to research coal gasification.[43] Standard Oil of New Jersey acquired the massive coal deposits with the intention of using them to develop "synthetic fuels from coal" that could supplement "traditional sources of petroleum energy." By 1971, Standard Oil of New Jersey owned "over 6 billion tons of coal reserves," earmarked for a future yet to arrive.[44]

Problems manifested immediately. The result of the energy industry reorganization was not more coal production. Despite the massive investments and the plans for increased output, coal production remained mostly flat in the four years after Continental Oil acquired Consolidation Coal— usually a little over 550 million tons per year.[45] By 1973, production for domestic markets was 85 million tons below U.S. consumption.[46] The reorganization also changed how the industry assessed the profitability of their different energy ventures, as a manager of the Tennessee Valley Authority noted in his testimony before the Senate Subcommittee on Intergovernmental Relations in August 1970:

> These companies that used to sell us coal are now controlled by people who are looking at the whole energy picture, and they do not really care—and they will tell you this—whether they sell the coal now or whether they keep it as reserves and convert it at some later date. Another aspect of it is that these same people that control the oil and coal also control the gas, and they are very rapidly acquiring the uranium deposits of this country. So that within a relatively short

time, relatively few people, a relatively few companies, are going to control the whole energy picture; and they tell you frankly that they won't open a mine unless you guarantee them the kind of return that they would get if they were selling gasoline."[47]

The energy companies sat on coal reserves rather than developing them unless the price was right. It represented "a major factor in the current coal shortage, a factor with tremendous ramifications for future energy policy . . . the companies that own the coal have other things to do with their money."[48]

This market dynamic, perhaps unsurprisingly, attracted the attention of antitrust experts, even those who had once dismissed the antitrust implications of the mergers. In 1967, Donald Turner, head of the Antitrust Division at the Justice Department, pointed out that the geographic markets in many of these mergers simply didn't appear to overlap, but by 1969 he had changed his mind. He wrote in the *Harvard Law Review* that the acquisitions could indeed fall under the Clayton Antitrust Act.[49] While the markets may not have appeared to overlap initially, the transformation of disparate fuels into energy muddied the lines between fuels and between markets from the perspective of the energy companies. Converting electrical generating stations to burn different fuels, while common, also lagged market shifts. As a result, the changing priorities of the companies could have a rapid impact on daily energy prices for consumers, as well as the general reliability of electric service, a serious concern by 1970. According to analysts, the transformation of the industry represented "a test of the nation's ability to make energy the servant rather than the master of us all."[50]

The nation's energy culture shifted, too. The conceptual shift from fuels to energy relied on ordinary Americans understanding fuels as sharing in a basic energy character, one that linked utility stockpiles of coal not only with the electric light in their house but with the gasoline used to power the cars on the street and with barrels of oil. The use of "energy" as a common language or measure that could bridge a wide range of fossil fuels, electric power, renewables, and more was relatively new in American political culture, even if the idea of substituting fuels for one another had been around for much longer.[51] The use of *energy* this way, to refer to a range of possible energy sources together, appeared rarely before the 1930s, and then only sporadically until the 1950s, where its use began to increase in government publications as interest in creating a unified national energy policy grew.[52] By 1970, energy had entered the political lexicon and the consciousness of many Americans. By the end of the decade, President Jimmy Carter would suggest that solving the problem of energy was necessary to hold onto the promise of the American century.

By the early 1970s, the nation's energy system looked very different than it had a decade before, but that was hard to see if you only looked at fuel consumption numbers. How Americans imagined the energy that powered their lives had changed in ways that reshaped how people would answer questions about who should be able to access energy and for what purpose. But Americans did not simply accept that coal and oil and gas and uranium had suddenly become energy because industry leaders said so. Over the course of the postwar decades, the way Americans lived with energy had changed, making it easier to imagine it as a new kind of thing.

One of the biggest changes was rooted in electric intensification. Electric power systems, as we have seen, had a way of obscuring where that electricity came from. But coal was not alone in becoming increasingly invisible. With the exceptions of gasoline and home heating oil, which still often went unseen as it pumped directly into tanks, Americans instead relied on a nebulous "power" that emerged from a complicated series of grids and wires. Kerosene, coal, and oil increasingly vanished from the domestic economy and even from people's memories of domestic spaces: shovelfuls of coal and tins of kerosene had been replaced with kilowatts.[53]

These new relationships had been cemented by popular images like Reddy Kilowatt, an electricity advertising figure that had grown in popularity since its creation in the 1920s.[54] Reddy Kilowatt, who often appeared on billing inserts and service notices as well as standard advertisements, explained how to live with electrical energy and in the process made tangible these shifts that would otherwise have been abstract, difficult to see, and dangerous to touch.[55] Sometimes the message was even less subliminal, such as an August 1970 cover of *Panorama*—a pull-out insert that came in Sunday newspapers across the South—which stated, "Coal is now power." An electric plug coursed up from a pile of coal to underscore the point.[56] These visual images helped Americans remap their energy relationships around the nebulous currents of power that figured more and more centrally in their lives. No longer confined to electric lighting, which lit larger and larger homes, electricity also powered televisions, air conditioners, hairdryers, and myriad other appliances.[57]

What the industry saw as the negotiating of risk, the federal government and energy consumers saw as a question of national interest and security. The nation's stability hung in the balance at a moment when stability appeared in short supply. A decade of social and cultural ferment was quickly giving way to deep-seated anxiety about the future of the United States and its political, social, and cultural institutions.[58] Antiwar protesters escalated their opposition to the war in Vietnam, particularly after the bombing of Cambodia in 1970, and faced an intense wave of repression. Black uprisings challenged racism and police brutality in cities across the country as President Nixon went on a "law and order" offensive. The greater participation of women in the formal economy—and particularly women's access to blue-collar employment—stoked anxieties about the future of what Robert Self has called "breadwinner liberalism": the employment and welfare regime that figured men's industrial employment as the anchor of single-income families. Efforts to decrease inflation pulled the country into a recession at the same moment the nation entered a decade that would become synonymous with "crisis."[59] Managing risk and navigating crisis would converge in the newly salient language of *energy security*.

The fuel crisis of the late 1960s and early 1970s—really the first years of the energy crisis—demonstrated that energy was indeed the nation's master. The energy crisis was not only a sudden confluence of problems with impact across the energy industry, as some scholars have argued.[60] Instead, the nation's descent into energy crisis signaled a crisis of governance, in part the outcome of deliberately pursued industrial strategies that transformed the economic structure of energy production in the United States. While these changes heralded a new era for industrial relations in the newly constituted energy industry, they also remade the basis on which the coal-fired social contract would be renegotiated.

As the ownership pattern suggested both new points of leverage and new quandaries about the nature of miners' power, it also helped push them toward organizing that focused on their political bonds with other Americans. While the coal-fired social contract had been undermined by its own contradictions, contradictions that had been unintentionally built into its structure, its collapse was also accelerated by the advent of an energy crisis, a political reality that would fundamentally shape miners' effort to renegotiate their relationship with the rest of the nation.

CHAPTER VI

Walk Out—Before They Carry You Out

On April 8, 1970, Joseph Stanish and Joseph Susick, both experienced miners, worked to extract the last possible load of coal from their section of Bethlehem's Ellsworth mine. Three hundred feet under the rolling hills of western Pennsylvania, and two miles from the portal, Susick operated the continuous miner while Stanish stood nearby with one hand resting on a post supporting the mine roof. Once they had finished, Susick began to back out the machine, when suddenly Stanish screamed, "Run for it!" Those were his last words, as the roof crashed down around him, crushing him beneath the rock. Susick made it a little farther away and was able to shield himself from the worst of the debris with the continuous miner he had operated only moments before, but the rock pinned his arm against the machine. Bleeding, his arm and leg broken, he waited an agonizing one and a half hours before his coworkers could free him. It took another two hours to recover Stanish's body. A nearby roof-bolter interviewed by investigators insisted none of the signs of an impending roof fall had preceded the accident—no fracturing posts, no noise to indicate the rock was shifting above them. Perhaps Stanish felt something with his hand resting on the post and, in warning Susick, saved his life.[1]

Bureau of Mines accident reports, like the one that catalogued Stanish's final moments, purported to narrate the events leading up to an accident, to explain what had caused it, and how it might have been prevented.

According to bureau investigators, the story of the accident at the Ellsworth mine began at 8 AM, when Stanish's crew entered the mine, and it ended when the investigators visited Joseph Susick in the hospital, where "he appeared to be recovering satisfactorily."[2] This narrative cast Stanish's death as a singular event, caused by bad risk management in the mine. It depoliticized his death.

Who was responsible for safe workplaces? Who was at fault for workers' deaths? Monthly safety competition newsletters framed safety as a personal responsibility. One such newsletter depicted a "good" and a "bad" miner in side-by-side panels, culminating in a final depiction of the "bad" miner crushed by a roof fall, screaming for help. The caption below read, "*I DID get hurt because I didn't do what I should. I put safety last.*"[3] Such depictions stripped safety decisions of the context of production demands, management pressures, and other factors that might lead a miner to "cut corners" on safety. Such representations also understated the extent to which safety underground was collective; explosions barreled through tunnels without consideration of who had ignited it, falling rock made no distinctions based on whose "fault" the fall was, and machines were shared across shifts and worked on by many hands. Framing safety as a matter of individual practice ignored the actual structure of work, especially in underground mines. Even though these fatal accident reports attempted to portray safety as procedural and technological, conflicts over safety cut to the heart a central American political dilemma in the 1970s: how to balance different interests in complex regulatory regimes.

Had Joseph Stanish been able, he might have begun the story of his death thirty-six years earlier, when a roof fall in a coal mine killed his father, a Polish immigrant.[4] Stanish was only nine at the time, but he began working in the mines ten years later, during World War II. In the decades that followed, death remained a constant, arms-length companion. The rock fall that killed Stanish in the spring of 1970 was the third fatal roof fall in the Ellsworth mine since Stanish began working there in the fall of 1964 and the fourth fatal accident at the area mines owned by Bethlehem in the previous year.[5] In March 1969, a roof fall in Bethlehem's No. 31 mine killed Clarence Watson in a nearly identical fashion, as he checked the roof before his crew began work. Four months later, Stephen Kovach also died in a roof fall in the No. 31, though his death was not even reported in the newspaper—perhaps because another miner, twenty-six-year-old Robert Carlson Jr., was electrocuted to death just hours later. A loading machine crushed Adam Petrisek, a mine mechanic from the same tiny three-thousand-person borough as Joseph Stanish, against a rib of coal in September. When he died, Petrisek was the third Washington County miner killed in a week.[6]

Between Petrisek's death in September 1969 and Stanish's death the following April, President Richard Nixon signed the Federal Coal Mine Health and Safety Act into law. Thirty days before the roof fall killed Stanish, the inspection schedules outlined in Title I and the interim safety standards outlined in Title III of the act should have come into force. Title I, §103(i) should have ensured a federal inspector visited the Ellsworth mine at least once every five days, and Title III, §302 should have given federal inspectors power to be sure Bethlehem implemented its already existing roof safety program. Had these standards been implemented as the law required, Joseph Stanish might have gone home to his wife and child that day. But the inspector did not visit the mine in April. Indeed, no federal inspector had visited the mine since December 22, 1969, before the act even became law, and management had the miners at the Ellsworth mine extracting coal that should have been left in to support the roof.[7] Stanish's death was not an isolated incident. In April 1970, twelve miners died in mines that *should* have been spot inspected but were not. Half of those deaths occurred in western Pennsylvania, in the same area where a growing reform movement sought to carry on the rebellion of 1969: the Miners for Democracy.[8]

Pressuring Congress to pass the Federal Coal Mine Health and Safety Act had taken a year of organizing, protesting, and striking by miners and their allies. Ultimately, forcing the executive branch, the companies, and the UMW to implement the new law and, thus, to recognize a new balance of the rights and obligations of coal-fired energy citizenship would prove even more challenging. In the months following the act's passage, the rate of death in the mines continued apace. June 1970 logged the worst safety record of any month since the Consol No. 9 disaster in November 1968. Reform-minded miners, both in the Miners for Democracy and the Black Lung Association, attributed the increase to lax enforcement by the Bureau of Mines and inadequate political will in the federal government more broadly. "Death Tolls Up—Inspections Down," summed up the Black Lung Association's newsletter, *Black Lung Bulletin*.[9] Companies sought and often received extensions on implementing new safety regulations. They also threw enormous sums of money into fighting miners in the courts on every possible point of law and fact. The Social Security Administration dragged its feet on awarding black lung benefits. And the Bureau of Mines' efforts to enforce the new safety act appeared, at best, half-hearted in comparison.[10]

From April 1, 1970, when the first provisions of the act were meant to take effect, reform-minded miners would take action to bridge the promises of the act and the day-to-day reality of their lives, continuing the process of renegotiating the coal-fired social contract. Was a wagon safe to place in service? Had the roof been properly supported? Did foremen insist on safety protocol, or did they cut corners? Had mine inspectors visited as required, and were they receptive to miners' safety concerns? From these workplace safety questions, which appeared technical or managerial, miners revealed how larger political questions about democratic administration in a coal-fired democracy had not been resolved by the Federal Coal Mine Health and Safety Act. Instead, these questions had only become more pointed, as the country's laws came into conflict with the energy system they were meant to govern. The democratic deficits of the coal-fired social contract came into full view.

The questions that miners raised in their efforts to enforce the Federal Coal Mine Health and Safety Act about the place, limits, and purpose of regulation in a democratic society were salient to a much wider group of Americans. Indeed, in the wake the Federal Coal Mine Health and Safety Act's passage, a decade of regulatory changed dubbed the "new social regulation" opened a new chapter in American administrative statecraft, and a new generation of public interest lawyers spoke out vociferously against the limits and failures of the regulatory frameworks and institutions constructed over four decades of New Deal liberalism.[11] Not least among them were Jock Yablonski's sons, Chip and Ken, two young labor lawyers who, along with their colleague Clarice Feldman, argued tenaciously in the courts that miners' safety activism was legitimate and protected by American law.

Chip and Ken Yablonski's ties to the coalfields and coal miners, and their motivation for involvement in a series of long and drawn-out cases, were clear. They had grown up in Clarksville, in western Pennsylvania, the sons of a miner-turned–union official, the grandsons of a Polish immigrant who had been killed in the mines. But they were also part of a group of public interest lawyers who supported the reform movement in this period. The growth of the public interest law movement formed one path that brought nonminers into the safety and reform movement.[12] Others arrived as part of a generation of young people, mostly college educated, who joined Great Society programs in Appalachia during the 1960s.[13] Tom Bethell was one of them: the son of a Massachusetts architect who left an editorial job at Houghton Mifflin in Boston to join the Appalachian Volunteers, eventually settling in Letcher County, Kentucky.[14] The organizing networks created by groups like the Appalachian Volunteers proved more durable than the programs themselves. Anticommunism and the Vietnam War drove a split in the group. Many Volunteers, including Bethell, resigned after a fellow Volunteer was fired for refusing induction into the army. The AV's opponents used the opening to cut the group's funding from the Office of Economic Opportunity.[15] In the long run, however, Bethell left his mark not through his work with the Appalachian Volunteers but instead by supporting miners' renewed efforts to claim their rights and democratize the coalfields. He turned his considerable research and writing skills toward the coal companies and the administrative state. Within a few years, he would direct the UMW's research office.

While reform-minded miners did have a growing number of allies, the pace of change was slow and the pace of legal challenges even slower. Miners measured that regulatory recalcitrance and judicial meandering in lives lost and bodies maimed. In the months following the passage of the 1969 act, the renegotiation of the coal-fired social contract stalled, and miners found themselves at a crossroads between the past and future of their work and the country's energy system. For miners, the politics of regulatory change was a matter of life and death, so they took it into their own hands: "Walk out—before they carry you out."[16]

Late at night on June 21, 1970, miners gathered at the entrances to dozens of mines in the ring counties around Pittsburgh. Many had copies of a list of mines classified as "especially hazardous" under the new safety law, compiled by the Bureau of Mines earlier that year. To receive the "especially hazardous" designation, a mine had to meet one of three criteria. The bureau classified as especially hazardous mines that emitted 100,000 cubic feet or more of methane daily—though some on the list, like the Maple Creek Mine, emitted around 1,750,000 cubic feet per day and put miners in an order of magnitude more danger. Others received the designation if they had recorded any kind of fatal or seriously disabling gas ignition or explosion in the past five years or if they had some other kind of "especially hazardous condition" present in the mine. All the picketed mines were on that list.[17] Ten thousand miners refused to work, idling almost every coal mine in western Pennsylvania, as well as some mines in northern West Virginia and Ohio.[18] The miners at Bethlehem's Ellsworth mine, where the roof fall had killed Joseph Stanish less than three months earlier, were among those who walked out.[19]

The miners had not taken such action lightly. A month before, members of the Miners for Democracy had gathered in nearby St. Clairsville, Ohio. The miners' concern grew as district after district reported that required federal inspections simply were not happening and that companies refused to comply with new safety standards. While miners reported numerous kinds of safety violations in the meeting, they were most concerned about the bureau's failure to inspect gassy mines. Each of these mines was another Consol No. 9 waiting to happen. The MFD resolved to act and to escalate their tactics as needed. They sent a telegram to President Nixon, which went unanswered. Then they sent a delegation to Washington to meet with Bureau of Mines officials and miners' congressional allies, but still, the required inspections did not occur.[20]

In early June, MFD members from western Pennsylvania gathered to discuss the situation. Those present included MFD chair Mike Trbovich, who worked at Jones & Laughlin's Gateway mine, and Lou Antal, local president at the Harmar mine, where a miner had been killed in April. They conceded their earlier efforts had amounted to nothing.[21] Believing they "had exhausted all administrative and legislative channels to get this Act enforced," they resolved to escalate their tactics.[22] The MFD would take the protests to the mines themselves.

As soon as the courthouse opened on June 22, the morning after the pickets appeared, lawyers for U.S. Steel, Bethlehem, Republic, and Jones & Laughlin—the major steel companies whose captive mines remained idle—filed for injunctions to force the miners back to work.[23] They had good reason to believe their filings would meet success. Only three weeks earlier, the Supreme Court had issued a consequential ruling, known as *Boys Market*, which limited the ability of workers to strike while under a collective bargaining agreement with a grievance procedure—even if, like the UMW's contract, the agreement did not contain a "no strike" clause.[24]

Federal District Judge Wallace Gourley called the case before the bench the next day, as many mines remained idle. Gourley had deep ties to the area. Born in Wellsville, Ohio—just five miles or so from the Pennsylvania border—where Gourley's father worked for a time rolling steel, Gourley went to law school and moved back to Washington County in 1929, where he started in private practice. During the New Deal he took a position in the county district attorney's office and ultimately, with the benefit of labor endorsements, won a seat in the Pennsylvania State Senate during World War II. Harry Truman nominated a forty-one-year-old Gourley to the federal bench in 1945.[25] Gourley called upon these long-standing connections, and particularly his long acquaintance with Jock Yablonski, to try to ease the way of the companies' complaints through his courtroom and to get the miners back to work while attempting to paint himself as a friend of labor: "Jock Yablonski wouldn't want things done this way. He was one of my oldest friends. I knew him from a kid. His son knows that too."[26] But as it turned out, Jock's son was there in the courtroom, and he very much disagreed.

Chip Yablonski had been called to court by some of the miners who had been served subpoenas, and he was the only lawyer in the room who understood the nature of the dispute. The company lawyers had been too busy tracking down the picketers and serving subpoenas. The UMW lawyers were primarily interested in protecting the union from fines and other legal action, and indeed, they saw the involved locals as dangerous dissidents who threatened Boyle's strained hold on power.[27] As the company and union lawyers went back and forth, insisting they could not answer what the walkouts were about, Yablonski finally asked to speak—and Gourley let him, but not before insisting once more that "if your father were here, he would tell them all to go back to work." Though less than six months had passed since his father's murder, Yablonski didn't respond to Gourley's jab. Instead, he tried to redirect the court's attention: this wasn't a dispute between coal miners and coal operators—so *Boys Market* didn't apply. It was a dispute "between coal miners and the United States government."[28] The intent of these walkouts was political. Miners aimed to safeguard their lives by forcing the federal government to meet their obligations to the nation's coal miners under the new act.

By late June, however, the act was not so new anymore. The Bureau of Mines had been dragging its feet on implementation since winter. March 2, 1970, the deadline to promulgate new regulations, came and went. The Bureau of Mines took no public action until Ken Hechler, two fellow members of Congress, and Johnny Mendez, a miner and reform activist from southern West Virginia, filed suit against the Department of the

Interior in the Washington, DC, District Court. A week after they filed the lawsuit, Interior Secretary Walter Hickel published a list of fixed penalties for safety violations, which in attempting to quiet complaints in fact violated the act's requirement that penalties consider a variety of contextual factors, like the mine's record of previous violations. Then, on April 1, one month late, Hickel finally published the new coal mine regulations.[29] As Hickel dragged his feet, Nixon ousted Bureau of Mines Director John F. O'Leary in March—a move that the *New York Times* strongly implied came at the request of the coal operators. Nixon would not replace O'Leary until nearly the end of October, when Elburt Osborn, a geochemist and administrator at Penn State University, stepped into the role. Nixon had squandered almost nine months looking for a "qualified Republican" to head the unit, during which the bureau fumbled on enforcement of the new safety law.[30]

Despite coal mine safety being the largest problem facing the bureau at the time of his appointment, Osborn had no experience in coal mining. His work had focused on metallurgy, ceramics, and blast furnace technology—including work with Bethlehem Steel while he was on the faculty at Penn State.[31] According to Tom Bethell, the Bureau of Mines was underfunded, understaffed, and "brutally sabotaged by the policies of the Department of the Interior," and the state bureaus performed so poorly that "state [mine] inspections may be of no practical use to either operators or miners."[32] The line of culpability, Bethell argued, went to the highest officials in the land, including the president, although Bethell felt that President Nixon was "presumably . . . beyond prosecution"—a prescient legal question that would be put to the test amid the Watergate scandal in coming years.[33] Chip Yablonski insisted that with the Bureau of Mines "in shambles," the companies violated the act "with impunity and without penalty."[34]

Back in the U.S. District Court for the Western District of Pennsylvania, James Mullen, a member of the Local 1248 safety committee at U.S. Steel's Maple Creek Mine, was sworn in to explain why he was on strike. It was a long story. For almost a year, a live high-voltage cable had been sitting in water, giving a dangerous "kick" to anyone who got too close. Water had gathered in the mine's escapeways, too. Motors ran without brakes, and the repair shop had fallen behind on repairing carts—known as "shop wagons"—used to haul coal around the mine. According to Mullen, no fewer than 325 shop wagons that should have been out for repair were in use in the mine.[35]

On April 30, a month after the act's interim safety standards were supposed to have come into effect, one of those shop wagons malfunctioned. The side door opened mid-trip, caught on a switch, and whipped around, derailing the cars behind it and striking Mike Gaydos in the temple, killing him.[36] Even after Gaydos' death, the shop cars remained in service. They were being "smash[ed] up" faster than the shop could fix them. In the week before the June 22 walkout, there had been eight wrecks in the mine. But U.S. Steel went to great lengths to keep the mine in production. Maple Creek produced the highest-quality high-volatile coal of all the mines U.S. Steel owned, and that high-volatile coal was an essential ingredient in steel production. The coal from Maple Creek fed the biggest coking ovens in the world, the Clairton Works ten miles downstream on the Monongahela River.[37]

The Maple Creek mine was dangerous, and the miners were afraid for their lives.[38] So when Gourley pressed Mullen to explain what he was striking about, Mullen replied simply: "This health and safety act.... The inspector is not enforcing it."[39] Gourley responded with condescension: "You have a collective bargaining agreement, my friend.... There is nothing I can do." He wanted to send the matter to arbitration and out of his courtroom. When pressed by the miners and Yablonski, Gourley suggested "a march on Washington."[40] Mullen was livid. "Every time we take it step by step it goes against us. We never win.... Do you mean the men has got to work under them conditions? ... I don't think it's justice. I don't think it's justice at all."[41] With the law meant to protect them going unenforced, miners felt they had no other recourse than to withhold their labor. It took two and a half hours of testimony and argument, with Chip Yablonski challenging Gourley's logic at every turn, but eventually Judge Gourley acceded that his initial decision to grant the injunctions might have been too hasty. He simply didn't know the new law well enough. As Gourley saw it, the basic legal question of the whole dispute was whether the 1969 act had the power to overrule the miners' 1968 collective bargaining agreement. He vacated the orders and told everyone to come back the next morning once he'd had a chance to read the law more closely.[42]

Feeling emboldened, Chip Yablonski went home to refine his argument for the next day, to turn the day's chaos into an orderly case that would present the miners' action as a legitimate form of recourse when the federal government failed to protect them. He was up most of the night. As he scoured case law and statutes, he stumbled across something surprising in an even more surprising place: Section 502 of the Labor Management Relations Act of 1947, widely referred to as Taft-Hartley.[43] Taft-Hartley was better known for restricting union activity and setting harsh limits on unions' power, but in §502, Yablonski saw a provision the MFD might make use of. Section 502, the second to last in the provisions of the law, outlined four instances in which Taft-Hartley would not apply to U.S. labor relations. Three regarded forced labor, clearly inserted to protect the law from challenges under the Thirteenth Amendment.[44] But it was the fourth that drew Yablonski's attention: "nor shall the quitting of labor by an employee or employees in good faith because of abnormally dangerous conditions . . . be deemed a strike under this Act."[45]

Although more than two decades had passed since Taft-Hartley became law, this fourth provision was little tested. The National Labor Relations Board applied §502 for the first time in 1956 and by the early 1960s had circumscribed its application, replacing the "good faith" standard with a requirement that dangerous conditions had to in fact objectively exist.[46] That significantly increased the difficulty for workers to defend their lives with walkouts protected under the provision, but Yablonski realized that the miners had a distinct advantage over most other workers: the Federal Coal Mine Health and Safety Act, which had written into the nation's statutes exactly what constituted an abnormally unsafe mine. Yablonski believed the Bureau of Mines' list of especially hazardous mines, on which all the struck mines appeared, were by definition "abnormally unsafe" when the bureau had failed to inspect them as required.[47]

Gourley, however, had already made up his mind to reissue the injunctions by the time court resumed the morning of June 24. Yablonski tried to make his case, but Gourley kept cutting him off. From Gourley's perspective, the act did provide remedies for unsafe conditions, but they had to be pursued by the Bureau of Mines and not in his courtroom. Moreover, he contended that an act signed in 1969 could not change the substance of a collective bargaining agreement that had been signed in 1968. By this reasoning, the collective bargaining agreement and the safety laws operated in separate realms, and mine safety committees would need to pursue both forms of relief, under law and contract, separately and simultaneously.[48] When Chip Yablonski suggested miners might die because of the injunctions, the judge responded with derision: "Every day in our lives when one of us gets up we are subjecting ourselves to death. . . . So I think your statement that if the Court would grant an injunction it would be sending the men to their death, you are saying what only our God can say. You have your remedy under the law, and you shall follow it."[49]

In the coming days, the Third Circuit Court of Appeals rejected Gourley's reasoning as underdeveloped and hasty, an oversimplified interpretation of a complex system of labor law.[50] Gourley's written opinion and statements from the bench, however, suggested another motivation for his quick decision making: the country needed the coal. "I cannot hazard the possibility that our national economy is going to fall apart and our national defense will be affected.... I am not going to allow our national economy to hit the wall any harder than it has been hit, or affect one man's life for a second that is serving in the armed forces and protecting this democracy."[51] He made this argument even as his draft opinion, which he read aloud in court, acknowledged that the miners had refused to work because they believed their own lives were in danger. Chip Yablonski insisted miners had a legitimate right to act in defense of their lives. Gourley told him to take it up with the Court of Appeals. In a moment of exasperation, he made his position clear: threat to the national economy and defense superseded the actual dangers faced by coal miners. "I'm trying to avoid a national catastrophe.... Can't you see what would happen to the United States if all the coal mines were shut?"[52]

His fear that the walkouts would spread and perhaps shut down most of the industry was likely amplified by a second series of walkouts that had sprung up across southern West Virginia. Those were organized by the Disabled Miners and Widows of Southern West Virginia, a new organization led by Robert Payne, a miner who had been disabled after receiving severe burns in a 1967 mine accident. While the walkouts in southern West Virginia began the same week as the ones in western Pennsylvania, their object, at first appearance, differed. Where the MFD had walked out to prevent future casualties, the Disabled Miners and Widows sought a liberalization of the UMW Welfare and Retirement Fund's benefits, to compensate those whose injuries and losses it was too late to prevent.[53] Both, however, were strikes opposing the structural violence of the nation's energy system, both had substantially slowed the flow of coal from some of the country's richest coal seams, and both fell outside the traditional bounds of a labor dispute between employer and employee, the kind of disputes collective bargaining agreements were meant to handle. The 1969 act, meant to ease these tensions, appeared to have exacerbated them. Rather than try to dirty his hands to help make the new mine safety regulations function as intended, Gourley signed the injunctions and ordered the miners back to work.[54]

With the UMW more concerned with shielding the union from liability than with defending miners' right to strike over safety, Chip Yablonski and Clarice Feldman prepared an emergency appeal to the Third Circuit. Without Gourley to interrupt them, Yablonski and Feldman developed a fuller version of their argument based on Taft-Hartley §502. If the court failed to recognize the applicability of §502 in this case, they contended, it left miners in an "unconscionable dilemma: if they obey the orders to return to work, they do so at great risk to their lives and safety; if they refuse to work in unsafe mines pending lengthy arbitration proceedings, they face the risk of [being held in] contempt." Such a dilemma would deprive them of a meaningful right to refuse unsafe work.[55] The Third Circuit, rather than affirming this reasoning, instead poked holes in Gourley's opinion, which they concluded was both procedurally and argumentatively faulty. They reversed the injunctions and ordered a new hearing on the matter.[56]

Chip Yablonski quickly recognized those holes had more substance than was readily apparent. Procedurally, Gourley had deprived the miners of their rights to testify about the safety conditions in the mines in court. The Third Circuit had insisted that miners had this right. Before a judge could decide whether a matter should fall to the contract mechanisms for resolving safety disputes as required by *Boys Market* or should be dealt with under the provenance of the Federal Coal Mine Health and Safety Act, the safety issues themselves had to be evaluated. Yablonski wrote to the members of the appellant locals and, in effect, to the Miners for Democracy: "This decision is more than just a victory. It is not only a defense against future injunctions, but it is also a sword—before a company can get an injunction in such a case again, you will have the right to try their safety record in open court, before the public."[57] It was a consequential victory that opened new possibilities for industrial action in a period where workers' on-the-job organizing was more likely to be legally constrained.

If the Third Circuit's decision was a sword that would allow miners to go on the offensive against unsafe mines and to hold the broader nation to account for failing to keep its promises to coal miners, the necessity of that weapon was underscored by the safety record of Pennsylvania's bituminous coal mines in the following months. The pressure to keep up production was amplified as a combination of walkouts, increased summer utility loads, high steel demand, and the regular annual miner's summer holiday drew down coal stockpiles and the threat of blackouts and brownouts loomed.[58] No Consol-size accident occurred, but the fatalities piled up as they often had, in ones and twos that rarely received media coverage outside the coalfields.

"In Washington," wrote Tom Bethell, the Appalachian Volunteer turned freelance journalist, "there is a tendency to see human beings as statistics, which is one of the troubles of Washington. North Vietnamese are body counts . . . and miners dying in preventable accidents—they are statistics too. The figures are bad, but they are just figures, and the killing goes on."[59] These figures, so often marshaled to present the seeming inevitability of miners' deaths, concealed the humanity of the people behind them: Henry Chileski, crushed to death when the belt of a loading machine pulled him into its works; George E. Moore, killed by a roof fall in Republic Steel's Newfeld mine on July 24; Thomas Kmetz, fatally electrocuted in Republic's Banning No. 4 on August 10; Nick Kalanavich, crushed beneath a coal car at a Rochester & Pittsburgh loading facility on the same day; Thomas E. Josephson and Robert McFall, killed in separate roof falls on the same day in September; Lavern Link, only twenty-five, who died after his head got caught in a machine on October 20, fracturing his skull, snapping his neck, and crushing his chest; Russell Cogley, who fell to his death at the Blacksburg Tipple on November 9; Duane Hutchinson, killed by a roof fall on November 20, the two-year anniversary of the Consol No. 9 disaster; Philip Orsini, Daniel Campbell, and Joseph Gedraitis, who died together in a massive roof fall at Republic's Russelton mine on December 1; Richard Childs, killed by a roof fall at Republic's Clyde mine only two days later; George Schokora, who died in a machine accident on December 12. When Thomas Sholtis, injured in an October roof fall, eventually succumbed to his injuries in March 1971, he was the thirtieth bituminous miner in western Pennsylvania and the 260th coal miner in the United States killed in workplace "accidents" in 1970, as the number of federal mine inspections fell far short of targets.[60] Concluded the *Black Lung Bulletin*: "It's murder."[61]

Bethell contended the same numbers that concealed the banal horror of death in the mines obscured a deeper story about the relationship between these deaths and the nation's energy choices. He continued: "Miners die because mines are unsafe, and mines are allowed to remain unsafe because we need the coal; we need it in record tonnages . . . so miners die. And because they die in ones and twos, no one seems to mind too much. But once in a while, they die in wholesale lots."[62] The next "once in a while" came on December 30, 1970, two years after the Consol No. 9 disaster and a year to the day after President Nixon had signed the Federal Coal Mine Health and Safety Act into law.

Around midday on December 30, A. T. Collins made his way out of the Finley Coal Company's No. 15 mine to eat lunch and retrieve some supplies. Although the sky was gray that day in Hyden, Kentucky, the air cold and windy, it must have felt good to get some time outside of the No. 15, where the small crew worked a cramped and dusty thirty-inch coal seam.[63] But eventually, Collins had to make his way back in. The roaring began as he approached the mouth of the mine. Well, it wasn't exactly a roar. But Collins found it difficult to describe when he tried to recall it later. It was unlike any sound he had ever heard. "Maybe what a tornado would sound like," he supposed.[64]

Perhaps the sound was also difficult to recall because of what followed: "a great blast of hot air and smoke and flying coal and coal dust and scraps of wood" flew out from the depths of the mine, "and the steel rollers from the conveyer belt tore loose with the rest of the debris and came flying out too." The explosion flung Collins back "fifty or sixty feet."[65] Charles Finley, the mine's owner, was eating lunch too, sitting safely in his office. He recalled hearing "something like a windstorm." He looked out the window of the office trailer to see the same smoke, coal, wood, and steel that A. T. Collins described blasting out every entrance to the mine.[66] And when James Collins, a second-shift miner, arrived at the mine that afternoon, he discovered that not only was he now out of another job—only three months after being laid off from the Frigidaire plant in Dayton, Ohio, because of the recession—but that he had suffered a far more devastating kind of loss. His brother Lonnie, working first shift, had perished deep inside the earth.[67]

It took rescuers hours to recover the first bodies. Working late into the evening, they proceeded slowly, "grop[ing] through the blackened interior of a mountain."[68] Because they did not have equipment to deal with the incredibly high concentrations of carbon monoxide they encountered on entering the mine tunnels, extra ventilation had to be installed first. Then they had to make their way through the cramped tunnels, often barely high enough to crouch in, in some places blocked by debris. Rescuers loaded the bodies onto trailers, usually used to haul coal, to bring

Figure 6.1 Rescuers recover the bodies of killed miners in Hyden, Kentucky.
Source: Photo by Jeanne Rasmussen, JRP 4/6.

them back to the surface.[69] Once recovered, each body was subjected to a brief, "superficial" postmortem exam by Dr. William R. Beasley of the Frontier Nursing Service before being loaded into a trailer and being transported to Hyden Elementary School, where a temporary morgue had been established. The bodies were laid out on the floor of the gymnasium.[70]

Beasley determined that of the thirty-eight men who had died, the overwhelming majority had been killed instantly by the initial blast, which would have ripped "through the narrow coal seam like bullets through a gun barrel."[71] Many of the victims' bodies were covered in burns that testified to the intensity of the flames and heat.[72] Dr. Beasley was "quite sure" that at least five men had survived the explosion only to succumb to carbon monoxide; the proof, he pointed out, was the distinctive redness of their skin—the telltale sign of carbon monoxide poisoning. Because of the intensity of the carbon monoxide, they had survived "minutes at most." The one remaining body proved a gruesome mystery: "when Dr. Beasley pressed on his chest, water came out his mouth and nose." Dr. Beasley hypothesized a terrifying account of the man's last moments to explain how he had drowned in a mine filled with fire and carbon monoxide: perhaps "he had been able to find water to take refuge in from the heat, but then, trying to breathe, had taken in only carbon monoxide and had fallen back, still trying to breathe, and his lungs filled with water."[73] But Dr. Beasley couldn't be sure. The body was loaded and taken away with all the other corpses as a group of newly widowed wives looked on. As the bodies were driven away, the mine's owner, Charles Finley, who "seemed not to be especially upset," could be heard complaining to gathered press. Finley apparently believed be had "plenty of insurance," that the financial burden of the disaster would fall on the state, and that ultimately he would not be held responsible for what had happened in his mine. He instead took the opportunity to complain about the burdens of the 1969 act to reporters.[74] County Judge George Wooten, who had been at the Finley mine all evening, also heard the comments. Enraged, he beat Finley so badly he had to be carried away from the mine site.[75]

In the coming days, heavy snowfall blanketed the hillsides as volunteers struggled to dig into the frozen ground, and the community struggled to cope with the loss—especially the thirty-three women who had suddenly been widowed, the ninety-seven children who depended on them, and the other kinds of relations and dependencies that both private and state compensation were quick to overlook.[76] Carl Mitchell, a mine mechanic who happened to be above ground and well away from the mine entrance at the time of the blast, wept as he conceded to a reporter that although he'd known many of the men who were killed for more than a decade, he would be unable to attend all the funerals. There were just too many of them. Mitchell vowed he would "never go into another mine again."[77] George Wooten promised that the county "would dig the graves and save the widows that expense," but many families nonetheless ended up in debt from funeral expenses. They received at most $725 for funerals that cost as much as $2,000. The Kentucky Workmen's Compensation Fund expedited payments but also had widows who desperately needed the money sign away rights to increased compensation if investigators declared that operator negligence caused the disaster. "Without the aid or assistance of a lawyer," the women likely did not know the rights they had signed away.[78] Moreover, the Bureau of Mines neglected to inform the widows of their right to have a full autopsy performed on their husbands' bodies, which they would need to qualify for federal black lung payments. A congressional investigation later discovered that no additional autopsies had ever been performed, excluding the families from possible black lung compensation of up to $306.10 per month.[79]

Everyone familiar with the No. 15 mine knew it was dangerous. In the six months before the explosion, it received forty-three cited violations (more than double the national average of nineteen), measured respirable dust levels more than ten times the legal limit set by the 1969 act, and had three serious accidents.[80] On August 12, a drill frame cut into a high-voltage cable, igniting an electrical fire. Rufus Whitehead and Mack Collins quickly cut off the electrical power and doused the fire with limestone. But unbeknownst to them, the fire had spread into the hydraulics and inner tube of the drill. When it suddenly exploded, it sent pieces of rock and metal through the air like shrapnel, permanently blinding Whitehead—who received the worst of the hit from the debris—and bursting one of Collins's eardrums. The next accident was fatal. Three months later, twenty-four-year-old Charlie Wagers requested maintenance help to repair his tractor, which was stuck in reverse. The mechanic tried twice to fix the contacts, which sometimes sent the vehicle into reverse when Wagers tried to drive it forward. Instead of management taking the defective tractor out of service, Wagers was left to continue his work.[81] As he maneuvered around a corner, the tractor malfunctioned again and "lurched backward," crushing Wagers's skull against a rib of coal.[82] On December 15, just two weeks before the mass casualty explosion that drew national attention, Sammy Henson received an electrical burn on the hip from a short-circuit on a loading machine serious enough to require him to go on disability. The Finleys did not report Sammy Henson's accident to the Bureau of Mines until the nation's attention intensified scrutiny of their safety practices—or, more aptly, malpractices.[83] Congressional investigators concluded: "It was generally known that the lives of the men were in danger."[84]

Repeated accidents caused by poorly maintained equipment spoke to the Finleys' disregard for the lives of the miners they employed, but further digging into the Finleys' relationship with the Bureau of Mines revealed a wider web of complicity. Regulatory failures stood as standard operating procedures, and inspectors seemed more concerned with maintaining coal production than protecting miners' lives. Perhaps nothing illustrated that better than the aftermath of the horrific accident that killed Charlie Wagers on November 9. The next day, November 10, an investigator from the Bureau of Mines visited the Finley No. 15. But for some reason, the bureau did not issue an imminent danger order to withdraw the dangerous tractor from service until November 13, three days later, a Friday. The mine did not operate over the weekend, and the equipment was allowed back in service on Monday. Bitterly, the committee observed that "no coal production was lost," but it took four months for the Bureau of Mines to fine the Finleys for the dangerous conditions that killed Wagers, and in the end, that fine was a measly $10,000.[85] A November 1970 spot inspection found the levels of toxic and volatile dust underground more than eleven times the limit legally permitted, creating a "virtual certainty that each miner exposed for a period to its environment would have contracted some development of . . .'black lung' disease."[86]

Whether the danger came from dust or machines, the violation notices suggested that inspectors went to great lengths to allow the mine to remain in operation, offering extensions of the deadline to bring the mine into compliance with safety standards. Inspectors granted six such extensions to the Finleys between the small explosion that disabled Whitehead and Collins and the December 30 explosion.[87] The inspections themselves left much to be desired: often the inspectors did not even go in the mine, or they inspected a small section and only marked those sections of the mine in violation when it would have been reasonable to find similar conditions throughout. The committee concluded that only "a gross and exceedingly negligent dereliction of responsibility" on the part of both the Bureau of Mines and the operator allowed the mine to remain open long enough for the December 30 explosion to occur.[88]

These failures were exacerbated by the Bureau of Mines' mishandling of the initial investigation. Elburt F. Osborn, the new Bureau of Mines chief who had been in his role for only two months, bungled the local hearing in Hyden. He insulted a local lawyer and told the audience, "Don't criticize the Finleys," because "I'll bet many mines have just as bad records as [they do]." And besides, he insisted, it was not the bureau's job "to levy criminal penalties against mine operators."[89]

The Bureau of Mines instead blamed the disaster on two of the men underground that day: shot firer Walter Bentley and foreman Walter Hibbard, both of whom were now dead. The bureau justified this blame because the pair had used Primacord, an explosive fuse illegal in underground mining, to simultaneously blast over one hundred sticks of dynamite in a large twenty-five-by-thirty-foot section of the mine roof, even though the limit on blast holes was set by law at twenty per explosion, and even though blasting while miners were underground was illegal. Investigators asked Finley if he thought using that much dynamite was permissible. Even though the law clearly stated it was illegal, Finley responded, "Depends on conditions."[90] One mine inspector likened Finley's blasting process to a game of Russian roulette. Except in this version, he explained, an additional bullet was added for each exacerbating factor: loose coal dust, dry air, inadequate fire mitigation in the mine, and a drop in atmospheric pressure.[91] Just one of those factors significantly increased the risk of an underground explosion. All of them had been present in the Finley mine on December 30. Why would Bentley and Hibbard have engaged in a process so likely to kill them? As became clear over the months of investigations, the mine's owner, Charles Finley, had pressured his workers to bend the law to meet production goals. The bureau's mishandling threatened to turn a delicate situation into a farce, and national lawmakers, journalists, coalfield activists, and miners alike perceived it as illegitimate.[92]

Bethell, a tenacious researcher and elegant writer, set to work on his own report on the Hyden disaster, one that situated it in the nation's broader energy system. On the one hand, the Finleys, with their "nineteenth century attitude," made for well-cast villains in an old story of operators versus coal miners. Their callous disregard for miners' safety in pursuit of production, Bethell concluded, was in large part responsible for the thirty-eight deaths on December 30, as well as the earlier death of twenty-four-year-old Charlie Wagers, and for the disabling injuries suffered by Whitehead, Collins, and Henson. But Bethell also insisted this old story had a new context: the role the liberal regulatory state was meant to play in balancing miners' rights against the nation's dependency on coal for electric power and other consumer goods made from steel.[93] The failure of federal and state agencies to effectively intervene under the auspices of the act before the disaster had occurred cemented Hyden's place in a growing crisis of governance by undermining the legitimacy of the coal-fired social contract. Bethell concluded: "The system under which coal is mined in this country is beyond justification and must be radically altered."[94] Bethell sent his report to the Bureau of Mines on January 26, 1970, less than a month after the disaster had occurred, before the agency had issued their own report and three months before the congressional investigation, which ultimately adopted much of Bethell's language into the final committee report.

The Hyden disaster, Bethell argued, couldn't accurately be summarized as *only* a violation—even a *series* of violations—of the 1969 act. Instead, he charged, the "miners were victims of institutional manslaughter," and the culpability extended far beyond the Finleys. Institutional manslaughter, in Bethell's mind, encompassed both "a company which operated in persistent violation of the . . . Act of 1969, but also . . . a complacent, negligent bureaucracy which extends to the highest offices of the federal government and refuses to serve in the public interest."[95] The idea that workplace death constituted a violation of the "public interest" was not only asserted by Bethell's report but reappeared across discussions of the disaster, from the county judge promising that the cost of the graves would be paid for by the public to the congressional hearings that took place in July 1971.

This contested notion of public interest was really a way of querying the proper relationship between the nation and its coalfields, between coal miners and energy consumers. Public interest, in the aftermath of Hyden, worked in two ways. First, it portrayed the right to a safe working environment as the fundamental right of the American coal miner and therefore a matter that should be protected by legal protections as well as labor contracts. Second, it suggested coal was a particular kind of commodity in which the public had special interest because of its role in electricity production, a reformulation of longstanding claims that located the special national interest in coal in its central role in the nation's energy system earlier in the century. Politicians tasked with investigating the disaster relied heavily on this second meaning, while miners and their advocates were more likely to rely on the first.

In fact, these dual forms of public interest were co-constituted. Most disparagers of mine safety regulation pointed to the purported "potential for crippling an essential industry" and the threat "of widespread . . . blackouts due to a coal supply rendered insufficient by extensive mine closings [for safety reasons]."[96] Supporters of additional regulation pointed to the intimate connection between coal and national strength as a primary motivator. Concluded the congressional committee that investigated the Hyden disaster: "A strong law is necessary to protect the men who extract one of our nation's most vital resources."[97] Once again, what miners saw as their most basic and fundamental rights were tied to the coal they produced. "A coal minner is like a sold[i]er," wrote the disabled miner James Gilliam. "The mines is the back bone of the nation." Gilliam developed his analogy to explain why miners were entitled not only to the right to "run for [our] lives," like a soldier overwhelmed at the front by enemy fire, but also "a little help from the government," the same way the government promised to support a soldier who "gets to wher he cannot go any fother." And should the nation doubt coal miners' status, well, there a miner was like a soldier too, just doing "a good job for thir count[r]y. And you just let eather one of thim pull back and quit and see what happen to o[u]r nation."[98] Miners were able to organize inside this public interest dichotomy that saw workplace safety as a set of rights owed to them as workers performing an obligation of citizenship: providing the nation with that fundamental national energy resource, coal.

The Congressional Subcommittee on Labor recognized the potential for an investigation of the Hyden disaster to expand into "oversight hearings into the administration of the Federal Coal Mine Health and Safety Act." At the beginning of the hearings, Chairman Dent took care to clarify their purview would remain narrow, "confined to the Hyden disaster."[99] As the many layers of the administrative state's failure to prevent the disaster became visible, the hearings opened up a seemingly contradictory set of narratives: on the one hand, the inefficacy of "the strongest health and safety regulation ever drafted in the United States," which had been implemented as the nation recognized "the power [of miners] ... to shut off every electric light in the country," and on the other, the simultaneous demand for even *stronger* regulation.[100] The Subcommittee on Labor's most basic conclusion echoed Bethell: "The disaster could have been prevented and—by any reasonable yardstick—danger could have been foreseen."[101] The disaster had demonstrated the limits of the 1969 act, which had both failed to prevent the explosion and to impose what miners saw as meaningful penalties for it. And it did so at a scale that was more visible to the rest of the nation than the slower but seemingly relentless killing ongoing in western Pennsylvania. For every major disaster, however, hundreds of miners were killed in ones and twos. And those deaths did not only occur in relatively small, nonunion outfits run by would-be coal barons but also in large mines integrated into global energy and steel conglomerates.

The safety strikes, by which miners hoped to secure enforcement of the Federal Coal Mine Health and Safety Act, never reached the size of the 1969 black lung strike. But they continued to break out across western Pennsylvania and nearby areas of Ohio and West Virginia despite the operators' attempts to secure injunctions. Their impact combined with a series of other events limiting coal stockpiling in the spring and summer of 1971. Some of those events were predictable, like the miner's annual summer holiday. Others entailed more uncertainty, like the rail strikes that summer that limited the availability of coal cars to transport fuel to generating stations. Still other contributing factors fell somewhere in between, like increasing air quality regulations that subjected the chemical composition of coal deliveries to more scrutiny. In the background lurked a series of interconnected challenges, which stretched across different fuel sectors, that Americans increasingly referred to as the "energy crisis."[102]

Histories of the energy crisis do not usually have much to say about death. But they should. Behind the growing sense of crisis lay miners' insistence that their right to live could not be suspended simply because the country needed the coal. Coal miners insisted they were modern, rights-bearing citizens entitled to the same quality of life as other Americans.

The miners of Local 1248, who worked in U.S. Steel's Maple Creek mine, made their case to the broader nation when ABC filmed an hour-long special program about their fight to make their mine safer. According to the miner Mickey Britvich, the safety walkouts were part of a larger fight for "freedom and democracy." His coworker Josh Descaro explained: "We are not the 1920s coal miner. We are not the man that goes in and drives a mule for his dust or his gas or no matter what. We are men that—We want to live! We don't just want to live to work in a mine. We want to live and have families and have a regular life just like anyone else that isn't a miner. We want to make it safe in the mines so we can consider our job as safe as a man that is a lawyer, or a doctor."[103] But of course, a coal mine was much more dangerous than a law firm. Indeed, it remained by far the most dangerous workplace in the United States, whether injuries were measured by frequency or severity.[104]

Interpreting the miners' words, the program's presenter observed, "The coal face is where nature takes its revenge, where man pays for what he steals from the earth in life and blood."[105] The singular "man" was really a sleight of hand, although the crew was sympathetic to the miners. It conjured a traditional form of literary conflict rather than the energy choices of a democratic society. It suggested that the man who stole and the man who paid were one and the same, rather than a country of more than 205,000,000 people with a wide variety of relationships to coal, the electricity it generated, the steel it helped forge, and the profits it garnered. It cast almost as tragic the man's relationship with the fuel that would kill him. And in any case, by the end of the program, U.S. Steel's vice president of coal operations insisted to viewers that the company's mines were among the safest in the country—a dubious claim, given that Mike

Gaydos had been killed in the mine only a year before and miners had testified to the mine's atrocious conditions in court, by 1971, for at least three years in a row.[106]

The program aired on May 22, 1971, and a week later, federal officials arrived at the Maple Creek mine to conduct the inspections required by the 1969 act. Their presence testified to the MFD's organizing in the area, as well as the local leadership's refusal to be cowed by the companies, the courts, or even their union leadership into accepting noncompliance with the act's most basic protections. But it was not enough to save Dan Gaudiano's life.[107]

Dan Gaudiano, also a member of Local 1248, was an experienced miner. He had worked in U.S. Steel's coal mines since 1940, meaning he had been there when the UMW succeeded in turning the captive mines into union shops the same day that Japan bombed U.S. territories in the Pacific. He struck in 1943. He was able to keep working through coal's big slump in the 1950s, and as demand for coal increased rapidly in the late 1960s, he was still there, cleaning the tracks so the motormen could haul coal out of the mine more safely. On June 1, 1971, while the inspectors were in the mine, a locomotive crushed Dan Gaudiano. The motormen never saw him. Indeed, no one saw what happened, but according to the Bureau of Mines fatal accident report, the mine superintendent and the general foreman "observed evidence of an accident." What this actually meant was that as they drove along the mine tunnel, they found Gaudiano's head, then his right foot, then his torso, and finally his left leg scattered along the tracks. The investigators theorized he must have been "lying in the middle of the roadway," though they could not answer why an experienced miner would have been lying on the tracks. It might have been a medical emergency, like a heart attack or some complication of undiagnosed black lung, but no autopsy was performed, even though enough of Gaudiano's body had been recovered to make such an examination possible.[108]

After discovering Gaudiano's dismembered body, management sent most of the shift home immediately. But three members of the Local 1248 safety committee—including James Mullen—stayed behind to help conduct the mandated fatal accident investigation.[109] Ruth Gaudiano, Dan's wife, now a widow, drew comfort from her friends and neighbors and their surviving family, friends, and community.[110] Dan's brother, Art, would soon be back at work in the mine where his brother had been torn apart.[111] Dan Gaudiano had not only lived to work in the mines. He was a valued member of his local community as well as an integral part of the nation's energy system: a union member, a parishioner at the Leisenring Presbyterian Church, and part of the local volunteer fire department.[112] In the same way that the story of Joseph Stanish's death had not begun when he entered the mine for work the day he was killed, the story of Dan Gaudiano's death did not end when his family laid him to rest. It lingered in the holes his death tore in his family and community.

Gaudiano's death certainly cast a new light on U.S. Steel's claims about the relative safety of their mines when, later that June, the company was back in the Federal District Court for Western Pennsylvania. There had been another safety walkout at the Maple Creek mine, this time after miners had discovered that one of the mine foremen, Paul Smorada, had falsified inspection logs, putting everyone's lives at risk. It fit a pattern of dangerous behavior by Smorada over the preceding months: interfering with the dispatcher's control of mine traffic, insisting a miner work with a faulty machine, and getting into a physical altercation with a worker who challenged him.[113] U.S. Steel's lawyer insisted he wanted "to place on the record . . . the fact that the U.S. Steel Corporation . . . has been considered by others, to be one of the safest operations of any mine. This corporation goes to all lengths to have safe mines."[114]

The miners called to the stand regarded these repeated remarks about how safe the mine was with disgust. They contended that U.S. Steel went to great lengths to keep numbers falsely low, treating miners on site for serious injuries and dissuading them from receiving workers' compensation, meaning that severe accidents were never logged as lost-time incidents.[115] Moreover, a safety record meant nothing if the practices that made it possible fell by the wayside, if methane was allowed to accumulate in the mines to five times the normal level with miners underground, or if negligent foremen were transferred to mine faces that had already had two recent gas ignitions. It only took one explosion to blow up a mine, the workers in it, and the company's safety record along with them.[116] Besides, as James Mullen, a member of the safety committee, testified, if the mine was so safe, Dan Gaudiano would still be alive. If management had assigned Gaudiano a partner, like they were supposed to, he would not have been alone when he fell on the tracks earlier that month. "If he . . . had a heart attack, the buddy could have drug him [off the track]. If he fell down and got hurt, he could drag him [off] the track." If management had really cared about safety, Mullen insisted, "Would you go down and pick him up piece by piece like we did?"[117]

To the extent the mine's safety record had improved, Local 1248 President Nick DeVince said, it was the miners and their safety committee who had made it safer and who had forced the Bureau of Mines to begin applying the 1969 act.[118] The ABC special on the Maple Creek mine had gotten this much right: a corner had been turned in the miners' struggle to survive their workday. "A new day is dawning for America's coal miners," the presenter concluded.[119] When that "new day" finally arrived, it would be thanks to miners like the members of Local 1248, who resisted pressure from both the companies and the courts to "put that pound of coal ahead of safety."[120] As miners sought to hold the federal government accountable for the promises made in the 1969 act, however, they would also increasingly be confronted with the broader changes in the U.S. energy system and the reality that their union had become an obstacle to coal-fired democracy rather than an instrument used to achieve it. And they also had to contend with the fact that the dangers of coal increasingly were felt above ground, with surface mining quickly turning much of central Appalachia into a sacrifice zone.

CHAPTER VII

If Letcher County Was a Pie ...

The rebellion of 1969 made clear to the broader country that the coal mine was a place defined by violence. But while national attention was focused on the way that violence entombed men underground and entered their lungs, coalfield residents contended with another way they were being consumed by the nation's energy appetite: the growth of surface mining, often referred to as strip mining, which in the postwar decades had devastated the Appalachian environment.

Ruby Caudill knew firsthand how these forms of energy violence fit together. Her home in Letcher County, Kentucky, stood at the base of a mountain in the process of being strip-mined. At least three times—first in October 1970, again that December, and then in July 1971—rock and mud slides threatened her family and home. The most recent had buried her fruit trees, cattle pasture, and barn, but she insisted the second slide, in December 1971, had been the most frightening. "I could just hear the big rocks go boom. I thought the mountain was collapsing." She and her husband, Bert, an underground coal miner, sold their cattle at a loss. They tried to sell their land, but because of the slides, its value had plummeted more than 75 percent. The insurance company refused to pay out for any of the damage, insisting to Ruby that the predictable outcome of surface mining was in fact "an act of God." With the mountain "slipping down on top of us," Ruby knew the couple had to move, but with the land devalued, the property had become a prison.[1]

As the mountain loomed ominously above, coal dust stole the breath of Ruby's family members. Her brother, Willie Milton, died in December 1970—right around the time of the second slide—after eleven years disabled with black lung. By the time he died, "only half his right lung was left."[2] To add insult to injury, he spent the last year of his life fighting to get the black lung benefits the Federal Coal Mine Health and Safety Act entitled him to. Black lung benefits applicants from eastern Kentucky waited longer for the Social Security Administration to process their claims than applicants in most other regions of the country. When black lung finally claimed Willie, he was one of more than 18,000 Kentucky claimants awaiting decision in their case.[3] His widow did eventually get the benefits he was owed, and much of the lump sum, according to Ruby, went to paying off the debts that Willie had incurred in death: outstanding hospital bills, funeral home expenses, a tombstone to ensure he would not be forgotten.[4] Ruby probably saw her own future in her sister-in-law's predicament. Her husband also had black lung, bad enough that it started showing up on X-rays two years earlier, bad enough that he woke up at night coughing and unable to breathe. Bert's black lung benefits hadn't shown up yet, either. Since they needed the money, he kept working in the underground mines, which was likely to make his black lung worse and thus kill him sooner.

Bert interpreted the situation as a violation of his property rights: "A man doesn't have any say so over his property."[5] His comment seemed to carry the weight of his family's decades entangled with coal. Bert was born in eastern Kentucky in 1919. A census-taker who came the next year listed his father, Henry H. Caudill, as a farmer in the 1920 census. But by the time an enumerator returned in 1930, Henry was working in the mines along with a few of his neighbors.[6] Henry Caudill would appear in the census just one more time in 1940, this time listing his specific occupation in the coal mines—a trackman. But soon he became part of another statistic: one of the 1,266 miners killed on the job in 1941, when a slate fall crushed him to death.[7] It's impossible to discern with certainty a causal relationship between these few data points created over two decades, but it is suggestive of the enclosures described by the historians Steven Stoll and Chad Montrie that consolidated landholdings and increased rates of absentee ownership in the region. In the process, Appalachian farmers were pushed into the coal mines.[8] The rock and mud cascading down the mountain as strip mining fractured it apart fit into a longer history of displacement that might have been written into the very land deed that made Bert and Ruby homeowners or to which they were pressured to agree in an effort to avoid economic hardship. Still, Bert maintained, "They can get that coal without tearing up the whole mountain."[9] But the company that owned the mineral rights could extract the coal any way it chose. Miners' land, like their lives, appeared to matter less than the profits and electricity that coal could generate.

From Ruby and Bert Caudill's experience, we can trace the contours of a much larger transformation. On the Appalachian landscape, the inequalities of the coal-fired social contract had produced what Jock Yablonski's campaign had once aptly described as "environmental mayhem."[10] Certainly, coal mining and combustion had caused visible environmental damage since it was first popularized for industrial use in the eighteenth and nineteenth centuries. The same coal that turned Pittsburgh into a great spectacle of coal-fired industrialism had also made it possible to describe, as the *Atlantic Monthly* did in the years after the Civil War, as "hell with the lid taken off."[11] Visitors to the coalfield state encountered coal camps, which had to be smelled to be believed and where black dust collected everywhere.[12] Surface mining wasn't a new practice, either. But in the decades after World War II, new surface mining techniques allowed operators to expand the practice in parts of Appalachia where rough terrain previously made it impracticable.[13]

The longstanding environmental devastation driven by coal mining accelerated. Between 1965 and 1970, strippers mined out an area the size of Delaware, as much land as had been strip mined in all years before 1965 combined.[14] By early 1971, the pace of strip mining was breakneck. Almost 50 percent of active strip mining permits had been issued since May the previous year.[15] For Warren Wright, the director of the community development–focused Council of the Southern Mountains, the growth of strip mining represented just the latest episode of energy resource grabbing by the nation's politicians: "from the lowest to the highest level they were in on the original stealing of the coal fields and have never been anything but handmaidens, prostitutes for the builders of mineral empire." Wright scorned those who insisted "that the mountains must be ruined for the benefit of what they call 'the rest of the nation.' A Letcher County operator told me personally that West Virginia and eastern Kentucky had to be sacrificed, written off."[16]

As black lung and mine accidents marked the underground accrual of coal-fired energy inequality, massive aboveground machines turned mountains into sacrifice zones for cheap electric power. Bulldozers, augers, loaders, shovels, and trucks left impacts that could be seen from miles away and tasted in the water. Towering hundreds of feet in the air and usually requiring only one or two people to operate, the stripper machines stood in as a physical monument to the displacement of underground mining labor in the postwar years and its replacement with destroyed hillsides. Watching a strip crew work made clear how disruptive the process was. A small group of workers, leaving the rest to watch from the hillsides, first cleared brush, trees, and scrub materials from the land. Then, with heavy equipment, they removed the topsoil and rock that blocked access to the coal seam. Finally, the crew set large explosives, fracturing the coal seam into pieces that could be trucked out of the mine. The process destabilized hundreds of millions of years of geological sedimentation.

The eastern Kentucky folk singer Jean Ritchie described what followed: "The hillside explodes with the dynamite's roar . . . and the mountain comes a'sliding so awful and grand."[17] Once the coal was removed, the overburden and topsoil was dumped back in without much ceremony, leaving a "barren moonscape" in its wake.[18] The Kentucky-born writer and activist Wendell Berry compared the aftermath to apocalypse and war: "It is a geologic upheaval. . . . It is a scene from the Book of Revelation. It is a domestic Vietnam."[19] The destroyed mountains transformed regular events, like rainstorms, into menaces. With old root systems and sedimentation destroyed, the hillsides could absorb less water, meaning that rain rushed to the valley floor much quicker than it otherwise would have. The water loosened the soil as it went, releasing chemical waste and dislodging massive stones. It all rushed down the hill in a thick, acidic, muddy sheet, burying anything in its path.[20]

Miners were among the first to experience these environmental consequences. Lee Peterson had worked in the mines of eastern Kentucky for twenty-eight years. He described to the journalist Jerry Demuth how strip mining had wrecked the soil. The practice left the hillsides so vulnerable to erosion that each time it rained mud cascaded down into the valleys and flooded people's homes. Ellis Bailey, a miner disabled with black lung, spoke bitterly of "streams which now bleed the rusty color of mine acids" and stands of trees that were gone forever. "They can't put it back," he lamented. "They can never put it back like it was before."[21] Other

Figure 7.1 Hanna Coal Company, "The Silver Spade," 1967.
Source: UMWPC 170/15.

residents echoed this wide range of environmental concerns: toxic streams, greater numbers of rockslides, good stands of timber destroyed, soil robbed of the nutrients that made it fertile. The blasting could shift the underground water tables people relied on for their wells of drinking water.[22] Demuth typed in his notes: "'When you wound the mountain, you kill the valley,' mountain people say."[23]

In that barren moonscape, many miners came to see yet another violation of their rights as citizens: the right to "clean air, clean water, [and] open spaces" that President Nixon had outlined in his 1970 State of the Union address.[24] Everett Tharp, a disabled miner from eastern Kentucky, placed these rights "to enjoy a decent place to live, to enjoy pure air, pure water" alongside the others that had been at the center of coal miners' struggles for decades: "to preach equality, justice, equal opportunity, and equality of law enforcement." And Tharp insisted that those rights "negate[d] the right of a few individuals to contaminate the processes of nature."[25] Tharp, like many coal miners who opposed strip mining, adopted the framework of environmental rights while also connecting the scars on the land to a wider struggle against what many saw as the persistence of unequal citizenship in a coal-fired nation.

Many miners conceived of the way strip mining violated their rights through the lens of housing and property rights, frameworks legible to a much wider group of Americans. Antistripping activists understood housing and property rights in regionally specific ways shaped by the legacy of the coalfield state. Lee Peterson insisted of strip mining, "I'd rather lose my job tomorrow than see this happen to my land."[26] But in eastern Kentucky, "broad form" land deeds often divided property ownership into surface and mineral rights in ways that made it difficult for ordinary people to prevent the coal operators' wanton destruction. Tom Bethell, the Appalachian Volunteer–turned–freelance journalist, uncovered how this form of deed was rooted in older formations of coalfield power in his adopted home of Letcher County, Kentucky. He went digging into the origin of the broad-form deeds and found that they had originated in the offices of coal company lawyers. Although the "traditional wording of such deeds predates the invention of strip mining by half a century," Bethell concluded, "they convey nothing of any value to the surface owner but give the mineral-rights owner free rein to remove coal any way he chooses."[27] Jean Ritchie's anti–strip mining song "Black Waters" put it even more plainly: "I own my land, but my land's not my own."[28]

When companies could not leverage broad-form deeds to mine the land with impunity, they resorted to other familiar tactics: threats, harassment, and violence.[29] Jimmy Sands recounted how one stripper pressured people to sell by "blasting and throwing heavy rock over on me and damaging my property," including when children were outside, potentially in the path of the debris. After each round of blasting, the operator "[went] around and ask[ed] the neighbors whether they'd like to sell their property or not."[30] This tactic put residents in physical danger, with rocks flying overhead and deafening sounds echoing through the narrow hollows; it also threatened to turn the promise of homeownership into a prison by pushing down the value of the land for any other use, as had happened to Ruby Caudill. When activists engaged in civil disobedience to halt surface mining on Clear Creek, Kentucky, the operators "brought in their gun thugs, they had 18 at one time, and they started shooting at us." It wasn't the first instance of violence. There had already been two confrontations between one area family and a bulldozer operator. After the second incident, the company sent two guards to the property armed with carbine rifles and German shepherds. The guards set the dogs on the landowner, who had to fend them off with a stick as the guards shot over the top of his head.[31] The activists felt they had no choice but to arm themselves and shoot back. The violation of property rights, however, was only one of several ways that strip mining violated the rights of citizenship.

Many miners also insisted that surface mining had stripped them of their right to meaningful rest and recreation and withered their relationships with the land. That was especially true for coal miners, contended John Tiller:

> If there was ever a class of men on the face of the earth that deserved a bit of peace and quiet, a bit of beauty in their hours off from work, it would be your coal miner. Go with me into a modern day mine where I work. And you don't see too good, there's too much dust there. It's an unreal world. . . . You never hear, you never see. And yet those same men who have to go through the stress and strain of this hellish type of job, for 8 long hours—they're forcing him to come out into another hell. . . . He has nowhere to go for recreation. . . . The miner works under great stress and strain. The fear of death is *always* with him. Each shift that he goes into the mine, he never knows whether again he'll get to see daylight. Certainly that man deserves to come back out and see his beautiful mountains untouched.[32]

Tiller argued this violation had effects that slowly rippled out into the larger energy system by causing miners' productivity to decline. Where operators blamed the new regulations of the Federal Coal Mine Health and Safety Act for falling productivity, Tiller insisted the explanation lie elsewhere, in the fact that miners moved from one hell to another without respite.[33] Johnny Grigsby's father relied on the therapeutic hours he spent working in his fields after he'd been disabled following twenty-two years in the mines. And Johnny believed that when the strippers destroyed the nearby mountain and, with it, his father's cornfield, "considering how much he valued that and what it meant to him, because that is what he worked for, it was just like watching a person, just like almost fade away."[34]

Arnold Miller, president of the West Virginia Black Lung Association and a strip mining abolitionist, also foregrounded the right to leisure in his critique. According to Miller, "hunting and fishing" were "the only recreation mountain people have . . . and strip mining wipes it out." Miller's anger pulsed through his words as he insisted, "Don't talk about regulating strip mining to me, just stop it."[35] Hunting and fishing, as recreational activities, also attuned participants to the impact of strip mining on the region's animal inhabitants. Joe Sumpter explained that in forests once rich with deer and bear, a hunter near strip-mined areas would now be "lucky to hit a squirrel."[36] Ed Mallacoat, who opposed strip mining even though he worked in one, lamented the destruction of the area's creek ecosystems. "There used to be good fishing around here," he told Jerry Demuth. "Now there's nothing. The water is poisoned or it's too shallow and the fish burn up. There was one creek where we could dive and not touch bottom. Now it's two feet deep."[37]

Such experiences might appear regional—but these ecological relationships did not exist in isolation. The scarring of the Appalachian Mountains and the polluting of its waters were intimately linked to the nation's coal-fired energy system, to a nation whose appetite for electric power and consumer products made from steel had grown rapidly across the preceding decade and appeared poised to continue that growth. Increased consumption didn't necessarily produce big gains in coalfield employment—thanks to mechanization and strip mining, which had radically reduced the mining workforce—but it *did* exacerbate coal-fired inequality. In particular, the fact that the Tennessee Valley Authority purchased much of eastern Kentucky's strip-mined coal underscored for residents the political nature of strip mining.[38] One protest song adapted the tune of the Black spiritual "Swing Low, Sweet Chariot" to draw attention to strip mining's role in the larger energy system: "They're going to turn our mountain homeland to acid-clay / Coming for to bury my home / To make a cheaper rate for the TVA / Coming for to bury my home."[39]

While homes could be destroyed in massive slides, in most cases "burying" a home was not a quick or simple act. Instead, as Rufus Brooks discovered, the process was drawn-out and painful, much like the black lung that had disabled him. Although Brooks had once been one of the best baseball players in southern West Virginia, after nearly thirty-five years in the mines a short walk left the fifty-two-year-old gasping for air. But even if he still had been able to play, the baseball field near his home was covered with rocks that had plummeted down the hillside in the months since the strip mine opened. His home, one in a row of thirteen, had been inundated with water and mud and rock four times within a month of the mine's opening and three times the month after. These regular deluges left the walls of his home damp to the touch and the furniture covered in mildew. The smell constantly irritated his wife, Jennie. Brooks also had to replace his furnace, damaged in one of the mudslides. The owner of the strip mine promised to pay for it and repair the house, but the cold came first. The new furnace cost Brooks a steep $439, more than double the amount he would have collected each month in black lung benefits. And the mine owner never did pay Brooks like he promised.[40]

Strip mining destroyed both physical houses and Appalachian claims to homeownership, both of which figured centrally in liberal social policy of the period.[41] Strip mining was not only an affront to miners in their lives as workers but also challenged the idea of equal citizenship in a country where the right to decent housing was often tied to one's status as a homeowner.[42] Clifton Bryant, a disabled miner and the chair of the Cabin Creek Area Citizens Union, considered the fact that "strip mining . . . is destroying wild life, & the health, life, and property of most of the people who live in this area" evidence of "disregards for our constitutional rights."[43] Rufus Brooks convened meetings in the basement of his church, where he and his neighbors "organized as citizens . . . who wish to abolish strip mining." But sometimes they had to pump out water and clean up mud instead, because when the mountain came down on their homes, it flooded the church basement, too.[44]

Even as strip mining destroyed the homes of people like Brooks and flooded the spaces they relied on to build civic community, it also limited opportunities to build new, much-needed housing. In the most affected counties, Richard Cartwright Austin noted, "housing cannot be built because there is no safe place to build it."[45] The region already faced a serious housing shortage, and strip mining exacerbated the problem.[46] Ed Mallacoat directed Demuth's attention to a nearby mountain as they spoke, where once nine homes had stood: "now there's none."[47] Mountain households were disposable in the name of low energy prices for consumers elsewhere. The mechanized coal industry ensured that coal was readily available to generate the electricity that ran the nation's cities, but coalfield residents paid an increasingly hefty environmental price, as Jock Yablonski had put it during his ill-fated campaign: "a terrible legacy of polluted rivers and streams, ravaged hillsides, and hideous slag heaps" that "robbed the coal miner of the rich, natural environment of his homeland."[48]

The reality of miners' lives defied the easy math that pitted miners' "jobs" against the Appalachian "environment." Bert Caudill surely knew the costs of coal: it had claimed his father and his brother-in-law and was slowly taking his breath away. On the issue of strip mining, as with black lung, the UMW leadership was out of step with miners. Boyle's administration had defended strip mining by claiming he was also defending miners' jobs. The historian Chad Montrie has shown how as opposition to surface mining grew, so did Boyle's dismissiveness of efforts to abolish the practice.[49] By early 1971, amid intensifying coalfield unrest, Boyle announced UMW support for federal regulation of strip mining as a necessary pairing to the Federal Coal Mine Health and Safety Act. Stricter underground mining regulations came with a hefty price tag that incentivized operators to turn to strip mining, inflicting on the land the damage they could no longer inflict on miners' lungs and bodies.[50] Although Boyle remained hostile to the stripping abolitionists, their activism forced him to change his position and to echo key points of their argument.

Still, Boyle's open hostility to the stripping abolitionists continued. The nation faced a choice, Boyle contended. Congress could regulate environmental damage—rather than halt it, as the abolitionists demanded—or the country could have "power blackouts." If the logic of stripping abolitionists was pushed "to its true conclusion," Boyle argued, underground mining would have to be abolished as well: "That might end water pollution, gob heaps and other similar problems. It would, however, also end modern American society and the jobs of most Americans including those of coal miners."[51] It was an argument for business as usual that adapted the idea of balancing the burdens of energy production with the benefits of its consumption, further underscoring the connection between the harms built into underground mining practices and those inflicted on the land by strip mining. Just as with black lung, in evaluating the possible paths forward, Boyle refused to recognize how the perceived legitimacy of the coal-fired social contract had unraveled around him.

The disquiet many miners expressed about strip mining pointed to a fuller understanding of how the nation's changing energy system had undermined and delegitimized the coal-fired social contract. Many miners doubted that strip mining supporters really cared about creating jobs. They saw stripping as a continuation of the process of underground mechanization, which in previous decades had put hundreds of thousands of miners out of work.[52] Because strip-mined coal was substantially cheaper by the ton than coal mined underground, companies actively closed underground mines to open stripping operations. But even as miners challenged the effort to cast strip mining as job creation, it also put some miners in what felt like an impossible position. Ed Mallacoat, who had been in the mines since 1946, was moved from a deep mine to a strip mine in 1968: "Strip mining is destroying the land," he said, "but it's the only work there is. So you're hurting yourself whatever way you go."[53] Charles York, a factory foreman, worked fourteen- and fifteen-hour days rather than go to work in a strip mine—the only other job available near his home. "I can't see strip mining, tearing up the country for just a few dollars."[54] Some, like the black lung activist Arnold Miller, even questioned if the men working in the strip mines should be allowed into the UMW, if they had the requisite coal-fired (and coal-circumscribed) citizenship that underground miners did. "These workers are predominantly from out of state," he said, suggesting that strip mine workers would not have to live day to day with the decimated hillsides and polluted drinking water that stripping created. "They are skilled heavy equipment operators who would have no trouble finding work."[55] Miller's formulation oversimplified a more complex story, and he would later change his position, recognizing the importance of surface miners as union members. While miners' opinions on strip mining varied—some favored greater regulation, others full abolition—they increasingly saw the environmental inequalities it created as a companion to the embodied inequalities that accrued underground.

Surface mining was rapidly becoming more central to the American energy system, and the scars already visible on the land only hinted at a possible future of total destruction. Antistripping activists drew on the spectacle of giant machines gnawing away at the mountains to metaphorically portray the industry as a voracious monster set on consuming the region. They created flyers that asked, "If West Virginia was a pie, how much would the strippers eat?" The number corresponded to the amount of land that could be destroyed by strip mining if the practice wasn't halted. Some counties, like Boone and Mingo, in southern West Virginia, could be "100%

destroyed by the strippers."[56] Appalachian activists escalated their resistance to the practice, occupying strip mining sites, organizing their communities to retain mineral rights, and sabotaging mining equipment.[57]

Growing Appalachian opposition to strip mining filtered into broader public consciousness at the dawn of the environmental decade, a moment when Americans were more concerned with the state of their environment than ever before.[58] The growing opposition to the practice concerned the Department of the Interior, which felt that land protection and energy development were "alternative national goals" that had to be balanced. Elburt Osborn, Nixon's new Bureau of Mines director, felt "the aroused citizen does not see or hear the whole story" about the contributions that coal mining made to American society. Additionally, energy consumers were less likely to think of the demands that their projected future consumption placed on the nation's energy resources, which seemed rather abstract from all-electric living rooms.[59]

More immediately visible were the scars on the land. What made consumers uncomfortable, Osborn felt, was that "the economics of mineral recovery has led us to turn more and more to surface excavation of ore, so that miles of unsightly open pits now mar the beauty of the countryside." But the problems didn't stop there: "acid runoff water from these areas enters rivers and streams, creating additional pollution problems." And finally, mineral processing further down the supply chain exacerbated the "corruption to the environment." As a result, lamented Osborn, nearly everything Americans encountered about the mining industry was unflattering.[60] With Americans' attention squarely focused on environmental impact, Osborn felt that Americans had missed the central role that coal played in their lives and all the "luxuries" it made possible. He insisted the public didn't understand the true meaning of their demands for energy, which were "so voracious that world mineral consumption during the last half-century has exceeded previous mineral consumption in the history of mankind."[61] Osborn's outlook both tied miners to coal and sought to temper Americans' growing demands for environmental protection. This perspective, which saw environmental protection and energy production as counterposed values that had to be balanced, operated as the baseline assumption in national politics.

Miners and antistripping activists, including some national environmental groups, saw another possibility. Following the establishment of Miners for Democracy, some environmentalists saw "the beginning of a much stronger role to be played by the UMW in environmental health and safety matters" by "bettering the quality of miners' environment both inside and out of the mines."[62] Richard Cartwright Austin, a Miners for Democracy supporter as well as an anti–strip mining organizer, directly tied this possibility to the historic struggle against the coalfield state: "As West Virginians liberated themselves from the mine thugs of the past, they will liberate themselves from the monster, earth-destroying machines of the present."[63]

The primary problems facing the Appalachian environment, environmentalists and miners agreed, were, first, the inattention to the dangers of underground mining, which resulted in the deaths of hundreds of miners each year, and, second, the ecological ravages of strip mining, which cannibalized miners' jobs and rendered the landscape ecologically unviable, robbing citizens of a landscape long revered for its breathtaking beauty.[64] As Ruby and Bert Caudill's experience made clear, for miners and their families, their rights as citizens remained irreversibly entangled with the nation's energy system. That same energy system continued to violate the rights they believed were theirs, the ledgers of its inequalities to be found in miners' lungs, in the region's graveyards, and on the land itself. Austin warned the nation that the "plagues" of coal-fired inequality had a way of spreading: "for centuries," the aftermath of strip mining would "spread its constant erosion and siltation through the river systems of the east and Midwest, spreading the plague to those who now receive the coal and the power."[65]

Austin's warning about the ravages of inequality traveling through the nation's river systems proved prescient, and not only as toxic sediment made its way from the mountain headwaters to the wide, gliding waters of the Ohio and Mississippi Rivers. The country would soon be confronted with horrifying evidence that the ecological violence of strip mining was difficult to contain and that it exacerbated longstanding environmental impact of coal mining in the region, particularly the dangers that accompanied waste storage.

Mine waste had long imperiled mining communities around the world. Above or below ground, once coal had been cut or blasted from the surrounding rock, workers had to clean and prepare it for shipment. The cleaner the coal, the lower the sulfur and ash content, the lower per-Btu cost of transporting the coal from the mine. The cleaner the coal, the more it was worth. Or, to look at it another way, the coal gained value by stripping away the impurities that made it harder to use in coking ovens and power plants. The waste—often called "gob"—was then dumped into piles around the mine. As these massive piles grew, they mixed with rainwater and could transform into a toxic slurry that could render the gob piles unstable. Impoundment dams could help contain the waste, but companies often cut corners on their construction and maintenance, and failures were too common for comfort. The danger of accumulated mining waste garnered worldwide attention in 1966, when an unstable waste pile above the village of Aberfan, Wales, collapsed. Waves of black slurry, about twice the density of water, rushed down to the village like an avalanche, engulfing homes, infrastructure, and most horrifying of all, a primary school full of children. One hundred and forty-four people were killed, including 116 children—nearly half of the school's enrollment.[66] Many coalfield residents in the United States saw the potential for their communities to become another Aberfan. In West Virginia alone, activists documented more than 120 coal mining refuse piles.[67]

While mine waste came from both underground and surface mines, strip mining greatly exacerbated the dangers it posed in two ways. First, surface mining simply increased the amount of waste produced, creating larger and more dangerous waste piles. Second, as we have seen, surface mining transformed the mountain ecosystem, especially the capacity of soils to absorb water. That increased the chance of liquefaction: of a water-soaked solid transforming into the same heavy liquid that had caused such devastation in Aberfan. The residents of Saunders, West Virginia, and a series of other small towns along Buffalo Creek, where the Pittston Company ran a group of mines, had lived in fear of an Aberfan-like disaster for years as water, sludge, slate, and other waste collected behind a series of haphazard impoundment dams upstream.

The psychic toll that the persistent danger inflicted could be read from an impassioned plea Pearl Woodrum wrote to West Virginia's governor in 1968: "Please send someone here to see the water and how dangerous it is. It scares everyone to death. We are afraid we will be washed away and drowned. They just keep dumping slate and slush in the water and making it more dangerous . . . for God's sake have the dump and water destroyed. Our lives are in danger."[68] Her letter passed from office to office until it ended up with the Logan County prosecutor, who did nothing. According to a later investigation, the only outcome of Mrs. Woodrum's plea was that the Water Resources Division of the Department of Natural Resources encouraged the company to build an even larger third dam, "thus compounding the dangerous situation Mrs. Woodrum had exposed to official scrutiny."[69]

Four years later, Denny Gibson made his way out onto that very dam—Pittston's No. 3 impoundment dam—a few minutes before 8 AM on Saturday, February 26, 1972. It was his third trip that morning: he was keeping a close eye on the rising water level. Several days of rain had brought the slurry nearly high enough to crest the top of the dam, and when Gibson stepped out of his truck this time, he realized the ground was "really soggy, like mush." He noticed "water oozing through the loose refuse piles on the top of the dam" and "large cracks and slumps on the downstream face . . . near the center of the dam."[70] He turned his truck around and sped off the impoundment, racing down to the valley, honking his horn to wake up anyone he could. But the dam gave way only minutes later, at 8:05 AM, taking the two smaller impoundments below along with it.

Pearl Woodrum lost power as the dam collapsed. Overtaken with fear, she scrambled for the hillside, and when she turned to look back, she saw the water. It rushed down in "the awfulest looking waves," sweeping her home down the hollow.[71] Within two minutes, the town of Saunders, located right at the dam's base, had been washed away. The catastrophic failure unleashed over 132 million gallons of coal slurry—the equivalent of two hundred Olympic swimming pools—onto the sixteen small coal towns dotted along the Buffalo Creek Hollow. The thirty-foot-high wave of dense black water killed at least 124 people, injured another 1,121, and left more than 80 percent of the hollow's population homeless.[72]

The tiny town of Saunders had been on edge for days by the time the dam finally collapsed. Some people "were up all night long," according to Jack Kent, the strip mining superintendent for Pittston's Buffalo Division: "They were out on their porches. Their lights were on."[73] Others had already fled farther down the hollow, to the Laredo schoolhouse about three miles away, though in the end, it would not be far enough. The flood inundated Laredo, too.[74] Still, when the dam gave way on Saturday morning, many people in the hollow were still in bed and unable to flee quickly enough to escape the wall of black slurry. Because the valley lacked proper alarm systems, warning traveled through word of mouth or through the repeated, desperate honking of car horns as drivers raced to escape the flood. As Bertha Glend made coffee, she "heard a neighbor, three houses down, yelling 'water water.'"⁷⁵ Most people, however, had no warning at all. Leroy Lambert, another Pittston coal miner, was eating breakfast with his family when the electricity went off. They looked outside, where "not far up the valley they could see a wall of black water hurtling a church house in front of it down the hollow towards them." Henry Kilgore "happened to look out the window and see water and debris pouring into [his] yard." Within moments, "a near neighbor's house came floating by. The neighbor was standing in the door with her 18-month-old baby in her arms screaming for help. There was no way to help them, and they were drowned. The whole family saw them go under."⁷⁶

Years of rumors and speculation about the dam's impending collapse also meant that even some residents who were warned in time failed to evacuate until they could see the deluge approaching—and by then it was too late. Anna Bailey's son had to convince her that the dam had really burst this time: "He said, 'I'm not joking, it's true. Get out.' . . . Even my husband said it wasn't true—they say the dam breaks every time it rains."⁷⁷ In addition to years of rumors, company officials had insisted as late as 6 AM that morning that things were under control. "We're working on it," Steve Dasovich told a gathering of miners two hours before the collapse. He insisted "the safest place . . . would be in the mines."⁷⁸ A neighbor relayed this conversation to Newson Bailey, as "there was no danger and that everyone could go to work." But later, while Newson Bailey ate breakfast with his family, neighbors shouted, "The water is here!" While the Baileys managed to jump "in their car . . . reaching high ground in safety," a second car just "behind the Bailey family did not make it and all that vehicles' occupants were killed." Later, Newson Bailey learned his oldest daughter and seventeen-year-old grandson had been killed and that his youngest grandchild "was found buried in the mud." Although "the mud was . . . caked inside the baby's lungs," the child managed to survive.⁷⁹

On the second day after the "avalanche of water" had swept through the hollows, bodies were recovered as far as twenty-four miles downriver. Rescue workers, National Guardsmen, and surviving residents desperately combed the wreckage for the missing.⁸⁰ Several hundred remained unaccounted for more than two days after the dam's collapse. Some of the missing would eventually be found hiding on the hillsides, wearing only bedclothes in freezing winter temperatures, or seeking refuge with relatives. One boy, who had lost most of his family, was found "caught in the branches of a tree."⁸¹ Others remained buried in the rubble or in cars that remained submerged underwater.[82] By March 1, just four days later, chickenpox had begun to spread in the school housing survivors; public health officials began a precautionary vaccination program against typhoid among displaced residents, and the whole hollow smelled of "rotting flesh."[83] Governor Arch Moore imposed a public health quarantine on the area, which simultaneously emphasized the serious health risks caused by the disaster while also limiting independent investigators' access to the area. Residents viewed the quarantine as a way for Governor Moore to avoid public scrutiny for his handling of the crisis.[84]

Once more, an elementary school became a morgue, this time in Man, West Virginia. "Twisted bodies" were brought and identified before being loaded for storage in refrigerated trucks.[85] Down the hall, survivors huddled in classrooms on army surplus cots. But even survival was little relief. Wayne Brady Hatfield, a disabled miner, survived the flood but lost "his wife, daughter, and grand-daughter, all swept away by the turbulent water"—all only a year after his only son had been killed in Vietnam. Hatfield described the harrowing moments as he fled the rising water and realized he would be unable to save most of his family. "I run out through [the rows of houses] until the water got up to under my arms. Then I see'd that I couldn't make it . . . I grabbed the baby and went upstairs, and . . . I said Lord have mercy."[86] Rufus Brooks just wanted a chance to say goodbye to his home, the one he had worked for decades to own, the one that had been under constant threat from the nearby strip mine for nearly a year. Brooks was thankful that, amid all the loss around him, his family had escaped uninjured. But the house was gone, knocked off its foundation and into another building, the slow creep of the damp and mildew and odor with it. It now sat "forlornly by the side of Route 16, a large letter X marking it as one of the hundreds of homes along the hollow to be razed."[87] Once the damage had been tallied, Brooks's home was one of 546 in the hollow destroyed by the flood; the water damaged an additional 538, leaving virtually no structure untouched by the flood's wrath.[88]

As the bodies were pulled out one by one and the horrifying stories of escape and survival began to emerge, the question of who was to blame began to accompany open grief. The company claimed the dam was simply "incapable of holding the water God poured into it," a claim met with rage and intense scrutiny. The residents had every reason to be skeptical of the company's story. Pittston's safety record was one of the worst in the

Figure 7.2 Survivors gather in the ruins of their homes.
Source: UMWJR 58/11.

country, and they seemed to spend more effort waging an ideological fight against mine regulation than in making their mines safer. In 1971, nine miners were killed in Pittston's mines. Another 743 suffered serious disabling injuries, and the company had been cited for five thousand safety violations. The dam had partially failed before, too, in 1971, though a second impoundment dam below held, a flood narrowly averted.[89] Five months earlier, the company acknowledged the need for improvements to the dam—specifically the addition of emergency spillways—to state regulators but had never acted on their own recommendation. But despite this atrocious safety record, the hugely profitable company had paid only $275 in fines. *Total*.[90] Area residents came to believe they would have to determine what had caused the dam failure on their own.

Miners drew on their own years of experience and interaction with the dam. Some believed that, just like the Hyden explosion had been triggered by a combination of bad conditions and the use of illegal explosive materials, perhaps the failure of the Buffalo Creek impoundment dam resulted from the illegal use of dynamite to blast holes in the dam to release water amid the heavy rain. Miners took ABC camera crews to the destroyed impoundments and "pointed out . . . evidences [sic] such as cable and drill holes." The men believed that when Pittston tried to relieve pressure on the dam, "something went wrong, and the whole section gave way." Other witnesses had reported hearing an explosion. One resident who lived close to the base of the dam "saw debris hurled hundreds of yards across the valley just before the river of water and mud broke way" and considered it to be evidence that the flood had been triggered by blasting.[91] In the end it turned out Pittston *had* tried to install a drainage pipe at the last minute to alleviate pressure, sometime after darkness fell the day before the collapse. It also turned out there *had* indeed been an explosion, manmade, though not with dynamite but with negligence: compacted mine waste generated heat, and the refuse behind the dam was so deep and so hot that as the cold rainwater made its way to the depths, it turned to steam, increasing the pressure, and finally triggering an explosion.[92]

The national media framed the preventable disaster as an inevitable tragedy by now familiar to coal mining communities, a narrative that suggested coal-fired inequality was likewise inevitable. One reporter asked Congressman Ken Hechler if "these people" had "gotten to where they're so used to living in the shadow of disaster, floods, coal mine tragedies, that they kind of take it for granted."[93] Such questions mirrored the naturalization of mine disasters that had taken place in the wake of the Hyden explosion just over a year before. State officials also suggested that the disaster stood beyond explanation to deflect blame, drawing on a narrative of a wild, vicious, and untamable landscape that echoed responses to the Consol No. 9 disaster. In the wake of the devastation, Governor Arch Moore addressed the public: "Why do all the bad things have to happen to West Virginia? As a governor, I . . . these are acts of God. And, uh, where he picks to undertake to deliver his message for whatever reason it may be . . . I don't know."[94]

Survivors pointed the finger back at the governor: "Our leader in Charleston / Yes we blame you / We dumb Hillbillies / Understand politics too."[95] Shirley Marcum, who lost fifty-two of her neighbors in the hardest-hit town of Lundale, likewise scoffed at Moore's explanation. "I didn't see God a-driving them slate trucks up there and wearing them hard hull caps. I did not see that at no time . . . I don't believe it was an act of God. It was an act of man."[96]

Casting the disaster as an "act of God" not only legally limited the liability of the company or the culpability of state and federal agencies but also presented as ineluctable an energy system where some benefited while others died. It allowed Americans to believe that the attainment of consumer citizenship did not entail offering a citizenship of broken promises to someone else. And to accomplish this sleight of hand, coal-fired liberalism drew on a longer tradition of what one historian has described as "conflating the man-made and the natural."[97] Surrounded by the twisted irons that had once been bridges, the utility poles that had been pulled from the ground as though they were little more than weeds, the house timbers scattered like matchsticks, it might have been tempting for a just-arrived journalist to limit the story of the devastation to the hollow. When the coal-black mud sucked at the boots of relief workers, or an official shook a spray can that hissed as it released paint in a quick X on the ruins that had once been someone's home, or a bulldozer worked to clear roads covered with a mix of sludge and keepsakes, it was easy to see the power of the water. Seeing the structures of coal-fired inequality took a little more work, but they were all around if you looked.

Coalfield residents were quick to note that the impact of the destruction was felt unequally and that the disaster was far from natural. One song about the disaster charged listeners with looking for "who takes our coal but don't share in the fear," if they wanted to understand what had happened.[98] Congressman Ken Hechler echoed this sentiment, placing the disaster in a longer history of energy extraction when he pointedly observed that in one of the affected communities "the only building left is the company store."[99] The *Baltimore Sun*'s cartoonist Tom Flannery depicted federal and state officials standing alongside the coal operators to survey the aftermath. From the safety of the hillside, they surveyed the damage before them: a riverbed replaced with the debris of destroyed lives. "Oh well," the men lament, "they were only coal miners." In the background, the coal preparation plant, where the very waste that had been unleashed on the hollow had been separated from the coal, stands ready for another shift.[100] In this image, miners doubtless saw an updated form of an old dehumanization: a boss who warned a miner to keep the mule safe from falling slate underground, a miner who retorted, "What about me? What if the rock

'Oh Well, They Were Only Coalminers'

Figure 7.3 Tom Flannery, "Oh Well, They Were Only Coal Miners." Source: *Baltimore Sun*, March 6, 1972. Used with permission.

falls in on me?" and the operator's response, "I can hire another man; I've got to buy that mule."[101]

Survivors' narratives underscored the connection between the disaster and this longer history of energy violence through their vivid descriptions, which echoed those given by miners who had survived explosions, fires, and cave-ins underground. Sue Looney's recollection of the moment she realized something was wrong evoked the miners' memories of the moments preceding underground explosions: "I heard a horn blowing and then a loud thundering sound." Other comments focused on how coal deindividualized its victims by covering them with black dust and slurry. Looney described "a man, who came up" out of the coal slurry so "dirty, you couldn't tell who [he] was . . . all he could say was *I've lost my little boy*." Pittston miner Ray Farley was asleep in bed with his wife, Frankie, with their two young children asleep nearby when "the water hit their house," knocking it off its foundation, "and turned it around." Ray broke open a window and was able to get his son to shore. He returned for his three-month-old daughter and was carried two hundred yards downstream before he could reach the safety of the hillside with her. Covered in "black stuff," she could not be recognized by relatives, who insisted that Ray had "saved

IF LETCHER COUNTY WAS A PIE . . . [231]

the wrong baby," while his wife "had been stranded . . . all of this time, with debris piling up around her . . . and bodies floating by."[102] Such descriptions emphasized that the dangers of mines and the horrors of the flood existed along a continuum of energy violence. It was no accident that these towns were clustered on the valley of this particular hollow or that the waste had been dumped above them with little regard for their safety. And as the communities mourned, company officials were "conspicuously absent." Instead of making meaningful amends for the lives they had destroyed, they set to work repairing the railroad tracks "to get the coal moving again."[103]

Miners felt that once again they had been viewed as expendable by federal and state officials, the companies, and their own union. Buffalo Creek joined a long and growing list of place names that anchored preventable coalfield disasters in public discourse. It joined, most recently, Farmington, the town closest to the Consol No. 9 mine, and Hyden, the location of the Finley No. 15 mine. When Governor Arch Moore appointed a nine-person ad-hoc committee to study the disaster that included five representatives of the very agencies whose performance would be under scrutiny, alongside three "independent" members who had previously voiced support for the coal industry or who used coal in their own firms, many coalfield activists feared the committee would do little more than paper over a mass murder.[104]

Believing they could not trust the institutions meant to represent them to meaningfully investigate the disaster, activists convened their own "Citizens' Commission" along with a wider group of area residents. The commission was organized by the black lung and disability activists who had built the Black Lung Association, the Disabled Miners and Widows Association of Southern West Virginia, and the Miners for Democracy. They were joined by environmentalists, health care workers, religious leaders, and civil rights lawyers.[105] The civic response, Ken Hechler noted, "gives eloquent testimony, I think, to . . . a new spirit abroad in both West Virginia and throughout the entire area, which demands that human rights be protected, and that the safety and health of the people be protected." The people of West Virginia were "tired of being pushed around."[106]

The commission raised the kinds of questions one would expect of such an inquiry: why did the dam fail? Who was responsible? What could prevent it happening again? The answers to these questions were as predictable as they were horrifying. The dam failed because it "never should have been built," because a host of federal and state agencies failed to intervene even though they had been warned of the dangers the dam presented at least twice in the prior five years, and because although the dam was in violation of at least three different regulations that already carried the force of law after 1969, the Pittston Coal Company felt it could use the dam without fear of legal consequences.[107] As Tom Bethell combed through long and arduous administrative reports, he found one unanimous conclusion among investigators: "shock" at how inadequate the dam was and certainty that the dam would fail. By any measure, the disaster had been preventable: estimates for Pittston to have constructed the dam properly ranged from $50,000 to $200,000—a pittance for the fourth-largest coal company in the country.[108]

While the commission did ultimately find twelve individuals from both the company and the county, state, and federal government responsible for the disaster, they also recognized that systemic issues went beyond these individuals who might be held directly liable for the murder of 124 people, the destruction of homes and property, and the trauma inflicted on the survivors.[109] The crux of the problem lay in the structure of the coal-fired social contract and the state it powered. And while Pittston, which primarily produced metallurgical coal exported for overseas steel production, was an outlier by the early 1970s, with coal overwhelmingly going to electricity production, it remained braided through the larger energy system and a globalizing political economy: "every ton of coal [Pittston produces] brings dollars to the state treasury, the UMW welfare fund, and Pittston's stockholders. Compared to the urgency of moving coal to the fantastically profitable Japanese and European markets, the human needs of the Buffalo Creek community have faded into insignificance."[110] But equally, the commission doubted that the communities of Buffalo Creek were the only such communities "subsidizing" the nation's energy system with their lives.[111]

As a result, while the commission set out to collect and evaluate evidence, its members "felt if we were a Citizens' Commission, we could not merely be a fact-finding group . . . citizens need to bring the government to accountability."[112] So they also outlined a series of larger-stakes questions about the unequal nature of energy citizenship and the possibility for justice in an energy system where much of the country had a strong interest in cheap coal, given the energy crisis looming on the horizon. What would it take for government to truly represent the people of the coalfields?

How could the residents of Buffalo Creek get justice in an energy system organized to leave them carrying the burdens of coal production as the financial, industrial, and energetic benefits accumulated elsewhere?

The Citizen's Commission came up with a long list of recommendations. Recognizing that the disaster was one of systemic regulatory failure as well as driven by Pittston's greed and negligence, the recommendations focused on accountability for both the company and the regulatory agencies that had failed to act to prevent the disaster. But the recommendations also demonstrated activists' insistence on the political character of their demands. In a list of twenty-one recommendations, two dealt with engineering interventions, and one urged Pittston to be more responsive to the needs of the victims. The other eighteen aimed to redress the democratic failures of the coal-fired social contract through equal and impartial application of the law, expanded state involvement in the mining sector, democratization of decision making over reclamation and redevelopment of the hollow, and enforcement of the individual property rights that had been usurped by the coal operators. These demands made clear that both securing justice for the residents of Buffalo Creek and preventing a similar disaster from occurring elsewhere had less to do with the dam's engineering than with reapportionment of political power and affirmation of citizenship rights for miners and their communities.[113]

Critically, several of the demands were not only made on those the commission felt were culpable for the disaster and thus the murder of at least 124 people. They also extended to the way the residents of mining communities ought to act in their role as citizens. The commission entreated citizens to "diligently search out presently existing dangers to their lives and property . . . and . . . take such action as may be necessary to remove the dangers," to individually and collectively support government officials who were "known to be diligent in [their] public responsibilities and in trying to serve the interests of the citizenry," and, finally, to engage in careful democratic deliberation of "facts and findings," yes, but also the "broad questions contained in this Report."[114] In other words, the commission called for a renewal of the practices of democratic citizenship.

But just getting the justice of recognition proved an uphill battle. Pittston lowballed settlement offers for people who had lost loved ones and homes. Bitterly, one survivor observed, the company tried to "satisfy" people with a check for $10,000 or $12,000 "when they've lost their life's earnings. It just doesn't work that way."[115] And the initial loss and hardship didn't come close to representing the totality of the agony. At least a dozen people suffered from acute psychological stress so severe they required hospitalization. Many more dealt with alcohol and drug addiction, and social workers cataloged increases in divorce, interpersonal violence, and domestic abuse.[116] Ultimately, organizers looked to the lawyers who had aided them in the black lung movement. They reached out to Harry Huge, who was representing an organization of disabled miners and widows in court as they fought to liberalize and revise the UMW welfare and pension system, but the case ultimately landed in the hands of Huge's colleague, Gerald Stern, who had cut his legal teeth on voting rights cases in the Civil Rights Division at the Department of Justice. Stern recognized that for the organizers to "meet publicly, and openly, to plan an attack on a coal company, especially one which was one of the largest employers in their county," was no small feat. He deeply admired their commitment to giving democracy content.[117]

Pittston ultimately settled out of court for $13.5 million.[118] Stern was thrilled; it was more than he had ever expected to win.[119] But Tom Bethell cast the figure in a different light. He estimated it amounted to fifty cents or a dollar from each ton of coal Pittston produced that year—barely a "blip" on the company's radar in a year of record coal prices and not enough to damage them financially at all. "The company just goes on making money," he said, "and the people who really wind up paying for the disaster... are the people who are buying Japanese-manufactured products.... You get the little old lady in California driving a Toyota made out of Japanese steel which is made out of Pittston's coal."[120] Although in this case the coal's international sojourn made it harder to see, the coal-fired social contract—its inequalities, its consequences—were with Americans when they turned on their lights or started their cars. When a person in Memphis turned on their bedroom light powered by the TVA, they were connected to Ruby and Bert Caudill, even if they couldn't hear the terrible roar the mountain made when it came down so frightfully. And the driver in California that Bethell gestured to was tied to Rufus Brooks, who lost his home even though he escaped with his life, even if she couldn't feel it beneath the gloss of the paint.

In the coalfields, the Buffalo Creek disaster solidified the connection between an emergent environmental politics, the fight for safe workplaces, and a longstanding desire to make the promises of energy citizenship real. The people who brought these threads of coalfield activism together were the very people who lived at the places where they overlapped. They understood their citizenship had been extracted at the coalface and that the coal-fired social contract had been written in blood. And they also believed it was precisely that sacrifice which entitled them to write it anew and, in the process, make the promises of coal-fired democracy real.

CHAPTER VIII

Jobs, Lives, and Land

Two months after Ken Yablonski found his father, mother, and sister murdered, he and Chip issued a warning to the nation: "America's lights may go out this fall" unless the U.S. government recognized miners' "fundamental right to be represented by men of their choosing."[1] This fundamental right for union members to elect their own leadership was relatively new in U.S. labor law, secured little more than a decade before.[2] Miners' claim on democratic representation, however, stood in a longer American political tradition immediately legible to most Americans. Their claim also expressed the intimate connection miners saw between industrial and political rights. And critically, the Yablonskis' warning recognized how miners' claims on the nation remained tied to their role in the nation's energy system.

The Labor Department took more than two years to order a new election. By then it had also become clear that far more was at stake in the new vote than the election rights outlined by Landrum-Griffin.[3] In between Jock Yablonski's murder and the Labor Department's May 1972 order, miners' activism continued to renegotiate the coal-fired social contract, in the process renewing their aspiration for a truly democratic energy citizenship. Still, reform-minded miners recognized that their union's leadership represented a major barrier in achieving their demands. Tony Boyle remained obstinate, even as the announcement of a rerun election unified several

[237]

threads of coalfield activism under the banner of the Miners for Democracy.

Because of the tactics that reform-minded miners employed in defense of their lives, their land, and their rights, the media commonly referred to the MFD as rebels and dissidents. This label helped place the miners within a broader upsurge of rank-and-file activism by union members across the United States that defied the business-as-usual of the country's labor relations.[4] A nationwide wildcat strike by postal workers in 1970 secured their right to collective bargaining and a substantial wage increase.[5] Autoworkers at General Motor's Lordstown plant struck against layoffs, speedups, and the monotony of assembly line work in March 1972. The miners' courage in standing up to Boyle and his regime, even after he ordered Jock Yablonski's murder, proved contagious, especially when the MFD became the first group of reformers to take over their union that December. The MFD's 1972 victory ignited a wave of efforts to democratize the nation's unions, like Ed Sadlowski's campaign in the steel landscape of South Chicago and Gary, Indiana. As the historian Jefferson Cowie has written, "rebel" also described a new generation of miners, often Vietnam veterans disillusioned by their experiences in Southeast Asia, who bristled at authority—be it the authority exercised by their commanding officer or their foreman.[6] The MFD's role in this broader upsurge of rank-and-file activism proved critical in shaping the trajectory of labor politics in a tumultuous decade.

Amid the ferment, it was easy to miss another narrative in which the Miners for Democracy belonged. The miners' rebellion also emerged from a deep and, by the 1970s, well-established conception of energy citizenship. In defying an undemocratic and deadly energy system, miners embraced a long tradition of viewing protest as an act that connoted and conferred citizenship, that strengthened the social contract rather than unraveling it. And as much as youthful rebellion, miners often conceived of their actions as an act of solemn duty. Bob Gergley situated his activism within these narratives as he recorded a radio spot to urge his fellow miners to support the MFD's slate in the new election, scheduled for December 9, 1972. With his quiet, measured voice—one clearly unaccustomed to public speaking—he appealed to the miners' shared democratic political tradition, calling forth the rights and obligations of American citizenship. Voting for the Miners for Democracy was a vote for "freedom from fear" and the belief that "everyone should have the right to express their opinion without being intimidated." At the heart of Gergley's appeal stood a belief that "no man should bear the miseries of a coal miner, let alone be cheated of his rightful benefits." He recognized that his fellow miners were often "uneducated and think there is not much we can do," but he also felt it was "surely" their collective duty to "stand up for what is right."[7]

For miners like Gergley, the effort to democratize the UMW was not a rebellion but instead represented a patriotic duty and the opportunity to restore the proper balance of rights and obligations of citizenship in the nation's energy system. Reform-minded miners like Fred Scott bitterly decried the public perception of miners as "Arsonists, Rioters, Animals, Conspirators, and destructive militants." While the public often "cannot visualize a miner as a human being," Scott contended, miners had "worked and fought and became a part of our nations Heritage."[8] Although what miners often saw as patriotic duty increasingly overlapped with open defiance of the very social contract they sought to reinvigorate, the MFD's 1972 campaign stood as a demand to revisit the relationship between the country's energy system and the substance of democratic citizenship, a final step in the renegotiation of the coal-fired social contract.

The MFD placed *democracy* at the core of that relationship. Democracy, to reform-minded miners, certainly encompassed the right to fair elections for union leadership positions, but it was also much more: a political culture, a social form, a set of practices and habits, and an organizing experiment intimately tied to their own citizenship claims and American identity.[9] The MFD contended that the most egregious marks of coal-fired inequality—black lung, workplace death, and environmental degradation from strip mining—resulted from an out-of-balance social contract and that those inequalities could only be alleviated with democratic participation. Democracy had the conceptual power to encompass a broad set of rights, obligations, and practices that stretched across the many spheres of Americans' lives from home to work, from the union hall to the halls of government. Specific places and issues gave miners' democratic imagination content: union reform, political participation, safety campaigns, and ecological protections. These issues represented more than a series of concurrent problems to the MFD. Their vision of democracy reflected their belief that coal-fired electric power yoked together the futures of the nation and its coal miners. Miners had come to understand a wide range of issues, from black lung to the destroyed mountainsides, as holistic evidence of an unjust and unviable energy system.

The MFD's invocation of wholesale democratic renewal could not be extricated from the broader political landscape of the era, particularly the rights revolution that expanded the scope of the claims that Americans made on their government and that reshaped the way many Americans imagined political community.[10] The MFD argued that workplace safety—the right to survive the workday—was not just a condition of steady production or an issue to be negotiated in the contract but a right conferred by and representative of full citizenship. Black lung and mine disasters violated that right to life, making sure that the shadow of death accompanied miners wherever they went and linking their access to the social citizenship of the mid-twentieth century to their participation in an energy system likely to kill them. The ecological devastation of strip mining knitted together a plethora of rights violations: new notions of environmental rights still being tested in the courts, older notions of a right to subsistence, the right to leisure, the right to decent housing. Their conception of democracy, rooted in the coal mining workplace, also fit into a broader moment in national and global politics. It came to rest on three pillars—jobs, lives, and land. Using this framework of jobs, lives, and land, the Miners for Democracy attempted to reimagine the possibilities of coal-fired democracy in the United States.

The Miners for Democracy braided these connected struggles, but they also had to contend with a union leadership who put their own power and financial gain ahead of miners' lives and aspirations. Boyle's corruption ran deep: day-to-day thuggery in the union; his manipulation of the 1969 election; his illegal political donations; his connection with the Yablonski murders, which was still being uncovered in the courts; and his role in the mismanagement of the UMW Welfare and Retirement Fund, which had deprived pensioners of benefits. However, the reformers never allowed Boyle's corruption to stand apart from the broader energy system in which he operated. Instead, the MFD argued Boyle's corruption had intensified as the limits of his political imagination ran up against the changes to the country's energy system. Boyle, they contended, was "old, flaccid, and venal."[11]

Alone, charges of corruption might not have resulted in Boyle's ouster. Older miners in particular remained skeptical of corruption charges. In the mid-twentieth century, the labor movement's critics politicized corruption, broadening the definition so much that it included political activities by workers that were in fact legal.[12] Miners who had been working for twenty-five or more years remained all the more skeptical because charges of corruption had also been leveled against John L. Lewis throughout his career. While those charges were sometimes true, especially those related to Lewis's role in mismanagement of the Welfare and Retirement Fund, most miners strongly associated Lewis with the wars that had been fought to unionize the coalfields and the gains that industry-wide bargaining had made in earlier years. They associated charges of corruption with antiunion politics and reaction against miners' own organizing and bargaining successes.[13] Even beyond the "climate of fear and intimidation" that percolated throughout the union, substantial support persisted for Boyle right up to his final moments in office.[14] One miner, Leonard Sergeant, insisted that while he—and indeed, everyone—knew Boyle had "done wrong," he still planned to vote for him. He conceded: "This is a funny thing for a man to say who believes in democracy as much as I do, but we can't afford democracy in this union."[15] Not all of Boyle's support could be chalked up to intimidation or patronage.

Despite the political mire that the charges of corruption waded into, the reformers did not shy away from pointing out the layers of corruption that pervaded the UMW. Still, the MFD refused to accept that the problem was *only* corruption. Corruption, they charged, was an outgrowth of a broader contempt for miners' political agency. Harry Patrick, a mine mechanic and MFD organizer, lambasted his district president for suggesting miners could "choke on too much democracy."[16] After all, Patrick insisted, "What was he really saying with that statement? In essence, that the lowly coal miner is too stupid to select his own leadership and that a country that was built on the principles of freedom had no right to impose its laws on the UMW."[17] The miners saw the reform of their union as intimately connected to a national democratic crisis that left them "no more optimistic about the future of the United States than anyone else."[18]

Yet it was precisely optimism that the Miners for Democracy called forth as they gathered in Wheeling, West Virginia, in May 1972 to nominate their candidates for the newly reordered election. Hundreds attended; raucous debate ensued and sometimes descended into bitter personal politics. It had been a rough couple of years. Much was at stake, and tempers were on edge. Nonetheless, Patrick attested it was "much more democratic than anyone ever dreamed was possible."[19] He left the Wheeling convention as the MFD nominee for secretary-treasurer. At forty-one, still young for someone soon to be elected to one of the union's top offices, Patrick had never attended a convention of any kind before, nor had he been part of any level of elected union leadership. A self-described "something of a rebel" known for being a bit hot-headed, Patrick had instead gained national recognition a year earlier, when he challenged the leadership's attempt to send miners back to work under a new national agreement no one had been allowed to read, let alone ratify. For Patrick, "Miners for Democracy" was an idea as much as an organization.[20] The man who had helped keep that idea alive in western Pennsylvania, Mike Trbovich, secured the vice presidential slot, though he was bitterly disappointed that he had not been chosen for the presidential nomination. That nod went to Arnold Miller.

Figure 8.1 Arnold Miller visits the grave of a striker killed by mine guards on Paint Creek, West Virginia, in 1913.
Source: Rick Lee, *Goldenseal.*

By 1972, Arnold Miller was well known in coalfield politics, particularly in southern West Virginia: a member of the Miners for Democracy, the leader of the West Virginia Black Lung Association, and an outspoken opponent of strip mining. He was born into a coal mining family along Cabin Creek in the spring of 1923, a decade after the area's miners had won a union, a nine-hour day, and other concessions following a year of violent conflict. But Miller's early years were some of the darkest for West Virginia's miners, with the coal industry in a protracted crisis and a new wave of company repression following the warfare in West Virginia during 1920 and 1921.[21] At sixteen, he began working in the mines, but by 1944, he was a twenty-one-year-old machine gunner on the beaches of Normandy. He was shot in the face during the battle, and despite many rounds of plastic surgery, his face bore the scars of that day for the rest of his life. But he bore the scars of the mines too. After two more decades in the mines, Miller discovered he had black lung, which left him with a choice: "Quit and get out of the mines or stay in them and die"—though in the end, he would die in 1985, only sixty-two, from pneumonia and a stroke, conditions certainly worsened, if not directly caused, by his coal-related ailments.[22] The growing cadre of national observers interested in the miners' reform movement would consider Miller a figure who rose from "obscurity" to suddenly head one of the most important democratic movements in the country.[23] One reporter described Miller as an exception to a half-century-old rule that meant "history [was] imposed" on the coalfields, a description that denied the political agency of people like Miller, let alone taking seriously the possibility that he had something to show the country about the limits and possibilities of a coal-fired democracy.[24]

Democracy. Arnold Miller had spent a lot of time thinking about it, even if he wasn't the kind of person most Americans saw as a political thinker. He anchored much of that thought to the writings of John Muir, a writer who emphasized the interconnected nature of the universe, a writer whose work he had encountered "long before I knew any people who called themselves environmentalists."[25] His own view of democratic politics reflected that idea of interconnection. It rested on "the principles this country was founded on" and the way people lived with and exercised them. For Miller, there was no disentangling his democratic politics from the coal he mined or the union of which he was part. He got involved with black lung activism before he even knew it had disabled him. He went to Charleston as part of the 1969 black lung strike because he felt it was his obligation to those who had already been disabled. Once the strike had ended, he continued helping miners access black lung testing, donating hundreds of dollars of his own wages each month. When the first leader of the Black Lung Association, Charles Brooks, became too ill to organize, Miller became the organization's president. The promises of compensation contained in the West Virginia and federal black lung programs, after all, were meaningless if miners couldn't get their disability recognized—and for the miners of West Virginia, high rates of claim denials demonstrated that recognition proved hard to come by. When Miller finally got tested himself in January 1970, his heart came under so much stress he had to be hospitalized. The doctor estimated his lungs had 65 percent impairment.[26] For the rest of his life, the fight for each breath would remind him of the importance of democracy: "Every time I breathe, it's a reminder of what it's like to be sold out all of your life."[27]

After he made the decision that he didn't want to die in the mines, in 1970 Miller took a part-time job with Designs for Rural Action, a Charleston-based group that had received War on Poverty funding. He worked helping to set up some of the group's educational programs and acted as a liaison between the program's staff, who were not from Appalachia, and the local communities. Miller recognized that, on the one hand, the program workers were fellow citizens driven by "moral concern and decency" and that, on the other, Appalachian coal communities didn't want or need saving: they could do it themselves "collectively, together, with a little bit of help here and there."[28] During the same period, he also organized against surface mining, as he watched a stripper disembowel a mountain in view of his home on Cabin Creek, and he served on the Buffalo Creek Citizen's Commission in 1972. He also sat on the editorial board of the *Miner's Voice*, a reform-movement monthly in the coalfields. These activities reflected a broad tapestry of democratic practices that together shaped how Miller would come to define what it meant to democratize his union and the nation's energy system.

Miller also believed strongly in the power of the franchise. In 1969, Miller ran Jock Yablonski's campaign in the southern West Virginia coalfields, and he organized enough election observers in his district that it was one of the few regions with a relatively reliable vote count. Yablonski won the district by a wide margin. Miller believed that just like the union leadership had ceased to represent miners' rights as workers, the state

Figure 8.2 "Run for Office?"
Source: *Black Lung Bulletin*, January 1972, MFDR 44/35.

government had failed to represent miners' rights as citizens. In 1970, he ran for the West Virginia House of Delegates, reflective of his belief that coal miners "should be active in the political structure of our state."[29] It was an uphill battle. Miller lived in a rural, unincorporated area of Kanawha County, also home to the state capitol, Charleston. He ultimately fell short of the votes needed to advance to the general election, but Miller hoped his 1970 run would set an example for other miners. On that count, he succeeded.[30] The Black Lung Association's newsletter often insisted on the need for miners to participate in politics. Asked one 1971 article: "Can't coal miners represent *themselves* in the legislature?"[31] A cartoon caption in another read: "These politicians don't do anything for miners—we'll have to run for office ourselves."[32] In 1972, at least five miners—some disabled, some working—ran for the West Virginia House of Delegates on a shared platform that included the abolition of strip mining and improved mine safety laws. Sara Kaznoski, one of the Consol No. 9 widows, and Jeanne Rasmussen, the miners' ally, journalist, and wife of the black lung clinician Dr. Donald Rasmussen, put themselves forward as McGovern delegates for the Democratic National

Convention.[33] Miller maintained, "I hope someday before I cross over the divide to see ninety percent of the people vote. Then I think we'll have a truly representative government." Like Bob Gergley, Miller did not see the MFD as a group of radicals: "My own opinion of miners," he said, "rather than radical, they've been too damn tolerant."[34] What national commentators cast as a rise from obscurity had in fact been a life deeply engaged with some of the nation's most important citizen-making institutions—military and union—and with democracy as a political process, as a social form, as an everyday practice, and, perhaps most of all, as John Dewey had once described it: a set of moral connections between people.[35]

As Miller emerged at the forefront of the most important union reform movement in the country, his vision of what democracy meant, along with the democratic imaginations of the MFD's members and supporters, would leave a mark on the United States at a moment of great uncertainty, at a moment when Americans had become more conscious than ever of the energy system on which they depended. According to the journalist John Hoerr, "The public now must realize that if there is uneasiness or restlessness or revolt in [the coal industry], it can never rest happily with the knowledge that the electric juices of its happy home will continue to flow unimpeded."[36] Americans had to come to grips with the fact that even though they didn't *see* coal as often, it remained present in their lives and, equally, that so did the political actions and imaginations of the nation's coal miners. The MFD wanted the nation to take the lives of miners as seriously as they took the threat of electricity shortages: "They talk about the lights going out in the cities of the United States and the low stock piles, but they say nothing of the 78 miners who had their lights put out [at the Consol No. 9] and the many others thru out the industry."[37] Junior Hicks, a disabled miner from West Virginia, was tired of waiting on promises: "I think we ought to shut their lights out and get what we want."[38] They recognized it was their hand on the proverbial light switch that gave them political power, and the MFD saw an opportunity not only to advance coalfield struggles for jobs, lives, and land but also to address the broader political crisis gripping the nation. According to Harry Patrick, the MFD's movement wasn't just about cleaning up the UMW; it was about ensuring "better government" for all Americans: "This union . . . should lead the fight to protect the environment, it should be the leader in the fight against wars like the ones in Vietnam . . . [in] forcing the companies to pay their fair share of taxes so our kids can go to better schools."[39]

This perspective helped reformers navigate a turbulent period in U.S. politics, a stagnating industrial economy, and an international political situation balanced on a knife edge between the Cold War and decolonization. The reform movement was indeed embedded in these larger stories. As tensions over the American war in Vietnam escalated, reformers like Mike Trbovich gave antiwar speeches that called into question the United States' self-proclaimed goals in Southeast Asia. Using a formulation that echoed the critiques of many Black antiwar activists, Trbovich asked an antiwar gathering at Macalester College how the United States could be fighting for democracy in Vietnam if union members in the United States couldn't even elect their own leaders: "They preach democracy all over the world . . . and yet here in the United States in the midst of this so-called democracy we have a dictator who operates with impunity."[40] Vietnam veterans who felt they had been treated as expendable by their government returned to the mines to find they were apparently expendable underground as well as overseas, making them one of the MFD's key pillars of support in the 1972 campaign.[41]

As calls for civil rights transformed into demands for Black power and a global struggle for decolonization interwove demands for democracy and self-determination, Black, Indigenous, and Chicano miners played critical organizational roles in the reform movement while also criticizing the fact the MFD elected an all-white slate.[42] Indigenous and Chicano miners figured more prominently in the western fields, while Black miners like Robert Payne, Charles Brooks, and Bill Worthington led important organizations like the Black Lung Association and the Disabled Miners and Widows of Southern West Virginia.[43] Johnny Mendez, a working Mexican American miner from southern West Virginia, was the most prominent working member of the reform movement in an area of the coalfields better remembered for the activism of disabled miners like Arnold Miller and Robert Payne.[44] Black disabled miners, like Rufus Brooks, whose home was destroyed in the Buffalo Creek disaster, organized against strip mining. Bill Finley, a Black miner from western Pennsylvania who strongly criticized the MFD's failure to include Black candidates on the slate, also volunteered to campaign for the MFD among Black miners in McDowell County, West Virginia—a stronghold of Black political life in Appalachia.[45] Like many Black labor activists in U.S. history, Black MFD supporters navigated the sometimes tense relationship between building the organizations to which they committed their time and skill and ensuring that those organizations addressed the challenges specifically faced by Black workers.[46] Black and other minoritized miners played a critical role in organizing and in the reform movement despite its limits because they, too, believed in democracy—and saw its potential to address persistent issues of employment discrimination and underrepresentation in union leadership.[47]

Democracy as a unifying principle heightened the importance of the jobs, lives, and land platform because it gave a clear content to the MFD's vision of democracy at a moment where globally the meaning and future of democratic politics were uncertain, contested, and thus apt for reconfiguration.[48] The MFD consciously situated their claims to democracy in an American tradition of political rights that would have been instantly legible to citizens outside the coalfields. Jobs, lives, and land closely mirrored life, liberty, and property, which since the founding of the United States in the eighteenth century had been widely accepted as foundational to the American political experiment without ever having a settled meaning. Contestation over the relationship between these natural rights and the nation's political development sat at the center of some of the largest fissures in the nation's history. Claims about the character and content of these rights had been marshaled to abolish slavery, extend voting rights to African Americans and women, and legalize labor unions. The jobs, lives, and land platform distilled these abstract natural rights into a set of concrete demands. It tied the Miners for Democracy's key platform document— the "Miner's Bill of Rights"—to a deeper American political tradition in content as well as form.

The genealogy of the "Miners' Bill of Rights" explicitly called back to the nation's founding myths. It sought to cement the union reform movement as quintessentially American, thus seeking to avoid the toxic political atmosphere that had seriously undermined the labor movement in the postwar years. During the 1950s Red Scare, anticommunist witch hunts targeted some of the nation's most prominent labor leaders and advocates, usually with the support of union officials.[49] But the MFD's alignment could not be reduced to tactical positioning. The charges of "communism," "outside agitators," and "dual unionists" came regardless, even at the height of U.S.-Soviet détente. Far from an expedient rhetorical move, the tripartite set of claims—of rights to jobs, lives, and land—reflected real shifts in how reform-minded miners understood the relationship between energy, political life, and the nation's economy. The Miners for Democracy, as an organized expression of these beliefs, contradictory and contentious as they were, opened a brief period of unprecedented change inside the United Mine Workers, which allowed miners to question the norms of their industry even as they sought to intervene in the way that their jobs mediated the relationship between the nation's energy system and their lives and land.

The "Miners' Bill of Rights" defined exactly what democracy and citizenship meant in a coal-fired energy system. The foundational right on which democracy and citizenship were built was "a safe and healthy working environment" because safety, the MFD contended, was "the right to life itself." Certainly, the MFD saw the companies as a major obstacle to safe mines, but it was the failure of democratic institutions—the federal and state governments and their own union—which they ultimately saw as more concerning. Those were the very institutions that could contravene the companies' drive for profit. Instead, coal miners had been left to face industrial slaughter in an age of "tremendous technological progress"— one that could "send men to the moon and back safely" but could not ensure a miner would survive a shift underground. The federal government had proven itself more interested in "crime on the street" than in the crimes being committed underground each day, and the UMW had enabled that inattention.[50] The consequences of that inattention were underscored for Mike Trbovich as the MFD composed the Miners' Bill of Rights, when his friend and coworker Tony Gallo was pulled into a roller and crushed to death—only a month before Gallo had planned to retire.[51]

The MFD platform focused its attention on the union's relationship with the federal government to ensure miners' safety. They demanded that "law-and-order" be applied on the job and insisted that they would put the government on notice: "no coal will be mined unless it is mined in working conditions that meet the letter and spirit of the law." To effect this change, the MFD looked not simply to new leadership at the international but to the everyday activity of the membership: extending the authority of local safety committees to evaluate the safety of a worksite and to take an active and leading role in dust sampling. While miners were certainly up against "production-oriented" bureaucracy in their union and the federal government, the MFD recognized that miners had significant leverage over the federal government, which didn't need any more energy problems to deal with—like unanticipated coal strikes.[52]

The "right to life itself" extended beyond ending the maiming and killing in the mines. It also extended to the black lung crisis and the rights of disabled miners. Addressing the problem required the MFD to gesture simultaneously in two directions. First, they pointed out that disabled miners had sacrificed "their health to produce coal for America's needs," and, as such, they were entitled to a pension and benefits that allowed them and their families to live "not just decently, but well." The MFD would not accept an energy system in which union leaders, politicians, and operators felt "content to discard these human beings." They demanded investments in regional hospitals and black lung clinics and an expansion of the tests, procedures, and care covered. The MFD also sought to upend the moral calculus that had prioritized cheap energy over miners' lungs and limbs. If compensating disabled miners offered restitution for the harms of the nation's energy system it was too late to undo, the MFD also contended that the black lung compensation program set up in the 1969 Federal Coal Mine Health and Safety Act was "totally inadequate," for it was not acceptable "merely to pay a man once his health has been destroyed by dust." If the right to life was to have content, "the conditions that cause black lung must be stamped out."[53] The MFD refused to accept a mining industry and energy system where disability was "an inevitability."[54]

If disability was preventable, the MFD contended, so were the other harms of coal extraction. The Miners' Bill of Rights turned its attention to the problem of surface mining, which the Kentucky antistripping activist Harry Caudill had described as "an ecological nightmare of unimaginable dimensions [that] suddenly looms everywhere."[55] Strip mining extracted energy and wealth from the region, offered little employment in return, and devastated the landscape. By 1972, however, surface miners made up nearly a third of the UMW's membership, and the MFD could not afford to alienate them. Miller, a stripping abolitionist, was forced to moderate his position. Addressing strip mining required careful consideration of the relationship between miners' work and the broader environment. The Miners for Democracy's effort to straddle both the ecological and jobs crisis was not only the product of Miller's own staunch antistripping position but a response to a volatile situation that was exploding across the Appalachian coalfields—sometimes literally, like one 1972 incident where someone dynamited a $250,000 bulldozer—as Appalachian residents rose up against the destruction of their home.[56] From the MFD's perspective, the expansion of strip mining was both a source of environmental degradation *and* a source of displacement for underground miners, since it took far fewer workers to strip coal out of the ground than to extract it with underground mining methods, even in highly mechanized underground mines. Bringing together both underground and strip miners to draft the platform, "The Miners' Bill of Rights" ultimately argued that:

> No group is more concerned about protecting our country's streams and countryside than members of the UMW. Coal miners must live where the coal is mined and they are the group that suffers when the land is raped and the streams are polluted. There is no question that irresponsible coal operators are putting profit before responsibility. There are many areas, particularly in mountainous terrain, where coal companies have failed to claim or restore the land. This has resulted in the destruction of coal miners' homes and property. UMW Miners for Democracy believes that strong reclamation laws are required to force coal operators to reclaim the land that is strip mined. Our primary concern is to ensure that BOTH jobs and land are protected.
>
> We believe that proper reclamation requirements are essential and that new union jobs would be created if the laws were expanded and enforced. . . . Expanded reclamation requirements . . . should be enacted and all reclamation work should be done by UMW members under contract.
>
> Many coal operators believe the word reclamation means spreading a little grass seed on exposed rock. To MFD, reclamation means restoring the land to constructive use. The UMW must insist on restoration. Where reclamation is absolutely impossible, coal operators should not be allowed to ravage the land.[57]

The statement articulated a clear vision in which energy jobs and environmental protection were not at odds and aligned the MFD environmental platform with the environmentalist concerns for "quality of life," which drove early policy efforts for clean air and water.[58] It stood in stark contrast with an increasingly common framework that saw energy production and environmental protection as opposing goals that had to be balanced in national policy rather than pursued together. In doing so, it suggested that both job loss and environmental destruction were a manmade disaster driven by the same underlying cause. They laid the blame for the clearly apparent environmental destruction taking place on the Appalachian hillsides with the coal companies and with the state and federal governments that had failed to protect their citizens' jobs and land through proper regulation. The problem was a coal-fired social contract out of balance, not *necessarily* the coal itself.

The MFD rejected the idea that miners' jobs had to come at the expense of the environment. Indeed, the practice of strip mining was not only a major source of environmental destruction across Appalachia, but it also furthered the process of mechanization, replacing underground mining employment with fewer jobs that were more akin to heavy construction jobs. According to James Stenger, who drafted an internal report for the MFD on the growing energy crisis, "a strong environmentalist stance" was the best defense for coal miners' jobs because the implementation of strong environmental regulations would force the externalized costs of coal production—including miners' lungs, lives, and land—to be considered in energy production and policy decisions. The companies had ignored the "real costs of energy production by charging it up on our major public asset—the environment." But rather than seeing miners as intrinsic to this cycle of ecological destruction, which implicated both industry and government, in the age of environmentalism, Stenger identified the very existence of externalities as potential leverage: if the real cost of ecological destruction was passed on to the consumer, "a serious conflict would develop between the need for energy and the ability of the consumer to pay for it. This would force the development of really clean production technologies—the only real cheap technologies."[59] By identifying environmental protection as a point of political and bargaining leverage rather than a liability for future employment, moreover, the MFD turned the old administration's approach on its head; Boyle had spent the bulk of the 1960s campaigning against air and water pollution regulations alongside his antinuclear campaign. The MFD, in contrast, sought to defend jobs by defending the land.

The MFD campaign literature specifically targeted to strip miners furthered this argument. It foregrounded Miller's interest in restoration but promised to "protect jobs and the land" by fighting for stronger reclamation laws. He cited his successful work to have the West Virginia reclamation laws amended so they would have "teeth." Because under the amended laws the operators "were required to reclaim the land and post bonds to see that they did," the MFD claimed that "the number of men working on reclamation in the state has tripled." Miller promised that "all reclamation [would be] done under UMWA contract."[60] Surface miners like Bruce Patton came out in "support [of] Miller's position on responsible mining. Coal miners and their families live where the coal is stripped. They're the ones who suffer from irresponsible mining.... Miller's position makes sense. It means job protection."[61] While this platform stopped short of full abolition, some antistripping activists believed that if reclamation laws could be made strict enough, it would halt the surface mining entirely and in effect would have the same impact as an outright ban.[62] This vision of the coal mining workplace imagined a new relationship for miners with the land, one in which extractive labor went hand in hand with intensive restorative work.

The MFD's position, that it was possible to produce coal in a way that was compatible with robust environmental protections, easily appears anachronistic—even outlandish—to us today, where our understanding of coal's polluting effects includes, and indeed centers on, the carbon dioxide released by burning coal for energy. While a growing body of historical scholarship on climate change and climate science has shown that knowledge of the role of greenhouse gases in global heating existed by the 1970s, this science was not understood by most ordinary people (in part because the energy companies suppressed information or engaged in disinformation campaigns), and it did not figure centrally in American environmental politics of the decade.[63] Given that the wide-ranging impact of coal production and consumption was most powerfully observed in the direct vicinity of mine and combustion sites, as well as in growing concern about coal's sulfur content, the MFD's focus on expanding underground coal production, reclaiming strip sites, protecting water supplies, and developing technology to clean coal before combustion reflected the policy priorities of clean air and water and was in line with other environmentalists of the time.

While certainly outdated, the MFD's position on strip mining nonetheless emerged from a regulatory environment that had placed a heavy emphasis on cleanups of air and water: a reclamation of public resources and an intervention in public health crises caused by pollution.[64] Their position allowed them to wed opposition to strip mining to their mine safety platform, to connect the Hyden disaster with the devastating flood on Buffalo Creek. Their approach to confronting the harms wreaked by the coal-fired social contract countered the idea that the dangers of the mining workplace emanated from the volatile gases and unstable rock formations and mining waste that coal mining produced. Instead, the MFD charged that the reason that mines were unsafe was because the government and the companies had made them so. The "Miners' Bill of Rights" centered on the disjuncture between the terms of the coal-fired social contract as it had been negotiated in the aftermath of World War II and the rights that miners felt were their due as the nation's coal-producing citizens.[65] The MFD was a union reform movement but also an effort to restructure power in the region to better represent miners in their role as energy citizens, people whose bonds with the rest of the nation ran along coal-fired electric power lines.

Arnold Miller, Mike Trbovich, and Harry Patrick spent the next six months taking the MFD's campaign "to the bathhouses," a campaign site meant to emphasize their connections with the rank and file.[66] Harry Patrick explained that the strategy was simple: "We'll always be on the offensive. Let them hammer away that we're communists." The MFD focused their attention on "the progressive things that make a union."[67] Being on the offensive, however, entailed a lot of self-defense. Arnold Miller understood that Boyle or his supporters might resort to violence once again and that, especially as he traveled outside the reform movement strongholds, his life was in danger. But he firmly believed "we had to demonstrate that we're not going to be intimidated by this fear. . . . No one's going to tell me where to go in this country."[68] Campaign staff wanted to hire Miller a bodyguard. Such concern was understandable. As the *Boston Globe* columnist Mary McGrory quipped: "Running against Boyle is a hazardous business, almost as hazardous as mining coal."[69] Miller refused the extra protection: "I faced danger all my life."[70] Of himself, Trbovich, and Patrick, he insisted, "We're all combat veterans . . . capable of handling ourselves in a tight spot."[71] Still, campaign staff installed new, more sophisticated locks on Miller's doors and placed a spotlight in the backyard to make it harder for an intruder to approach the house unseen. Miller's travel reservations were placed under pseudonyms, and when he went to campaign in Alabama, four state police were on hand to assure his safety.[72] In some regions, he let it be known he was armed as he traveled. Since he had "some reputation as a combat veteran," he felt any potential attackers would know he could defend himself.[73]

If Miller emphasized his experience as a machine gunner to try to ward off potential attacks, the campaign also emphasized the military service of all three MFD candidates to paint them as citizens who understood their obligations both to their fellow miners and to the broader country. Bob Gergley felt the slate gained credibility in two ways—first, because they had "over eighty years' experience collectively in the mines," and second, because "each has fought for their country."[74] It was only one of the ways that reform-minded miners used the space opened by the campaign to articulate the relationship between their status as coal miners and their status as citizens and the way that these identities were inextricable from each other. The Pennsylvania miner Fred Scott warned that allowing "demagogues" to continue to run the union would "create pollution and ruin our Democratic way of life." He denounced "men who would demerit their rights and liberties as free Americans to spread Nepotism and Despotism into the ranks of the labor force." Instead, Scott called for "a program for equal rights and justice" because "every mine worker in our nation must now take a stand for his freedom and rights as an American citizen."[75] Another MFD miner, Bill Singer, justified his support for the MFD because he was "an American citizen."[76] Virgil Debaum believed that Boyle's corruption, by robbing him of "his pension, his pride, his dignity, and his membership in a powerful working man's union," had infringed on his rights as an American.[77]

When miners cast their votes in early December, MFD voters did so conscious of these wider meanings of their decision, of the history in which it was embedded, and of the future they hoped to build. Indeed, many older miners saw themselves as protecting the legacy of the struggles in the 1930s and the way they saw those struggles as written into the nation's laws by Franklin D. Roosevelt.[78] One miner, recalling the days before the New Deal, recounted having "to see 4 gun thuggs whip my father [and] call there self Peace Officers for the big Coal Co." In this miner's view, President Roosevelt had put a stop to that thuggery, and Tony Boyle didn't have the right to undo it. He hoped the MFD would kick out Boyle and that miners could elect people who would *really* represent them in the halls of government.[79] These sentiments spoke to the fact that miners could see the structure of coalfield power, negotiated decades earlier, collapsing around them. The boundary between efforts to democratize the union and broader concerns about the future of American democracy often blurred, as did the rights of citizenship with the rights of union membership.

Labor Department officials began counting the ballots in their Silver Spring, Maryland, office on December 12, 1972, guarded by an "elaborate" security detail, under the careful eye of election observers from Boyle's office and the MFD as well as the national media. The first votes counted came from Ebensburg, Pennsylvania—Boyle's campaign headquarters. Officials removed seventeen ballots from the box. Miller received ten, and Boyle only seven.[80] By the end of the first shift, however, Boyle led Miller by 553 votes.[81] For the rest of the week, 120 Labor Department vote tabulators would work around the clock, forty to a shift, to count 126,707 votes.[82] Miller took the lead by the end of day two, as Boyle struggled in locals where he had thought he would win big, and Miller's lead widened further on day three of the count.[83] By the end of the week, it was clear that the MFD had won even though the Department of Labor had yet to certify the vote. Walter Cronkite, of CBS News, informed the nation that Boyle's headquarters looked "pretty gloomy."[84]

In their home just southeast of Beckley, West Virginia, Donald and Jeanne Rasmussen—two of the reform movement's biggest supporters—prepared for a Christmas party. They were thrilled with the vote returns. The Christmas party would also be a victory party. Arnold Miller, along with Mike Trbovich and Harry Patrick, planned to drive down from the vote count in Silver Spring to celebrate, but the snowy weather was making it difficult. Still, even without the guests of honor, the mood was jubilant. Many of the attendees were miners who had given every spare minute of the previous six months to secure Miller's victory. Then the phone rang. Eight miners, a section crew who would have been working as a group, had not returned for the 4 PM shift change at Itmann, a massive mining complex operated by a subsidiary of Consolidation Coal.[85]

At the Rasmussen house, the joyful atmosphere quickly turned solemn. Dan Burleson, the vice president of the Itmann local and district co-chair of "Miners for Miller," quickly left the party to make the treacherous drive through the snow to the mine site, to await news from the rescue crews searching for the missing miners.[86] Over the coming hours, the events that turned a night of triumph into a sobering reminder of energy violence would become clearer. When the men had not returned, mine management went underground to investigate but were quickly turned back by heavy smoke at the entry to the section where the miners had been working. Rescue teams made their way into the mine, installing ventilation to clear out smoke, methane, and carbon monoxide as they went. It took nearly three hours to find the first miner. Larry Bailey had managed to put on his self-rescuer, which allowed him to breathe despite the gas and crawl 550 feet up the mine tunnel. Despite serious injuries, he was alive. Thirty minutes later, rescuers found the rest of the crew. Two others had survived the blast with severe injuries and burns. The blast had killed the other five: shuttle car operator and local union president Bill Hatfield, roof bolter Teddy McMillion, general laborer David Meador, and two young brothers, Nathan and Larry Akers, only twenty-seven and twenty-four years old.[87] Arnold Miller did not make it to the Rasmussen party. Instead of celebrating, he spent seven hours the next day at the Itmann mine, demanding answers and "express[ing] his disgust." Miller was sick of "telegrams of regret, people saying they're sorry."[88] Boyle appeared to wash his hands of the whole thing; he resigned the presidency that weekend—before the Labor Department had even certified the vote tally.[89]

News media quickly picked up on the fact that the Itmann mine complex was operated by a subsidiary of Consolidation Coal, in turn owned by Continental Oil. The media were equally quick to remind the public that Consolidation Coal also owned the Consol No. 9 mine in the northern reaches of the state where seventy-eight miners had been killed four years earlier.[90] But as was so often the case, media focus on the "major" disasters obscured the everyday violence of the mining workplace, and the Itmann mining complex was plenty violent on its own. In 1972, four other miners had already been killed in the Itmann mines. A roof fall killed Roger Sizemore in January.[91] Two months later, a collapsed mine rib pinned Van Crockett Dillon, who survived long enough to reach the ambulance but died of internal bleeding on the way to the hospital.[92] The chief electrician in the Itmann No. 2 was crushed to death in July, and in November, beltman Van Shrewsbury Jr. became ensnared in a cable that pulled him under a runaway mine car, killing him instantly.[93] In addition to the fatal accidents, three miners had been injured in a smaller January explosion. In the eleven and a half months leading up to the December 15 explosion, the Bureau of Mines had ordered workers withdrawn from the No. 3 mine four times and cited the company for eighty-nine safety violations.[94]

According to J. Davitt McAteer, an MFD supporter, this kind of safety record fit into a pattern of energy inequality that could be traced through company profits as well as the nation's energy system. Continental Oil/ Consolidation Coal made profits by "get[ting] the coal out at all costs"—and then leaving miners and their communities to pay the bill. As President Nixon deployed street lighting around Washington, DC, "in an effort to make the nation's Capital safe [with] electricity generated from coal mined in West Virginia," in the coal towns of Logan County, West Virginia, streetlights were nonexistent.[95] This disparity, to McAteer, underscored that the "safety" offered by electric illumination was not a safety on equal offer to all Americans. Instead, West Virginia miners died to make Washingtonians feel more secure. It was an old story, but Arnold Miller, who had spent a lot of time thinking about what it might take to democratize a coal-fired society and who had devoted years of his life to making the promises of coal-fired democracy mean something for the workers who mined that coal, was now the president-elect of the United Mine Workers.

By Monday morning, Miller was back in Washington, DC, for his first television interview as the UMW's president-elect on NBC's *Today Show*. He castigated Consolidation Coal for its abysmal safety record and made it clear that since the Bureau of Mines didn't seem particularly interested in enforcing the law, miners would have to take things into their own hands: "The general public in this country had just as well face up to the fact that coal is vital to everything in this country. And they may be asked to pay a little bit [more] so we can provide a decent benefit program for miners. This is the way I see it, and this is the way that the membership accepted during the campaign. . . . We think it's time that everyone be a little bit more concerned about the coal miners in this country."[96]

As the MFD took over the UMW's Washington offices that winter, it was clear that the MFD's victory marked the end of one era and the beginning of a new one. Miners, exhilarated with their victory, wandered the halls, some wearing hardhats. One miner sat down at Boyle's old desk, sarcastically imitating the way Boyle had signed "sweetheart contracts"—agreements that relieved companies from royalty payments in the name of preserving their market competitiveness. His joke was met with cheers and guffaws. The mood was festive.[97]

Behind the exuberance, the results of the 1972 election revealed the uneven geography of the reform movement as well as some of the challenges that Miller would confront during his years in office. Although Miller carried 55.5 percent of the vote overall, he won only ten of the union's twenty-two districts. The voting patterns reflected years of organization building and political struggle. Miller's support was most heavily concentrated in districts where the fight for black lung legislation had been the strongest and where the ratio of pensioners to active miners was more even. Miller's largest margin of victory came in the anthracite district of eastern Pennsylvania, where he won 83 percent of the vote, but he handily won most of West Virginia, Pennsylvania, Ohio, and Virginia. Other key victories came from District 15 in Colorado and New Mexico, as well as Illinois, which he carried by a nearly 2–1 margin. Boyle carried both Kentucky and Alabama, as well as the Plains districts, Arkansas, and most of the West.[98] This geography represented coming challenges: deepening organization in Alabama, where the state's coal operators had been steadily increasing their role in coal export markets; organizing the western states as the geography of coal production and thus the potential geography of miners' power, began to shift; and, finally, organizing the growing number of nonunion outfits across Appalachia.[99]

Even in the MFD strongholds throughout central Appalachia, coalfield unrest continued, and the energy crisis loomed ever larger. The MFD administration would have to contend with the fact that democracy was not an idea that could be applied like a salve. For all the MFD's attempts to transform the traditional American appeal of life, liberty, and property into a concrete set of demands around economic security, workplace safety, and environmental protection, miners' definition of democracy, rights, and citizenship also remained malleable and thus unsettled. Precisely because the stakes of the 1972 election extended far beyond Boyle's ouster and instead marked miners' reimagination of their relationship with the rest of the country, the election results could hardly be expected to resolve the deeper challenges facing the renegotiated coal-fired social contract.

PART FOUR

Bounding
(1973–1981)

Third Interlude

East and West

The United Mine Workers convened their December 1973 constitutional convention under incredible circumstances. The country was entering the second month of an Arab oil embargo, accompanied by escalating production cuts meant to censure the United States for its support of Israel in the 1973 Arab-Israeli War. The Organization of Petroleum Exporting Countries (OPEC) had also raised prices earlier in the fall, amplifying the impact of these actions in international oil markets.[1] By the end of October, the United States faced a constitutional crisis as well, after President Nixon ordered the firing of Archibald Cox, the Watergate special prosecutor. Impeachment investigations were well underway by the time miners' elected delegates gathered in December, calling into question Nixon's ability to exercise legitimate authority over the nation's energy system. It was indeed an auspicious moment for the miners to rewrite their constitution, the *Pittsburgh Post-Gazette* concluded: "The energy crisis suddenly has hit the American public hard, with oil shortages pointing directly to coal as an absolutely essential long-range answer. Obviously, the attitudes of the men who go deep into the bowels of the earth to extract this fuel are important, as is the ongoing philosophy of their union."[2]

As turmoil engulfed the United States, the UMW put their hard-won democracy to the test, outlining their understanding of the renegotiated coal-fired social contract in a hotel ballroom in downtown Pittsburgh. The delegates came prepared to redefine themselves, their place in the labor movement, and in the nation. The UMW's new president, Arnold Miller, having completed his first year in office, was no exception. He used his first "State of the Union" address to offer a version of the nation's history with the coal miner at its center. Some of Miller's interpretations would have been familiar to anyone who had long been listening. He presented miners as "the front-line troops" of the nation's industrial growth, workers toiling in dark, dirty, and dangerous mines "to fuel the nation's progress." He also placed coal miners in a settler-colonial genealogy of men who "helped tame the western frontier"—another rhetorical strategy the UMW had deployed in earlier years to affirm miners' political status. Yet he also noted that around the convention hall one could meet miners who were the grandchildren of people who had been enslaved and expect to encounter a wide array of foreign accents. These facts, to Miller, illustrated his belief that the union was a citizen-making institution, one that cemented in miners' understanding of their own national belonging an obligation to serve the nation.

Miller drew on this understanding to make clear that the UMW was "the finest group of working men in the world" ready to "come to the nation's aid," prepared to help right an "upside down system of allocating the nation's energy resources." As the country faced an energy crisis, he affirmed that the nation could rely on American coal miners to help solve a heady problem. But the fact that miners served the nation first, he argued, now needed qualification: "No coal miner today is willing to repeat the history of his father and his grandfathers who labored their lives away in the bowels of the earth to fuel the nation's progress and reaped as their reward a back bent like a stunted tree and lungs . . . full of coal dust. The pick and shovel days are over."[3]

Miller's speech read as a natural outgrowth of his own political thought as well as the swell of miners' activism that had ended with his election the previous December. But equally, it read as a rebuff to President Nixon's address on the energy crisis one week earlier. Nixon, in announcing a series of measures intended to draw down the nation's oil consumption, had reiterated his commitment to energy independence because this kind of independence, he argued, best summed up the nation's "essential character." Once the United States became truly energy independent, Nixon said, "Americans will not have to rely on any source of energy beyond our own" to ensure the "plentiful supplies of energy which helped to build the greatest industrial nation and one of the highest standards of living in the world."[4] However, Miller's speech and four years of coalfield rebellion made clear that the burdens and benefits of the United States' coal-fired energy system had accrued unequally. Nixon's "Project Independence" masked a second story of *dependence* on cheap American coal and the miners who extracted it. It was miners, Miller contended, as much as coal that had created national prosperity. What Nixon and many others cast as supply-and-demand problems with short-, medium-, and long-range implications, Miller presented as evidence of a system of "upside-down" priorities and energy system inequality. The time had come, Miller said, "to bring the blessings of coal—not merely to the nation and the giant corporations—but to the men who mine it." Modern coal miners were modern citizens, unwilling to sacrifice their lives, bodies, and land with nothing to show for it.[5]

After affirming that coal miners' role in energy production defined their national belonging, Miller also outlined the UMW's vision of what the renegotiated coal-fired social contract entailed in language fitting the historical moment: energy security. The UMW's new leadership understood that the atmosphere of national emergency might be presented by industry and political leaders as a justification for backsliding on mine safety and environmental protection. Miller moved quickly to assert his opposition to any gutting of miners' hard-won rights. In exchange for extracting coal from the nation's massive reserves to power the country, miners insisted they were entitled to the protection of robust and responsive regulatory structures to guard miners' lives and land as well as more meaningful representation in the federal government. Miller contended that these changes, rooted in coalfield struggles and workplace organizing, would democratize the nation's energy system and make it more secure.[6]

For Miller, the nation's energy insecurity resulted from decades of government failure to curb oil companies, which had pursued their own profits at the expense of the public. President Nixon, Miller charged, offered only "makeshift solutions like turning down our thermostats [while] he leaves the long-range decision on energy to the people who got us in this mess in the first place."[7] The UMW would undertake an extended set of legislative activities with its newly formed Coal Miners' Political Action Committee, or COMPAC. Additionally, drawing on his longstanding belief that miners should represent themselves in political offices, Miller said that coal miners would start running for office. "We proved this year that coal miners can run an International Union," Miller told the gathered delegates. "In the years to come, I think we'll prove that coal miners can help run a State legislature too, or a Congress."[8] In Miller's vision, energy security came from recognizing the rights and obligations citizens had in a democratic energy system, a vision that reflected miners' democratic aspirations and their desire for a greater political voice in the nation.

According to the coalfield "fighting preacher" James Somerville, who offered a prayer to the convention chock full of political argument, coal miners—"stewards of this black gold"—had been presented "a new kind of opportunity, a new potential, a new power, perhaps even greater than that which this union has had in the time of war."[9] But although responses to the energy crisis often evoked the memory of World War II and Cold War visions of national security, the energy at the center of policy debates in the 1970s was not energy for making war but instead for stabilizing a society whose bonds appeared increasingly frayed.[10] Americans increasingly understood industrially, commercially, and residentially consumed electricity as basic to social functioning, political governability, and economic prosperity.[11]

Because of energy's undeniable importance in nearly every facet of American life, and because coal was the country's most bountiful fossil fuel, the nation's energy system would remain intimately tied to the workers who mined it for the foreseeable future. According to Russell Train, the Environmental Protection Agency's administrator, "During your lifetime, and for at least the next generation of miners, most of America's energy must come from coal." Because much of the "load" of energy security would be borne "on [miners'] shoulders and on those of the new miners you must train," he insisted that the nation "must do whatever is necessary to insure the health and safety of the miners and their families, and the integrity of the environment in which they live." Train's vision sought to reframe coal mining as a new form of energetic "husbandry." By relying on coal, energetic growth could be managed for political, social, and environmental stability, and that stability would, in turn, be secured by allowing coal miners to play a larger role in the nation's energy governance.[12]

The convention demonstrated that coal miners were operating with a new understanding of the coal-fired social contract, one that emphasized American dependency on coal. It was also true that the United States' energy dependencies were global and shifting. And it was equally true that the U.S. energy system increasingly depended on petroleum, too. The 1970s and the energy crisis emphasized, once again, the connections between the Appalachian coalfields and the global energy system of which they were part. While the energy crisis, as miners knew, was about much more than oil, and while politicians worried about not only oil but also natural gas shortages and utility financing, the oil shock of 1973 came to be seen as an energy crisis all its own. The oil-centric narrative of the crisis often threatened to obscure the way other fuels, political processes, and social formations also called into question the energy-intensive liberalism of the New Deal Order. The oil shock's distorting impact on many Americans' understanding of how their energy system worked was a form of what the historian Christopher Jones has termed "petromyopia."[13]

Yet the politics of coal and oil were intimately linked. By 1973, power over the world's oil supply had largely shifted from the major oil firms and into the hands of OPEC nations. At the same time, Nixon moved the dollar off the gold standard, the long-range impact of U.S. efforts to promote international steel production came to fruition, and U.S.-Soviet détente shifted global trade patterns. These larger changes, combined with the toll of the American defeat in Vietnam, were harbingers of declining American hegemony.[14] Although the changing politics of coal was most visible domestically during the 1970s, it didn't take much digging to connect the U.S. coalfields with global oil politics.[15] Americans would largely make sense of coal's global entanglements by describing a world torn between East and West, deploying Orientalist language, imagery, or metaphors to make such claims legible.[16] As the Nixon administration stared down OPEC in the fall of 1973, they concluded that the United States *could* match the Arabs in the global energy scene. They could make the United States "the Saudi Arabia of coal."[17]

What did it mean to suggest that the United States was the Saudi Arabia of coal, as would be claimed many more times before the end of the decade?[18] For most commentators who deployed the idea, it referred to the size of nation's coal reserves compared to almost every other coal-producing nation. Usually left implicit was the power that asymmetry lent the United States to shape global coal prices and markets, particularly for metallurgical coal exported globally for steel production. While the prices for exported U.S. coal did increase enormously during the decade, coal in the United States remained a largely domestic affair. Becoming the Saudi Arabia of coal was meant to signal *independence* of the U.S. energy system from Arab oil producers rather than to emphasize the *dependence* of U.S. trading partners like Japan on the United States' ability to set coal prices. President Gerald Ford painted coal as "an *American* answer—not one based on uncertain resources in faraway lands with different ideas and diverse interests. It represents our hope for the future."[19]

Coal's advocates had long portrayed coal as uniquely American, though that depiction obscured the fraught history of the eastern coalfields and the persistence of contested sovereignty claims to western reserves. While coal had been mined in the American West for decades, its use had been relatively marginal compared to the more energy-dense bituminous and anthracite coals found east of the Mississippi River. It was also located far from the largest coal-consuming markets. However, as air pollution regulations tightened, western coal became more appealing. Although western coal was usually far less energy-dense than eastern coal, it also, on average, contained far less sulfur—one of the key pollutants targeted by the Clean Air Act.[20] This low-sulfur coal seemed tantalizingly close to the surface, much easier to strip out with giant machines compared to the rough terrain that defined much of the Appalachian landscape. But the coal companies would have to navigate the political terrain of Indigenous and federal landholding, as well as the land claims of ranchers who relied on vast swaths of the area for grazing their herds.[21]

The westward shift in U.S. coal production unleashed similar, related political processes as the shift in oil power to the Middle East. Anticolonial claims on resource sovereignty not only shaped *international* energy markets, but they also challenged the structure of energy production within the United States' claimed territory, particularly the Great Plains and Southwest. Indigenous nations across the West—especially the Hopi, Navajo, Crow, and Northern Cheyenne nations—drew on Third World examples like OPEC to prevent another colonial resource grab on their land and, sometimes, as described by the historian Andrew Needham, to get "a piece of the action" in the new coal boom.[22] In 1975, one wing of the movement for resource sovereignty created a self-styled "Indian OPEC," the Council of Energy Resource Tribes, or CERT, to help ensure that the wealth generated by extracted tribal energy resources stayed in Indigenous hands. In the pages of the *Atlantic*, Wallace and Page Stegner dubbed these resource nationalists the "Arabs of the Plains."[23] The specter of the "East" and the Orientalism that shaped the United States' relationship with Middle Eastern nations also molded the politics of coal as the locus of the nation's coal production shifted westward. While Indigenous energy nationalists drew on OPEC's model and reportedly sought advice from OPEC advisors, designating the leaders of CERT as the "Arabs of the Plains" also drew together two connected histories of racialization and empire to suggest that greedy "others" withheld energy resources at the expense of "real"—settler—Americans.[24]

The UMW, with its base of power in the East, struggled to adapt to this changing geography. The UMW had always been relatively weak in the West, and many of the companies opening mines in the region went to great lengths to hire workers who they believed would be unlikely to unionize. The new MFD leadership pledged to organize the Western fields, but the cultural divide between the Eastern and Western coalfields was substantial. Moreover, the geography and work practices of the big strip mines that dominated the region amplified the challenges of organizing. Miners often rode to work on company buses, sometimes two or more hours away from their homes, and the "big sky" landscape facilitated company surveillance over large swaths of territory. Work in the Western strip mines also tended to be isolating—sitting alone while driving a large truck, communicating over the radio—and knowing the boss was listening.[25] The UMW faced internal challenges too. While the UMW had an important minority of Indigenous membership in the West, issues of discrimination within the union as well as on worksites persisted, sometimes driving a wedge between Indigenous and white members.[26] For all these reasons, the new UMW leadership ultimately failed to fulfill their campaign promise to organize the West, a fact that seriously undermined the union's bargaining power later in the decade. Increasingly, the American coal that industry leaders and politicians were looking to as an integral part of solving the nation's energy problems was no longer union coal.

The threat that loss of union density in the industry posed was amplified when the Southern Company—one of the country's largest utilities, providing electricity across the South—planned to import coal from South African at the cost of $47 million, with the first ship due to arrive in Mobile, Alabama, in July 1974.[27] The company attested that the imported coal would be low in sulfur and then burned in pilot plants where Southern would "study methods of purifying smokestack discharges," thus helping the company meet new environmental quality standards.[28] According to a senior executive at Southern, South Africa was "the only place in the world" with coal low enough in sulfur to meet Florida's clean air requirements.[29] This claim was spurious. There were low-sulfur coals available in other countries too, including the United States. The industry members interviewed by the *United Mine Workers Journal* suggested the real story was about keeping prices low and avoiding signing long-term contracts, the kind that would result in the opening of new mines.[30]

The move by Southern sent shockwaves throughout the United Mine Workers, particularly in Alabama, where many coal miners had once worked extracting iron ore, only to be laid off when the region's steel companies began importing iron ore from Venezuela instead.[31] With the new leadership at the head of the UMW, however, and with increased opposition in the United States to South Africa's apartheid regime, the response to these threatened imports differed from the UMW's response to Venezuelan imports in the 1950s, instead emphasizing the human suffering that made the South African coal cheap.[32] Arnold Miller told the press, "South African coal is cheap for one reason only . . . because it is mined at the expense of human beings."[33]

The UMW response not only highlighted the potential for imported coal to cause layoffs in Alabama mines but also suggested that if the Southern Company was allowed to import South African coal over coal produced by union miners in the United States, it was subsidizing "slave labor" under the apartheid regime. "Slavery in the South went out a long time ago," recounted Howard Tedford, an Alabama miner. "We don't believe in slavery . . . it's my information that this coal is produced under slave labor conditions."[34] Miners reviled the working and living conditions in the South African coal camps—concentration camps, the UMW insisted—that worked men six days per week "until they are disabled," after which the miners were deported without ceremony. "South African Miners Live, Suffer, and Die in Slavery," read the text above a photo essay.[35]

The message was clear: importing South African coal didn't just threaten the jobs of U.S. miners; it also threatened to strengthen apartheid and its own form of coalfield autocracy. The struggle to protect jobs was connected to the South African fight for freedom. That sentiment was echoed by Mrs. John Marchant, a miner's wife and head of the Coalition to Stop South African Coal: "There are two fights, one here in this country, fighting the company for our jobs, the other in South Africa where the people are fighting for their freedom."[36] Arnold Miller warned that the Southern

Company's actions were but "the beginning of a dangerous trend." Consolidation Coal had also reportedly been scouting South African coal reserves.[37] It was, according to Miller, "a trend which American miners must bitterly oppose, for our own sake and for the sake of our exploited brother miners in South Africa."[38]

The possibility that the nation with the world's largest coal reserves might start importing coal and that companies might justify that importation by referencing tightening environmental regulations revealed something unsettling. In the *Journal*'s coverage as well as in the statements made by miners, the unease was palpable: coal imports threatened to break apart the political relationships that bound U.S. coal miners to the rest of the nation. Arnold Miller argued that the Southern Company had threatened the relationship between coal and the nation's future and that if the imports proceeded, the American energy crisis would be "solved through the misery and suffering of South African miners."[39] One rank-and-filer argued the companies would use the South African coal to generate electricity in the case of a strike, undercutting miners' leverage over the nation's electric power system (and how convenient that the national contract was due to expire that year).[40] In the 1950s and 1960s, UMW had tied the uniquely "American" qualities of coal to its purported affinity for free enterprise. But in the 1970s, the UMW emphasized using American coal in the United States as a core element of energy democracy both by denying financial support to the apartheid regime and by ensuring the continued salience of the coal-fired social contract in the United States. No one expressed the miners' position more clearly than Tom Youngblood, a miner from another Alabama local, who chastised the Southern Company Board of Directors at their annual meeting: "If you owe your allegiance to this country, then you get your coal from it."[41]

Still, the *Erredale* sailed into the port of Mobile, Alabama, on August 16, 1974, loaded with coal. Miners gathered with picket signs reading "Stamp Out Slave Labor" by the docks as the longshoremen unloaded the coal "under police guard." FBI agents were also on hand. The ship sailed under a British flag, but the Coast Guard confirmed to protesters the coal was South African. Later, the company would try to claim it was, in fact, Australian.[42] Despite the protests, the imports from South Africa continued, as did the UMW's criticism of them.[43] The imports hinted at the contingency of the national character of coal-fired energy in the United States, even as the UMW's MFD leadership had foregrounded miners' power as flowing from their political ties to other Americans. At the very moment the UMW had latched on to those coal-fired bonds between Americans as a primary source of the union's power, the changing geography of coal production called the viability of that perspective into question.

CHAPTER IX

Rights and Obligations

On the second day of the UMW's 1973 convention in Pittsburgh, a delegate interrupted Vice President Mike Trbovich, the day's presiding chair: "We delegates who sit in the back and toil in the underground coal mines are not used to this powerful source of illumination," he said. "We understand that it is for the convenience of the news media, but we are willing to share half an hour with the lights on and possibly then half an hour off."[1] Later that afternoon, after miners had switched off not only the lights but also the heat, Trbovich brought the issue to the open floor of the convention: "I thought it was only fair [to turn on the lights] . . . the people at Channel 13 . . . took all night to set up their cameras and equipment." The camera operators, he pointed out, were "in a bind now with their employer." But finally, somewhat exasperated, he conceded, "We leave it up to you people. . . . You will decide whether the lights shall stay on or they will go off."[2] It was one of many seemingly tangential debates at the convention, which journalists described as everything from freewheeling, if they felt charitable, to chaotic, if they did not.

Delegates ultimately voted to turn the lights on so the news crew could broadcast, allowing the new leadership could fulfill its pledge to transparency as they sought to reform their union. In later days, organizers managed to dim the bright lighting, which made it hard to see from the stage and generated so much heat that speakers joked about the water bill the union must be running up as delegates sought to relieve themselves with a cool drink.³ The exchange evoked the convention's spirited atmosphere, but surely no one could have missed the echoes between Trbovich's comment—"You will decide whether the lights shall stay on or they will go off"—and the broader political moment, where, as another speaker noted, the UMW had its "finger on the light switch of the nation."⁴ In the delegates' minds, whether the lights should stay on or go off was not a settled question, and the very fact that the matter was the subject of debate and ultimately left to a vote demonstrated the place that energy, broadly defined, had come to occupy in the miners' democratic imaginations.

The exchange captured coal miners' increasingly sophisticated understanding of energy democracy: the belief that the people who produced energy should have a meaningful say in its apportionment and use and that access to energy should be considered a core promise of democratic governance. Democratic relationships of energy, they believed, might translate not only into a more democratic union or workplace but a more democratic way of life. The MFD had argued for this position throughout their campaign. Now miners had to figure out how to put it into practice. How would they turn an upside-down mode of energy governance right, ensuring energy fairness not only for themselves but their communities? Previous versions of the coal-fired social contract had left this balancing act largely to federal administrative agencies, but miners, whose experience of federal regulation left them well aware of its limits, increasingly sought to hash out the meaning of energy fairness at the grassroots.

During the months of the OAPEC oil embargo, miners attempted to put the renegotiated coal-fired social contract into practice. Their actions revealed their own theory of the relationship between energy and power, one that fit into a schema of broader working-class and progressive critiques of how expanding corporate influence undermined American representational democracy. Miners also drew on arguments made by public interest lawyers like Ralph Nader, one of the miners' allies in the black lung fight of 1969. Yet miners' understanding of energy democracy was also rooted in their longstanding conception of energy citizenship, a way of thinking that transcended these critiques as much as they reflected them. After all, corporate power could not explain the contention in the hall over the lights.

The exchange instead indicated that, in an age of energy crisis, the classic organizing question—*who decides?*—could not be confined to the energy workplace or even the energy industry. It fell outside the boundaries of traditional conceptions of post–World War II industrial democracy entirely. Energy democracy had to encompass multiple sites of energy decision making, engage structures of power that included multiple fuels, and force a broader group of Americans to reckon with the energy bonds that shaped their political community. Energy democracy had the potential to reshape the kinds of claims that different Americans could make on one another and allow them to once again confront difficult questions about the rights and obligations of citizenship in an energy-intensive society. Most pressingly, energy democracy in the age of oil panics would have to confront a difficult question: what happened when rights and obligations came into open conflict? Miners, well accustomed by this point to seeing their everyday lives as part of a much broader energy system, were better prepared than most Americans to meet that challenge. Miners had developed rhetorical tools to expose energy flows as not just physical processes but also forms of political and moral connection.

By the winter of 1973–1974, the nation's political and moral connections were frayed, and the belief in the federal government's capacity for "good government," a belief that had spurred miners to democratize their union, seemed more tenuous than ever. To address the energy crisis, miners adapted a tactic that had worked comparatively well in forcing the Bureau of Mines to enforce the 1969 Federal Coal Mine Health and Safety Act: taking government into their own hands. If the state wouldn't ensure energy fairness, the union would. The UMW believed that workplace action could be a tool for democratization and social policy making, and indeed, the several preceding years seemed to have proven them right. However, while the union's actions during the 1973–1974 embargo did result in some redistribution of energy resources, the country's changing political climate undercut their efforts. As the conservative crusade against the New Deal order began to erode support for midcentury liberalism and dovetailed with the impact of energy industry consolidation, the union's traditional power in shaping the terms and enforcement of the nation's social contract eroded, even though serious concerns about Americans' ability to access oil and natural gas should have *increased* the miners' political power. Those same processes ensconced energy decision making outside of the public institutions that miners saw as central to securing recognition of their status as energy citizens.

During the acute phase of the energy crisis in 1973–1974 and in its immediate aftermath, the relationship between the rights and obligations of energy citizenship was tested in three ways. Coal miners in eastern Kentucky voted to join the United Mine Workers and struck for fourteen months before the operating subsidiary of the southern electric utility Duke Power would sign a UMW contract. In the winter of 1974, facing gasoline shortages and restrictions, miners walked off the job to secure a greater allotment of gasoline for coal-producing regions amid national shortages. And finally, the federal black lung program, understood as a program to make reparations for the harms of the nation's coal energy system, came before the Supreme Court. The justices had to determine if the program represented a proper way of rebalancing the burdens and benefits of a coal-fired society. In these three seemingly separate events, the country put the renegotiated coal-fired social contract to the test.

In June 1973, the miners at the Eastover Mining Company's Brookside Mine voted 113 to 55 to join the UMW. Eastover, a subsidiary of North Carolina-based utility Duke Power, refused to sign the UMW's standard bituminous coal agreement. In July, the miners struck; they would be out on strike until the following April. Immortalized in Barbara Kopple's Academy Award–winning documentary *Harlan County, USA*, the strike has mostly been remembered for the role it played in shifting gender roles inside the UMW.[5] But her footage also offers a window into the UMW's rank and file as miners and their communities debated key issues that surrounded the project of organizing energy workers. Although the first oil shock of the 1970s played no major part in the narrative that Kopple ultimately presented, the Brookside strike was inseparable from the broader context of energy crisis.

The stakes of the organizing campaign were high for the United Mine Workers as well as the Eastover miners. If the UMW was going to have the power to enforce the renegotiated coal-fired social contract, the union needed to organize the growing number of nonunion mines across the country. Eastover's location in Harlan County, Kentucky, held much symbolism. Four decades after Bloody Harlan, the conditions in the area's nonunion mining towns demonstrated that coal miners' citizenship rights were not something that could be taken for granted. The situation in Harlan proved to the UMW's new secretary-treasurer, Harry Patrick, that "the great ideals this country was founded on—democracy, equality, and justice for all" had not been fulfilled because "the Brookside strikers and their children sit in jail for trying to build a union while the president of Duke Power violates every safety law on the books . . . and goes scot free."[6]

The origins of the Eastover strike lay in the energy industry's restructuring that took place from 1963 to 1971. In the wake of the fuel shortages that followed the frenzy of mergers, Duke Power began a process of partial vertical integration—taking control of their supply chain. In late 1970, Duke formed two new subsidiaries to oversee the utility's entry into the coal business: Eastover Land Company to oversee reserve acquisitions and Eastover Mining Company to handle the mining operations. Brookside, part of this initial investment, was placed under the management of Norman Yarborough, who had been charged with massively expanding the operation to meet Duke's growing coal requirements. He later recalled, "At the time we bought it there was twenty-one men working there . . . the idea was to . . . put about three or four hundred people to work down there."[7] Within three years, the Eastover Land Company had acquired more than 21,000 acres of coal reserves in four counties in eastern Kentucky for Duke Power, and the Eastover Mining Company was already mining coal from the operations in Bell, Knox, and Harlan counties and had $24.6 million in production commitments.[8]

Yet despite the promise that the mountains of eastern Kentucky held for Duke Power, by early 1974, more than three years after the company had purchased its Harlan operations, Duke still had to report to its shareholders that coal production was "under development." The reason: "a strike which has idled the Brookside mine since July 26, 1973."[9] The strike soon gathered national attention as it became clear that amid the coal boom in eastern Kentucky, the resulting new outside investment, and the opening of new mines as nonunion shops, the vestiges of the old coalfield state had stirred back to life. Miners lived in company housing without running water. Management downplayed workplace injuries, and every day, the miners' families worried if their loved ones would make it back alive. As the strike dragged on month after month, the reminders piled up. Police dragged strikers and their family members to jail when they tried to block roads to prevent scabs from entering the mine. Judges issued injunctions to help the company maintain production. Gun thugs shot into miners' homes.[10]

As old resentments stirred, Yarborough insisted, "We're not going to have the violence of the 30s. The conditions are *not* the same."[11] Anxieties about the return of open conflict carried real weight. Many of the miners, their family members, mine management, and other community members had lived through that violence themselves, many as young children. Yarborough, for example, had moved to Harlan County with his family in the 1930s from rural Alabama, when he was a teenager.[12] Some older miners and retirees had been participants in the events that earned the period the name "Bloody Harlan." They knew what the company men, gun thugs, and state police were capable of, and they knew what it meant to have to defend the value of their lives at the end of a gun.

Miners and their families drew on these memories and experiences as they debated how to escalate pressure on the company and how to respond to instances of company and state violence. At one gathering of the Brookside Women's Club—the UMW women's auxiliary—one older woman urged, "Let's not let it happen, to come back to the 30s, because I was here. I've seen children hungry, crying for something to eat, and . . . oh, I can't, I can't take it." Nearly in tears, she gathered herself before continuing. "I'll be out [on the picket line]. . . . If I get shot, they can't shoot the union out of me."[13] Lois Scott, one of the most vocal members of the Brookside Women's Club, was a child in Harlan in the 1930s, the daughter of a union organizer. She remembered how the company gun thugs harassed her family, banging on the door at night, shining lights into the house, turning over mattresses looking for union paraphernalia, and playing cruel psychological tricks on the family.[14] During the 1973–1974 strike, she resorted to carrying a gun in her bra because "well, you'd be crazy not to." When a scab shot and killed Lawrence Jones, a young striking miner born nearly two decades after the worst of the violence in Bloody Harlan had ended, older men demanded revenge, drawing on their experience of the 1930s to make sense of what had happened. These responses emphasized how the strikers and their supporters in Harlan County understood the fragility of their rights and their access to meaningful redress of grievances.

In some ways, the story of Eastover was quite simple: an intransigent company, bent on meeting the demands of the changing marketplace, felt that its employees' right to a collectively bargained contract would inhibit their capacity to compete and overlooked the "benevolence" of capitalist development. Yarborough, meanwhile, extolled his efforts to place "our people . . . my people" into better housing, but Carl Horne, the president of Duke Power, wanted the union "off our backs."[15] The company was emblematic of southern antiunionism. As the UMW organizer Houston

Elmore described, "Duke Power is a Southern, conservative company. Less than ten percent of their employees in their power plants and their line crews are organized."[16] Duke Power, he felt, was worried about unionization drives spreading into the Carolinas, where the company was based; however, by the early 1970s the antiunion movement among southern companies was on the offensive, not the defensive. As the historian Nancy MacLean has shown, conservatives like James Buchanan targeted the United Mine Workers as unfairly benefiting from a "labor monopoly" at the expense of social welfare in Appalachia.[17] By the end of the 1970s, a group of southern and neoliberal conservatives would be in power, and workers would be the ones trying to hold onto what they had already won in the chilled political environment. But the energy crisis reveals another layer to the story, at once a microcosm of the larger trends in the industry and the U.S. economy *and* a moment of truth for the newly reformed United Mine Workers. Could the messy power and process of rank-and-file democracy so powerfully on display throughout the 1973 convention hold up to the fast pace of industrial change and political crisis that miners faced throughout the early years of the energy crisis?

The complaints at Brookside were familiar. In addition to pay below the UMW wage scale, there were safety complaints and an overwhelming sense that the miners were expendable to the company. As one striking miner described, "I got hurt there at Brookside about a year ago. I got about three hundred pound of steel on my head. And they took me to the hospital, sewed my head up . . . and I was off one day. And the superintendent sent a fellow over, said, uh, 'Get him to come on back up here and work.' Said, 'We'll make it easy on him so he won't lose no time.' And I went back up there and it knocked me out of compensation or anything . . . I got my head busted open. That's the way they want you to work down there."[18] Women raised concerns as well, saying that, like miners' wives across the country, the women of Harlan County didn't want "their husbands going into these scab mines with the rock a-falling and running these here motors with no brakes . . . they go in there praying that they get out and they feel like maybe their prayers would be answered sooner if they were working under a UMWA contract."[19]

But the protection the Brookside women sought from the union also extended beyond the mine face. For Lois Scott, "Duke Power's control over these men that voted in the UMW contract" represented a violation of their "constitutional rights" as "American citizens." She compared herself to the "protesters calling 'Impeach Nixon! Impeach Nixon!'"—except when miners and their families exercised their rights, they got threatened by company gun thugs.[20] At a moment in history when the negotiation of labor contracts between industrial firms and large national unions had been so deeply institutionalized into the structures of private industry, strikers and the members of the Brookside Women's Club claimed labor rights as citizens to protest against a structure of coalfield power rather than as a claim to a seat at the negotiating table. It was a more expansive imagination of workers' rights than the statutory, contractual framework of U.S. labor law.

Moreover, compared to the way older miners used a narrative of the state as the "muscle man" for the company, a narrative that had been a key organizing tool for the UMW in the 1930s, by the 1970s, younger miners often used taxation to understand the relationship between themselves and the state as well. Betrayal of the democratic promise of government could be traced in the tax dollars that went to pay the wages of state police and fill the gasoline tanks of their police cars, which were driven to break up their picket lines: "tax money at work breaking organized labor," one striker described. The strikers' power was emblazoned on the buttons they wore each day to the picket line—"UMWA Coal Power." When some of the Brookside miners traveled to the New York Stock Exchange in April 1974 in an effort to warn investors of the risks of owning Duke Power stock during a strike amid the energy crisis, they carried signs which read "The nation needs coal, not Duke Power."[21] The slogan presented Duke Power as an obstacle to the fundamental energy relationship represented by that coal: the relationship between coal miners and the nation they powered.

Miners, in claiming their citizenship at Brookside, thus insisted that a labor dispute that from one perspective appeared to lie squarely in the terrain of private-sector industrial relations belonged in the realm of public interest. The days the miners spent appealing to Duke Power stockholders in New York City were especially telling. While it might be tempting to label the effort as a union corporate campaign, a strategy that had become an increasingly important part of the labor movement's repertoire during this period, the appeals of the Brookside miners differed from typical corporate campaign strategies. Corporate campaigns sought to expose the corruption, mismanagement, or conflicts of interest on a corporation's board of directors to gain organizing or bargaining leverage. But the UMW focused on the place of the Brookside miners in the nation's energy system.[22]

Figure 9.1 Members of the Brookside Women's Club.
Source: Photo by Earl Dotter, www.earldotter.com.

Miners called forward an image of civic sacrifice in their appeals and pointed to the nation's electrical supply as a target rather than Duke Power's profit line. "A lot of people don't understand that that electricity burning over there, there's somebody dying every day for it. There's one man dies every day."[23] In one sentence, the miners were able to deftly connect their experiences working—and dying—in the Appalachian coal seams with the omnipresent energy that appeared so much more easily controlled when called forth by a light switch. The filtration of this idea into the mainstream of American politics was captured by a 1974 article written by Fred Harris, a former chair of the Democratic National Committee and senator from Oklahoma. The rights violations in Harlan County couldn't all be blamed on Duke Power, Harris insisted. "We're all involved," he wrote, "and we're burning up people to make electricity."[24] This strategy tied Duke Power into a broader critique of the nation's energy system and slowed the corporation's strategy of expansion into the energy industry. By the end of 1974, their stock was performing well below book value, and in 1975, faced with concerns over their ability to raise investment capital, they began the process of selling off the Catawba nuclear power station, strategically located south of Charlotte, North Carolina, and Duke's largest nuclear power investment, to a cooperative of wholesale buyers. Duke also halted construction on two other nuclear plants, and the size of their coal reserves stagnated.[25]

The Brookside miners extended their interpretation of the strike's relationship to the broader energy system beyond their ability to halt coal shipments. In going on strike, they also protested an energy system that had kept them in energy poverty. Across Harlan County, miners lived in company housing that fell far below the expectations of workers in their wage bracket nationally. Their houses lacked, among other things, running water. Kopple captured a mother giving her young daughter a bath in a bucket; the girl, who could no longer fit all the way into the bucket, listened to her mother fantasize about how after the strike they would have "a big ol' bathtub" with hot, running water.[26] Greater access to energy in their homes was integral to how the Brookside miners and their families understood the stakes of their struggle.

By the time Duke Power signed the UMW contract, the strike had demonstrated how energy relationships could be leveraged both against company profits and against the flows of electricity keeping lights on across the United States. The strike also showed how different forms of energy could be leveraged against one another: the fear of dwindling stockpiles strengthened the miners' claims on a union contract that would have more fairly distributed access to energy in Harlan County—whether that was the lighting in better housing or the power to run a water heater and pump water out of the ground directly into the house. That miners made such claims amid a nationwide move toward energy austerity was truly remarkable, but it was made possible by their relative energy poverty compared to the average working family. On the picket line, one miner captured the vision of a positive future on his sign, consciously echoing the assassinated liberal politician Robert Kennedy: "Some miners," the sign read, "see things as they are and ask why? We see things as they should be and ask why not?"[27]

In February 1974, as the Brookside strike entered its ninth month and the United States entered its fifth month under oil embargo, miners in nearby West Virginia began to feel the pinch of gasoline shortages. On February 20, Governor Arch Moore prohibited selling gasoline to any motorist whose vehicle had more than a quarter-full tank of fuel. State residents quickly complained: that was unreasonable and unworkable in a mountainous and rural state like West Virginia.[28] Coal miners appeared to have been among the most affected by this rule. After miners had broken the power of the coalfield state earlier in the twentieth century, the number of miners who lived in company-owned housing began to decline. As a result, the distances between miners' homes and the mines in which they worked had increased dramatically. It wasn't uncommon to travel fifty miles each way to work on isolated mountain roads. Many miners required half a tank of gasoline to travel to and from work each day.[29] With limited supplies, curtailed filling station hours, and now the quarter-tank rule, some miners worried they wouldn't be able to make it back to work.

At the Maitland No. 1-G mine, owned by Continental Oil's subsidiary Consolidation Coal, concern about the potential impact of the quarter-tank rule spread quickly. Many of the miners lived forty or more miles away from the mine, across the state line in Tazewell County, Virginia. To get home required ascending into the heights of the Blue Ridge Mountains, with at least three steep grades that required sustained power from their car's engine. One miner, unable to secure enough gas for the journey, slept in his car overnight at the mine. The miners walked off the job the next day. Danny Deskins, the union local president, emphasized they weren't striking against mine management. "We know they can't remedy our situation," he explained, but "we've got to find someone that will."[30] They called a mass meeting that weekend where three hundred miners gathered to decide what to do about the fuel situation.[31]

After the meeting, Deskins telegrammed the UMW's Washington office, explaining that "the miners are in a desperate position due to the fact they cannot get gas to get to work." Many filling stations were out of gas entirely. Those that did have fuel available, the miners explained, made it inaccessible by "jacking the price on each gallon." The miners requested that Miller take the matter to the relevant members of Congress and that he invoke the clause of their contract that allowed for up to ten "mourning days," during which production would be idled.[32] Traditionally, the mourning period was to emphasize the need for safety in the mines by cutting off the nation's supply of coal—sometimes in the wake of major disasters, other times to mark the accumulated devastation of energy system violence. The last time the union had actually used the mourning days, however, was in 1969, following the death of John L. Lewis.[33] The District 29 miners' request thus underscored the severity of the fuel situation.

Miller took two days to reply to the miners' telegram, by which time things had escalated dramatically.[34] On February 25, the day after the weekend meeting, forty-eight area mines were closed, not for safety violations or management infringements but because the area's miners were incensed over the disproportionate impact that gasoline shortages were having on them. Faced with long, winding stretches of roads through unforgiving terrain, miners now also contended with rationing, shortened filling station hours, and price gouging. They believed Governor Moore's quarter-tank edict was unjust. Making matters worse, shift times often prevented miners from filling up in gas stations even when they were open.[35] Although the union had called for mandatory staggered service hours, the UMW found most "stations were pumping last week only between 8–10 a.m., opening too late for miners going in for the day shift and closing before they were headed for home"—and that was if they had gasoline at all.[36] On March 1, the UMW office called every one of the 119 gas stations in District 29. Twenty-seven percent had no gasoline at all; an additional 18 percent had under a thousand gallons; a further 37 percent had fewer than five thousand. This included stations like the Gulf Oil station in Iager, which had 215 gallons on hand on March 1. Before rationing, the station sold around ten thousand gallons each day. Coal operator–owned filling stations reported that they had enough to provide for their employees, but such stores were notorious across the area for exploiting miners and their families.[37]

The Federal Energy Office (FEO) and West Virginia state authorities were completely excluded from the energy logistics responsible for making sure gasoline reached the most affected areas. This information was, instead, completely in the hands of the energy companies. As the UMW surveyed shortages across the southern part of the state, they discovered "neither FEO nor the state had . . . comprehensive data on wholesale and retail outlets; no maps existed, for example, pinpointing distributors, bulk plants, etc."[38] Gas station owners also lacked "effective statewide association . . . individual owners fear getting the short end of the supply stick." The filling station owners argued they were powerless to rectify the situation. Some began "lobbying miners to stay out," believing the miners had a better chance of forcing the government or the energy companies to act. Unlike the miners, the filling station owners, who were connected to the consumption end of the energy industry but owned no stake in production, worried they were "at the mercy of . . . distributors, the major companies, state and federal officials." In their eyes, "the miners' political power was providing the necessary leverage to buckle the Governor and force [the Federal Energy Office] to re-allocate for West Virginia."[39] The gas station owners' position spoke to the power of miners as energy workers with organization.

Though his position would later change as he came under increasing state, industry, and public pressure to end the strike, in its early days, Arnold Miller castigated the state leaders, federal government, and, most of all, the energy companies for causing the shortages. The energy companies, he argued, were, in the midst of the crisis, "still consolidating their economic and political power. . . . They have no real fear of public reaction. . . . And they couldn't care less about West Virginia."[40] In the context of ongoing industry restructuring, he pointed out the "absurdity" of the energy crisis: "producers of one fuel—coal—can't get to work because of inadequate supplies of another fuel—gasoline."[41] From February 25 to March 14, from 16,000 to thirty thousand miners were on strike each day. At the strike's peak, nearly two hundred mines across the state were closed. Observers worried the strikes might soon spread into neighboring Kentucky as bituminous coal production from one of the world's richest coal seams effectively ground to a halt.[42] Twenty-one percent of the country's coal miners worked in the ten West Virginia counties most affected by gasoline shortages, and those miners produced about 85.6 million tons of coal each year—15 percent of total national production.[43]

By March 7, the UMW leadership convinced Governor Arch Moore to lift the quarter-tank restriction for miners, who traveled much longer distances to work than most other workers in West Virginia, and persuaded the energy companies to ensure an adequate amount of fuel was trucked into the mining areas. Arnold Miller unsuccessfully implored miners to return to work: "Gasoline is now pouring into the Southern part of the state. . . . I am confident that I can obtain adequate gasoline on a fair and equitable basis not only for UMWA members but for all other West Virginians."[44] Miners rejected the concession as inadequate. On March 10, miners held a mass meeting in Boone County and "overwhelmingly" voted to continue their strike until Arch Moore scrapped the quarter-tank limit.[45] Although Miller continued to appeal to the miners to return to work, he also presented these demands to the public, courts, and state as legitimate.[46] It was an adaption of the tactics that Miners for Democracy had employed before taking power: suggesting that a reinvigorated UMW could intervene when the state and the companies had failed not only miners but also citizens. It blurred the lines between the different ways in which miners, as energy citizens, could interact with different axes of power.

Miller's administration also challenged the implicit idea of democratic energy administration that the federal government had created in the previous months. The union, in Miller's view, was more capable of democratizing energy access than the federal institutions responsible for allocating fuel resources under the Emergency Petroleum Allocation Act or the agencies like the Federal Energy Office that had been created at the executive level in response to the oil embargo and subsequent fuel shortages. The federal government had crafted these agencies and laws with a specific vision of energy democracy in mind: "to make sure that the fuel shortage does not fall with unfair severity on any region or on 'independent' refiners and distributors not affiliated with major oil companies."[47] These programs set allocations at the state level and relied heavily on voluntary cooperation to make them work, similarly to Nixon's other price stabilization programs.[48] These policy interventions were meant to stabilize price relationships in the fuel sector and assure fuel allocations. However, they also opened up a new space to question how those decisions were made. The strikers, leveraging their ability to withhold energy to effect a change in petroleum allocation processes, remade the meaning of those programs from the bottom up.

Not everyone saw things the way the miners did. Some painted the strikers as un-American for transgressing the energy austerity felt by many working-class Americans while at the same time failing to meet their obligations to extract coal. With each day that passed, the UMW noted, "our nation loses more than 200,000 tons of vitally needed coal."[49] As the stoppages continued into their second week, the impact on industry intensified, deepening the rift between the union leadership—under increasingly heavy fire to get the miners back to work—and the strikers, who continued to argue that the disproportionate impact of the shortages required immediate and non-negotiable remedy.

By the strike's third week, Ellis England, a West Virginia miner and strike leader, appeared on a local radio program hosted by Dan Lucas to answer West Virginians' questions about the now-protracted strike. England was a polarizing figure. Introducing him on the show, Lucas noted how England had been called "everything from Robin Hood to a radical" and "even had a gentleman who referred to [him] as an anarchist."[50] The severity of the strike's perceived transgression became apparent as Lucas questioned Ellis about the strike's intentions. "Are you an outlaw?" Lucas queried. England insisted he was not, but Lucas continued to press him: "A union outlaw. You know outlaw (quote, unquote). I don't mean a criminal, you know, being chased down by the law. I'm talking, Ellis, are you an outlaw, are you a union radical?"[51] Lucas's comment, dripping with implied anticommunism, also spoke to a system of adjudicating right and wrong that had been upended and couldn't be defined by the bounds of legislation and common law. Nor could it be contained within the question of the collectively bargained labor contract. This exchange, however, becomes intelligible when viewed from the perspective of competing views of what energy democracy meant and how it should be carried out.

Since 1968, black lung strikes had snowballed into safety strikes, which then grew into political strikes and had now expanded into strikes over energy access. The apparent 1950s "peace" in the coalfields had disappeared entirely, and the weakness of the old-regime form of collective bargaining suddenly found itself on full display. After all, one of the miners who called in to challenge Ellis on the radio was right when he said, "Nowhere in that contract does it call for a strike of any kind. A gas strike to me is illegal so . . . I think we ought to go back to work."[52] Many miners supported the strike, however, even if they were critical of figures like England. One miner who spent most of a three-page letter to Arnold Miller complaining about the wildcat leaders nonetheless felt "the ¼ tank strike was justified."[53] Like the black lung and safety strikes in previous years, which had challenged the boundaries between workplace and politics structured by the postwar system of industrial relations, the gasoline strike pointed to how the transformed industry had blurred the lines between worker and citizen, producer and consumer, in new ways and how energy served as a key bridge by which miners could negotiate these new muddy waters. One of the strikers captured the tension when he joked with a reporter that striking "was my patriotic duty. . . . Like the President said, I was just conserving my energy."[54]

Miners' employment in the energy industry contractually bound them, as part of the national BCOA-UMWA agreement, to produce coal—coal that overwhelmingly went to providing the nation's electricity. But miners also believed it was their right as energy citizens to commute to and from work without running out of gas. They also felt that being forced to sleep in the mine bathhouse or having a gas station attendant poking his head into their car to check the fuel level violated that right. The fact that miners occupied both roles was the basis of their claim to a greater allocation of the nation's gasoline, an argument that the union's leadership accepted and used as they tried to devise legal reasoning that could be used in a suit against the Federal Energy Office. Chip Yablonski, now the UMW's general counsel, concluded miners did in fact have a legal claim to higher allocations because the "miners were engaged in energy production."[55] Most people felt it was the obligation of miners to produce coal in a moment of national energy crisis, but miners insisted that obligation came with the corresponding right to gasoline.

The gasoline shortages, miners contended, had been produced by the failures of energy governance, leaving the energy companies to profit while miners suffered the indignities of energy shortages. As the energy crisis spurred increased demand for coal production during 1973, energy companies invested in new mines and ordered additional shifts at mines that had previously operated below capacity. These changes translated into increased gasoline demand as more miners drove to and from work, but the Federal Energy Office relied on old, pre-embargo numbers to determine "baseline" energy use. Although the Federal Energy Office had a goal of supplying the southern coalfields at 83 percent of normal usage—9.13 million gallons a month, based off the 1972 consumption numbers—the UMW research office concluded that 83 percent of estimated need would have totaled about 12.7 million gallons of fuel. As a result, instead of receiving 83 percent of normal use, the southern coalfields were receiving 73 percent.[56]

Not only did estimates fall far short of actual need, but the promised gasoline rations didn't appear to be reaching the region at all. In late January, the FEO ordered the major energy companies to supply 1.18 million gallons of extra gasoline, but by mid-February, the gasoline had yet to arrive. As the acute shortage deepened, the FEO ordered another injection of energy on February 19—"a 'booster-shot' amounting to 3.98 million gallons." Instead, on February 20, Governor Moore instituted the quarter-tank rule, and less than five days later, he also ordered gas stations to close on Sundays.[57] Tom Bethell, now the UMW's research director, wrote that of the 9.13 million monthly gallons promised, "during the past 2–3 months of shortages, they have been getting only about 6 million gallons per month," or about 40 percent of pre-embargo consumption. He concluded that "neither the quarter-tank rule nor any other conservation measure will be sufficient to prevent widespread dislocation of the area's economy sooner or later."[58] While the UMW worried that waging war against the FEO would destroy the miners' claim that "UMWA members want [energy] fairness for everybody," Moore's restrictions appeared to work in favor of the energy companies, which the UMW believed were hoarding fuel to drive up prices, rather than in the public interest.[59]

The UMW charged the energy industry with usurping authority that should belong to the state, even as they remained critical of the West Virginia and federal government's distribution plans. Inequities in energy access seemed even more undemocratic in such an energy-rich region of the country, even if coal could not be pumped into miners' gasoline tanks. Bethell argued that miners, like Americans across the country, believed "the whole gas shortage is contrived by major companies who are hoarding/storing supplies while whipsawing the public and the government in order to get wide-scale price increases."[60] That perception was amplified when the companies appeared to negotiate with small deliveries of fuel. Continental Oil, which owned Consolidation Coal, delivered 650,000 gallons of gasoline from their storage facility in Roanoke, Virginia, in early March.[61] Following this incident, UMW officials doubted the ability of the FEO to "guarantee that the flow of gas into West Virginia will be distributed equitably."[62]

Although the energy companies and the state and federal governments appeared to be the target of the strikes, the first companies affected severely enough to take the matter to court were not energy but steel companies.[63] Energy industry diversification might not have stabilized the nation's energy supply efficiently, but it certainly helped insulate the companies' bottom lines. Steel firms, on the other hand, relied on quite specific qualities of bituminous coal, which were abundant in southern West Virginia; the process couldn't easily substitute other fuels—or even other coals.[64] As the strike entered its third week, U.S. Steel indicated that unless production resumed, and quickly, "it may need to furlough more than 50,000 steel workers because of its decreased supplies of metallurgical coal."[65] The steel industry began a full legal and legislative campaign against the striking miners and the UMW.

Bethlehem Steel led efforts to appeal for legislative change that would prohibit strikes in the energy industry. On March 11, Bethlehem Steel's president, Lewis W. Foy, called for "emergency labor disputes legislation . . .

which would prohibit any strikes in protest of energy related problems."[66] In this extreme demand, Foy acknowledged the strike was indeed fundamentally about the energy crisis. The legislation Bethlehem sought was not confined to an injunction against strikes at their mines, nor was it concerned with securing coal supply for steel production, but instead chose to exploit the energy crisis to upend an entire system of industrial relations that had—grudgingly, on the part of the companies—accommodated contracts without a no-strike clause.

As Bethlehem appealed to legislators, Armco Steel led the charge to the courts. They filed a request for temporary restraining orders in the U.S. District Court for the Southern District of West Virginia. Chief Judge Dennis Knapp denied the request to enjoin the United Mine Workers, concluding that neither the Emergency Petroleum Allocation Act nor the Sherman Act gave the court the authority to issue an injunction against the union in this particular dispute. The companies then appealed their case to the Fourth Circuit Court of Appeals. They demanded relief, insisting that although the strikers' stated aims were to compel "the executive branch of the Federal Government . . . to change certain . . . regulations . . . affecting the allocation, distribution, and sale of gasoline," to achieve these ends, they had instead inflicted mayhem on the economy, causing "economic damage to the plaintiffs, those who do business with them, and the public in general." Since the steel industry had "no power over the allocation and distribution of gasoline, and are wholly unable to grant to the defendants the demands which are the avowed object of the strike," the companies called on the Appellate Court to reverse the District Court's decision.[67]

The request came before Appellate Judge Hiram Emory Widener Jr., a Nixon appointee. Where Chief Judge Knapp had concluded that the restraining orders fell outside judicial authority based on the laws cited, Widener took the time to develop a substantive, seventeen-page opinion on why he did have the authority to grant the relief the companies requested. The basic problem, as Widener distilled it, was whether he could restrain picketing when miners "cause severe areawide and national economic disruption which will force the representatives of the executive branch of the government to treat them with respect . . . as soon as the United States sees that the [miners] have a sufficient supply of refined petroleum products."[68] The *Boys Market* decision, which prevented most strikes during the life of a collective bargaining agreement and which UMW counsel Chip

Yablonski had successfully outmaneuvered in the past, loomed large. In the western Pennsylvania safety strikes nearly four years earlier, Yablonski had been able to evade a *Boys Market*–style injunction by opening the possibility that a safety strike did not meet the Taft-Hartley definition of a strike, since it protested abnormally dangerous working conditions. Here, he attempted a similar maneuver—making the case that the gasoline wildcats were not subject to injunctive relief because they were not really a labor dispute between employees and employer and, thus, that the UMW's contract didn't really have a way to arbitrate it.[69] This time, however, Yablonski was unsuccessful.

Widener granted the injunction, echoing nearly verbatim the argument presented by the company counsel. The striking miners, he agreed, were indeed outlaws because they put "their whims" above the law, in defiance of the 1973 Emergency Petroleum Allocation Act. This action, he concluded, in full agreement with the companies, unfairly targeted "the flow of bituminous coal in interstate commerce . . . as a source of energy." It also defied the court's view of democracy, Widener concluded, since the Emergency Petroleum Allocation Act was an extension of power by a democratically elected government. He drew a fundamental distinction between the "disruption" caused by the fuel shortages and the "disruption" caused by the miners. One was an expression of Nixon's "law and order"; the other was antithetical to that order.[70] The reasoning tied employment law and energy regulation together in the context of the energy crisis. Widener believed there was a public interest not only in protecting the contract obligations of employers but also in ensuring that energy democracy was carried out by the body that had the vested power to do so: the federal government. The ruling rested on the braiding of three legal threads—the Sherman Act, a pillar of antitrust legislation; the authority to regulate flows of energy, which had been instituted by the Emergency Petroleum Allocation Act; and the common law precedent that prevented tortious interference with the employment contract. This reasoning formed a legal basis by which labor relations could be tied to flows of energy, even when multiple energy sources and infrastructures were in play, and even when that workplace activity extended to matters of political and democratic concern.[71]

Despite Widener's ruling, the showdown ended with what appeared to be a victory for the miners. Within forty-eight hours of the ruling, and with violence on the picket lines escalating, striking miners began to return to work, but with substantial concessions from the state and federal governments.[72] Governor Moore was forced to lift the quarter-tank cap, meaning miners could now fill their tanks completely, and the Federal Energy Office promised 18 million gallons of increased gasoline supplies for the state in March, around three times the amount West Virginia had received in February.[73] The gasoline wildcat and its outcome raised in an even more dramatic way the basic question of democracy that had driven the December 1973 debate over the convention hall lights: *who decides?* As the nation wrestled with the energy crisis, miners distilled questions of energy production, distribution, and use into questions about the changing relationship between energy and the country's democracy at the grassroots, in administrative and political institutions, and in the courts.

The first peak of the energy crisis from 1973 to 1974 demonstrated how the transformation of coal into energy reflected a transformation of coalfield power—from coal into energy, from coal miners into energy workers. It also shaped the balance of power with which miners would contend as they bargained their subsequent national contracts in late 1974 and 1977–1978. The wildcat gasoline strike resulted in what appeared to be a major political victory for the miners despite Widener's injunction, since they did ultimately secure gasoline concessions. But miners also lost more than ten million dollars in wages during those weeks, draining down savings they would need for the expected strike later that year when their contract expired.[74] That tension reflected the challenges of organizing within the framework of the coal-fired social contract, which had been forged and contested in many different places—the national collective bargaining agreement, legislation, jurisprudence, and, of course, energy flows. Democratic reforms inside the UMW encouraged a new generation of miners to take politics into their own hands as they sought to rebuild their union. But those reformers found it increasingly difficult to enforce the renegotiated coal-fired social contract in a decade of energy crisis. The energy crisis emboldened miners to claim what they saw as their rights, but it also intensified the nation's scrutiny of how well miners appeared to meet their obligations to mine coal.

For the miners to articulate their wide-ranging conception of their place in the energy system during the gasoline wildcat strike required a great amount of abstraction and fluidity. This shift toward a notion of energy unmoored from its original fuel form was striking, since so much of the organizing in the union had revolved around very material perils: toxic coal dust, crushing slate, massive slag heaps. While talking about *energy* allowed miners to emphasize the interconnectedness and substitutability, it also made coal, that shiny black rock, more invisible than ever—even as industry leaders and government officials invoked it as the nation's "great black hope" that could solve the energy crisis.[75] This seeming paradox relied on the increasingly widespread notion that different fuels would soon become substitutable for one another and that coal might soon provide gasoline.

But when *Usery v. Turner Elkhorn Mining Co.*, a case challenging the constitutionality of the landmark Black Lung Benefits program established in 1969, finally came before the Supreme Court's bench in December 1975, the nation would be reminded just how much the materiality of coal still mattered. As miners and miners' widows and dependents claimed benefits for the dust disabling and killing them, the companies, the states, and the federal government fought over the constitutional way to split the bill for the nation's embodied energy debts.[76]

The response to the new black lung benefits program attached to the Federal Coal Mine Health and Safety Act of 1969 had been overwhelming. Although the Social Security Administration received "only a few weeks' notice" that the agency would administer the massive program, within one month of the program's enactment, disabled miners and their widows filed more than one hundred thousand claims. Delays plagued the program's early days, and when the SSA denied more than 50 percent of claims, disabled miners returned to their local Social Security offices in protest. These protests were amplified by working miners who continued to walk off the job as the new law failed to alleviate the safety crisis unfolding underground. Government agencies, coal miners, and union and company leaders all sought to find the proverbial balance point between lives lost, kilowatts delivered, and profits made—though each group valued the various elements of that equation differently. At the national level, the federal government distilled into dollar costs this rich fabric of protest, contestation, and negotiation unfolding at the grassroots. The dollar costs added up quickly, a testament to the generations of suffering miners and their families had endured for the country's coal-fired energy system—and which continued to accumulate.[77]

By 1971, only two years after the program's creation, more than $533 million in compensation had already been paid to miners who were "totally disabled" or their widows, even though a substantial proportion of claims had been denied. The payout cost failed to capture lingering debate over the criteria for receiving benefits and the policies and procedures for program administration. However, the high cost and high rates of claim denial focused national scrutiny on the program, and in 1972 Congress passed the Black Lung Benefits Act (BLBA) to better facilitate payments and claims processing.[78]

The BLBA aimed to further redress the inequalities of the U.S. energy system through financial redistribution, recognizing that coal mining remained both dangerous and necessary. The BLBA allowed a wider range of surviving family members to claim death benefits and extended black lung benefits to surface miners, who had previously been excluded. It also committed $10 million to the construction of new black lung clinics in the coal regions. Reflecting the demands of the Black Lung Association, which had led the Social Security office protests, the BLBA also made it harder to deny claims and allowed claimants to introduce a wider range of evidence in support of their claim. The General Accounting Office estimated that in its first year alone, the BLBA amendments would result in the payment of an additional $954 million to miners and their widows. By increasing the annual benefit payout more than four and a half times, the black lung compensation program would become a more than $1.2 billion annual program, with the federal government footing approximately one-third of the cost where state compensation programs and company payments fell short. Although the burden of payments was ultimately meant to fall to the states and the companies, the BLBA conceptualized the federal government as the guarantor of the program. This focus on immediate payment at great expense and with much confusion reflected an increasing understanding of the importance of stable coal production to meet the nation's energy needs as the future of oil and natural gas appeared increasingly uncertain. And when state programs failed to materialize and companies balked at paying their share of claims, the federal government continued to increase its payments, which by the mid-1970s had reached nearly one billion federal dollars annually.[79]

The BLBA was immediately challenged in the courts by companies that felt it was unfair they be expected to pay black lung benefits to disabled former employees and their widows and dependents. They contended that the BLBA held them unexpectedly liable for working conditions that were legal at the time they had taken place. The federal government argued the justification for such retroactive liability was that the uneven costs of an imbalanced moral economy exacted on miners' bodies had in fact accumulated as operators' profits. The extraordinary recovery of the industry's profitability across the 1960s, in this logic, had directly resulted not only in the disabling of workers and their premature deaths but also destabilized the nation's largest domestic source of energy. But this line of thought, countered the coal companies' counsel, ignored "the legislative history of the Act as being a national obligation and recognized as a moral obligation by the government." Both parties agreed that black lung benefits were more than an expanded worker's compensation program. They were a necessary form of "reparations." The question at stake was not whether the benefits should be paid but on whom the obligation to pay fell.[80]

Justice Thurgood Marshall delivered the Supreme Court's opinion upholding the constitutionality of the 1969 act and the 1972 amendments. He rejected the operators' claims. Their obligation to pay was indeed fair and constitutional. The Supreme Court, in a 6–2 decision, recognized the black lung program as standing in a legislative tradition of moral economy, "adjusting the burdens and benefits of economic life." Rather than acting as a deterrent for companies still running mining operations or as an arbitrator of a company's past "blame-worthiness," the Supreme Court held instead that the black lung program as expanded by the BLBA was "justified as a rational measure to spread the costs of the employee's disabilities to those that have profited from the fruits of their labor, the operators and the coal consumers." Reparations to coal miners for the unequal bodily costs of energy production that they had borne would come through a combination of state, federal, and industry funds.[81] The U.S. Supreme Court affirmed such legislative efforts as a proper realignment of the burdens and benefits of the country's energy system through economic mechanisms. This decision reflected an understanding beyond the coalfields that citizenship in a coal-fired democracy entailed both rights and obligations. But as malaise settled over the national mood and the country's politics, the optimism that the UMW could bring into being an era of just energy governance slipped away, and by the early 1980s, the coal-fired social contract would be hollowed out.

CHAPTER X

Revolution of Declining Expectations

As Jimmy Carter crossed the United States seeking reelection in 1980, he stopped in West Frankfort, Illinois, to give an energy policy speech atop one of the nation's largest industrial graveyards. On the site of a mine explosion that killed 120 miners in 1951—and that was now back in production because of the increased utility demand for coal—Carter thanked coal communities for their "great contribution" to the United States' industrial history and—he hoped—its energy future. Carter chose the site of one of the country's worst mine disasters to promote his plan for a national energy policy, to affirm that "America indeed is the Saudi Arabia of coal." He appealed to miners to see their fates bound up with the coal they extracted: "I believe that you recognize that coal production is . . . good for you and for your families, with a sustained income and a healthy life." The importance of coal extended far beyond the coalfields, he reminded them, for production of the nation's most abundant fossil fuel was central to the "economic and national security of the United States."[1]

Carter's West Frankfort speech wasn't enough to win him reelection a month later. His one-term presidency was in many ways defined by the energy crisis, which he presented as an existential threat to an American way of life built on fossil-fueled affluence. Between 1977 and 1979, three major upheavals destabilized the nation's energy system, including the coal-fired social contract that had undergirded the New Deal order. The best

Figure 10.1 Jimmy Carter goes underground in West Frankfort, Illinois, while on the campaign trail.
Source: Associated Press.

remembered of these upheavals was the 1979 oil panic. Revolution in Iran sent global oil prices surging for the second time in six years, confirming that the events of 1973–1974 had not been an anomaly. Similarly consequential were the complete breakdown of labor relations in the coal industry and the 1979 accident at the Three Mile Island nuclear generating station. These events called into question the viability of the nation's energy system and undercut the legitimacy of the institutions that had governed it. Coal presented a particularly vexing problem for the federal government. While coal, and especially its labor troubles, contributed greatly to the nation's energy problems, most also saw coal as part of any viable resolution to the energy situation. American democracy still drew on imagined coal-fired stability.

Carter chose to visit West Frankfort not only because of the history it represented but because coal-generated electric power tied the West Frankfort community to his home state of Georgia. Orders from the Georgia Power Company had reopened the mine. Carter credited his leadership: during his governorship, Georgia "made a basic decision . . . that our electric power would stick with coal," he told the West Frankfort audience. The Georgia Power Company expanded its coal use as fuel prices spiked in the fall of 1973 and the federal government sought to encourage coal conversion.² As Carter appealed for miners' votes, he described how those energy relationships intertwined with other forms of commercial and political exchange: "I have a special deal with you, right? As a Georgian, good customer, and also as President."³

But if Carter chose a site that emphasized his energy connections to the miners in West Frankfort, his visit also underscored how a decade of energy crisis had shifted the national conversation on the relationship between coal and the country's democracy. In drawing a line between the old, deadly coal industry represented by the West Frankfort disaster and modern American energy production represented by the mines' reopening, Carter conspicuously overlooked the more recent disaster at the Consol No. 9, just twelve years earlier. Carter never visited the site of that disaster. The deadly explosion at the Consol No. 9 mine had faded from the American public's memory, even though it explained so much about why the nation's coal-fired energy system looked the way it did. While the Consol disaster had brought national attention to the moral crisis at the heart of coal-fired liberalism, the reopening of the West Frankfort mines suggested that eastern coal, thought to be in decline, could still power a presidency.

Indeed, Carter suggested coal had the power to lift the malaise that he believed had settled over the country. The reopening of the West Frankfort mine, he insisted, was proof positive that coal could be mined and burned more safely and "that this country can produce more and discover more and conserve more energy, and that we can use American resources, American knowledge, and American jobs to do it." To safeguard the nation's future, he argued, Americans would "have to accept coal as both a clean fuel and a safe fuel."⁴ In making his case for increased coal use, Carter minimized the basic problems of danger and pollution that had driven more than a decade of coalfield activism and guided federal regulatory reforms. This statement, meant to project national optimism, also hinted at how a decade of energy crisis had circumscribed the country's energy imagination. Three successive presidential administrations had neither successfully raised expectations for national energy policy as a positive good nor had appeared up to the task of governing diminished expectations. Although Carter's national energy program spoke to a distant future potential for renewables and other "nonconventional" forms of energy, the United States in the meantime would turn "to plentiful coal, while taking care to protect the environment."⁵

Whether such a transition was possible drew doubt from many quarters. And from that doubt reemerged the basic tensions that had characterized the U.S. energy system for much of the century: labor unrest, environmental degradation, the expansion of corporate control, the moral unease at the suffering of the nation's miners, and the difficulties of democratizing energy access and production simultaneously. Coal industry labor relations had deteriorated to the point of being entirely broken, and low mining productivity reflected it.[6] A deepening understanding of the impact of burning coal on the global environment tied coal combustion to acid rain, to the release of carcinogenic trace elements, and to the "greenhouse effect," where carbon dioxide accumulated in the atmosphere, threatening to upend temperature norms and rainfall patterns—what today we know and live with as climate change.[7] Coal was dangerous and dirty. Its compatibility with democracy, freedom, and equity was questionable.

Yet it became difficult to imagine a real alternative. Although Carter insisted the energy crisis represented the end of an era where abundance could be taken for granted, these years perhaps better demonstrated how the pursuit of abundance also set limits on the country's energy imaginaries, including those of the nation's unionized coal miners. Compared to the 1973–1974 oil crisis, where coal miners effectively leveraged their position within the nation's energy system to pursue their vision of coal-fired democracy, the UMW struggled to navigate the late 1970s, and the union found that its ability to secure a seat at the table had declined substantially. With energy security and workplace democracy at odds in a nationally visible way, the rights and obligations of energy citizenship once again became the subject of contestation. In the coalfields, these years of crisis shrank the bounds of acceptable workplace action and diminished miners' political expectations as the country reckoned with the political quandaries built into the nation's coal-fired democracy.

When Carter addressed the nation in April 1977 about the energy crisis and the need for the development of a national energy policy, he claimed the nation faced a "problem unprecedented in our history."[8] Despite the looming threat of another 1973, he contended that to worry about gas lines and Middle Eastern politics missed the deeper, structural crisis, which would "test the character of the American people, and the ability of the President and Congress to govern this nation." The problem went deeper, and it demanded that the nation finally reckon with the real environmental and geopolitical costs of energy, which could no longer be kept "artificially cheap" by allowing the externalities of production to be foisted on the landscape, to run off into the water, and to be emitted into the air.[9] By treating the crisis as "the moral equivalent of war," he also attempted to call forth memories of large-scale mobilization during World War II. He hoped to remake the American political ethos "in every town and every factory, in every home and on every highway and every farm," through a planned energy transition.[10] In placing coal at the center of that vision of energy transition, Carter repeated the decade's familiar political claim about the place of coal in American life as a source of independence and security.

Carter planned to double coal production within a decade. The General Accounting Office (GAO) assessed Carter's plan as ambitious but likely unattainable. True, the country had a lot of coal, and "we will mine it of course," the GAO concluded, "but it is not quite that simple."[11] Doubling coal production would require opening between 438 and 825 new mines and securing capital investment of $26.7 million to $45.5 million. The industry would need to recruit between 288,300 and 531,600 new miners—if mining equipment could be manufactured quickly enough to put them to work. And through it all, miners' productivity would have to increase rapidly after it had been declining for eight straight years. The GAO doubted the country could meet these benchmarks, especially if commitments to environmental protection and workers' health remained in place. The report exposed concerns over whether the renegotiated coal-fired social contract and the wider expansion of pollution control measures could accommodate such increased use of coal.[12]

Whether Carter's proposed expansion of coal use was feasible or not, his framework of energy transition signaled an end to a particular way of life, one that took as given fossil-fueled abundance. Carter reframed the energy crisis from an imbalance of supply and demand to an existential crisis about the fate of the nation. His national energy policy plan foregrounded the need for national soul searching and hard choices. This approach departed from his predecessors, who had generally framed domestic energy use in cornucopian and utopian terms, even in moments of uncertainty. During the 1973–1974 oil shock, for example, Nixon's proposals for energy conservation had cast it as a problem of dependence that could be countered by increasing domestic supply and that still involved energy-intensive spectacles of space travel. Where permanent alterations in national energy use might be necessary, Nixon had marshaled the long tradition of American conservationism, a tradition that supported a relatively robust regulatory framework for resource management in the nation's forests and called forth ideas like "sustainable yield" that should not have so easily mapped onto fossil fuel supply. In November 1973, Nixon had also sought to assure the public by authorizing new energy development projects that were accompanied by assertions such as "we want enough energy so that America is not dependent on any other country. But we want this to be a beautiful country, and we can have both."[13]

Carter attempted a different approach. Appearing before a national television audience in a cardigan in April 1977, he attempted to grapple with the limits of American high-energy capitalism. How would the American obsession with growth adapt to the age of limits? He argued that dependence on fossil fuels, particularly oil and natural gas, left the country economically and politically vulnerable. In the short term, Americans' energy use might increase its dependence on Arab nations the United States viewed as unreliable after the 1973–1974 embargo, but in the long term, he argued, "we would not be able to import enough oil from any country, at any acceptable price."[14]

The viability of economic growth through energy conservation was uncertain on its own terms. It is difficult to imagine it emerging at another point in American history than from the ominous period of stagflation in the 1970s, when the U.S. economy defied Keynesian economic expectations: inflation and unemployment grew, while the economy stagnated and even contracted. Although Carter appeared to have the economy in hand by the time the energy crisis peaked for a second time, the national mood struggled.[15] Carter stared down a looming deadline that threatened his plan to increase the country's dependence on coal: the December 6 expiration date on the UMW's national bituminous contract. One commentator noted that "the moral equivalent of war" threatened to become Carter's "equivalent of the Vietnam war," as he faced a threat of open insurrection from the "front-line troops" of energy policy: the nation's coal miners.[16]

As winter approached in 1977, coal-fired stability seemed further out of reach than ever. Indeed, it appeared almost laughable. Labor relations in the industry had broken down completely, especially the resolution of everyday workplace disputes between miners and management. In the five years since the democratization of the UMW, nearly unabated, seemingly random work stoppages had defied increasing pressure to limit workers' ability to strike at the local level while under contract. Even in a decade remembered for wildcat strikes and rank-and-file militancy throughout the labor movement, miners struck three to five times more frequently than other workers by the late 1970s.[17] Before the MFD's takeover, wildcats often reflected miners' dissatisfaction with workplace governance procedures, which they had little say in crafting, since they did not get to ratify their collective bargaining agreements. But beginning with the 1974 bituminous agreement, the rank and file *did* vote on whether to ratify the contract before returning to work, and not only did the wildcats continue—they increased.

Wildcat strikes called into question the Carter administration's energy plan. The industry saw in the chaos an opportunity to undercut the miners' democratic claims, decrying the "new democracy" as "the new anarchy."[18] Among the wider public, one journalist observed, the unrest drove "some serious skepticism about added dependence on coal."[19] If Carter was to achieve his vision of national energy security, then labor peace would have to be restored in the coalfields, but peace was nowhere to be seen. When the contract expired on December 6, 1977, the United Mine Workers of America walked off the job. The strike lasted nearly four months and halted half the nation's coal production. The energy impacts of the strike were felt most acutely across Appalachia and the Rust Belt, the regions most dependent on union-mined coal, as miners shot at coal barges and national guardsmen were called in to escort priority coal deliveries, treating Americans to warlike images from the home front.

By the late 1970s, the meaning of energy security had shifted from an earlier idea of defense mobilization capacity to instead signify the way that energy powered particular visions of consumer citizenship and provided a certain element of social cohesion. As miners' industrial action increasingly appeared at odds with national energy stability, their labor rights became profoundly politicized. The UMW had staked claims to political power on the basis of coal's role in national security for decades, going as far as to say that miners were the "frontline troops" of national energy policy. The union had much to lose by being considered an unreliable security ally, but the thousands of young miners joining the industry seemed increasingly unimpressed with this national security role, focusing instead on the erosion of their right to strike while under contract.[20]

The "battle line" strike of 1977–1978, usually remembered as one of labor's last stands in the face of a strengthening ongoing employer offensive, highlighted the growing mismatch between the geography of coal production and the geography of UMW organization.[21] The Bituminous Coal Operators Association (BCOA), with whom the UMW negotiated the national bituminous contract, primarily represented operators across the eastern coalfields, despite the national shift westward in production. The BCOA also disproportionately represented the steel companies that were increasingly marginal to the sector overall, particularly as steel plants began to close and relocate. By contrast, the utility companies that burned the majority of the nation's coal had far less representation at the bargaining table. By 1977, the percentage of U.S. coal mined under UMW contracts had dropped to 50 percent, from a peak of 90 percent in 1945.[22]

The regional disparities in the strike's impact emphasized the importance of place in how the energy crisis was felt, how it was imagined, and how people thought it might be resolved. The nine-state region most affected by the strike—Ohio, Pennsylvania, Indiana, Michigan, West Virginia, Kentucky, Tennessee, and the western portions of Maryland and Virginia—relied on coal for more than 90 percent of its electric power, and more than half of that electricity went to industrial use.[23] Although the portion of UMW coal in total national production had been falling over time and losing tonnage to the western coalfields, the fact that the United States lacked "an integrated nationwide system for moving coal around" amplified union power in the region.[24]

Security concerns exacerbated distribution problems. Miners and other strike supporters had intimate knowledge of the terrain as well as the railroads and rivers. By February, one power company had secured 27,000 tons of coal upriver, only to find that the barges could not bring it down to the generating station because "six of the barges have been fired upon, and the barge operators fear other attacks from people sympathetic to the mineworkers."[25] Around the region, "dozens of coal trucks" had been "forced at gunpoint to dump their loads." In one desperate case, federal officials responded to a "frantic call from the power plant in Logansport, Ind[iana,] saying that it would run out of coal in two days." Carter dispatched the army to deliver three hundred tons of coal from a nearby base. The exasperated UMW leadership tied the outbreak of violence to a longer history, one that hinted at the coal-fired social contract's flagging legitimacy: "We may see the 1930s again," one official commented to a reporter. "These miners have fought the Army before."[26]

Moving power across the national grid was a little easier than moving coal along rivers, railways, and roads—and a less likely target for sabotage. Damaging electric infrastructure would have obscured the moral distinctions that miners often made in allowing coal through for hospitals, which often had the ability to burn coal in their own emergency power systems, but not allowing coal to pass through to generating stations. One miner told *Time*, "If anybody tries to move coal to power plants around here, there's going to be hell to pay. We've been letting coal go through for private homes and hospitals all along, but we've got to draw the line somewhere."[27] The most affected states, however, were also among the largest energy consumers. Other regions didn't have the capacity to sustain the diversion of power across the grid in the long term or to increase it much further if the power plants that remained on line had to shut down. Trying to avert political catastrophe, Energy Secretary James Schlesinger hoped to put off rationing power among the states as long as possible.[28]

The ability to "wheel in" power across state lines seriously undercut the effectiveness of picket lines, armed confrontations, and effective sabotage, even if the loss of market share to the western coalfields and the formation of energy conglomerates were primarily responsible for miners' loss of power in the sector overall. Still, these power-sharing arrangements and the new stream of coal flowing from nonunion mines in the West were not entirely successful. Economists hoped that the increasingly "flexible" economy would be able to respond to the regionalized shortages, but cutbacks in power access were already underway across the nation's industrial heartland: a 30 percent reduction in electric power consumption resulted in a 15 percent reduction in employment.[29]

Just eight months after Carter's address on the energy crisis, the nation found itself in the uncomfortable position of simultaneously looking to coal as the nation's first defense against an energy crisis and being forced to confront the fact that the rights and obligations of energy citizenship remained unsettled. Miners saw a nation attempting to curtail their rights, especially their right to strike over local issues—one of the most powerful tools miners had to enforce their contract—as well as mine safety regulations. The federal government, as well as energy consumers, saw miners as unwilling to fulfill their national obligation of providing fuel for industrial growth and electric power.

Because most Americans encountered coal exclusively in the form of electricity, the political questions at the heart of the strike traversed the nation's electric power grids. Miners increasingly competed with the electrical utilities, entities with which they had very few channels for direct interaction, over who would define the narrative of energy crisis. During the strike, the utilities went on the offensive as disorganization in the UMW press office diminished the impact of miners' voices and demands on broader political discourse.[30] Utility leaders argued that "between the coal mining industry on the one hand [and] the independence of energy on the other," the utilities represented "a connecting force," the reaction that turned dirty black coal into bright and clean electricity.[31]

Not all "dirty black coal," however, was equal. Electricity could, *potentially*, be produced from a wide range of coals—from "river coal" anthracite dredged from the Susquehanna River in Pennsylvania, to deep-mined bituminous coal from Alabama, to the lower-grade lignite coal strip-mined in North Dakota. But the particularities mattered. The chemical composition of bituminous coal varied so much across the North American continent that, according to one utility executive, burning western coal in a plant designed for eastern coal was akin to "burning regular gasoline in a car that's supposed to use only unleaded gasoline."[32]

Utility companies shaped public perceptions of the energy crisis through voluntary conservation programs and mandatory power cuts, which could both be incorporated into powerful advertising and media campaigns to sway public opinion. These actions communicated powerful messages about the priorities of and for power.[33] Through these programs, utilities recast the narrative of blackout from a symbol of systemic uncertainty to an omen of recession and energy austerity. In the wake of a massive 1977 blackout that plunged New York City into chaos, utilities intervened in the narrative of the coal strike and energy crisis by leveraging fears of decline: job loss, declining consumption, a world without growth.[34]

Power cutbacks, or the threat of them, were particularly concentrated across the Rust Belt and Appalachia. Typists and secretaries at the Westinghouse Electric world headquarters had reverted to carbon copies as management switched off electric copying machines. Some of the building's elevators were taken out of service, a quarter of the lights shut off.[35] Voluntary participation in energy conservation, particularly among retailers, communicated the potential of the coal strike's impact to spread into other sectors. While some observers doubted Energy Secretary James Schlesinger's claim that the strike could put 3.5 million people out of work, the message of the blackout in the context of stagflation threatened unemployment.[36] "People are getting worried," one department store head explained. "I think it's because of the possible loss of jobs in industry and the fact that this whole thing could snowball."[37] Coal strikes had a wider impact than strikes in most other sectors. In auto, for example, the interruption of a single part's production might radiate out to the industry because it was impossible to build cars without them, and local areas around factories affected by substantial layoffs might suffer economically, but the threat of a coal strike loomed even larger. Electricity shortages might affect areas and industries with no seeming connection to the coal industry or coal communities; the potential to snowball was exponentially larger. Less than a year after Carter announced "the energy problem" to be a problem of limits, a darkened workplace signaled austerity and recession.

As the strike lumbered into its third month in late February, negotiations between the UMW and BCOA reached a breaking point, and the Carter administration, which had bet big on coal for their national energy plan, was split over how to resolve it. Some cabinet members advocated for federal seizure of the mines, while Trade Advisor Robert Strauss fell firmly in support of the operators. Energy Secretary Schlesinger stood behind the BCOA as well and argued the president should invoke the Taft-Hartley Act.[38] "The coal strike," he argued, had "taught the nation the absolute necessity of achieving long-term stability in the mines . . . the industry is just going to have to be induced to institute proper labor relations."[39] Yet in contrast to the wildcats of the previous decade, the 1977–1978 strike fell well within the UMW's contractual rights. When Schlesinger demanded federal intervention to induce "proper labor relations" in the nation's mines, he instead suggested a narrowing of miners' democratic rights. Those advocating for Taft-Hartley knew that invoking it couldn't solve the whole crisis, but it might ensure a basic level of energy stability, at least for a time, as the nation confronted fuel shortages, a fragile economic situation, and uncertainties in the international oil markets as rebellion against the Shah's rule erupted across Iran.

The administration's threat to invoke Taft-Hartley only spurred miners' defiance. Pete Bizok, who had worked underground since World War II, insisted that "Taft-Hartley is OK for wartime. But it's not going to get me down there except at gunpoint. Even then, no gun can make me work faster than I want to, and I can work awful slow when I put my mind to it." David Forms, a former local president from West Virginia, pointed out that miners could easily sabotage expensive machinery if forced back to work: "You've got $250,000 pieces of equipment in each of these mines, and it wouldn't take much to tear them up."[40] This statement would not have been taken as an idle threat: in the strike's first week back in December 1977, a bomb destroyed an $180,000 auger.[41] If the administration was going to get miners back underground, they would have to operate in a way that miners saw as legitimate, and that meant respecting miners' democratic rights when calling upon them to fulfill their obligations to the nation's energy system.

At the end of February, Carter brought the UMW and BCOA negotiators to the White House along with his energy secretary and advisers and the governors of the twelve states most heavily affected by the strike. The stakes were high: the UMW's democratic but lengthy ratification process meant that restoring full production would take at least thirty days. Meanwhile, one of Schlesinger's aides commented, "The power is just draining away."[42] Carter's efforts came to naught. UMW negotiators presented the rank and file with a proposed contract, which miners overwhelmingly rejected. Carter finally invoked Taft-Hartley on March 6, 1978, as the strike was poised to enter its fourth month. He justified his decision by claiming he was taking action to prevent the United States from becoming an "innocent victim" of a "total breakdown" in industrial relations.[43]

Yet his announcement, in emphasizing the obligations of miners, inadvertently admitted that far from being an "innocent" bystander, the United States had benefited profoundly from past curtailments of miners' rights. "The difficult and dangerous work of coal miners," Carter said, "has helped America prosper and grow strong." Carter acknowledged that strength was built on coal even as "miners, their parents, and their grandparents paid an unfair and bitter price for working in the mines," and even as he conceded that further improvements in miners' working conditions were needed.[44] Still, Carter insisted miners had an obligation to help preserve the country, "which is now in danger." The nation's labor laws, he suggested, existed not only to protect workers but also "to protect our Nation." He then admonished miners for—as he saw it—defying the rule of law. "In times of crisis," he continued, "the law binds us together. It allows us to make our decisions openly and peacefully and it gives us, through the courts and legal procedures, means to resolve disputes fairly.

Respect for the rule of law ensures the strength of our Nation. The law will be enforced."[45]

Under intense presidential pressure, individual firms inside the BCOA broke ranks with the negotiation hardliners, splintering the traditional bargaining structure. Federal arbitrators identified the original Gulf Oil subsidiary, Pittsburgh and Midway, as a "wedge company" that they believed could be convinced to settle their own contract in advance of a national agreement. Traditionally, smaller companies who were not members of the BCOA had followed the UMW-BCOA agreement rather than deal with the expense of bargaining individual contracts. By offering an alternative to the BCOA agreements, however, arbitrators opened a new avenue for piecemeal transformation of the mining workplace outside the purview of the extensive, mature national agreement.[46] The old, top-heavy system of industry-wide bargaining had increasingly locked out other parties to the energy regime who were not included in the collective bargaining process, such as many electric utilities. The fragmentation of the national bargaining structure signaled the decline of the UMW and the diffusion of sectoral power across the different points of energy governance, including mines, utility plants, and grid infrastructure. Within a decade, the BCOA would splinter. Representing more than 130 member companies in 1978, by 1988 it would represent a mere fourteen firms.[47]

Miners finally accepted a new contract on March 24, 110 days after they had walked off the job. Many observers of the strike argued that the strike was not the emergency suggested by the invocation of Taft-Hartley, the mobilization of the army and the National Guard to secure coal shipments, or the tales of "layoffs and dark streets" emerging from across the Midwest.[48] But as people across the country disputed the strike's impact and questioned the Carter administration's response, the strike remade the fabric of labor relations in the coal industry. Despite the impressive compensation boost—37 percent over three years—the 1974 provision for an annual cost-of-living adjustment was removed, a substantial blow in the era of stagflation. Industry also took the day on the rule changes and finally succeeded in reintroducing production-based incentive plans for the first time since 1945, a major blow to mine safety efforts.[49]

Perhaps no change in the contract better signaled the remaking of coalfield power than the restructuring of the health care system that had been in place since the establishment of the landmark 1946 UMW Welfare and Retirement Fund. The new health care plans introduced copays and reordered the funding structure for one of the most important regional health systems. According to Curtis Seltzer, with the shift to company-based plans, private insurance had "little interest in building a coalfield medical infrastructure, raising the quality of healthcare, or maintaining the clinics and hospitals organized over the years by the Fund." In the aftermath of the strike, one hospital in southern West Virginia closed entirely, and sixty or more doctors left the region.[50] The 1978 agreement hollowed out key elements of the coal-fired social contract.

The wage increases also obscured other important on-the-ground issues not directly addressed by the contract, particularly housing. Toward the end of the 1970s, housing problems had once again emerged as a key issue of contention, one that could not be solved by raises, since at stake were key issues of absentee land ownership, the safety and viability of the land in areas subject to surface mining, and the lack of affordable housing options in reasonable proximity to jobs. The housing crisis was particularly acute in central Appalachia, where 80 percent of miners still lived even as production shifted west. Land shortages for home building (attributable both to excessive corporate land holdings and ecological degradation), an underdeveloped construction industry, insufficient lending capacity among regional banks, and federal programs that seemed to work at odds with one another further exacerbated the problem. Laid across the region's difficult terrain, they together caused a severe housing shortage.[51]

And finally, in the strike's aftermath, miners met renewed contempt from industry leaders. John Corcoran, a former chair of Consolidated Coal, argued that negotiations had been "severely hampered by the fact that the new officers of the Union tried to make the bargaining function a completely democratic process without understanding the consequences of their actions."[52] What industry leaders painted as too much democracy, however, was perhaps better described as an incomplete process of energy system democratization. The limits of the UMW's efforts to build robust coalfield democracy is often attributed to interpersonal rivalry or Arnold Miller's unwieldy attempts at administering a union where he faced substantial opposition from the remnants of Boyle's old guard. But more consequential was the fundamental underlying problem: the balance of power in the industry and at the bargaining table had become substantially skewed. The miners who had demanded the moral attention of the nation just a decade earlier found the prospect had, structurally, become much more difficult. The 1977–1978 strike was a watershed moment in the history of the

American coal industry because it cast in clear terms the rebalancing of power that had delimited the boundaries of energy citizenship over a decade of energy crisis.

In May 1978, Carter formed the President's Commission on Coal to study the problems that had led to the breakdown in negotiations over the winter. Despite a relative loss of power in their bargaining structure, miners remained a liability in a fragile energy system. The commission was composed primarily of five voting members: one representing labor, one representing industry, and three representing the "general public" as an interested party in coal's place in the nation—a composition that reflected the logic of the Guffy Coal Acts passed more than four decades earlier.[53] Although set up as an inquiry into the problems facing the coalfields and the industry, the commission more accurately functioned as a seminar for labor, industry, the federal government, and the public to reevaluate the rules of the energy game as the coal-fired social contract appeared to disintegrate around them.

The core problem before the commission, Carter suggested, was to explain how Appalachian coal, the bedrock of the nation's energy system, the fuel that "fired the furnaces that made this Nation a great industrial power... fueled the engines that first connected from sea to shining sea the people who live in the great land area of the United States," had become a liability rather than an asset. Carter placed the importance of the commission on par with "discussing with one of our major allies the strength of NATO." Energy security, he affirmed, was a "war, and in this war, the most formidable defense weapon in our arsenal is coal."[54] In addition to the war analogy, Carter also appointed Willard Wirtz, a former secretary of labor, to the commission. Carter lauded Wirtz for his expertise, which extended "back to his membership on the War Labor Board during World War II."[55] Although posed in the language of 1970s politics, the commission grappled with the question that had been at the heart of modern American politics across the previous century: could coal really serve as the baseload fuel for a democratic society?

Some questioned whether the commission had the political will or authority to do anything at all and cast doubt on its democratic legitimacy. Beth Spence, a UMW ally and member of the Appalachian Alliance, used her testimony to press the committee on their supposed purpose when "it was set up without any input from rank-and-file coal miners and other ordinary coalfield citizens. It has no mandate to develop legislation. . . . It lacks the authority to subpoena corporate financial records and other documents that might actually shed some light on the problems we face." Such a commission, she scoffed, "is hard to take seriously."[56] The entire goal of the commission, as its mandate laid out, was at odds with her own vision of reclaiming energy citizenship for Appalachia: "the kind of democracy envisioned in this country's Constitution—a democratic system in which we have much more direct control of our own resources and can develop them in a planned, rational way, minimizing the damage and maximizing the benefits."[57] Despite the power of her critique, the Appalachian Alliance represented a minority of the voices considered by the commission.

In contrast to Spence's pessimism, many coal miners and the UMW's leadership embraced the commission and its purpose. Arnold Miller enthusiastically endorsed the project, particularly after viewing its interim report: "For such an illustrious group of this nation's energy leaders to advocate some of the same solutions to the nation's energy problems that I have been calling for since the first energy crisis in the early 1970s is both encouraging and gratifying."[58] Miller repeated a claim that he had made in the early years of his presidency: that miners could "end the energy crisis that cripples our country" so that "once again America shall truly be the independent democracy it was created to be."[59] Those rank-and-file members who testified appeared to accept that their seat at the table of energy decision making was premised on meeting their obligation to provide the nation with a stable energy source. The UMW's slogan, "America can solve its energy problems . . . let us do it!," evoked the image of miners committed to national service.[60] Miners' hopes for the commission, however, ultimately posed more fundamental questions about the relationship between coal and democracy than most commission members were willing to entertain. The commission seemed less inclined to ponder new forms of energy governance that might give miners and people living in Appalachian energy-producing communities a greater role in shaping the national energy plan.

As far as possible, the commission focused on analyzing the recent wave of wildcat strikes and the bitter feelings unleashed during the national coal strike—and it was more concerned with developing failsafes to avert a future coal catastrophe at its weakest point, labor relations. Although a decade of miners' activism left a strong impression on the nation's laws and regulatory administration, the commission struggled to make sense of coal's democratic paradox, that the burdens and benefits of coal went hand in hand, even if they fell across the nation's citizens unequally. Carter had admitted as much when announcing the commission:

> In West Virginia it's long been known that what was under your land was the key to your prosperity and sometimes the cause of your problems. . . . For a long time the hills of West Virginia were abused. . . . Your creeks and your rivers were polluted, your land was scarred and left raw, and too many of those who dug the wealth from under the ground were left poor and sick after their labors were completed. In recent years we've learned how to stop this devastation, learned how to restore the hills as we have extracted their wealth, learned how to make life safer and more prosperous for those who bring it out of the earth. The land and the people of Appalachia have sacrificed much . . . to our national development. And I'm determined that in the future this land and its people will share in the benefits of meeting our nation's needs.[61]

Carter used language that echoed the UMW reform efforts begun a decade earlier and the growing environmental consciousness of the nation, but he did not plan to meet these new social and environmental obligations by changing the conditions of coal production. Instead, he proposed a five-year program of "impact assistance," consisting of $675 million in grants and securities to back $1.5 billion in loans to "offset some of the social and economic costs of increasing coal production." He also promised to enforce already-on-the-books laws regulating air pollution and strip mining but argued that the rest would come from private sector capital investment, research, and development. Carter insisted that even amid "the rising demand for coal to meet our nation's energy needs," the nation had also begun to "heal" the scars that the industry had historically inflicted on West Virginia's workers and their land. But the very regulations that Carter looked to were the ones that many politicians, when faced with oil shortages, argued should be removed in order to exploit the nation's coal resources to their fullest.[62]

By the time the commission delivered their final report two years later, little progress had been made on setting a national energy policy. Still, the members of the commission felt that "domestic and world events [had] broadened and heightened the significance of the Commission's mandate."

They pointed to a new round of OPEC price increases, which raised oil prices to nearly ten times the highs of 1973 and drove domestic inflation; the partial meltdown at Three Mile Island, which "raised new doubts about public acceptance of nuclear power as an alternative to oil"; and "the revolution in Iran and the Soviet invasion of Afghanistan," which the commission believed endangered the world's oil supply in new ways.[63] The commission argued that a stable, "independent" energy system for the coming "decade of dangerous energy vulnerability" depended on coal.

To this end, the commission recommended immediately halting new use of oil and natural gas by electric utilities and dedicating $15 billon in federal funds to convert already existing oil and natural gas generating stations to coal. This plan, the commission argued, could reduce oil and natural gas use by utilities by 40 percent in a decade and ensure all regions of the country shared the costs of reconversion equally. In heavy industry, the commission called to increase coal use by prohibiting oil and natural gas use in industrial boilers with five-megawatt capacity or greater. They looked to the Interstate Commerce Commission to induce coal use by lowering coal transit rates on the nation's railroads and to state utility regulators to implement programs designed to attract capital investment for coal-fired infrastructure. These changes, contended the commission, would also disincentivize coal imports from South Africa, Poland, and Australia, which could sometimes be cheaper than rail transport in some coastal markets. The federal government should further intervene by developing a new industry capable of producing "significant quantities of synthetic fuels" by the 1990s. Most of all, if this political promotion of coal was going to succeed, the commission argued, the federal government would have to act as guarantor of "environmental integrity, stability in labor-management relations, and adequate living conditions in mining communities."[64] The recommendations nodded to miners' aspirations and, environmental concerns aside, the recommendations, under the guise of state authority, appeared to support industry's vision for expanded coal use through a friendly regulatory landscape that shifted its focus from the externalities of coal to the impossibility of an alternative.

In the last two years of Carter's presidency, the short-range coal supply problems faded, but the long-term challenges of coal development came back into view. If coal was going to solve the energy crisis as Carter hoped, its production would have to expand rapidly and go far beyond serving as the nation's primary source of electricity to also deliver long-promised synthetic fuels.[65] But as productivity declined in the nation's mines despite massive capital investment, coal production goals slipped further out of reach. Operators insisted these productivity declines were the result of safety and environmental regulations and that the regulations would have to be undone, at least in some measure, in order to allow the industry to meet demand.[66] But actual supply was not the problem, it turned out. The industry had 150 million tons of untapped capacity and far more in undeveloped reserves sitting idle. Coal executives worried they would not be able to sell the coal if it were mined, given strengthening air pollution regulations.[67] Coal struggled to keep its place in the country's new regulatory landscape, driven by Americans' expectations for environmental quality and workplace safety. According to one political scientist, by the end of the 1970s coal constituted a form of "ambiguous abundance."[68]

Coal-fired abundance appeared even more ambiguous as greater public focus fell on how coal combustion decimated public health in communities around generating stations and wreaked havoc on the environment in the places where particulates released during coal combustion, heavy with condensation, fell back to earth as acid rain. Externalities accrued on both the production and consumption sides of the coal-fired energy system that Carter hoped would secure the nation's energy future. Miners had fought for years to make the human costs of mining coal visible, but *burning* coal also inflicted serious harm.[69] The federal government opened the books of its moral calculus, but its methods yielded ambiguous answers: "In principle," the General Accounting Office reported, "the external costs . . . should be internalized into the price of coal wherever possible. . . . In practice, this is difficult to do . . . how do you include the cost of a human life when coal pollution causes premature death?"[70] Was it possible to internalize the cost of an electricity customer's own asthma to the price of the electricity they used in their home?

That question was thorny enough on its own, but in a multifuel energy system where electricity might also be generated from oil and natural gas, the GAO's energy calculus also considered the importance of energy security. If coal's price was adjusted to reflect externalities, coal wouldn't be particularly cheap anymore. In a world of expensive coal, oil and gas might become attractive alternatives, further exacerbating the vulnerability of the nation's energy system to supply disruptions in international markets. The costs of coal production, measured in the damage to public health and the nation's environment, had to be balanced against the energy security it provided.[71] Carter had framed the energy crisis as "the moral equivalent of war," and war had a way of rebalancing the ledgers of risk.[72] The revolutionary upheaval in Iran beginning in 1978 only increased the appeal of coal as a way of limiting the risk of dependence on international oil. As oil prices went soaring for the second time that decade, Carter desperate to appear as though he had the domestic energy situation under control: "This time our country has been ready," he said, "and you've not seen the world brought to its knees by a temporary shortage of oil."[73]

Many understood, however, that the energy problem ran deeper and that it was not an Iranian problem but an American one. The malaise that had settled across American society emphasized the crisis as part of a national tragedy. Congressman Nick Rahall, a Democrat who represented the southern West Virginia coalfields, described the energy crisis as self-inflicted:

No one forced us into this predicament. The sheiks in Abu-Dabi [sic] didn't force us to drink their oil. They didn't force it down our throats and say, "Here, drink up." No one forced us to build nuclear power plants. . . . No one has forced us to price our coal out of the competitive world markets. No one forced us not to develop a synthetic fuels program many, many years ago. No one forced us not to convert our oil and gas-burning facilities to coal. No one forced us to do these things. We did it to ourselves, and we have no one to blame but ourselves.[74]

These were not mere problems of geology. They called into question decades of energy decision making that had prioritized cheap energy above all else.

But energy wasn't cheap, a fact that the country had finally been forced to acknowledge. The best Americans could hope for would be that their energy system could be made dependable—and that would require investment in infrastructure, yes—but also for the nation's energy citizens to accept their obligations to one another. Arnold Miller, still trying to temper the fallout from the bitter breakdown in labor relations the previous year, admitted that coal miners' obligations in solving the problem went further than most: "We recognize the heavy responsibility that a commitment to coal places upon us," he wrote. Miners had to "guarantee . . . to the American people that their faith in us will be justified."[75] Grudgingly, the federal government had to agree. While "coal can be a problem in terms of dependability," Assistant Secretary of Energy Alvin Alm conceded, it was "still our most stable fuel by far."[76]

With oil now understood to be a source of energy insecurity, coal's most immediate competitor for electric power generation was nuclear power. Nuclear power's contribution to the national energy mix in the late 1970s still fell far short of the optimistic predictions of earlier decades, but nuclear optimism among its supporters proved persistent, and the country had the technological knowhow to ramp up nuclear power if it chose to. As Carter increasingly gravitated toward a dual-strategy solution based on coal and nuclear power to make the United States "independent" from foreign oil, it became clear that early tensions between nuclear power and the coal industry had been pushed to the background temporarily, rather than resolved.

In the interim, public opposition to nuclear power development had grown.[77] Mounting concerns about nuclear accidents, radioactive waste, and nuclear weapons proliferation led people who understood the dangers of coal to recommend it over atomic power. Ralph Nader, although increasingly critical of coal as a power source, nevertheless suggested it was preferable to nuclear power. Coal's problems, he argued, were technical, while nuclear power's problems were existential. Nuclear power had the potential to fuel weapons proliferation, and the threat of nuclear catastrophe loomed large. "Were a catastrophe to occur . . . nuclear power plants all over the country might be shut down—forever," wrote Nader. "The nation would then be faced with simultaneous radioactivity and energy crises."[78] Even leading environmentalists like Barry Commoner, who advocated for the development of renewable sources, argued that coal should serve as a bridge fuel to a solar-powered future. He appeared to prefer the known dangers of coal to the possible impact of a nuclear catastrophe.[79]

The problems of coal, however, were not as "amenable to technical solutions" as Nader suggested. A growing body of research pointed to "increasing atmospheric concentrations of carbon dioxide—resulting, in part, from the burning of fossil fuels," which "could result in the warming of the Earth's atmosphere" within a century. Others placed the timeframe for rapid changes in climatic conditions at less than fifty years. Such a problem, trapped in coal's carbon bonds, defied the technical fixes that had helped reduce sulfur dioxide emissions during the burning process or the improvements in land reclamation practices (which still fell far short of returning the land to its pre-mining state).[80]

The UMW ultimately navigated the reinvigoration of the atomic menace under new leadership. Arnold Miller—plagued by health problems, his authority undermined by political fractiousness in the union's head office, his democratic spirit withered by isolation—suffered a heart attack and finally resigned his position in the fall of 1979. He was replaced by Sam Church. Church, a one-time mine electrician from Matewan, West Virginia, had supported Tony Boyle until his last days in office but quickly moved up through the union's ranks and became Miller's running mate during his successful reelection bid in 1977. He assumed the presidency upon Miller's resignation in November 1979.[81]

In early 1980, just three months into his presidency, Church launched a critique of nuclear power that echoed Boyle's antinuclear crusade as much as it echoed the critiques of Nader and Commoner. He insisted that while coal had problems with safety and environmental damage, "the costs of coal use are well known." Worried that a "new pro-coal consensus" would "be dragged down by nuclear power," Church demanded that Carter decouple the fate of coal from the future of nuclear power. "If the administration wants to support a nuclear bailout, it should be proposed as a separate program," since "future attempts in the Congress to make nuclear power safe will greatly increase its cost." The costs of the returning atomic menace were not only questions of liability and construction costs, Church argued, but rather "the health and security of [not only] UMWA members, but all Americans." One only had to look to Three Mile Island, where "just yesterday there was another radiation leakage."[82]

The partial meltdown of the Three Mile Island-II reactor near Harrisburg, Pennsylvania, in March 1979 had only been the beginning of a more protracted crisis for the facility and the United States' commercial nuclear power program. Both Metropolitan Edison, the utility company that owned the facility, and the state and federal governments bungled their handling of the aftermath, quickly eroding public trust. A Nuclear Regulatory Commission–ordered report suggested the accident, which "might well have been relegated to 30-second shots on the network news and inside pages of metropolitan dailies," had instead taken a place beside "certain other functional structures on the modern American landscape—the bridge at Selma, Alabama; the Watergate Complex; the Texas Schoolbook

Depository in Dallas." Three Mile Island, they argued, had "slipped into an unprojected half-life," a reminder of "steep depressions in our national lifeline."[83] The Three Mile Island crisis exposed the structural weaknesses of existing energy regulation to the wider public and made freshly salient the problem of bodily and environmental risk in energy decision making.[84] The accident thus affirmed what miners had been saying for a decade, since the black lung strike that had shut down the West Virginia coalfields in the early months of 1969: assessing the risks of the country's energy system could not be left to technocrats. They had to be subjected to political mediation. Energy was firmly a subject of democratic concern.[85]

The political questions raised in the aftermath of the disaster rested implicitly on questions about the balance of benefits and burdens in the nation's energy system, questions that miners had played a large part in making legible. The Three Mile Island accident, however, reshaped the narrative of energy disaster in American politics and miners' efforts to focus on the workplace as the site of the energy disaster, like when a mine exploded. Radioactive contamination couldn't be seen, only detected with instruments or felt through its cumulative bodily and environmental impact. Residents contended with doubt and mistrust about whether radioactive contamination had in fact occurred and struggled to prove with certainty the cause and extent of harm.[86] In many ways, the danger of radiation found its closest analogy in black lung, the public health disaster that accrued slowly and could only be detected after irreparable harm had occurred. But as this form of contamination dovetailed with miners' efforts to portray themselves as reliable partners in the nation's energy future, miners' workplace safety was subjugated to defending the public from nuclear harm.[87]

The accident at Three Mile Island propelled antinuclear politics back to prominence within the United Mine Workers. At the union's convention that fall, the delegates charged with reporting the activities and recommendations of the UMW's legislative arm, COMPAC—the Coal Miners Political Action Committee—reported "the economic, health and safety, and environmental disadvantages of nuclear power far outweigh any advantages it may have." They worried that nuclear waste and potential nuclear accidents might harm future generations. To these delegates, continued development of nuclear capacity seemed like an unnecessary risk, given "that Three Mile Island sits on top of the nation's largest anthracite reserves."[88] The delegates unanimously voted to support the committee's report, which included a resolution that reaffirmed the union's opposition to nuclear power development "until adequate safeguards against radiation poisoning are developed; until safe, permanent waste sites are devised; and until protection against a catastrophic nuclear power plant accident is assured."[89]

One year after he had formed the President's Commission on Coal, Carter ordered a presidential commission to investigate the accident. The commission ultimately found that the fundamental problems were "people related," rather than the technical problems of "equipment safety," which figured powerfully into the public imagination of the accident. They were quick to clarify that this assessment referred not to basic human fallibility but instead to "the structural problems in various organizations," the "deficiencies in various processes, and . . . a lack of communication." Together, these problems "revealed problems with the 'system' that manufactures, operates, and regulates nuclear power plants."[90] Amid a general decline in Americans' confidence in ruling institutions and the ability of the federal government to do the work of governing, the regulatory system took the blame for a set of failures that went much wider and for which industrial management was at least equally responsible. It was another major setback in the Carter administration's effort to meet the nation's energy challenges. In July 1979, four months after the accident, Carter acknowledged the country faced a "nearly invisible threat"—and not from radiation. "It is a crisis of confidence," Carter told the country in an address that became known as the "malaise speech." That crisis had eroded the country's faith in the future, Carter contended, and was "threatening to destroy the social and political fabric of America."[91] At a historic crossroads, the future of the United States would be determined by how the country's citizens solved the energy problem.

Little more than a decade after Lyndon B. Johnson had warned that without coal to fuel it, the furnace of freedom could run cold, the entropic nature of the U.S. energy system appeared to have come into full view. The turn to coal in the late 1970s was "a matter of necessity rather than choice," according to the assessment of the General Accounting Office. "If it were strictly a matter of choice, coal's decline relative to other fuels would continue." Coal was "dangerous and difficult to extract," it was "bulky" in a streamlining economy," and, most of all, it was dirty, whether viewed from southern West Virginia, the Powder River Basin, or a street near a coal-fired power plant in a densely populated area.[92] Coal's place in the

Figure 10.2 Miners picket at the 1980 Democratic National Convention.
Source: UMWPO 219/1.

nation's energy system had come at high cost: morally, ecologically, socially, politically, and financially.

Still, coal's promoters, from the United Mine Workers to the National Coal Association to President Carter, continued to hail coal as the nation's energy cornerstone, no matter how heavily opinion weighed against it. The most viable alternatives, oil and nuclear, were simply too volatile. Petroleum may have been fueling globalization by powering container ships, semi trucks, airplanes, and automobiles and by producing the kinds of petrochemicals and plastics that became integrated into almost every facet of daily life. But it was only possible because, hidden away in the Appalachian hillsides—and increasingly in the West—coal miners continued to power the nation. Coal, once king, by the end of the 1970s found itself less monarch than fallback.

By 1979, James Schlesinger equated this narrowing of energy expectations to a "decline in our historic expectations."[93] He echoed Carter's address just the month before, where the president had emphasized how the effort—and failure—to meaningfully grapple with the energy crisis had made "clear that the true problems of our Nation are much deeper—deeper than gasoline lines or energy shortages, deeper even than inflation or recession."[94] The myth of cornucopian energy had contorted American politics in strange ways, unsustainable ways. Michael Koleda, the executive director of the President's Commission on Coal, argued that the "naivete" and "luxury of temporary abundance" had allowed the American system of politics to "compartmentalize our thinking and policies with respect to energy, the economy, the environment, and national security."[95] Efforts to govern a highly integrated energy system from a variety of administrative agencies at the federal and state level, from private sector boardrooms, and from union offices had substituted management for politics, malaise for freedom. "How will the American society respond to this revolution of declining expectations?" Schlesinger wondered: "I do not know."[96]

The nation's unionized coal miners, dwindling in number as nonunion Western surface mines rapidly expanded, adjusted to the new world of lowered expectations by largely retreating from two decades of efforts to intervene in various ways in national energy policy across fuels. Ronald Reagan entered office in January 1981 and immediately signaled he would slash the budget of the federal black lung program by $2 million over five years, condescendingly referring to the hard-won black lung benefits as an "automatic pension."[97] Such a devaluing of miners' lives had provoked rebellion just a decade before, but Reagan's effort was met much more quietly. Opposition failed to gain traction like the black lung movement that had halted production in the West Virginia coalfields in 1969.[98] The largest action that took place was a two-day strike on March 9 and 10, 1981, invoking the contract's memorial day clause. Although Reagan's proposal enraged miners, the organizational basis and political will to mobilize, with a few notable exceptions, dissipated in the face of the rapidly consolidating power of the firms and the westward shift in coal production. The 1981 black lung amendments that were passed months later in December eliminated two key "presumption" clauses that assumed black lung disability in miners who had respiratory or pulmonary disability and had also worked fifteen years in the mines, or ten years for those who had died from respiratory disease. These clauses had been essential in helping miners and their widows claim black lung benefits—now they were gone.[99]

The democratic flourishing of earlier years had opened a brief window that allowed miners to challenge basic assumptions about the character of the coal-fired democracy written into the nation's social contract. By 1980, that window had closed once more as operators, union leadership, and the government insisted on labor stability in the name of energy security. As a result, the nation's coal-fired social contract had ossified and withered, further constraining the energy and political imaginaries of those bound by it. Instead, UMW President Sam Church wrote to his members that "*COAL IS THE ONLY SOLUTION*" to the nation's energy problems.[100] It was an American coalfield version of the infamous neoliberal idiom: *there is no alternative.*

Under Church's leadership, the UMW made one major last effort to leverage coal against the atom as the second anniversary of the partial meltdown at Three Mile Island approached in March 1981. With the national bituminous agreement expiring the day before the anniversary, the UMW once again saw a chance to use the atom as leverage, this time by using a deepening antinuclear sentiment to shore up support for the miners' contract battle. Under the auspices of the Labor Committee for Safe Energy and Full Employment—a coalition of fifty-seven unions that had begun discussing the development of "an independent energy policy for the labor movement"—the UMW sponsored a major rally to coincide with the second anniversary of the accident.[101] The rally would "dramatize the concerns of working people about the continued use of nuclear power." The organizers' major demands including keeping Unit 1 on Three Mile Island offline, protecting the Susquehanna River from any radioactive waste, a jobs guarantee for displaced nuclear workers as part of a larger public works program, and, finally, to "support the United Mine Workers of America in their effort to gain a decent contract."[102] The unions that signed on to the event represented more than six million workers and declared themselves the "safe energy wing" of the U.S. labor movement.[103] Church encouraged rank-and-filers of the UMW to attend because the event would provide "a national audience to which we can show that miners are ready to provide a safe and alternative energy source—coal."[104]

Church's goal to present coal miners as ready to fulfill a role as productive energy citizens, to "show our organization acting in a constructive manner toward an objective that benefits everybody," included an insistence that the UMW and BCOA would settle a contract without a strike for the first time in fifteen years.[105] But Church's plan was thwarted when the UMW bargaining team failed to reach an agreement with the BCOA. Miners walked off the job the day before the rally.[106]

Although the UMW-led labor coalition organized the rally specifically to increase the miners' leverage in the case of a strike, the timing also drew the UMW's attention away from rally mobilization. Most of the rally mobilization came not from the miners but instead from civil rights, women's, and environmental groups, as well as from organizing public employee unions across the East Coast. Church, intended to be one of the key speakers, sent his secretary-treasurer in his stead so he could focus on bargaining.[107] While some diversion of attention to the new strike was inevitable, it also conveyed the difficulty of actively participating in energy politics, while in their communities, UMW miners were increasingly under threat from deindustrialization, the western drift in coal production, and the opening of greater numbers of nonunion mines.

The rally appeared to herald the end of a remarkable era of coalfield politics not only because of the decreased presence of the miners at a rally they had helped organize but because it appeared to signal the UMW was willing to exchange a decade's worth of hard-won safety and environmental protections to solve the energy crisis. Church, in his appeal to miners to attend the rally, insisted that, compared to nuclear power, coal was "safer and cleaner."[108] The Pennsylvania branch of COMPAC argued that "electricity generated by coal is cheaper and far less hazardous to the general public than nuclear power."[109] The UMW speaker at the rally echoed the political ethos of Tony Boyle when he suggested that the more than one hundred thousand coal miners who had been killed on the job in the twentieth century were "nothing compared to the hundreds of thousands who would be affected by one nuclear meltdown." This framework cast occupational health and safety for miners as a separate issue from radioactive waste, cancer and birth defects caused by radiation exposure, and the potentially catastrophic impact of a future meltdown—rather than seeing them as emerging from the same basic problem of energy system inequality. In the shadow of Three Mile Island, the steam stack, rather than the mine face, had come to embody "the grim visage of death in whose shadow we stand."[110]

By declaring coal the "only solution," Church also helped close off debate over how that coal would be produced. After all, he appealed to miners, "your families, the labor movement, our American heritage, and all of humanity itself" was depending on coal and the workers who mined it.[111] Instead of using these claims to demand safer working conditions or less environmentally destructive energy practices as the reformers had just a decade before, the UMW marshaled the danger of the atom in a way that appeared to justify the danger of the mining workplace. With the vision of a better future dimmed, suddenly the UMW leadership's portrayal of competition between coal and the atom seemed a race to the bottom, together careening toward social and ecological ruin. Within a decade, the biggest energy crisis the country had ever known affirmed the indelible link between energy and modern American citizenship, even as it circumscribed the range of futures that energy citizens, especially coal miners, could imagine for themselves.

Conclusion

Energy Citizenship in Transition

Across the United States' most coal-fired century, coal miners contended with a challenging question: what should democratic citizenship mean in an energy-intensive society? They did more than most to answer it, too, and in the process, coal miners, as well as the coal they mined, reshaped how the country imagined the possibilities and limits of its democracy. Miners also made it possible to conceive of *energy citizenship*, where the rights and obligations of national belonging flow through the U.S. energy system. Through their workplace organizing, political activism, and resistance to an energy system fueled by their deaths, miners secured the rights of citizenship, although the belonging that citizenship conferred remained tied to the coal they extracted. Over the course of the twentieth century, miners leveraged this connection to demand the extension of basic constitutional rights to the coalfields, the enactment of safety regulations, expanded environmental protections, and redistributive policies to repair the harms wreaked by the coal-fired energy system. In their insistence that a coal-fired energy system could indeed be made truly democratic, they revealed the nation's energy system as contingent, as a product of choices and power.

Although miners looked to the coal-fired social contract to address the inequalities of the country's coal energy system, from our vantage point more than half a century later, it seems reasonable to question if a coal-fired democracy could ever have lived up to the promise of equal, democratic citizenship. The autocratic character of coalfield government at the turn of the twentieth century may be easy to see from a twenty-first-century vantage point. The abuses of the coalfield state, after all, grate against the most basic of democratic impulses. Coal company towns are a stock trope used to ridicule, for example, tech capitalists who propose creating on-site, company-owned housing for workers.[1] It is harder to reckon with the democratic failings of later decades. From the New Deal to the Great Society, modern American liberalism drew enormous amounts of power, both literal and figurative, from an energy system that normalized a great deal of violence. Miners and their communities, often the most affected by that violence, both vociferously resisted its normalization and became deeply invested in liberal visions of American democracy. That contradiction is a genuine one, and it fits with a growing set of scholarship in U.S. history rethinking the consequences of American liberalism. This scholarship emphasizes how the zenith of the country's welfare regime and commitment to public investment also perpetuated and deepened racial injustice, engendered novel forms of economic inequality, and drove new forms of environmental destruction.[2]

The coal-fired social contract, the energetic underpinning of modern American liberalism, has never been fully dismantled, but it has been gutted. Its substance has in part been replaced by coal industry propaganda and climate denialism, which has gained a foothold in Appalachia in recent decades. The power of coal industry campaigns is amplified by decades of political disinvestment and company economic intervention that has limited alternative forms of development in the region and, with it, limited employment opportunities for people who do not want to leave their homes and communities for a job. As Sylvia Ryerson has shown, coal industry groups have gone to great lengths to recruit Appalachian coal communities into a "pro-coal" camp, one which co-opts the language of energy citizenship while gutting its substance.[3] But the rest of the country should remember that what happens in Appalachia is not just an Appalachian story. If miners' place in the United States has been tied to coal since the early decades of the twentieth century, it is only possible because the rest of the United States, too, was tied to coal through the electricity and steel it produced.

Miners' identification with coal can also be read as identification with the coal-fired social contract, an uneasy reminder for a country that for so long has neglected its debts—debts, it is important to remember, that are still being incurred. Since Ronald Reagan's inauguration, more than 1,700 coal miners have been killed at work. And as has been the case throughout the history of the United States' coal-fired energy system, most of those miners died in ways that did not attract national attention: crushed against ribs of coal, buried under falling rock, electrocuted, thrown from a bulldozer as it cascaded down three hundred feet from a high and unstable embankment. One miner bled to death underground after a belt roller pulled his arm off.[4] But some of those deaths also resulted from major disasters.

On April 5, 2010, a massive explosion tore through the Upper Big Branch mine in southern West Virginia. The blast killed twenty-nine miners, the worst U.S. mine disaster since the 1970 Hyden disaster, forty years earlier. Like Hyden, Upper Big Branch was nonunion. Miners contended with poor ventilation, standing water, and blatant disregard by management for safety regulations. Adam Morgan had only worked at the mine for two months before it killed him. In those short eight weeks, he complained to his father and uncle about the conditions in the mine: the poor ventilation led to high dust levels and methane concentrations; the standing water in the mine passageways was so deep he came home wet up to his chest. Because he was still a trainee, Adam should never have been left alone in the mine, but he confided to his father, Steve, that he was often left by himself. Steve Morgan had worked in union mines for twenty-nine years, so he told Adam how to explain to management he wouldn't work in unsafe conditions. Instead of listening to his concerns, management told Adam that "if you're going to be that scared of your job ... you need to rethink your career." Steve tried to convince Adam to quit, but the mine blew up first.[5]

With national attention focused on West Virginia in the aftermath of the disaster, the persistent dependence of the United States on miners and the coal they extracted resurfaced. "Your families paid the ultimate price for a job our nation depends on," Hilda Solis, the U.S. labor secretary, told the family members of the miners who had been killed.[6] She was echoed by George Miller, a California Democrat and the chair of the House Committee on Education and Labor, who insisted that the coal industry "makes our country strong, makes our country free. . . . Coal mining is not an optional economic activity. This country desperately needs the coal, the coal mines, and the miners who engage in this very dangerous occupation."[7] But when Steve Morgan tried to go back to work two weeks after the disaster, he couldn't stop thinking about Adam. "I worked seven days and I was just getting more and more ill thinking about Adam. . . . [I] had panic attacks, anxiety, and depression. . . . And I'd get, you know, angry too."[8]

In the decade following the 2010 Upper Big Branch mine disaster, U.S. coal production appeared to decline precipitously, dropping around 45 percent between 2011 and 2021. That decline was not driven by a recognition of the danger that coal posed to the workers who mined it but rather by tightening environmental regulations and declining mine profitability. But even following this decline, the amount of coal the United States produces remains staggering. Total production in 2021 nearly equaled production highs from World War II.[9] It was less that coal had been consigned to history than, as one black lung clinician put it, "history [is] going in the wrong direction."[10] Black lung, a preventable occupational disease, surged among coal miners, particularly in underground mines, during the first decades of the twenty-first century, taking less time than ever for miners to progress to the deadliest stages of the disease.[11] The decimation of the industry's union density, already visible by the early 1980s, continued. In 2015, the last union miners in eastern Kentucky were laid off.[12] In the contemporary United States, most coal is surface mined in the West by nonunion miners. Of the ten largest coal mines operating in the United States during 2021, only one—number ten—lay east of the Mississippi River.[13]

At the same time, by the end of the 2010s, change did appear to be looming, both in the structure of the fuels markets and in the country's growing use of renewables. First, the "fracking revolution" reinvigorated U.S. oil and natural gas production, offering domestic growth markets in other fossil fuels besides coal.[14] With the growth of the climate justice movement, a better public understanding of the severity of the climate emergency, and major public investment by the Biden administration, by 2022 the United States began a meaningful buildout of alternative energy sources like wind and solar.[15] Although coal has experienced (and ultimately survived) many past downturns, the Energy Information Administration predicted that coal's decline would continue.[16]

The UMW seemed to agree. In 2021, the union issued its "Energy Transitions Initiative," an outline to the union's plan to help the nation's coal miners and their families navigate a shift that now seemed inevitable. "Change is coming," the union's statement read, "whether we seek it or not."[17] While echoing longstanding and controversial calls for new and expanded ways to use coal that will not emit so much carbon, the initiative also calls for new job creation without uprooting or breaking apart families, for reinvestment in the coalfields' social and physical infrastructure, and funding commitments to cover displaced miners' wages, pensions, health care, and education benefits.[18]

UMW President Cecil Roberts voiced skepticism toward calls for "just transition," a labor-environmentalist framework for phasing out dangerous and destructive industries while also ensuring workers in those industries had pathways to other employment. He told the National Press Club in 2021, "I wish people would quit using that. There's never been a just transition in the history of the United States."[19] Many in the labor movement disagree with Roberts's disavowal of the just transition model—including activists in the coalfields, in heavy industry, and in other fossil fuel sectors.[20] A growing number of coal miners and former coal miners are building new solidarities and rekindling old ones as they imagine new ways of life "after coal."[21] But I understand where he's coming from: if we understand the declines in coal production during the 2010s to be evidence of an energy transition already underway, there is little evidence to suggest that the broader country has the political will to foreground justice for coal communities. Just as the decision to move away from coal is the result of policy choices, the opioid epidemic ravaging deindustrializing communities, rising poverty and increased suicide rates in coal country, allowing coal companies to renege on contracts and cleanup obligations by declaring bankruptcy—those resulted from policy choices too. The UMW insists on the importance of keeping miners and their families "whole."[22] Certainly, that means doing no more harm, but it must also entail reparation of past injustices.

If we want to build a just future in the country that coal made, we need a real reckoning with history. A history of the modern United States that takes the agency and political subjectivity of coal miners seriously helps us make sense of a troubling paradox: that coal fueled the democratic imagination even as it undercut it, that coal miners helped build the country's democracy while workplace violence eroded it from within, and that miners used the same coal-fired energy system that was killing them to claim for themselves the rights of citizenship. The paradox of coal joins others in the nation's history: a slaving republic, an empire of liberty, and a coal-fired democracy.

For both better and worse, the United States bears the mark of coal. But more importantly, it bears the mark of coal miners. Miners, over the course of the American century, learned how to interpret geological strata, infrastructure, and regulatory minutiae and read from them questions about the nature of democracy, citizenship, and justice. Through their workplace organizing, their own brand of constitutionalism, their political imaginations, their aspirations for the future, their yearning for justice, and their belief in democracy, they shaped the United States and its energy system. They made it possible to see how energy citizenship has shaped the way Americans conceive of their rights and obligations to one another. As they attempted to answer the complex and often contradictory questions at the heart of political life in a coal-fired society, they left a lasting impression on how Americans define the content of democratic citizenship, an impression that will likely last longer than the country's coal-fired power plants.

The American age of coal appears to be fading, but the United States' coal-fired century will be with us for a long time. One thing I have learned from the coal miners in this book is that coal has a way of warping time. Even if the United States had stopped extracting, burning, and exporting coal as I wrote these words, the 38,000 or so workers who mined that coal would continue to carry it with them in their lungs, and that dust will kill some number of them.[23] The families of the workers killed in the mines will keep carrying the past with them. As one son of a miner killed in the 1968 Consol No. 9 explosion explained to the journalist Bonnie Stewart, "Forty years later, I'm still crying over it, so it just never ends I guess."[24] Another described watching rescuers race to save miners trapped in a flooded underground coal mine during the summer of 2002. The scenes, broadcast on television screens across the country, were too much to bear. He found himself sobbing on the couch, haunted by thoughts of his own father's last moments in the No. 9.[25]

The carbon emissions and other pollutants released from burning coal will be with us for even longer. American coal use has reshaped the global environment and altered the composition of our planet's atmosphere. The country is responsible for more than 20 percent of all historical carbon emissions, a staggering number that still shrouds the way the decades of American empire, interventions, and economic influence have shaped energy use and carbon emissions throughout the world.[26] Coal has entangled our past and future. That's one of the reasons reckoning with coal demands we examine its history as well as its future impact. The history of coal miners in the modern United States, however, reminds us that entanglement is not simply a matter of atmospheric chemistry but the product of both choices and contestation. It is profoundly political, and it still figures centrally in contestations over the nation's future.

At the same time, it is important to acknowledge that the questions raised by miners in this book about the nature of justice in energy-intensive societies extend beyond the United States and beyond its peculiar form of democracy, which just as often was not democratic at all. I see the echoes of those miners' questions everywhere. In 2014, the year I began the research that would eventually become this book, a coal mine fire in Soma, Turkey, killed 301 coal miners and injured at least 162 more. Over the years, as I researched and wrote, many more miners died, and like the miners in this book, their deaths were usually preventable. By the summer of 2022, Chinese miners contended with a spate of deadly accidents as their government pushed for greater coal production. China's National Mine Safety Administration set a goal of reducing mining deaths by 10 percent over the next three years, a move Bloomberg News argued was "necessary," the kinds of "tough policy trade-offs" that after eight years of living with this project felt familiar and sickening.[27] Tom Bethell's words from 1971 sounded in my ears: "The figures are bad, but . . . the killing goes on."[28] In those numbers, in considering each disaster as an individual travesty, we continue to miss the larger story: how coal-fired energy systems, in a wide range of political contexts, accrue inequality by normalizing extraordinary levels of violence. This reality, which extends beyond coal to nearly every aspect of global energy systems, demands we adopt new ways of thinking about the relationship between energy and political power as fundamentally mediated by workers' deaths.

In Sabinas, Mexico, a small city about three hours west of Laredo, Texas, graveyards continue to masquerade as coal mines. Hugo Tijerina died in one of those mines in August 2022, along with nine others, after water flooded the tunnels. Tijerina's brother-in-law, Juan Briones, still had to go to work at a nearby mine to support his family, as he had for the last sixteen years. Working in the area's small mines, he could earn about 2,700 pesos ($134) or a little more each week—far more than any other local employment could offer.[29] The state utility burned the coal he and his brother-in-law mined to generate electric power, in a move Mexico's president, Andrés Manuel López Obrador, suggested would make Mexico more energy independent and less unequal.[30] Independence and equality: those promises seemed distant to Briones as he descended underground for work each day. He resigned himself to his fear, knowing his options were limited, hoping his children wouldn't have to follow in his footsteps, remembering those he had lost: "When I'm working, down below, I remember all of them."[31]

While coal's role in global heating and the destabilization of the earth system underscores the ultimately illusory nature of efforts to create equality by burning coal, we should also be careful not to reduce the explanation for coal-fired inequality to carbon bonds. The global inequalities of decarbonization driven by the mining of critical minerals like lithium and cobalt look far too familiar. It doesn't take long, surveying the newspapers of the last decade, to find traces of how across the globe, the violence at the heart of the coal energy system has morphed into a new geography of energy violence, often overlapping with forms of what the geographer Noura Alkhalili has termed "enduring coloniality."[32] From the lithium triangle stretching across Chile, Bolivia, and Argentina to the cobalt pits in the Democratic Republic of Congo, energy system violence has so far been central to the renewable transition: mine collapses, lung disease, toxic soil, poisoned water, political violence exacerbated by extractivism.[33] The paradox of the United States' coal-fired democracy need not become the paradox of our decarbonized future, but changing course will require us to reimagine our energy sources, our political communities, and our connected histories.

Acknowledgments

Like all scholars, I have incurred many debts in the process of writing this book, though the largest one, without doubt, is the debt I owe to the miners whose voices inhabit it. Almost all of them have passed on, and it is not a debt I can repay directly, but I hope this book has helped honor their memories and their struggles.

My next debt of gratitude is to the community of scholars who have helped shape this project from the vaguely conceived idea it began as. Many people have shaped its final contours, though none as much as Jim Sparrow, Brian Balogh, and Karine Walther. In addition to their intellectual engagement, which both shaped and sustained my work, each embodied a generosity and kindness that I can only hope to pay forward. I am also deeply grateful for the many years of support and guidance I received from Fredrik Albritton Jonsson, Jon Levy, and Andrew Needham. My colleagues in Doha provided invaluable friendship and intellectual community as I finished this project. My thanks to Nadya Sbaiti, Vicky Googasian, Zahra Babar, Anne-Sophie Pratte, Firat Oruc, Noha Aboueldahab, Fatema Hubail, Sonia Alonso, Misba Bhatti, Suzi Mirghani, Maram Al-Qershi, Lynda Iroulo, Lamis Kattan, Eddie Kolla, Abdullah Al-Arian, and Carol Fadda.

Many other colleagues offered support, insights, and comments on this manuscript. For their comments on the full manuscript, I thank Sarah Jaffe and Ewan Gibbs, as well as those anonymous colleagues who served as peer reviewers for Columbia University Press. Thank you also to John McNeill,

David Painter, Joe McCartin, Katherine Benton-Cohen, Lane Windham, James Benton, Michael Kazin, and Toshihiro Higuchi for an incredibly helpful manuscript workshop at a critical writing stage. And thank you to the many colleagues who have read and commented over the years, especially Victor Seow, Anna Andrzejewski, Chris Jones, Tamara Fernando, Emily Prifogle, Barbara Welke, Lizabeth Cohen, Sara Pritchard, Ellie Shermer, Natasha Zaretsky, Ryan Driskell Tate, Agatha Slupek, Robert Suits, Caine Jordan, Guy Emerson Mount, Topher Kindell, Emily Masghati, Alyssa Smith, Andrew Seber, and Alejandra Azuero Quijano.

Linda binti Ridzuan Chun and Allie Penn both provided essential research assistance in the final stages of writing. I am also thankful for the assistance of the many archivists who supported my research at Penn State University, the Reuther Library, the Archives of Appalachia, the University of North Carolina, the University of Kentucky, the Ford Presidential Library, the Stapleton Library at Indiana University Pennsylvania, the West Virginia and Regional History Center at West Virginia University, the West Virginia State Archives, and the United Mine Workers of America. Special thanks are owed to Erin Lundy, James Quigel, and Harrison Wick. Thanks also to the Herb Block Foundation, Baltimore Sun Media, *Goldenseal* magazine, Earl Dotter, Lemley Mullett, and Tricia Gresner for help with images. Workshops and presentations at the Tensions of Energy Working Group, the University of Glasgow, the DC Labor History Seminar, and the Newberry Library Labor History Workshop all improved the final manuscript.

I am also grateful for the institutions that funded this research over many years: the University of Chicago, the Jefferson Scholars Foundation, the Mellon Foundation, Georgetown University and the Qatar Foundation, the Eberly Family Special Collections at Penn State University, the Walter P. Reuther Library, the Gerald R. Ford Presidential Library, the American Society for Environmental History, and the Western Association of Women Historians.

Finally, let me express my gratitude to Stephen Wesley, Alex Gupta, Michael Haskell, Rob Fellman, and the entire editorial and production team at Columbia University Press who have brought this project from proposal to manuscript to the book you hold now.

Abbreviations

In Text

ACLU	American Civil Liberties Union
AEC	Atomic Energy Commission
BCOA	Bituminous Coal Operators Association
BLA	Black Lung Association
BLBA	Black Lung Benefits Act
CCF	Central Competitive Field
CERT	Council of Energy Resource Tribes
COMPAC	Coal Miners' Political Action Committee
EPA	Environmental Protection Agency
FEO	Federal Energy Office
FOPC	Foreign Oil Policy Committee
FPC	Federal Power Commission
GAO	General Accounting Office
MFD	Miners for Democracy
MOIP	Mandatory Oil Import Program
NCA	National Coal Association
NCPC	National Coal Policy Conference
NIRA	National Industrial Recovery Act

NRA	National Recovery Administration
NRC	National Resources Committee
OCAW	Oil, Chemical, and Atomic Workers International Union
OAPEC	Organization of Arab Petroleum Exporting Countries
OCR	Office of Coal Research
OPA	Office of Price Administration
OPEC	Organization of Petroleum Exporting Countries
SEC	Securities and Exchange Commission
SFAW	Solid Fuels Administration for the War
TMI	Three Mile Island
TVA	Tennessee Valley Authority
UMW	United Mine Workers of America
WLB	National War Labor Board

In Notes

Archives

ARP	Archie Robinson Papers
JDC	Jerry Demuth Collection
JHP	John Herling Papers
JRP	Jeanne Rasmussen Papers
LCFSEFE	Labor Committee for Safe Energy and Full Employment Records
MFDR	Miners for Democracy Records
MRDP	Michael Raoul-Duval Papers
PPLR	Pennsylvania Power & Light Company Records
SOHP	Southern Oral History Program Collection
UMWAV	United Mine Workers of America, Audio-Visual Records
UMWJR	United Mine Workers of America, Journal Office Records
UMWPC	United Mine Workers of America, President's Correspondence with Districts
UMWPO	United Mine Workers of America, President's Office Records

Institutions

BCOA	Bituminous Coal Operators Association
BM	U.S. Bureau of Mines
BLS	U.S. Bureau of Labor Statistics
DMMR	Pennsylvania Department of Mines and Mineral Resources
DOI	U.S. Department of the Interior
DOL	U.S. Department of Labor
EIA	U.S. Energy Information Administration
JCAE	Joint Committee on Atomic Energy
MSHA	Mine Safety and Health Administration
OMB	U.S. Office of Management and Budget
PCC	President's Commission on Coal (1978–1980)
PCTMI	President's Commission on Three Mile Island
PDER	Pennsylvania Department of Environmental Resources
WVDM	West Virginia Department of Mines

Databases

AAA	African Activist Archive
APP	American Presidency Project
DHFDRP	Documentary History of the Franklin D. Roosevelt Presidency
MSHA-DL	Mine Safety and Health Administration, Digital Library
NBER	National Bureau of Economic Research
NCOH	Louie B. Nunn Center for Oral History
SHC	Southern Historical Collection
WVRHC	West Virginia and Regional History Center

Publications

BLB	*Black Lung Bulletin*
MV	*Miner's Voice*
NYT	*New York Times*
UMWJ	*United Mine Workers Journal*

Notes

Introduction. The Paradox of Coal-Fired Democracy

1. Lyndon B. Johnson, Proclamation 3789—National Coal Week, June 16, 1967, APP.
2. For recasting the end of Reconstruction as an overthrow, see Kidada E. Williams, *I Saw Death Coming: A History of Terror and Survival in the War Against Reconstruction* (New York: Bloomsbury, 2023).
3. Christopher F. Jones, *Routes of Power: Energy and Modern America* (Cambridge, MA: Harvard University Press, 2014); Peter Shulman, *Coal and Empire: The Birth of Energy Security in Industrial America* (Baltimore, MD: Johns Hopkins University Press, 2015).
4. Andrew Needham, *Power Lines: Phoenix and the Making of the Modern Southwest* (Princeton, NJ: Princeton University Press, 2014); Richard H. K. Vietor, *Energy Policy in America Since 1945: A Study of Business-Government Relations* (New York: Cambridge University Press, 1984). On electric utilities, see Richard L. Gordon, *U.S. Coal and the Electric Power Industry* (Baltimore, MD: Johns Hopkins University Press, 1975); Casey Cater, *Regenerating Dixie: Electric Energy and the Making of the Modern South* (Pittsburgh, PA: University of Pittsburgh Press, 2019). On steel, see Kenneth Warren, *The American Steel Industry, 1850–1970: A Geographical Interpretation* (Pittsburgh, PA: University of Pittsburgh Press, 1973). On the global oil context, see Giuliano Garavini, *The Rise and Fall of OPEC in the Twentieth Century* (New York: Oxford University Press, 2019); David S. Painter, *Oil and the American Century: The Political*

Economy of U.S. Foreign Policy, 1941–1954 (Baltimore, MD: Johns Hopkins University Press). On nuclear, see Brian Balogh, *Chain Reaction: Expert Debate and Public Participation in American Commercial Nuclear Power* (New York: Cambridge University Press, 1991).

5. The history of the social contract and social contract theory are far more extensive than I can treat in full here. For how the social contract has operated in modern U.S. history, I draw on Linda K. Kerber, *No Constitutional Right to Be Ladies: Women and the Obligations of Citizenship* (New York: Hill and Wang, 1998); Alice Kessler-Harris, *In Pursuit of Equity: Women, Men, and the Quest for Economic Citizenship in 20th-Century America* (New York: Oxford University Press, 2001); Julilly Kohler-Hausmann, *Getting Tough: Welfare and Imprisonment in 1970s America* (Princeton, NJ: Princeton University Press, 2017), 125–27.

6. The classic example of this assumption is Timothy Mitchell, *Carbon Democracy: Political Power in the Age of Oil* (New York: Verso, 2011). In developing my critique of Mitchell, I have relied on Needham, *Power Lines*; Jones, *Routes of Power*; Ann Norton Greene, *Horses at Work: Harnessing Power in Industrial America* (Cambridge, MA: Harvard University Press, 2008); Andreas Malm, *Fossil Capital: The Rise of Steam Power and the Roots of Global Warming* (New York: Verso, 2016); Dominic Boyer, *Energopolitics: Wind and Power in the Anthropocene* (Durham, NC: Duke University Press, 2019); Victor Seow, *Carbon Technocracy: Energy Regimes in Modern East Asia* (Chicago: University of Chicago Press, 2022); On Barak, *Powering Empire: How Coal Made the Middle East and Sparked Global Carbonization* (Berkeley: University of California Press, 2020); Laura Nader, "The Politics of Energy: Toward a Bottom-Up Approach," *Radcliffe Quarterly* 7 (1981): 5–6, reprinted in *The Energy Reader*, ed. Laura Nader (Malden, MA: Wiley, 2010), 314.

7. Practices of governance drawn from William J. Novak, *The People's Welfare: Law and Regulation in Nineteenth-Century America* (Chapel Hill: University of North Carolina Press, 1996).

8. On the limits of comparison, see Dino Drudi, "A Century-Long Quest for Meaningful and Accurate Occupational Injury and Illness Statistics," *Compensation and Working Conditions*, BLS (Winter 1997): 19–27; MSHA, "Coal Mine Fatalities, 1900–2023," https://arlweb.msha.gov/stats/centurystats/coalstats.asp; DOL, BLS, "The Safety Movement in the Iron and Steel Industry, 1900–1917," by Lucien W. Chaney and Hugh S. Hanna, Industrial Accidents and Hygiene Series No. 18 (Washington, DC, 1918), 29–32.

9. William Graebner, *Coal-Mining Safety in the Progressive Period: The Political Economy of Reform* (Lexington: University Press of Kentucky, 1976); Mark Aldrich, "Preventing 'the Needless Peril of the Coal Mine': The Bureau of Mines and

the Campaign Against Coal Mine Explosions, 1910–1940," *Technology and Culture* 36 no. 3 (July 1995): 483–518.
10. "Injury Rates in 1968," Holmes Safety Council, 1969, UMWPO 11/24.
11. Alan Derickson, *Black Lung: Anatomy of a Public Health Disaster* (Ithaca, NY: Cornell University Press, 1998); Barbara Ellen Smith, *Digging Our Own Graves: Coal Miners and the Struggle Over Black Lung Disease*, updated ed. (Chicago: Haymarket, 2020).
12. Ronald Eller, *Uneven Ground: Appalachia Since 1945* (Lexington: University of Kentucky Press, 2013), 3.
13. Robyn Muncy, "Coal-Fired Reforms: Social Citizenship, Dissident Miners, and the Great Society," *Journal of American History* 96, no. 1 (2009): 72–98; David Ekbladh, *The Great American Mission: Modernization and the Construction of an American World Order* (Princeton, NJ: Princeton University Press, 2009).
14. John Gaventa, "Appalachian Studies in Global Context: Reflections on the Beginnings—Challenges for the Future," *Journal of Appalachian Studies* 8, no. 1 (2002): 79–90; Barbara Ellen Smith, "The Place of Appalachia," *Journal of Appalachian Studies* 8, no. 1 (2002): 42–49.
15. Allen W. Batteau, *The Invention of Appalachia* (Tucson: University of Arizona Press, 1990), 1–2; David E. Whisnant, *All That Is Native and Fine: The Politics of Culture in an American Region* (Chapel Hill: University of North Carolina Press, 1983); Wilma A. Dunaway, *The First American Frontier: Transition to Capitalism in Southern Appalachia, 1700–1860* (Chapel Hill: University of North Carolina Press, 1996); Henry D. Shapiro, *Appalachia on Our Mind: The Southern Mountains and Mountaineers in the American Consciousness, 1870–1920* (Chapel Hill: University of North Carolina Press, 1986).
16. Barbara Kunkle, "Appalachia and the Imagination of Empire," Ph.D. diss., Bowling Green State University, 1998; Daniel Immerwahr, *How to Hide an Empire: A History of the Greater United States* (New York: Farrar, Straus and Giroux, 2019), 10–11.
17. Steven Stoll, *Ramp Hollow: The Ordeal of Appalachia* (New York: Hill and Wang, 2018), 3–7.
18. For a classic example, see Jack E. Weller, *Yesterday's People: Life in Contemporary Appalachia* (Lexington: University Press of Kentucky, 1965). For a historicization and critique of this narrative, see Rebecca R. Scott, *Removing Mountains: Extracting Nature and Identity in the Appalachian Coalfields* (Minneapolis: University of Minnesota Press, 2010), 169–206; Jerry Bruce Thomas, *An Appalachian Reawakening: West Virginia and the Perils of the New Machine Age, 1945–1972* (Morgantown: West Virginia University Press, 2010), 3–8.
19. William H. Turner, *The Harlan Renaissance: Stories of Black Life in Appalachian Coal Towns* (Morgantown: West Virginia University Press, 2021); William

Hal Gorby, *Wheeling's Polonia: Reconstructing Polish Community in a West Virginia Steel Town* (Morgantown: West Virginia University Press, 2020); Joe William Trotter Jr., *African American Workers and the Appalachian Coal Industry* (Morgantown: West Virginia University Press, 2022); William H. Turner and Edward J. Cabbell, *Blacks in Appalachia* (Lexington: University Press of Kentucky, 1985).

20. Paul Nyden, *Black Coal Miners in the United States* (Pittsburgh, PA: American Institute for Marxist Studies, 1974), 57–64.

21. Joe William Trotter Jr., *Coal, Class, and Color: Blacks in Southern West Virginia, 1915–1932* (Urbana: University of Illinois Press, 1990), 268; Ronald L. Lewis, *Black Coal Miners in America: Race, Class, and Community Conflict, 1780–1980* (Lexington: University Press of Kentucky, 2009); Karida L. Brown, *Gone Home: Race and Roots Through Appalachia* (Chapel Hill: University of North Carolina Press, 2019), 29–54.

22. Mildred Allen Beik, *The Miners of Windber: The Struggles of New Immigrants for Unionization, 1890s–1930s* (University Park: Pennsylvania State University Press, 1996); Charles B. Keeney, *The Road to Blair Mountain: Saving a Mine Wars Battlefield from King Coal* (Morgantown: West Virginia University Press, 2021).

23. Classic texts from this vein of scholarship include John Gaventa, *Power and Powerlessness: Quiescence and Rebellion in an Appalachian Valley* (Urbana: University of Illinois Press, 1980); David Alan Corbin, *Life, Work, and Rebellion in the Coal Fields: The Southern West Virginia Miners, 1880–1920* (Urbana: University of Illinois Press, 1981); Ronald D. Eller, *Miners, Millhands, and Mountaineers: Industrialization of the Appalachian South, 1880–1930* (Knoxville: University of Tennessee Press, 1982); Trotter, *Coal, Class, and Color*; John H. M. Laslett, ed., *The United Mine Workers of America: A Model of Industrial Solidarity?* (University Park: Pennsylvania State University Press, 1996); Daniel Letwin, *The Challenge of Interracial Unionism: The Alabama Coal Miners, 1878–1921* (Chapel Hill: University of North Carolina Press, 1998). For the later period, see Smith, *Digging Our Own Graves*; Paul F. Clark, *The Miners' Fight for Democracy: Arnold Miller and the Reform of the United Mine Workers* (Ithaca, NY: ILR Press, 1981); Curtis Seltzer, *Fire in the Hole: Miners and Managers in the American Coal Industry* (Lexington: University Press of Kentucky, 1985); Paul J. Nyden, "Rank-and-File Movements in the United Mine Workers of America, Early 1960s–Early 1980s," in *Rebel Rank and File: Labor Militancy and Revolt from Below During the Long 1970s*, ed. Aaron Brenner, Robert Brenner, and Cal Winslow (New York: Verso, 2010); James Green, *The Devil Is Here in These Hills: West Virginia's Coal Miners and Their Battle for Freedom* (New York: Grove, 2016); Thomas G. Andrews, *Killing for Coal: America's Deadliest Labor War* (Cambridge, MA: Harvard University Press, 2008).

24. Heber Blankenhorn, *The Strike for Union: A Study of the Non-Union Question in Coal and the Problems of a Democratic Movement* (New York: H. W. Wilson, 1924), 3.
25. Blankenhorn, *The Strike for Union*, foreword.
26. Blankenhorn, *The Strike for Union*, 110.
27. Blankenhorn, *The Strike for Union*, foreword.
28. Shannon Elizabeth Bell and Richard York, "Coal, Injustice, and Environmental Destruction," *Organization and Environment* 25, no. 4 (2012): 359–67; Michelle Morrone and Geoffrey L. Buckley, *Mountains of Injustice: Social and Environmental Justice in Appalachia* (Athens: Ohio University Press, 2011); Lara J. Cushing, Shiwen Li, Benjamin B. Steiger, and Joan A. Casey, "Historical Red-Lining Is Associated with Fossil Fuel Power Plant Siting and Present-Day Inequalities in Air Pollutant Emissions," *Nature Energy* 8 (2023): 52–61.

I. Civil War in the Coalfield State

1. Winthrop Lane, *Civil War in West Virginia* (New York: B. W. Huebsch, 1921), 11.
2. James Green, *The Devil Is Here in These Hills: West Virginia's Coal Miners and Their Battle for Freedom* (New York: Grove, 2015), 194.
3. Rebecca J. Bailey, *Matewan Before the Massacre: Politics, Coal, and the Roots of Conflict in West Virginia* (Morgantown: West Virginia University Press, 2008), 210–12.
4. "Twelve Men Killed in Pistol Battle in West Virginia," *NYT*, May 20, 1920; Green, *The Devil Is Here in These Hills*, 209–14; Bailey, *Matewan Before the Massacre*, 214–18.
5. Thomas G. Andrews, *Killing for Coal: America's Deadliest Labor War* (Cambridge, MA: Harvard University Press, 2008).
6. Lane, *Civil War in West Virginia*, 11.
7. For a critique of this understanding, Bailey, *Matewan Before the Massacre*, 254–55.
8. Christopher McKnight Nichols, *Promise and Peril: America at the Dawn of a Global Age* (Cambridge, MA: Harvard University Press, 2011), 123; David Alan Corbin, *Gun Thugs, Rednecks, and Radicals: A Documentary History of the West Virginia Mine Wars* (New York: PM Press, 2011), 9.
9. Amy Dru Stanley, *From Bondage to Contract: Wage Labor, Marriage, and the Market in the Age of Slave Emancipation* (New York: Cambridge University Press, 1998).
10. Stephen Skowronek, *Building a New American State: The Expansion of National Administrative Capacities, 1877–1920* (New York: Cambridge University Press,

1982), iix–ix, 4; Eric Jarvis, "Toward a New Deal for Coal? The United States Coal Commission of 1922," *Journal of the Historical Society* 3 no. 3 (September 2008): 457.

11. Lane, *Civil War in West Virginia*, 125.
12. Winthrop Lane, "The Black Avalanche," *Survey Graphic*, March 25, 1922, in Corbin, *Gun Thugs, Rednecks, and Radicals*, 17; Bob Johnson, *Carbon Nation: Fossil Fuels in the Making of American Culture* (Lawrence: University Press of Kansas, 2014), 86–87.
13. Lane, "The Black Avalanche," 21–22.
14. Steven Stoll, *Ramp Hollow: The Ordeal of Appalachia* (New York: Hill and Wang, 2017), 140–52.
15. Ronald Eller, *Miners, Millhands, and Mountaineers: Industrialization of the Appalachian South, 1880–1930* (Knoxville: University of Tennessee Press, 1982), 86–128; Drew A. Swanson, *Beyond the Mountains: Commodifying Appalachian Environments* (Athens: University of Georgia Press, 2018), 4–9.
16. Samuel Gompers, "Russianized West Virginia," in Corbin, *Gun Thugs, Rednecks, and Radicals*, 23–29.
17. Joe William Trotter Jr., *Coal, Class, and Color: Blacks in Southern West Virginia, 1915–1932* (Urbana: University of Illinois Press, 1990), 9–13.
18. DOI, U.S. Geological Survey, *Birth of the Mountains: The Geologic Story of the Southern Appalachian Mountains*, by Sandra H. B. Clark (Washington, DC: U.S. Geological Survey, n.d.).
19. David Alan Corbin, *Life, Work, and Rebellion in the Coal Fields: The Southern West Virginia Miners, 1880–1922* (Urbana: University of Illinois Press, 1981), 2–5.
20. Trotter, *Coal, Class, and Color*, 21.
21. Tara Zahra, *The Great Departure: Mass Migration from Eastern Europe and the Making of the Free World* (New York: Norton, 2016), 23–63; Marco Soresina, "Italian Emigration Policy During the Great Migration Age, 1888–1919: The Interaction of Emigration and Foreign Policy," *Journal of Modern Italian Studies* 21, no. 5 (2016): 723–46.
22. Edward B. Barbier, *Scarcity and Frontiers: How Economies Have Evolved Through Natural Resource Exploitation* (New York: Cambridge University Press, 2011), 368–462; Megan Black, *The Global Interior: Mineral Frontiers and American Power* (Cambridge, MA: Harvard University Press, 2018).
23. Wilma E. Dunaway, *The First American Frontier: Transition to Capitalism in Southern Appalachia, 1700–1860* (Chapel Hill: University of North Carolina Press, 1996), 246–48.
24. Barbara Kunkle, "Appalachia and the Imagination of Empire," Ph.D. diss., Bowling Green State University, 1998, 6–17; William Goodell Frost, "Our

Contemporary Ancestors in the Southern Mountains," *Atlantic Monthly*, March 1899.
25. Richard White, *Railroaded: The Transcontinentals and the Making of Modern America* (New York: Norton, 2012), xxix; Wolfgang Schivelbusch, "Railroad Space and Railroad Time," *New German Critique* 14 (Spring 1978): 31.
26. Manu Karuka, *Empire's Tracks: Indigenous Nations, Chinese Workers, and the Transcontinental Railroad* (Berkeley: University of California Press, 2019); Peter Shulman, *Coal and Empire: The Birth of Energy Security in Industrial America* (Baltimore, MD: Johns Hopkins University Press, 2015); Andrew B. Arnold, *Fueling the Gilded Age: Railroads, Miners, and Disorder in Pennsylvania Coal Country* (New York: New York University Press, 2014).
27. Kenneth Warren, *The American Steel Industry, 1850–1970: A Geographical Interpretation* (Pittsburgh, PA: University of Pittsburgh Press, 1973), 109–33.
28. Thomas Taro Lennerfors and Peter Birch, *Snow in the Tropics: A History of the Independent Reefer Operators* (Leiden: Brill, 2019), 215–16.
29. John Soluri, *Banana Cultures: Agriculture, Consumption, and Environment in Honduras and the United States* (Austin: University of Texas Press, 2005), 2–3.
30. Only in the Midwest and Ohio did fewer than half of miners live in company towns in 1920. U.S. Congress, House, Committee on Labor, *Investigation of Wages and Working Conditions in the Coal-Mining Industry*, 67th Cong., 2d sess., 1922, 50–53; Corbin, *Life, Work, and Rebellion*, 8; Eller, *Miners, Millhands, and Mountaineers*, 162–63.
31. Oliver J. Dinius and Angela Vergara, eds., *Company Towns in the Americas: Landscape, Power, and Working-Class Communities* (Athens: University of Georgia Press, 2011), 6–9; also see Crandall A. Shifflett, *Coal Towns: Life, Work, and Culture in the Company Towns of Southern Appalachia, 1880–1960* (Knoxville: University of Tennessee Press, 1991).
32. Elizabeth Anderson, *Private Government: How Employers Rule Our Lives (and Why We Don't Talk About It)* (Princeton, NJ: Princeton University Press, 2017).
33. John Gaventa, *Power and Powerlessness: Quiescence and Rebellion in an Appalachian Valley* (Urbana: University of Illinois Press, 1982), 89.
34. Harold Mostyn Watkins, *Coal and Men: An Economic and Social Study of the British and American Coalfields* (London: G. Allen & Unwin, 1934).
35. Carter Goodrich, *The Miner's Freedom: A Study of the Working Life in a Changing Industry* (Boston: Marshall Jones Company, 1925), 22.
36. Pennsylvania Department of Mines, *Report of the Department of Mines of Pennsylvania, Part II: Bituminous, 1905* (Harrisburg, PA: Harrisburg Publishing, 1906), vii; Russell Freedman, *Kids at Work: Lewis Hine and the Crusade Against Child Labor* (New York: Clarion, 1994), 47–58.

37. Lane, *Civil War in West Virginia*, 17–18.
38. Stephen H. Norwood, *Strikebreaking and Intimidation: Mercenaries and Masculinities in Twentieth-Century America* (Chapel Hill: University of North Carolina Press, 2002), 120–28; Elizabeth Ricketts, "The Struggle for Civil Liberties and Unionization in the Coal Fields: The Free Speech Case of Vintondale, Pennsylvania, 1922," *Pennsylvania Magazine of History and Biography* 122, no. 4 (October 1998): 330–35; for copies of some of these affidavits, see District 3 Records, United Mine Workers of America 3/32.
39. Interview with George Swain in *On Dark and Bloody Ground: An Oral History of the West Virginia Mine Wars*, ed. Anne T. Lawrence (Morgantown: West Virginia University Press, 2021), 67–68; Robert Shogan, *The Battle of Blair Mountain: The Story of America's Largest Labor Uprising* (New York: Basic Books, 2006).
40. Lane, *Civil War in West Virginia*, 17–18.
41. David E. Nye, *Electrifying America: Social Meanings of a New Technology, 1880–1940* (Cambridge, MA: MIT Press, 1992); Harold L. Platt, *The Electric City: Energy and the Growth of the Chicago Area, 1880–1930* (Chicago: University of Chicago Press, 1991).
42. On Barak, *Powering Empire: How Coal Made the Middle East and Sparked Global Carbonization* (Berkeley: University of California Press, 2020); Walter Benjamin, "On the Concept of History," in *Selected Writings*, vol. 4: *1938–1940*, ed. Howard Eiland and Michael W. Jennings (Cambridge, MA: Belknap, 2003), 392.
43. On the link between workplace and social violence, see Jeremy Milloy, *Blood, Sweat, and Fear: Violence at Work in the North American Auto Industry, 1960–1980* (Urbana: University of Illinois Press, 2017); Andrews, *Killing for Coal*, 122–56.
44. Ronald L. Lewis, *Black Coal Miners in America: Race, Class, and Community Conflict, 1780–1980* (Lexington: University Press of Kentucky, 2009), 15–19.
45. *Report of the Department of Mines of Pennsylvania, Part II: Bituminous, 1905*, xx–xxi.
46. Barbara Kopple, *Harlan County, U.S.A.* (New York: Criterion, 2006); interview with Luther Keen in *On Dark and Bloody Ground*, 113.
47. Melvin Triolo, *The Black Debacle: From a Thundering Voice to a Confused Whimper* (Parsons, WV: McClain Printing Co., 1991), 1–5.
48. Triolo, *The Black Debacle*, 5–6.
49. Triolo's account does not tell us what kind of accident it was, but statistically it was most likely it was a roof fall or haulage accident. On "combat" and "battle" analogies, see Paul Rakes, "A Combat Scenario: Early Coal Mining and the Culture of Danger," in *Culture, Class, and Politics in Modern Appalachia: Essays in Honor of Ronald L. Lewis* (Morgantown: West Virginia University Press, 2009), 56–87.

50. DOI, BM, *Coal Mine Fatalities in the United States, 1870–1914*, comp. Albert H. Fay (Washington, DC: GPO, 1916); DOL, MSHA, *Coal Fatalities for 1900 Through 2022*, MSHA-DL.
51. Eller, *Miners, Millhands, and Mountaineers*, 163.
52. Watkins, *Coal and Men*, 258.
53. Gaventa, *Power and Powerlessness*, 91.
54. Interview with Dewey Browning in *On Dark and Bloody Ground*, 79.
55. U.S. Congress, House, Committee on Labor, *Investigation of Wages and Working Conditions in the Coal-Mining Industry, Part 2*, 502–4.
56. Interview with Lana Blizzard Harlow in *On Dark and Bloody Ground*, 46.
57. Eller, *Miners, Millhands, and Mountaineers*, 171.
58. Eller, *Miners, Millhands, and Mountaineers*, 168–69; "Voting Population of McDowell County," *McDowell Times*, May 16, 1913.
59. Trotter, *Coal, Class, and Color*, 76.
60. "Voting Population of McDowell County," *McDowell Times*, May 16, 1913.
61. "Near Riot in Anawalt," *McDowell Times*, May 16, 1913.
62. Trotter, *Coal, Class, and Color*, 126. On interracial organizing and its challenges in the coalfields, see Daniel Letwin, *The Challenge of Interracial Unionism: Alabama Coal Miners, 1878–1921* (Chapel Hill: University of North Carolina Press, 1998); Brian Kelly, *Race, Class, and Power in the Alabama Coalfields, 1908–1921* (Urbana: University of Illinois Press, 2001).
63. Jennifer Keene, "A 'Brutalizing' War? The USA After the First World War," *Journal of Contemporary History* 50, no. 1 (2015): 78–99.
64. "Fears Are Relieved," *Charleston Daily Mail*, December 11, 1919; "General Increase in Coal Supply Reported," *Charleston Daily Mail*, December 12, 1919; Green, *The Devil Is Here in These Hills*, 193–95.
65. David F. Krugler, *1919, The Year of Racial Violence: How African Americans Fought Back* (New York: Cambridge University Press, 2015).
66. "Negroes Shot to Death by Mob After Murder in Logan," *Independent-Herald* (Hinton, WV), December 18, 1919. I first encountered Whitney and Whitfield's story in Trotter, *Coal, Class, and Color*, 125–26.
67. "Logan Mob Kills Two Colored Men," *Hinton Daily News*, December 17, 1919; "Negroes Shot to Death by Mob After Murder in Logan," *Independent-Herald* (Hinton, WV), December 18, 1919; "Murder Suspects Lynched in Logan," *Fairmont West Virginian*, December 16, 1919; Trotter, *Coal, Class, and Color*, 125–26.
68. Interview with John Wilburn in *On Dark and Bloody Ground*, 39.
69. Letwin, *The Challenge of Interracial Unionism*, 182–83.
70. Karin Shapiro, *A New South Rebellion: The Battle Against Convict Labor in the Tennessee Coalfields, 1871–1896* (Chapel Hill: University of North Carolina Press, 1998).

71. Lane, *Civil War in West Virginia*, 15.
72. Corbin, *Life, Work, and Rebellion*, 176.
73. Clayton D. Laurie and Ronald H. Cole, *The Role of Federal Military Forces in Domestic Disorders, 1877–1945* (Washington, DC: Center for Military History, 1997), 308–11, 322–23; Howard B. Lee, *Bloodletting in Appalachia: The Story of West Virginia's Four Major Mine Wars and Other Thrilling Incidents on Its Coal Fields* (Morgantown: West Virginia University Press, 1969), 74–75; "Governor Puts Mingo Co. Under Martial Law by Proclamation Issued This Morning," *West Virginian*, May 20, 1921; "Martial Law Order for Strike Field Signed by Harding," *Martinsburg Journal*, May 16, 1921.
74. "Interviews for and Against the State Constabulary Bill," *Wheeling Intelligencer*, March 3, 1919.
75. "Interviews," *Wheeling Intelligencer*, March 3, 1919; C. H. Quenzel, "A Fight to Establish the State Police," *Journal of Criminal Law and Criminology* 34, no. 1 (1943): 62–63; "W.Va.'s Labor Problems Are Now Becoming More Serious, Says State Labor Commissioner," *Wheeling Intelligencer*, March 1, 1919.
76. "Twelve Men Killed in Pistol Battle in West Virginia," *NYT*, May 20, 1920.
77. Merle T. Cole and Donald R. Davis, "Training the Troopers: Part 1, Before the Academy, 1919–1949," *West Virginia Historical Society Quarterly* 27, no. 2 (2013): 7.
78. Merle T. Cole, "'The Meanest Old Son-of-a-Bitch': J. R. Brockus of the West Virginia State Police," *West Virginia Historical Society Quarterly* 23, no. 3 (July 2009): 1–2.
79. Laurie and Cole, *The Role of Federal Military Forces in Domestic Disorders*, 314–16.
80. "Summary of the Principal Events Connected with Military Operations in the Philippine Islands, September 1, 1900 to June 30, 1901," in *Report of the Lieutenant-General Commanding the Army, in Four Parts, Part 2. Annual Reports of the War Department for the Fiscal Year Ended June 30, 1901* (Washington, DC: GPO, 1901), 51; Shogan, *The Battle of Blair Mountain*, 115.
81. McCoy, *Policing America's Empire*, 317.
82. McCoy, *Policing America's Empire*, 317.
83. McCoy, *Policing America's Empire*, 318.
84. Shogan, *The Battle of Blair Mountain*, 180–81.
85. "Gompers Defends Miners Protest," *NYT*, September 2, 1921.
86. "Armed Truce Holds in Logan County," *NYT*, September 8, 1921.
87. "Mob of 800 Miners Gather in Illinois," *NYT*, September 8, 1921; "Rainstorm Blocks Illinois Mine Army," *NYT*, September 9, 1921.
88. U.S. Congress, Senate, Committee on Education and Labor, *West Virginia Coal Fields: Hearings Before the Committee on Education and Labor*, Vol. 2, 67th Cong., 1st sess., 1921, 604.

89. U.S. Congress, Senate, Committee on Education and Labor, *West Virginia Coal Fields*, 604–5.
90. U.S. Congress, Senate, Committee on Education and Labor, *West Virginia Coal Fields*, 605.
91. Ronald W. Schatz, "Philip Murray and the Subordination of Unions to the United States Government," in *Labor Leaders in America*, ed. Melvyn Dubofsky and Warren Van Tine (Urbana: University of Illinois Press, 1987), 234–236.
92. U.S. Congress, Senate, Committee on Education and Labor, *West Virginia Coal Fields*, 606–7.
93. U.S. Congress, Senate, Committee on Education and Labor, *West Virginia Coal Fields*, 609–10.
94. U.S. Congress, House, Committee on Labor, *Investigation of Wages and Working Conditions in the Coal-Mining Industry*, Part 2, 50.
95. Selig Perlman and Philip Taft, *History of Labor Movements in the United States, 1896–1932*, vol. 4: *Labor Movements* (New York: Macmillan, 1935), 482–86.
96. U.S. Congress, House, Committee on Labor, *Investigation of Wages and Working Conditions in the Coal-Mining Industry*, Part 2, 503–5.
97. UMW Strike Invitation Card, reprinted in Heber Blankenhorn, *The Strike for Union: A Study of the Non-Union Question in Coal and the Problems of a Democratic Movement* (New York: H. W. Wilson, 1924), 16–17.
98. *Report of the Department of Mines of Pennsylvania, Part II: Bituminous, 1905*, xx–xxi.
99. U.S. Congress, House, Committee on Labor, *Investigation of Wages and Working Conditions in the Coal-Mining Industry*, Part 2, 504–5.
100. U.S. Congress, House, Committee on Labor, *Investigation of Wages and Working Conditions in the Coal-Mining Industry*, Part 2, 506.
101. John Higham, *Strangers in the Land: Patterns of American Nativism, 1860–1925* (New Brunswick, NJ: Rutgers University Press, 2002).
102. See, for example, Katherine Benton-Cohen, *Borderline Americans: Racial Division and Labor War in the Arizona Borderlands* (Cambridge, MA: Harvard University Press, 2009).
103. John H. M. Laslett, "A Model of Industrial Solidarity? Interpreting the UMWA's First Hundred Years, 1890–1990," in *The United Mine Workers of America*, ed. John H. M. Laslett (University Park: Pennsylvania State University Press, 1996), 14–16; Jennifer Egolf, "Radical Challenge and Conservative Triumph: The Struggle to Define American Identity in the Somerset County Coal Strike, 1922–1923," in *Culture, Class, and Politics in Modern Appalachia*, 88–117.
104. Laslett, "A Model of Industrial Solidarity?," 14–16.
105. "Propaganda Spread Among Foreign-Born Miners Answered by Union," *UMWJ*, May 1, 1922; Egolf, "Radical Challenge and Conservative Triumph."

106. Melvyn Dubofsky and Warren Van Tine, *John L. Lewis: A Biography* (Urbana: University of Illinois Press, 1986), 86–128.
107. Mildred Allen Beik, *Miners of Windber: The Struggles of New Immigrants for Unionization, 1890–1930s* (State College, PA: Penn State University Press, 1996).
108. Green, *The Devil Is Here in These Hills*, 291.
109. Green, *The Devil Is Here in These Hills*, 292–99; "'Treason' in West Virginia," *NYT*, May 30, 1922.
110. Green, *The Devil Is Here in These Hills*, 309–10; Dubofsky and Van Tine, *John L. Lewis*, 110.
111. Alan Singer, "Communists and Coal Miners: Rank-and-File Organizing in the United Mine Workers of America During the 1920s," *Science and Society* 55 (1991): 132–57; John W. Hevener, *Which Side Are You On? The Harlan County Miners, 1931–1939* (Urbana: University of Illinois Press, 2002); Caroline Merithew, "'We Were Not Ladies'": Gender, Class, and a Women's Auxiliary's Battle for Mining Unionism," *Journal of Women's History* 18, no. 2 (2006): 63–94.
112. Dubofsky and Van Tine, *John L. Lewis*, 111; Melvyn Dubofsky, *The State and Labor in Modern America* (Chapel Hill: University of North Carolina Press, 1994), 98–99.
113. John L. Lewis, *Hoover's Safest Tonic for Industry*, 1928, quoted in Dubofsky and Van Tine, *John L. Lewis*, 111.
114. Jerry Bruce Thomas, *An Appalachian New Deal: West Virginia in the Great Depression* (Morgantown: West Virginia University Press, 2010), 8–11.
115. On the CCF, see Branden Adams, "Coal Miners and Coordination Rights," *Law and Political Economy Project Blog*, July 15, 2021, https://lpeproject.org/blog/coalminers-and-coordination-rights.
116. U.S. Congress, Senate, Committee on Interstate Commerce, *Conditions in the Coalfields of Pennsylvania, West Virginia, and Ohio: Hearings Before the Committee on Interstate Commerce, Volume 1*, 70th Cong., 1st sess., 1928, 7.
117. U.S. Congress, Senate, Committee on Interstate Commerce, *Conditions in the Coalfields*, 14–15; Nancy MacLean, *Behind the Mask of Chivalry: The Making of the Second Ku Klux Klan* (New York: Oxford University Press, 1994). The UMW had, since 1924, a nationwide policy of expelling any member who joined the Klan, which was at its apex in the late 1920s.
118. John L. Lewis, *The Miner's Fight for American Standards* (Indianapolis, IN: Bell, 1925), 14.
119. U.S. Congress, Senate, Committee on Interstate Commerce, *Conditions in the Coalfields*, 18.
120. U.S. Congress, Senate, Committee on Interstate Commerce, *Conditions in the Coalfields*, 9.

121. U.S. Congress, Senate, Committee on Interstate Commerce, *Conditions in the Coalfields*, 17–19.
122. Hevener, *Which Side Are You On?*, 40.
123. "Protests Killing in Mines," *NYT*, June 14, 1931.
124. Mine Safety and Health Administration, "Coal Fatalities for 1900 to 2019," MSHA-DL.
125. Lewis, *The Miner's Fight for American Standards*, 14.
126. Lewis, *The Miner's Fight for American Standards*, 11–12.
127. Joseph H. Willits, foreword to Homer Lawrence Morris, *The Plight of the Bituminous Coal Miner* (Philadelphia: University of Pennsylvania Press, 1934), v.
128. Green, *The Devil Is Here in These Hills*, 292–99; "'Treason' in West Virginia," *NYT*, May 30, 1922.
129. Barbara F. Walter, "Why Bad Governance Leads to Repeat Civil War," *Journal of Conflict Resolution* 59, no. 7 (2015): 1242–72.
130. Blankenhorn, *Strike for Union*, 3.

II. National Problem, National Obligation

1. John L. Lewis, *The Miners' Fight for American Standards* (Indianapolis, IN: Bell, 1925), 188.
2. Lewis, *The Miners' Fight for American Standards*, 16.
3. Kiran Klaus Patel, *The New Deal: A Global History* (Princeton, NJ: Princeton University Press, 2016), 2.
4. James Gray Pope, "The Western Pennsylvania Coal Strike of 1933, Part I: Lawmaking from Below and the Revival of the United Mine Workers," *Labor History* 44, no. 1 (2003): 16–20.
5. Franklin D. Roosevelt, Fireside Chat (Recovery Program), July 24, 1933, APP.
6. Franklin D. Roosevelt, Statement on the Aversion of a Threatened Coal Strike, August 4, 1933, APP.
7. Melvyn Dubofsky and Joseph A. McCartin, *Labor in America: A History*, 9th ed. (Malden, MA: Wiley, 2017), 225; David J. Saposs, "Voluntarism in the American Labor Movement," *Monthly Labor Review* 77, no. 9 (September 1954): 967–71.
8. Lewis Lorwin and Arthur Wubnig, *Labor Relations Boards: The Regulation of Collective Bargaining Under the National Industrial Recovery Act* (Washington, DC: Brookings, 1935), 72; Pope, "The Western Pennsylvania Coal Strike of 1933."

9. James P. Johnson, "Drafting the NRA Code of Fair Competition for the Bituminous Coal Industry," *Journal of American History* 53, no. 3 (1966): 534.
10. Pope, "The Western Pennsylvania Coal Strike of 1933," 16–18.
11. "Clemency Sought," *UMWJ*, January 15, 1936. This euphemistic *UMWJ* description almost certainly refers to sabotage, not violence against people.
12. Johnson, "Drafting the NRA Code," 535.
13. Howard B. Lee, *Bloodletting in Appalachia: The Story of West Virginia's Four Major Mine Wars and Other Thrilling Incidents of Its Coal Fields* (Parsons, WV: McClain, 1969), 165.
14. Charles W. Jessee, "It Does Him Much Good," *UMWJ*, October 15, 1934.
15. "News and Views from the Rank and File," *UMWJ*, February 1, 1935.
16. Interview with Luther Keen in *On Dark and Bloody Ground: An Oral History of the West Virginia Mine Wars*, by Anne T. Lawrence (Morgantown: West Virginia University Press, 2021), 114.
17. Gus Joiner, "I Can Tell De World," to the tune of "I Can Tell the World About This," in *Coal Dust on the Fiddle: Songs and Stories of the Bituminous Coal Industry*, ed. George Gershon Korson (Philadelphia: University of Pennsylvania Press, 1943), 306.
18. *John L. Lewis and the International Union, United Mine Workers of America: The Story from 1917 to 1952* (Washington, DC: UMW International Executive Board, 1952), 52.
19. The right to unionize on offer in the NIRA's section 7(a) offered a relatively limited conception of industrial democracy, as would the Wagner Act that later replaced it. While the New Deal defined the rights of workers as statutory and contractual, most miners understood these rights as more akin to constitutional rights like those guaranteed by the First Amendment. See James Gray Pope, "Western Pennsylvania Coal Strike," 15–48; Howell John Harris, *The Right to Manage: Industrial Relations Policies of American Business in the 1940s* (Madison: University of Wisconsin Press, 1982), 29–30; Michael Goldfield and Cory R. Melcher, "The Myth of Section 7(a): Worker Militancy, Progressive Labor Legislation, and the Coal Miners," *Labor* 16, no. 4 (2019): 49–65. On the limitations of New Deal labor law as well as the Wagner Act's institutional and legal importance, see Melvyn Dubofsky, *The State and Labor in Modern America* (Chapel Hill: University of North Carolina Press, 1994), 128–30.
20. Judith Shklar, *American Citizenship: The Quest for Inclusion* (Cambridge, MA: Harvard University Press, 1998), 34; James Green, *The Devil Is Here in These Hills: West Virginia's Coal Miners and Their Battle for Freedom* (New York: Grove, 2015).

21. Other major gains were made in the textile industry and extended across the labor movement. However, the UMW probably had the largest individual gains, with more than 300,000 new or renewed members in the months after NIRA's passage. Dubofsky and McCartin, *Labor in America*, 223–30.
22. Robert H. Zieger, *The C.I.O., 1935–1955* (Chapel Hill: University of North Carolina Press, 1995), 22–24.
23. "Troops Again Move on Harlan County," *NYT*, September 29, 1935; John W. Hevener, *Which Side Are You On? The Harlan County Miners, 1931–1939* (Urbana: University of Illinois Press, 2002), 128–58.
24. Kevin J. MacMahon, *Reconsidering Roosevelt on Race: How the Presidency Paved the Road to Brown* (Chicago: University of Chicago Press, 2003), 121–22.
25. I. F. Stone, "Bloody Harlan Reforms," *Nation*, August 6, 1938, 121; D. D. Guttenplan, *American Radical: The Life and Times of I. F. Stone* (New York: Farrar, Straus and Giroux, 2009), 138.
26. Hevener, *Which Side Are You On?*, 181.
27. David E. Nye, *Electrifying America: Social Meanings of a New Technology, 1880–1940* (Cambridge, MA: MIT Press, 1992), x.
28. Ronald C. Tobey, *Technology as Freedom: The New Deal and the Electrical Modernization of the American Home* (Berkeley: University of California Press, 1997), 93–95; Abby Spinak, "'Not Quite So Freely as Air': Electrical Statecraft in North America," *Technology and Culture* 61, no. 1 (January 2020): 71–108.
29. Tobey, *Technology as Freedom*, 111–12.
30. Sarah T. Phillips, *This Land, This Nation: Conservation, Rural America, and the New Deal* (New York: Cambridge University Press, 2007), 100.
31. "'TVA: Electricity for All': Synopsis of the creation of the Electric Home and Farm Authority, December 1934," *Documentary History of the Franklin D. Roosevelt Presidency*, vol. 28: *Promulgation of the Tennessee Valley Authority*, Document 129, 590; Bob Johnson, "Energy Slaves: Carbon Technologies, Climate Change, and the Stratified History of the Fossil Economy," *American Quarterly* 68, no. 4 (2016): 955–79.
32. "'TVA: Electricity for All': Synopsis of the creation of the Electric Home and Farm Authority, December 1934," 591.
33. Phillips, *This Land, This Nation*, 100–1; Tobey, *Technology as Freedom*, 118–20; Gregory B. Field, "'Electricity for All': The Electric Home and Farm Authority and the Politics of Mass Consumption, 1932–1935," *Business History Review* 64, no. 1 (1990): 32–60.
34. "Mountain Life Problems Will Be Discussed," *Middlesboro Daily News*, February 13, 1934.
35. "We'll Need Them," *Charleston Daily Mail*, November 27, 1934.

36. Michael Bernstein, "Why the Great Depression Was Great: Toward a New Understanding of the Interwar Economic Crisis in the United States," in *The Rise and Fall of the New Deal Order, 1930–1980*, ed. Steve Fraser and Gary Gerstle (Princeton, NJ: Princeton University Press, 1989), 32.
37. Paul H. Hayward, "The Other Side of TVA," *Nation's Business* 22, no. 12 (December 1934): 23.
38. Hayward, "The Other Side of TVA," 24.
39. "Taking Away the Right to Earn," *Bluefield Daily Telegraph*, September 19, 1934.
40. "Coal Generated Electricity Flows Over Farm Lines," *UMWJ*, May 1, 1939.
41. "Fuller Warns of Danger in TVA," *Bluefield Daily Telegraph*, October 28, 1936.
42. Phillips, *This Land, This Nation*, 83–107.
43. A survey of the *UMWJ* from 1933 to 1943 yielded only a handful of articles mentioning the TVA. Searches of regional newspapers from Tennessee, Kentucky, West Virginia, and southwestern Virginia also yielded few comments by miners or UMW officials, even though the matter was openly discussed and of some concern in the region.
44. Hevener, *Which Side Are You On?*, 130.
45. U.S. Congress, House, Committee on Ways and Means, *Bituminous Coal Conservation Bill of 1935: Report to Accompany HR 9100*, August 14, 1935, 74th Cong., 1st sess., H. Rep. 1800, 3.
46. David M. Kennedy, *Freedom from Fear: The American People in Depression and War, 1929–1935* (New York: Oxford University Press, 1999), 323–31.
47. "Guffey Appeals for Coal Bill," *Plain Speaker*, August 21, 1935.
48. "Public Law 74–402, Chapter 824, 74th Congress, Session 1, An Act: To stabilize the bituminous coal industry . . . ," U.S. Statutes at Large, 49 (1935): 991.
49. *Ashwander v. Tennessee Valley Authority* 297 U.S. 288 (1936).
50. *Carter v. Carter Coal, et al.*, 298 U.S. 238 (1936), 243; "Ford Retains Lawyer Who Helped Kill the NRA to Lead His Fight Against the Labor Board," *NYT*, December 28, 1937, 7. For background on Wood's life and career, see Robert T. Swain, *Cravath Firm and Its Predecessors, 1819–1948* (New York: Priv. print. at Ad. Press, 1948), 326–30.
51. Ronen Shamir, "Managing Legal Uncertainty: Elite Lawyers in the New Deal," PhD diss., Northwestern University, 1992, 234–35.
52. "Hughes Hushes Lawyer, Loud Against New Deal," *NYT*, March 12, 1936; Frederick H. Wood, "Some Constitutional Aspects of the National Recovery Program," *American Bar Association Journal* 20, no. 5 (May 1934): 284–89.
53. *Carter v. Carter Coal Co. et al.* 298 U.S. 238 (1936), 331.

54. *Carter v. Carter Coal Co. et al.* 298 U.S. 238 (1936), 326.
55. *Sunshine Anthracite Coal Co. v. Adkins* 310 U.S. 381 (1940), 380–81.
56. *Sunshine Anthracite Coal Co. v. Adkins* 310 U.S. 381 (1940), 381.
57. Franklin D. Roosevelt to the Congress, February 15, 1939, reprinted in U.S. National Resources Committee, *Energy Resources and National Policy* (Washington, DC: GPO, January 1939), iii.
58. NRC, *Energy Resources and National Policy*, 5.
59. *Labor Laws and Their Administration: Proceedings of the Twenty-fifth Convention of the International Association of Governmental Labor Officials, Tulsa Oklahoma, September 1939*, Department of Labor, Bulletin 678 (Washington, DC: GPO, 1939), 77–78.
60. DOI, BM, *Coal Mine Accidents in the United States, 1941*, by W. W. Adams and L. E. Geyer, Bulletin 456 (Washington, DC: GPO, 1944), 1–2.
61. Alan Derickson, *Black Lung: Anatomy of a Public Health Disaster* (Ithaca, NY: Cornell University Press, 1998), 87–111; Mark Aldrich, "Preventing 'the Needless Peril of the Coal Mine': The Bureau of Mines and the Campaign Against Coal Mine Explosions, 1910–1940," *Technology and Culture* 36, no. 3 (1995): 517.
62. "Five Trapped Miners Saved," *Allentown Morning Call*, January 1, 1941; Henry Ward, "7 Killed, 34 Saved in Mine Explosion; 20 in Hospital," *Pittsburgh Press*, July 1, 1941.
63. Ward, "7 Killed, 34 Saved"; Hiram Brown Humphrey, *Historical Summary of Coal-Mine Explosions in the United States, 1810–1958*, BM Bulletin 586 (Washington, DC: GPO, 1960), 177–79; "Injured Are Better Today," *Indiana Gazette* (Pennsylvania), July 3, 1941.
64. "3 Mine Foremen Fined for Laxity," *UMWJ*, January 15, 1941, 20.
65. "Redding, Ramsell Freed," *Indiana Gazette*, September 18, 1942.
66. Humphrey, *Historical Summary of Coal-Mine Explosions*, 227.
67. U.S. Congress, House of Representatives, Committee on Mines and Mining, *Investigations in Coal Mines*, 77th Cong., 1st sess., February 20, 1941, 11–13, 35.
68. U.S. Congress, House of Representatives, Committee on Mines and Mining, *Investigations in Coal Mines*, 5.
69. U.S. Congress, House of Representatives, Committee on Mines and Mining, *Investigations in Coal Mines*, 5.
70. U.S. Congress, House of Representatives, Committee on Mines and Mining, *Investigations in Coal Mines*, 6.
71. U.S. Congress, House of Representatives, Committee on Mines and Mining, *Investigations in Coal Mines*, 36.
72. *Congressional Record*, House, March 13, 1941, 2235.

73. *Congressional Record*, House, March 13, 1941, 2231.
74. U.S. Congress, House of Representatives, Committee on Ways and Means, *Extension of the Bituminous Coal Act of 1937: Hearings Before the Committee on Ways and Means, House of Representatives*, 77th Cong., 1st sess., 1941.
75. U.S. Congress, House of Representatives, Committee on Ways and Means, *Extension of the Bituminous Coal Act of 1937*, 347, 338.
76. U.S. Congress, House of Representatives, Committee on Ways and Means, *Extension of the Bituminous Coal Act of 1937*, 48.
77. U.S. Congress, House of Representatives, Committee on Ways and Means, *Extension of the Bituminous Coal Act of 1937*, 4, 10–11.
78. On the farm and consumer cooperative movement, see Jennifer E. Tammi, "Minding Our Own Business: Community, Consumers, and Cooperation," PhD diss., Columbia University, 2012, 156–96.
79. U.S. Congress, House of Representatives, Committee on Ways and Means, *Extension of the Bituminous Coal Act of 1937*, 12.
80. U.S. Congress, House of Representatives, Committee on Ways and Means, *Extension of the Bituminous Coal Act of 1937*, 50.
81. U.S. Congress, House of Representatives, Committee on Ways and Means, *Extension of the Bituminous Coal Act of 1937*, 61.
82. U.S. Congress, House of Representatives, Committee on Ways and Means, *Extension of the Bituminous Coal Act of 1937*, 402; Sean Adams, "Making Coal Sharp: Gendered Consumers and Users of Mineral Fuel in the 19th-Century United States," *Journal of Energy History/Revue d'Histoire de l'Énergie* 6 (2021).
83. U.S. Congress, House of Representatives, Committee on Ways and Means, *Extension of the Bituminous Coal Act of 1937*, 402–3.
84. John L. Lewis, quoted in "Coal Miners Seek $1-a-Day Pay Rise," *NYT*, March 12, 1941.
85. U.S. Congress, House of Representatives, Committee on Mines and Mining, *Investigations in Coal Mines*, 35–39.
86. *Congressional Record*, House, March 13, 1941, 2237.
87. U.S. Congress, House of Representatives, Committee on Ways and Means, *Extension of the Bituminous Coal Act of 1937*, 6.
88. "Coal Miners Seek $1-a-Day Pay Rise."
89. *Congressional Record*, House, March 13, 1941, 2232–33.
90. U.S. Congress, House of Representatives, Committee on Ways and Means, *Extension of the Bituminous Coal Act of 1937*, 35.
91. "The Soft-Coal Strike," *NYT*, April 2, 1941, 2.
92. Melvyn Dubofsky and Warren Van Tine, *John L. Lewis: A Biography* (New York: Quadrangle, 1977), 391.

93. "Coal Accord Near, Disorder Flares," *NYT*, April 2, 1941; "4 Dead, 5 Wounded in Harlan Gunplay," *NYT*, April 3, 1941; "4 Killed, 25 Shot in Coal Mine Fight," *NYT*, April 16, 1941.
94. "Coal Trade Awaits Move by Roosevelt as Shortage Grows," *NYT*, April 13, 1941.
95. Dubofsky and Van Tine, *John L. Lewis*, 392–93.
96. Alan Derickson, "Participative Regulation of Hazardous Working Conditions: Safety Committees of the United Mine Workers of America, 1941–1969," *Labor Studies Journal* 18, no. 2 (1993): 25.
97. U.S. Congress, Coal Mine Inspection Act, Public Law 49–77th Congress, May 7, 1941; U.S. Congress, House of Representatives, Committee on Mines and Mining, *Investigations in Coal Mines*, 12–13.
98. Humphrey, *Historical Summary of Coal-Mine Explosions*, 229.
99. Derickson, "Participative Regulation," 29–30.

III. War and Peace

1. McAlister Coleman, *Men and Coal* (New York: Farrar and Rinehart), 205–6.
2. "Union Shop Granted for Captive Coal Pits," *Canonsburg Daily Notes*, December 8, 1941.
3. "Canonsburg Industry on War-Time Status; County Takes Action," *Canonsburg Daily Notes*, December 8, 1941.
4. U.S. Census Bureau, *1940 Census of the Population, Volume 2: Characteristics of the Population, Part 6: Pennsylvania-Texas* (Washington, DC: GPO, 1943), 157.
5. DOL, BLS, Division of Industrial Relations, *Strikes in 1941 and Strikes Affecting Defense Production*, Bulletin No. 711 (Washington, DC: GPO, 1942), 1.
6. DOL, BLS, Division of Industrial Relations, *Strikes in 1941*, 6, 12–13.
7. *UMJW*, December 1, 1942.
8. Nelson Lichtenstein, *Labor's War at Home: The CIO in World War II* (Philadelphia: Temple University Press, 1982), 72.
9. Melvyn Dubofsky and Warren Van Tine, *John L. Lewis: A Biography* (New York: Quadrangle, 1977), 418; William O'Neill, *A Democracy at War: America's Fight at Home and Abroad in World War II* (Cambridge, MA: Harvard University Press, 1993), 206.
10. O'Neill, *A Democracy at War*, 208–9.
11. Isador Lubin, "How the Miners Feel Now, Also Spot Survey of Public Opinion Toward the Coal Mining Dispute," confidential report, May 11,

1943, Document 95 in *DHFDRP, Volume 15: Coal Strikes, Labor, and the Smith-Connally Act, 1943*, Folder 002166-015-0255.
12. Coleman, *Men and Coal*, xvii–xix.
13. Draft of letter from William H. Davis to Philip Murray, November 18, 1941, Strikes and Labor Issues Subject File [March 1941–June 1943], President Franklin D. Roosevelt's Office Files, 1933–1945, Part 4: Subject Files, President's Secretary's Files, Folder 002184-038-1070.
14. Coleman, *Men and Coal*, xvii.
15. "Mines Idle Despite Plea for Weekend Production," *Wilkes-Barre Times Leader*, December 26, 1942.
16. Christopher F. Jones, *Routes of Power: Energy and Modern America* (Cambridge, MA: Harvard University Press, 2014), 46–85.
17. "Anthracite Outlook," *Wilkes-Barre Times Leader*, December 28, 1942; Thomas Dublin and Walter Licht, *The Face of Decline: The Pennsylvania Anthracite Region in the Twentieth Century* (Ithaca, NY: Cornell University Press, 2005), 87.
18. OPA, "Fuel Oil Rationing, Industry Instructions," Form OPA R-1114, 1942, Accession No. Pr32.4206.F95_2, ProQuest Congressional.
19. "Little Studies," *Wilkes-Barre Times Leader*, December 26, 1942.
20. "Garden's Heating System Converted from Oil to Coal," *Wilkes-Barre Times Leader*, December 26, 1942; Effie Welsh, "Do You Know That?" *Wilkes-Barre Evening News*, January 1, 1943.
21. NBER, Anthracite Coal Production for United States [M0117BUS-M601NNBR], NBER Macrohistory Database; Dublin and Licht, *The Face of Decline*, 85.
22. "Mines Idle Despite Plea for Weekend Production," *Wilkes-Barre Times Leader*, December 26, 1942.
23. "Peace at Ewen," *Wilkes-Barre Times Leader*, December 26, 1942, 10; for an account of the initial walkout, see "Company Head Discusses Miners' Pay," *Wilkes-Barre Times Leader*, December 3, 1942.
24. "Families in Lowlands Are Forced to Move; Highways Under Water," *Wilkes-Barre Times Leader*, December 31, 1942.
25. "Many Mines in District Work Today," *Wilkes-Barre Times Leader*, January 2, 1943.
26. "Mine Worker Is Killed by a Fall of Rock," *Wilkes-Barre Times Leader*, December 30, 1942; anthracite fatality statistics, DOI, BM, *Coal Mine Accidents in the United States, 1942*, by W. W. Adams and L. E. Geyer, Bulletin 462 (Washington, DC: GPO, 1944), 87; on wartime regulation and technological impact on anthracite mining, see Mark Aldrich, "The Perils of Mining Anthracite: Regulation, Technology, and Safety, 1870–1945," *Pennsylvania History* 64, no. 3 (1997): 377–78.

27. "1300 Employees Quit Work at Glen Alden Mine Here," *Wilkes-Barre Times Leader*, December 30, 1942.
28. "Pay Boost Demand Adds to Unrest Among Miners," *Wilkes-Barre Times Leader*, January 4, 1943.
29. Dublin and Licht, *The Face of Decline*, 86.
30. On outrages over price changes, I draw from E. P. Thompson, "The Moral Economy of the English Crowd in the Eighteenth Century," *Past & Present* 50 (1971): 73–136; James T. Sparrow, *Warfare State: World War II Americans and the Age of Big Government* (New York: Oxford University Press, 2011), 201–41.
31. "Striking Miners Study Labor Board Testimony," *Wilkes-Barre Times Leader*, January 16, 1943; J. R. Sperry, "Rebellion Within the Ranks: Pennsylvania Anthracite, John L. Lewis, and the Coal Strikes of 1943," *Pennsylvania History* 40, no. 3 (1973): 297.
32. "Striking Miners Study Labor Board Testimony," 15.
33. NBER, "Anthracite Coal Production for the United States."
34. "75,000 at Work in Pits: Strike Only Affects 15 Per Cent of the Industry's Tonnage," *NYT*, January 20, 1943.
35. Sperry, "Rebellion in the Ranks," 294.
36. Press release, January 19, 1943, Document 8 in DHFDRP, Vol. 15, Folder 002166-015-0008.
37. "Anthracite Shortage Develops as Miners Refuse to End Strike," *Messenger* (Owensboro, KY), January 8, 1943.
38. "Pleasure Driving Banned; Fuel Oil Cut 25 Per Cent," *Raleigh News and Observer*, January 7, 1943.
39. "Anthracite Shortage Results from Strikes," *News-Herald* (Franklin, PA), January 6, 1943.
40. "Enemy No. 1 on the Home Front: John L. Lewis," *Philadelphia Inquirer*, January 14, 1943; Sperry, "Rebellion in the Ranks," 294–95; Dubofsky and Van Tine, *John L. Lewis*, 420.
41. "East Coast Area to Get Soft Coal to Ease Anthracite Shortage," *Philadelphia Inquirer*, January 14, 1943.
42. "Nation-wide Dimout Hinted," *Pittsburgh Press*, January 24, 1943.
43. "John L. Lewis Fights a Strike," *Time*, January 25, 1943.
44. "We are Fighting WLB 'Dictatorship' Says Miner in Scathing Letter to FDR," *UMWJ*, July 1, 1943.
45. "Miners, Resentful of Quibbling, Buck-Passing, and Stalling on Coal Mine Wage Increase," *UMWJ*, June 1, 1943.
46. *Congressional Record*, March 13, 1941, 2240.
47. Coleman, *Men and Coal*, 226.
48. Coleman, *Men and Coal*, 229.

49. Quoted in Coleman, *Men and Coal*, 230.
50. UMW, "Suppose *YOU* Got Only 7 Hours' Pay for 8 ½ Hours in a Coal Mine!," *New York Daily News*, April 13, 1943.
51. UMW, "Suppose *YOU*," emphasis in original.
52. U.S. Congress, Senate, Special Committee Investigating the National Defense Program, *Investigation of the National Defense Program: Hearings Before a Special Committee Investigating the National Defense Program, Parts 12–15*, 77th Cong., 1st Sess., March 26, 1943 (Washington, DC: GPO, 1943), 7394.
53. UMW, "Suppose *YOU*," emphasis in original.
54. U.S. Congress, Senate, Special Committee Investigating the National Defense Program, *Investigation of the National Defense Program*, 7406; UMW, "Suppose *YOU*."
55. U.S. Congress, Senate, Special Committee Investigating the National Defense Program, *Investigation of the National Defense Program*, 7410.
56. Coleman, *Men and Coal*, 306; Harold Ickes to Colonel Marvin H. McIntyre, May 11, 1943, Document 91 in DHFDRP, Vol. 15, Folder 002166-015-00091.
57. U.S. Congress, Senate, Special Committee to Investigate Gasoline and Fuel-Oil Shortages, *Additional Report, Interim Report on Oil and Coal: Conclusion and Recommendations*, Report 59, part 3, 78th Cong., 2nd sess., 1944, 12.
58. Franklin D. Roosevelt, Executive Order 9332, Establishing the Solid Fuels Administration for the War, April 19, 1943, APP; Franklin D. Roosevelt, Executive Order 9276, Establishing the Petroleum Administration for the War, December 2, 1942, APP.
59. Coleman, *Men and Coal*, 245–46; William H. Davis to FDR, April 28, 1943, Document 37 in DHFDRP, Vol. 15, Folder 002166-015-0037.
60. Lubin, "How the Miners Feel Now."
61. "Overlapping Govt. Burrocracy Jurisdictions Prevent a Settlement of Coal Controversy," *UMWJ*, June 1, 1943; "WLB Holds Up Coal Wage Decision," *UMWJ*, October 15, 1943.
62. Coleman, *Men and Coal*, 261–78; Lichtenstein, *Labor's War at Home*, 165–71.
63. Dubofsky and Van Tine, *John L. Lewis*, 438–39.
64. Malcolm Ross and Richard Deverall to Harold Ickes, May 7, 1943, Document 90 in DHFDRP, Vol. 15, Folder 002166-015-0090.
65. Leo Fishman and Betty G. Fishman, "Bituminous Coal Production During World War II," *Southern Economic Journal* 18, no. 3 (1952): 393.
66. U.S. Congress, Senate, Special Committee to Investigate the Fuel Situation in the Middle West, *The Fuel Situation in the Middle West: Hearings Before the Special Committee to Investigate the Fuel Situation in the Middle West, January 7–8, 1943* (Washington, DC: GPO, 1943).

67. U.S. Congress, Senate, Special Committee to Investigate the Fuel Situation in the Middle West, *Fuel Situation in the Middle West*; Special Committee to Investigate Gasoline and Fuel-Oil Shortages, *Additional Report, Interim Report on Oil and Coal: Conclusion and Recommendations*, Report 59, part 3, 78th Cong., 2nd sess., 1944.

68. Coleman, *Men and Coal*, 262; U.S. Congress, Senate, Special Committee to Investigate the Fuel Situation in the Middle West, *The Fuel Situation in the Middle West*.

69. For examples, North Camden Coal Company, "Don't Say We Didn't Warn You," *Morning Post* (Camden, NJ), June 2, 1943, 22; Farmer's Union Cooperative Association, "Don't Take a Chance," *Lynch (NE) Herald-Enterprise*, June 3, 1943, 5.

70. War Production Board, Office of War Utilities, *Report on Voluntary Conservation Program for Electric Utilities*, approved July 14, 1943 (Washington, DC: GPO, 1943), 3–6; for a framework for examining the relationship between household labor and electric power systems, see Trish Kahle, "Electric Discipline: Gendering Power and Defining Work in Electric Power Systems," *Labor: Studies in Working-Class History* (2024): 79–97.

71. For example, the American Window Glass Company in Belle Vernon, Pennsylvania, "Miners Prefer Contract to Strike Truce: Tired of 'Promises' Is General Attitude," *Richmond (VA) News Leader*, June 3, 1943; a blast furnace near Birmingham, Alabama, "Blast Furnace Shut Down Because of Coal Shortage," *Binghamton Sun-Bulletin*, June 4, 1943.

72. "Sprague Calls Coal Conclave to End Crisis," *Newsday (Nassau Edition)*, December 31, 1943.

73. Memorandum, OWI, Richard Deverall to Secretary of Interior Ickes, n.d. (early June 1943), reprinted in Merl E. Reed, "Some Additional Materials on the Coal Strike of 1943," *Labor History* 23 (1982): 100.

74. Lubin, "How the Miners Feel Now."

75. Deverall to Ickes, n.d. (early June 1943), 100.

76. Coleman, *Men and Coal*, 270; Kathy Peiss, *Zoot Suit: The Enigmatic Career of an Extreme Style* (Philadelphia: University of Pennsylvania Press, 2011), 106–30; Sparrow, *Warfare State*, 184–88.

77. Coleman, *Men and Coal*, xix.

78. Honey Brook Lions Club to FDR, January 20, 1943, Document 14 in *DHFDRP, Vol. 15*, Folder 002166-015-0016; Lillian Williams to FDR, April 26, 1943, Document 33, Folder 002166-015-0066.

79. Frank McCoy to FDR, March 25, 1943, Document 24 in *DHFDRP, Vol. 15*, Folder 002166-015-0046.

80. Helen Assad to FDR, April 27, 1943, Document 35 in *DHFDRP, Vol. 15*, Folder 002166-015-0071; Dubofsky and Van Tine, *John L. Lewis*, 426–27.

81. William M. Jarvins to FDR, April 25, 1943, in *DHFDRP, Vol. 15*, Folder 002166-015-0064.
82. W. J. Carpenter to FDR, June 21, 1943, Document 173 in *DHFDRP, Vol. 15*, Folder 002166-015-0173.
83. Deverall to Ickes, n.d. (early June 1943), 99.
84. Coleman, *Men and Coal*, xvii.
85. Deverall to Ickes, n.d. (early June 1943), 102.
86. Sparrow, *Warfare State*, 196.
87. Bonnie E. Stewart, *No. 9: The 1968 Farmington Mine Disaster* (Morgantown: West Virginia University Press, 2012), 15.
88. Stewart, *No. 9*, 14–15.
89. E. A. Williams et al. to Senator Andrews, May 3, 1943, Document 791 in *DHFDRP, Vol. 15*, Folder 002166-015-00079; Coleman, *Men and Coal*, 280–81.
90. "Death and Injury on the Coal Mining Front," *UMWJ*, September 15, 1943.
91. Deverall to Ickes, n.d. (early June 1943), 97, 99, 101; the report leaked to the press and was reprinted in part under the title "Miners Slaves, Suppressed Report Claims," *Miami Herald*, July 12, 1943.
92. "WLB Seeks to Force UMW to Sign a Yellow Dog Contract," *UMWJ*, July 1, 1943.
93. Deverall to Ickes, n.d. (early June 1943), 101.
94. "4 Additional Bodies Found in Coal Mine," *Stars and Stripes*, January 1, 1946; on reconversion, see Lichtenstein, *Labor's War at Home*, 221–32.
95. "More Than 200 Miners Walk Out of Blast-Torn Havaco," *Bluefield Daily Telegraph*, January 16, 1946.
96. "Explosion Traps 270 W.Va. Miners," *Indianapolis Recorder*, January 19, 1946; Davitt McAteer, *Monongah: The Tragic Story of the 1907 Monongah Disaster* (Morgantown: West Virginia University Press, 2014).
97. "Five Dead, 200 Rescued, 65 Caught in Mine Blast," *Paducah Sun-Democrat*, January 15, 1946; "Coal Dust Caused Welch Blast; Bosses Praised," *Beckley Post-Herald*, January 17, 1946.
98. "Five Dead, 200 Rescued, 65 Caught in Mine Blast."
99. "Five Dead, 200 Rescued, 65 Caught in Mine Blast."
100. "West Virginia Mine Blast May Have Trapped 192," *Staunton Evening Leader*, January 15, 1946; "Mine Blast Worse Than Guns in War," *Tucson Daily Citizen*, January 15, 1946; "Blast Survivor Says War Was Easier on Him," *Idaho Statesman*, January 16, 1946. The reporting appeared in at least seventeen states.
101. Coleman, *Men and Coal*, 307; Harold Ickes to Colonel Marvin H. McIntyre, May 11, 1943, Document 91 in *DHFDRP, Vol. 15*, Folder 002166-015-00091.

102. John Ervin Brinley Jr., "Government and Labor: The Coal Industry, 1946–1947," MA thesis, University of Utah, 1967, 12–14; Jennifer Klein, *For All These Rights: Business, Labor, and the Shaping of America's Public-Private Welfare State* (Princeton, NJ: Princeton University Press, 2003), 197–98.
103. *United States v. United Mine Workers*, 330 U.S. 258 (1947).
104. "Julius Krug, HST's Interior Boss, Dies," *Tennessean*, March 28, 1970; Dubofsky and Van Tine, *John L. Lewis*, 461.
105. U.S. Congress, Senate, Committee on Public Lands, *Investigation of Mine Explosion at Centralia, Illinois: Hearings Before a Special Subcommittee of the Committee on Public Lands*, 80th Cong., 1st sess. (Washington, DC: GPO, 1947), 223.
106. Hiram Brown Humphrey, *Historical Summary of Coal-Mine Explosions in the United States, 1810–1958*, BM Bulletin 586 (Washington, DC: GPO, 1960), 209, 213; Robert E. Hartley and David Kenney, *Death Underground: The Centralia and West Frankfort Mine Disasters* (Carbondale: Southern Illinois University Press, 2006).
107. U.S. Congress, Senate, Committee on Public Lands, *Investigation of Mine Explosion at Centralia, Illinois*, 32–33, 215–16.
108. Dubofsky and Van Tine, *John L. Lewis*, 471.
109. Dubofsky and Van Tine, *John L. Lewis*, 470–71; U.S. Congress, Senate, Committee on Public Lands, *Investigation of Mine Explosion at Centralia, Illinois*, 438.
110. Humphrey, *Historical Summary of Coal-Mine Explosions in the United States*, 214.
111. U.S. Congress, Senate, Committee on Public Lands, *Investigation of Mine Explosion at Centralia, Illinois*, 298, 308–11.
112. Dubofsky and Van Tine, *John L. Lewis*, 471.
113. U.S. Congress, Senate, Committee on Public Lands, *Investigation of Mine Explosion at Centralia, Illinois*, 298, 308–11.
114. Hartley and Kenney, *Death Underground*, 156–74.
115. Richard P. Mulcahy, *A Social Contract for the Coalfields: The Rise and Fall of the United Mine Workers of America Welfare and Retirement Fund* (Knoxville: University of Tennessee Press, 2000); Ivana Krajcinovic, *From Company Doctors to Managed Care: The United Mine Workers' Noble Experiment* (Ithaca, NY: ILR Press, 1997), 41–42.
116. Dubofsky and Van Tine, *John L. Lewis*, 476–90; Robyn Muncy, *Relentless Reformer: Josephine Roche and Progressivism in Twentieth-Century America* (Princeton, NJ: Princeton University Press, 2015), 227.
117. Mulcahy, *A Social Contract for the Coalfields*, 141.

First Interlude: Between Deep Time and the Future

1. Robert S. Weise, "A New Deal in the Cold War: Carl D. Perkins, Coal, and the Political Economy of Poverty in Eastern Kentucky, 1948–1964," *Register of the Kentucky Historical Society* 107, no. 3 (2009): 307–10. Portions of this interlude are adapted, with permission, from Trish Kahle, "The Front Lines of Energy Policy: The Coal Mining Workplace and the Politics of Security in the American Century," *American Quarterly* 72 no. 3 (2020): 627–49.
2. Robert Vitalis, *America's Kingdom: Mythmaking on the Saudi Oil Frontier* (Palo Alto, CA: Stanford University Press, 2006).
3. Natural Gas Subcommittee of the Bituminous Coal Industry Committee, Proposed Plan for Federal Administrative Action and Legislation with Respect to Natural Gas, September 15, 1954, UMWPO 10/3.
4. Judith Stein, *Running Steel, Running America: Race, Economic Policy, and the Decline of Liberalism* (Chapel Hill: University of North Carolina Press, 1998), 197–210.
5. Richard F. Hirsh, *Technology and Transformation in the American Electric Utility Industry* (New York: Cambridge University Press, 1989), 57–70.
6. U.S. Congress, Senate, Committee on Interior and Insular Affairs, *Basic Data Relating to Energy Resources*, 82nd Cong., 1st sess., 1951, Senate Doc. 8, serial 11505, xvi.
7. Neta C. Crawford, "Pentagon Fuel Use, Climate Change, and the Costs of War," Costs of War Project, Watson Institute for International and Public Affairs, Brown University, June 12, 2019, https://watson.brown.edu/costsofwar/papers/ClimateChangeandCostofWar; Vaclav Smil, "War and Energy," in *Encyclopedia of Energy*, ed. Cutler J. Cleveland and Robert U. Ayres (Boston: Elsevier, 2004), 6:363–71.
8. U.S. Congress, Senate, Committee on Interior and Insular Affairs, *Basic Data Relating to Energy Resources*, xv.
9. Richard H. K. Vietor, *Energy Policy in America Since 1945: A Study of Business-Government Relations* (New York: Cambridge University Press, 1984), 46–52.
10. Walter R. Hibbard, remarks before the Mining and Metallurgical Society of America, New York City, September 20, 1966, UMWPO, 15/29; Christopher F. Jones, "The Materiality of Energy," *Canadian Journal of History* 53, no. 3 (2018): 378–94.
11. Giuliano Garavini, *The Rise and Fall of OPEC in the Twentieth Century* (New York: Oxford University Press, 2019), 89–92.
12. David S. Painter, *Oil and the American Century: The Political Economy of U.S. Foreign Oil Policy, 1941–1945* (Baltimore, MD: Johns Hopkins University Press, 1986).

13. Peter Shulman, *Coal and Empire: The Birth of Energy Security in Industrial America* (Baltimore, MD: Johns Hopkins University Press, 2015).
14. U.S. Shipping Board, Bureau of Construction, *Data Relating to the Diesel Conversion Program*, BC Report 104 (Washington, DC: GPO, 1932), 1–3.
15. DOI, OCR, Division of Economics and Marketing, *The Foreign Market Potential for United States Coal* (Research and Development Report No. 3), September 16, 1963, (Washington, DC: GPO, 1963), II1–III1.
16. DOI, OCR, Division of Economics and Marketing, *The Foreign Market Potential for United States Coal*, II1–III1.
17. Richard H. K. Vietor, *Environmental Politics and the Coal Coalition* (College Station: Texas A&M University Press, 1980), 17.
18. John L. Lewis, remarks to NCPC, April 3, 1963, UMWPO, 192/13; Michael F. Widman Jr., presentation, May 11, 1961, UMWPO, 13/16.
19. W. A. Boyle, statement to the Mines and Mining Subcommittee, House Committee on Interior and Insular Affairs, March 26, 1963, UMWPO, 12/24.
20. Widman, presentation.
21. FPC, *National Power Survey* (Washington, DC: GPO, 1964), 57–58.
22. "An Economic Credo for Americans," c. 1953, UMWPO 10/3.
23. Douglas A. Irwin, *Clashing Over Commerce: A History of Trade Politics in America* (Chicago: University of Chicago Press, 2017), 517.
24. Paul Averitt, Louise R. Berryhill, and Dorothy A. Taylor, *Coal Resources of the United States*, U.S. Geological Survey, Circular No. 293, October 1, 1953.
25. Sam H. Schurr and Bruce Netschert, *Energy in the American Economy: An Economic Study of Its History and Prospects* (Baltimore, MD: Johns Hopkins University Press, 1960), 12.
26. "An Economic Credo for Americans."
27. "Cooper Says Coal Exports to Be Raised," October 1, 1954, UMWPO 10/3.
28. "White House Report on Energy Supplies and Resources Policy," February 26, 1955, UMWPO 10/3.
29. Tom Pickett, press statement, March 1, 1955, UMWPO 10/3; "UMWA Criticizes President's Energy Report as Too General," press release, March 13, 1955, UMWPO 10/3.
30. Felix Belair Jr., "All Oil Imports Under Hard Curb," *NYT*, March 11, 1959; Dwight D. Eisenhower, Proclamation 3279, March 10, 1959, APP; Vietor, *Energy Policy in America*, 114–15.
31. Widman Jr., presentation.
32. Widman Jr., presentation.

33. Roger M. Olien and Diana Davids Olien, *Oil and Ideology: The Cultural Creation of the American Petroleum Industry* (Chapel Hill: University of North Carolina Press, 2000).
34. Vietor, *Energy Policy in America Since 1945*, 44–63.
35. Jennifer Klein, *For All These Rights: Business, Labor, and the Shaping of America's Public-Private Welfare State* (Princeton, NJ: Princeton University Press, 2003), 3–7.
36. Bob Johnson, *Carbon Nation: Fossil Fuels in the Making of American Culture* (Lawrence: University Press of Kansas, 2014), 63.
37. Lizabeth Cohen, *A Consumers' Republic: The Politics of Mass Consumption in Postwar America* (New York: Vintage, 2003).
38. W. A. Boyle, statement, March 26, 1963.
39. Ray Zell, "Passing Inspection," 1962, UMWJR, 60/6.
40. Ray Zell, "This Is War," 1962, UMWJR, 60/6.
41. "An Economic Credo for Americans."
42. Ray Zell, "Watch the Roof," 1962, UMWJR 60/6.
43. Thomas Dublin and Walter Licht, *The Face of Decline: The Pennsylvania Anthracite Region in the Twentieth Century* (Ithaca, NY: Cornell University Press, 2005).
44. August J. Lippi to Daniel J. Flood in Cong. Rec. 108 no. 36 (March 13, 1962), UMWPO, 21/22.
45. T. H. Price to John F. Kennedy, March 9, 1962, UMWPO, 21/22.
46. Ezra Johnson, Harold Bellamy, and Robert Carter to John F. Kennedy, March 23, 1962, UMWPO, 21/22.
47. C. E. Bean, directive, March 12, 1962, UMWPO, 21/22; Hugh White, directive, March 7, 1962, UMWPO, 21/22.
48. FPC, *1970 National Power Survey*, I-1-4.
49. Coal-by-Wire, television program, undated, c. 1953–1958, UMWAV box 14, digital file pstsc_09375_203.
50. Rebecca Bailey, *Matewan Before the Massacre: Politics: Coal, and the Roots of Conflict in West Virginia* (Morgantown: West Virginia University Press, 2008), 148–49, 167.
51. *Coal-by-Wire*.
52. U.S. Congress, Committee on Interior and Insular Affairs, Special Subcommittee on Coal Research, *Coal Research*, 84th Cong., 2nd sess., (1956), 1, 107.
53. U.S. Congress, Committee on Interior and Insular Affairs, Special Subcommittee on Coal Research, *Coal Research* (1956), 86.
54. 105 Cong. Rec. 19753.
55. U.S. Congress, House, Committee on Interior and Insular Affairs, Subcommittees on Mines and Mining, *Coal Research and Development Program: Hearings*, 86th Cong., 2nd sess., January 18, 1960, 68–70.

56. DOI, OCR, *Annual Report*, February 15, 1966. George A. Lamb, "The Office of Coal Research and Its Activities," Annual Meeting of the American Institute of Mining, Metallurgical, and Petroleum Engineers, Dallas, Texas, February 26, 1963, OnePetro; George Fumich Jr., remarks, Paonia Chamber of Commerce, Paonia, Colorado, February 2, 1966, UMWPO, 15/29.
57. DOI, OCR, *Report of the Office of Coal Research, February 15, 1963*, 10; DOI press release, April 11, 1962, UMWPO 3/11.
58. DOI, OCR, *Report, February 15, 1963*, 6.
59. A. H. Raskin, "John L. Lewis and the United Mine Workers," *Atlantic*, May 1963.
60. DOI, press release, April 11, 1962, 10, UMWPO 3/11.
61. Ray Zell, "A Growing Thing/Fertile Growth/Flowering Power/Heat Line/Coal Burning Plant," 1962, UMWJR, 60/6.
62. Melvyn Dubofsky and Warren Van Tine, *John L. Lewis: A Biography* (New York: Quadrangle, 1977), 518, 525–26.
63. Roger Hawthorne, "The Boyle Family and Montana," *Billings Gazette*, August 24, 1969.
64. Justin McCarthy, "W. A. Boyle Succeeds to Presidency," *UMWJ*, February 15, 1963.

IV. Atomic Menace

1. Gerard Delanty and Aurea Mota, "Governing the Anthropocene: Agency, Governance, and Knowledge," *European Journal of Social Theory* 20, no. 1 (2017): 9–38; Lewis L. Strauss, remarks to the National Association of Science Writers, September 16, 1954, https://www.nrc.gov/docs/ML1613 /ML16131A120.pdf.
2. Thomas E. Murray, "The Atom and a New Moral Maturity," May 26, 1955, UMWPO 8/2. Anthony Leviero, "Murray, New York Engineer, Is Named to Atomic Board," *NYT*, March 23, 1950.
3. Spencer R. Weart, *Nuclear Fear: A History of Images* (Cambridge, MA: Harvard University Press, 1988).
4. Natasha Zaretsky, *Radiation Nation: Three Mile Island and the Political Transformation of the 1970s* (New York: Columbia University Press, 2018), 1–14; Sarah E. Robey, *Atomic Americans: Citizens in a Nuclear State* (Ithaca, NY: Cornell University Press, 2022), 2–5.
5. DOL, Atomic Energy Study Group, *Labor Implications of Atomic Power* (Washington, DC: U.S. DOL, 1956).

6. Thomas E. Murray, Report to the JCAE on Completion of Seven Years as a Member of the AEC, circa 1957, UMWPO, 8/4; "Thomas E. Murray," *Physics Today* 14, no. 10 (October 1961): 79.
7. Wolfgang Saxon, "W. A. Boyle Dies; Led Miners' Union," *NYT*, June 1, 1985.
8. William L. Laurence, "Parley in Geneva Unveils Advance in Atomic Plants," *NYT*, August 14, 1955; Willard P. Owens, Report on the Second United Nations Conference for the Peaceful Development of Atomic Energy, October 6, 1958, UMWPO 8/4.
9. Owens, Report on the Second United Nations Conference.
10. Owens, Report on the Second United Nations Conference.
11. Weart, *Nuclear Fear*, 421.
12. Joseph P. Brennan to W. A. Boyle, April 14, 1969, UMWPO 193/4; "What Price Price-Anderson?" *UMWJ*, June 15, 1969.
13. Brian Balogh, *Chain Reaction: Expert Debate and Public Participation in American Commercial Nuclear Power* (New York: Cambridge University Press, 1991).
14. W. A. Boyle to Stephen Dunn, March 1, 1963, UMWPO 8/6.
15. David Ekbladh, *The Great American Mission: Modernization and the Construction of an American World Order* (Princeton, NJ: Princeton University Press, 2009), 196.
16. David E. Lilienthal, "Whatever Happened to the Peaceful Atom?," 1963, UMWPO 8/6.
17. W. A. Boyle, quoting Lilienthal, statement to the Mines and Mining Subcommittee, March 26, 1963, UMWPO 12/24.
18. Boyle, statement, March 26, 1963; OMB, *Budget of the United States Government for the Fiscal Year Ending June 30, 1964* (Washington, DC: GPO, 1963), 69, 233, 270–71.
19. Russell Olwell, *At Work in the Atomic City: A Labor and Social History of Oak Ridge, Tennessee* (Knoxville: University of Tennessee Press, 2007); Charles Thorpe, "The Political Economy of the Manhattan Project," in *The Routledge Handbook of the Political Economy of Science*, ed. David Tyfield, Rebecca Lave, Samuel Randalls, and Charles Thorpe (Philadelphia: Routledge, 2017).
20. Jayita Sarkar, *Ploughshares and Swords: India's Nuclear Program in the Global Cold War* (Ithaca, NY: Cornell University Press, 2022), 59–60.
21. Thomas E. Murray, remarks at St. Bonaventure University, October 4, 1957, UMWPO 8/4.
22. FPC, *National Power Survey, Part I: Guidelines for Growth of the Electric Power Industry* (Washington, DC: U.S. GPO, 1964), 77–80.
23. See Lawrence Glickman, *Free Enterprise: An American History* (New Haven, CT: Yale University Press, 2019), 2–4.

24. Thomas Kennedy to Jennings Randolph, August 22, 1961, UMWPO 8/ 6.
25. W. A. Boyle, Statement Before the JCAE, March 4, 1964, UMWPO 27/14.
26. R. W. Cook to Thomas E. Murray, reproduced in Thomas Kennedy to John L. Lewis, July 2, 1952, UMWPO 8/1.
27. R. T. O'Neill to John L. Lewis, July 19, 1957, UMWPO 27/20.
28. Roger Hawthorne, "The Boyle Family and Montana," *Billings Gazette*, August 24, 1969; "Closing the Coal Mines," *Billings Gazette*, August 25, 1969, 8; "Four Died in 1958 Cave-In of Mine," *Billings Gazette*, August 26, 1969.
29. Ben A. Franklin, "Boyle Controversy Grips the Miners Union," *NYT*, August 31, 1969.
30. J. J. Boyle to John L. Lewis, July 9, 1957, UMWPO 27/20; W. A. Boyle to J. J. Boyle, July 19, 1957, UMWPO 27/20.
31. W. A. Boyle to R. J. Boyle, July 22, 1957, UMWPO 27/20.
32. Hawthorne, "Closing the Coal Mines."
33. Hawthorne, "Four Died in 1958 Cave-In of Mine."
34. Glenn Seaborg to Chet Holifield, August 7, 1961, UMWPO 8/6.
35. Seaborg to Holifield, August 7, 1961.
36. Seaborg to Holifield, August 7, 1961.
37. See Kate Brown, *Plutopia: Nuclear Families, Atomic Cities, and the Great Soviet and American Plutonium Disasters*; Patricia Nelson Limerick, "The Significance of Hanford in American History," in *Terra Pacifica: People and Place in the Northwestern States and Western Canada*, ed. Paul W. Hirt (Pullman: Washington State University Press, 1998), 53–70.
38. Dwight D. Eisenhower, Annual Budget Message to the Congress: Fiscal Year 1961, January 18, 1960, APP.
39. Chet Holifield to Thomas Kennedy, August 16, 1961, UMWPO 8/6.
40. Kennedy to Randolph, August 22, 1961.
41. W. A. Boyle, "Statement on the Hanford Project," *UMWJ*, August 15, 1961.
42. Kennedy to Randolph, August 22, 1961.
43. Jennings Randolph to Thomas Kennedy, August 28, 1961, UMWPO 8/6.
44. Boyle, statement, March 26, 1963.
45. "UMWA Expels District 50!," *UMWJ*, March 8, 1968.
46. Rex Lauck to W. A. Boyle, July 29, 1963, UMWPO 27/12. This memo references Boyle's July 16, 1963, letter to the *Journal* office in which Boyle made the request, but this initial letter was not in the archives.
47. "What Price of Price-Anderson?," *UMWJ*, June 15, 1965.
48. James Jasper, *Nuclear Politics: Energy and the State in the United States, Sweden, and France* (Princeton, NJ: Princeton University Press, 2014), 43.
49. "Pandora's Box of Poison," *UMWJ*, March 1, 1968.

50. "6,000 Miners Dying from Atomic Exposure, Expert Charges," *UMWJ*, May 1, 1967.
51. Joseph Grego to Lyndon B. Johnson, October 26, 1967, UMWPO 34/6.
52. Edward Stearns to W. A. Boyle, February 1968, UMWPO 34/7; Local 7365 petition, c. 1967, UMWPO 34/6.
53. Local 7365 petition.
54. Kerman K. Lovelace to W. A. Boyle, February 20, 1968, UMWPO 34/6.
55. Jess Ballard to W. A. Boyle, May 20, 1968, UMWPO 34/7.
56. Mrs. Clarence Kirkendoll to W. A. Boyle, March 21, 1968, UMWPO 34/7.
57. W. A. Boyle to Mrs. Clarence Kirkendoll, March 25, 1968, UMWPO 34/7.
58. FPC, *1970 National Power Survey: Part I* (Washington, DC: GPO, 1971), I-6-2.
59. Local 1082, Resolution on Atomic Energy, November 25, 1967, UMWPO 34/9; *Proceedings of the Forty-Fifth Consecutive Constitutional Convention of the United Mine Workers of America* (Washington, DC: United Mine Workers of America, 1968), 9–12.
60. For the broader context, see Andrew Needham, *Power Lines: Phoenix and the Making of the Modern Southwest* (Princeton, NJ: Princeton University Press, 2014).
61. Peter H. Eichstaedt, *If You Poison Us: Uranium and Native Americans* (Santa Fe, NM: Red Crane, 1994), 54.
62. Robert Lifset, *Power on the Hudson: Storm King Mountain and the Emergence of Modern American Environmentalism* (Pittsburgh, PA: University of Pittsburgh Press, 2014), 12–14.
63. *Proceedings of the Forty-Fifth Consecutive Constitutional Convention*, 245–49.
64. *Proceedings of the Forty-Fifth Consecutive Constitutional Convention*, 102–3.
65. *Proceedings of the Forty-Fifth Consecutive Constitutional Convention*, 78–84.
66. W. A. Boyle, Labor Day Address, Wheeling, West Virginia, September 4, 1967, UMWPO 46/21.
67. W. A. Boyle, statement to House Committee on Interstate and Foreign Commerce, August 24, 1967, UMWPO 46/21.
68. Les Leopold, *The Man Who Hated Work and Loved Labor: The Life and Times of Tony Mazzocchi* (White River Junction, VT: Chelsea Green, 2007), 216–17.
69. Jeanne Rasmussen, "The Hot Edge of Hell," unpublished manuscript, undated, JRP 1/12.
70. "6,000 Miners Dying from Atomic Exposure."
71. W. A. Boyle, statement, February 18, 1969, UMWPO 46/22.
72. W. A. Boyle, testimony to Senate Labor and Public Welfare Committee on Coal Mine Health and Safety, February 27, 1969, in *The Fight for Coal Mine*

Health and Safety: A Documented History, ed. Ken Hechler (Charleston, WV: Pictorial Histories, 2011), 117–25.
73. "UMWA Expels District 50!"
74. James Nelson, *The Mine Workers' District 50* (New York: Exposition, 1955).
75. John L. Lewis to Thomas Kennedy, W. A. Boyle, and John Owens, December 27, 1961, UMWPO 191/10.
76. The UMW claimed District 50 had failed to make payments on loans that had been made for organizing efforts; District 50 insisted the UMW had expected too much in dues contributions. Memorandum, undated, circa 1966, UMWPO 191/10.
77. District 50 News Release, April 30, 1968, UMWPO 191/16.
78. "UMWA Expels District 50!"
79. "UMWA Expels District 50!"
80. These letters and telegrams were nearly unanimously supportive of the decision, unsurprising given Boyle's penchant for vindictiveness and retaliation. This correspondence, read within these limitations, remains illuminating for *how* writers voiced that support, UMWPO 34/4–16.
81. Harry Rossi and John Kutchman, to W. A. Boyle, April 2, 1968, UWMPO 34/5.
82. Steve Panak to W. A. Boyle, April 5, 1968; Joseph Yablonski to W. A. Boyle, April 10, 1968, UMWPO 34/5; telegrams from Locals 7922, 9926, and 7714; Kerman Lovelace to W. A. Boyle, February 20, 1968, UMWPO 34/6.
83. Tom Serra to W. A. Boyle, February 5, 1969, UMWPO 34/8.
84. Lee Roy Foltz to W. A. Boyle, April 10, 1968, UMWPO 34/8.
85. Farrell Whitlow, President LU 1284, to W. A. Boyle, February 9, 1968, UMWPO 34/7.
86. Elmer Hall to W. A. Boyle, February 13, 1968, UMWPO 34/7.
87. James Balsamelle to W. A. Boyle, February 9, 1968, UMWPO 34/7.
88. Edward K. Bright to W. A. Boyle, UMWPO 34/8.
89. Erne L. Bigham to W. A. Boyle, February 9, 1968, UMWPO 34/7.
90. Gerard C. Gambs, "The Coal Industry Meets the Challenge of the Nuclear Age," *Coal*, June 1965, UMWJR 13/6.
91. W. A. Boyle, testimony before the Senate Labor and Public Welfare Committee on Coal Mine Health and Safety, February 27, 1969, UMWPO 46/22.
92. Nelson Lichtenstein, *The Most Dangerous Man in Detroit: Walter Reuther and the Fate of American Labor* (New York: Basic Books, 1995), 220–21; Charles S. Maier, "The Politics of Productivity: Foundations of American International Economic Policy After World War II," *International Organization* 31, no. 4 (1977): 607–33.

93. David Nye, *Consuming Power: A Social History of American Energies* (Cambridge, MA: MIT Press, 1998), 210–15; Lizabeth Cohen, *A Consumers' Republic: The Politics of Mass Consumption in Postwar America* (New York: Vintage, 2003) 112–14.

94. Kenneth T. Jackson, *Crabgrass Frontier: The Suburbanization of the United States* (New York: Oxford University Press, 1985), 297.

95. W. D. Cobb, advertising memo, August 8, 1970, PPLR, 46/1; Needham, *Power Lines*, 6–7; these ads are representative of utility electricity advertising pre-1971. See Kirsten Moana Thompson, "Live Electrically with Reddy Kilowatt, Your Electrical Servant," in *Animation and Advertising*, ed. Malcolm Cook and Kirsten Moana Thompson (Cham, Switzerland: Springer International, 2019), 127–44.

96. EIA, "US Electricity Retail Sales to Major End-Use Sectors and Electricity Direct Use by All Sectors, 1950–2020," *Monthly Energy Review*, March 2021, table 7.6.

97. Sidney M. Milkis and Jeremy M. Mileur, eds., *The Great Society and the High-Tide of Liberalism* (Amherst: University of Massachusetts Press, 2005); Elizabeth Hinton, *From the War on Poverty to the War on Crime: The Making of Mass Incarceration in America* (Cambridge, MA: Harvard University Press, 2017); Destin Jenkins, *The Bonds of Inequality: Debt and the Making of the American City* (Chicago: University of Chicago Press, 2021); Lily Geismer, "Good Neighbors for Fair Housing: Suburban Liberalism and Racial Inequality in Metropolitan Boston," *Journal of Urban History* 39, no. 3 (2012): 454–56.

V. An Inherent Danger of Explosion

1. WVDM, *Official Hearing: Coal Mine Explosion, Consol No. 9 Mine, November 20, 1968*, WVDM Records, AR-1527, folder 17, West Virginia State Archives, Charleston, West Virginia; Bonnie E. Stewart, *No. 9: The Farmington Mine Disaster* (Morgantown: West Virginia University Press, 2012), 67.
2. WVDM, *Official Hearing*.
3. Robert Coles and Harry Huge, "Black Lung: Mining as a Way of Death," *New Republic*, January 25, 1969.
4. Ben A. Franklin, "The Scandal of Death and Injury in the Mines: Nobody Knows What the Cost of a Century of Neglect Has Been," *NYT*, March 30, 1969.
5. "78 Miners Entombed in Farmington No. 9 After Blasts Rip Workings," *Times-West Virginian*, November 21, 1968; Bill Evans, "Sealing of the Farmington Mine Is Complete," *Times-West Virginian*, December 1, 1968.

6. Romeo M. Flores, *Coal and Coalbed Gas: Fueling the Future* (Amsterdam: Elsevier, 2014), 167–233.
7. Stewart, *No. 9*, 44.
8. Ken Hechler, statement, March 19, 1969, in *The Fight for Coal Mine Health and Safety: A Documented History*, ed. Ken Hechler (Charleston, WV: Pictorial Histories, 2011), 137.
9. "Flaming Pit Entombs 15," *Charleston Daily Mail*, November 15, 1954; Stewart, *No. 9*, 36.
10. Stewart, *No. 9*, 15; see discussion in chapter 3.
11. Stewart, *No. 9*, 37–64.
12. Douglas Imbrogno, "Farmington No. 9: The West Virginia Disaster That Changed Coal Mining Forever," *West Virginia Public Broadcasting*, November 20, 2018, https://www.wvpublic.org/news/2018-11-20/farmington-no-9-the-west-virginia-disaster-that-changed-coal-mining-forever.
13. Imbrogno, "Farmington No. 9."
14. "Coal Mine Safety: 9 Comments," in *The Hurricane Creek Massacre* by Tom Bethell, January 26, 1971, MFDR 46/15.
15. "Coal Mine Safety: 9 Comments."
16. NCPC, report to membership, 1963, UMWPO 192/13.
17. "This One Won't Blow Up," *UMWJ*, May 1, 1967.
18. Justin McCarthy, "Our Heartfelt Sympathy Is Extended to the Victims of the Mine Disaster," *UMWJ*, December 1, 1968.
19. DOI, BM, *Historical Summary of Coal Mine Explosions in the United States, 1959–1981*, by J. K. Richmond, G. C. Price, M. J. Sapko, and E. M. Kawenski, Information Circular 8909, 1983, 30–31.
20. "A Test for Coal Miners," 1969, MFDR 23/35.
21. A. F. Tegen, "The Coal Producer and the Electric Power Industry," 38, presentation at the joint annual meeting of the Central Pennsylvania Coal Producers Association and the Eastern Bituminous Coal Association, Bedford Springs, PA, October 2, 1958, UMWPO 10/2.
22. Robyn Muncy, "Coal-Fired Reforms: Social Citizenship, Dissident Miners, and the Great Society," *Journal of American History* 96, no. 1 (June 2009): 72–98; Richard P. Mulcahy, *A Social Contract for the Coalfields: The Rise and Fall of the United Mine Workers of America Welfare and Retirement Fund* (Knoxville: University of Tennessee Press, 2000), 130.
23. Charles River Associates Inc., "The Economic Impact of Public Policy on the Appalachian Coal Industry and the Regional Economy. Part I: Profile of the Appalachian Coal Industry and Its Competitive Fuels."
24. EIA, "Electricity Net Generation, Total (All Sectors), 1949–2011," *Annual Energy Review*, September 2012; Tegen, "The Coal Producer and the Electric Power Industry."

25. Andrew Needham, *Power Lines: Phoenix and the Making of the Modern Southwest* (Princeton, NJ: Princeton University Press, 2014); Beth Gardiner, *Choked: Life and Breath in the Age of Air Pollution* (Chicago: University of Chicago Press, 2019), 147–54; Richard H. K. Vietor, *Environmental Politics and the Coal Coalition* (College Station: Texas A&M University Press, 1980), 127–54.
26. David E. Nye, *When the Lights Went Out: A History of Blackouts in America* (Cambridge, MA: MIT Press, 2010), 67–105.
27. Dan Edelstein, Stefanos Geroulanos, and Natasha Wheatley, *Power and Time: Temporalities in Conflict and the Making of History* (Chicago: University of Chicago Press, 2020), 26–27.
28. "Well Balanced," *UMWJ*, January 15, 1967.
29. Franklin, "The Scandal of Death and Injury."
30. McCarthy, "Our Heartfelt Sympathy."
31. "Old King Coal Returns!," *UMWJ*, January 15, 1968.
32. "Coal Mine Safety: 9 Comments."
33. NBC, "The Condition of the Coal Miner," August 4, 1970, transcript, UMWPO, 29/18.
34. Coles and Huge, "Black Lung."
35. W. A. Boyle to Stuart Udall, March 29, 1968, UMWPO 29/14.
36. NBC, "Condition of the Coal Miner."
37. Lyndon B. Johnson to President of the Senate and Speaker of the House, September 11, 1968, APP.
38. Michael D. Guillerman, *Face Boss: The Memoir of a Western Kentucky Coal Miner* (Knoxville: University of Tennessee Press, 2009), 40–41; Rowland Atkinson, "Ecology of Sound: The Sonic Order of Urban Space," *Urban Studies* 44, no. 10 (September 2007): 1905–17; Thomas G. Andrews, *Killing for Coal: America's Deadliest Labor War* (Cambridge, MA: Harvard University Press, 2008), 125.
39. Guillerman, *Face Boss*, 49–52.
40. Ken Hechler, statement, March 19, 1969, in *The Fight for Coal Mine Health and Safety*, 135.
41. W. A. Boyle, testimony to the Senate Subcommittee on Labor, February 27, 1969, in *The Fight for Coal Mine Health and Safety*, 117.
42. Lorin M. Kerr, "Coal Workers Pneumoconiosis: The Road to Dusty Death," presented at the 45th Consecutive Convention of the United Mine Workers of America, September 1968, Denver, Colorado, UMWPO 29/15; Disabled Workers Association of Clay County, "Black Lung Handbook: How to Get Your Rights," 1971, MFDR 10/11.
43. Jeff Goodell, *Big Coal: The Dirty Secret Behind America's Energy Future* (Boston: Houghton Mifflin, 2006), xx.

44. Barbara Ellen Smith, *Digging Our Own Graves: Coal Miners and the Struggle Over Black Lung Disease* (Chicago: Haymarket, 2020), 55.
45. "No Need to Delay Mine Safety Law," *Louisville Courier-Journal and Times*, January 26, 1969; Jim Lee to Archie W. Robinson, April 8, 1963, ARP 6/6.
46. Hechler, *The Fight for Coal Mine Health and Safety*, 74.
47. Hechler, *The Fight for Coal Mine Health and Safety*, 23.
48. Kenneth W. Hechler, "Insurgency: Personalities and Politics of the Taft Era," PhD diss., Columbia University, 1941.
49. Carter Taylor Seaton, *The Rebel in the Red Jeep: Ken Hechler's Life in West Virginia Politics* (Morgantown: West Virginia University Press, 2017), 108.
50. Seaton, *The Rebel in the Red Jeep*, 131.
51. Hechler, *The Fight for Coal Mine Health and Safety*, 23–24, 73.
52. Ken Hechler, statement, March 19, 1969, in *The Fight for Coal Mine Health and Safety*, 137.
53. Hechler, *The Fight for Coal Mine Health and Safety*, 74–75.
54. Hechler, *The Fight for Coal Mine Health and Safety*, 74–75.
55. Ken Hechler, statement, January 26, 1969, in *The Fight for Coal Mine Health and Safety*, 93–96.
56. Ken Hechler, statement, November 25, 1968, in *The Fight for Coal Mine Health and Safety*, 77.
57. Ken Hechler, statement, December 12, 1968, in *The Fight for Coal Mine Health and Safety*, 87.
58. Ben A. Franklin, "West Virginia Miners Demand Black Lung Compensation Law," *NYT*, February 12, 1969.
59. "East Gulf Miners Strike in 'Black Lung' Protest," *Raleigh Register*, February 18, 1969.
60. "Black Lung Walkouts—Many Area Mines Idle," *Raleigh Register*, February 19, 1969; "Laws Labeled Inadequate—'No Work Until We Get What We Want,' County Man Says," *Raleigh Register*, February 27, 1969.
61. Seaton, *The Rebel in the Red Jeep*, 217–19.
62. "12,000 Coal Miners Join Wildcat Strike," *NYT*, February 26, 1969.
63. "Federal Court Says It Lacks Power to Halt Mine Strike," *NYT*, March 2, 1969; Cong. Rec., 91st Cong., 1st sess., 1969: 8352–8353; 29 U.S.C. 103, Ch. 90, sec. 3, 47 Stat. 70.
64. W. A. Boyle, testimony, February 27, 1969, in *The Fight for Coal Mine Health and Safety*, 119–20, emphasis added.
65. Lewis E. Evans and Robert E. Howe to W. A. Boyle, January 2, 1969, UMWPO 29/16.
66. John Brennan to W. A. Boyle, January 31, 1969, UMWPO 29/16.
67. John Brennan to W. A. Boyle, January 31, 1969, UMWPO 29/16.
68. Brennan to Boyle, January 31, 1969.

69. John Brennan to W. A. Boyle, January 3, 1969, UMWPO 29/16.
70. Coles and Huge, "Black Lung"; on company doctor complicity, see Curtis Seltzer, "Moral Dimensions of Occupational Health: The Case of the 1969 Coal Mine Health and Safety Act," in *The Health and Safety of Workers: Case Studies in the Politics of Professional Responsibility*, ed. Ronald Bayer (New York: Oxford University Press, 1988), 242–70.
71. Lizabeth Cohen, *A Consumers' Republic: The Politics of Mass Consumption in Postwar America* (New York: Vintage, 2003).
72. Quoted in Coles and Huge, "Black Lung."
73. Coles and Huge, "Black Lung."
74. James A. Nuechterlein, "The Dream of Scientific Liberalism: The *New Republic* and American Progressive Thought, 1914–1920," *Review of Politics* 42, no. 2 (1980): 167–90.
75. "Coal Miners' Revolt," *NYT*, February 25, 1969.
76. "'Black Lung' Bill Is Signed by West Virginia Governor," *NYT*, March 12, 1969.
77. Alan Derickson, *Black Lung: Anatomy of a Public Health Disaster* (Ithaca, NY: Cornell University Press, 1998), 161–63.
78. Derickson, *Black Lung*, 161.
79. "The Black Lungers," *NYT*, February 3, 1969.
80. Ken Hechler, "Behind the Scenes on the Mine Safety Bill," January 5, 1970, in *The Fight for Coal Mine Health and Safety*, 274–78.
81. "Mathies Miner Killed in a Fall," *Uniontown Morning Herald*, November 20, 1968.
82. W. A. Boyle to Stuart Udall, March 29, 1968, UMWPO 29/14.
83. MSHA, "Coal Fatalities, 1900–2020," MSHA-DL; DOI, BM, Division of Coal-Mine Inspection, Annual Report for 1966, January 1967, UMWPO 11/23.
84. Richard Nixon, State of the Union Address, January 22, 1970, APP.
85. John Dewey, *Freedom and Culture* (New York: G. P. Putnam's Sons, 1939), 162.
86. PL 91–173, §202(b).
87. U.S. Congress, Senate, Subcommittee on Labor, *Coal Mine Health and Safety*, 91st Cong., 1st sess., 1969, 522–23.
88. U.S. Congress, Senate, Subcommittee on Labor, *Coal Mine Health and Safety*, 1969, 4.
89. U.S. Congress, Senate, Subcommittee on Labor, *Coal Mine Health and Safety*, 1969, 4.
90. Ken Hechler, statement, March 19, 1969, in *The Fight for Coal Mine Health and Safety*, 144; on longer history of actuarial approaches to workers' bodies, see Nate Holdren, *Injury Impoverished: Workplace Accidents, Capitalism, and the Law in the Progressive Era* (New York: Cambridge University Press, 2020).

91. U.S. Congress, Senate, Subcommittee on Labor, *Coal Mine Health and Safety*, 7–447.
92. U.S. Congress, Senate, Subcommittee on Labor, *Coal Mine Health and Safety*, 464.
93. Derickson, *Black Lung*, 170–71.
94. Smith, *Digging Our Own Graves*, 151–52; National Independent Coal Operators' Association, "Recommendations Concerning Rules and Regulations Governing Coal Mine Health and Safety as Found in Title 30, Part 75 of the Federal Register, Vol. 35, No. 61," March 28, 1970, MFDR, 44/11.
95. Barbara Kopple, *Harlan County, USA* (New York: Criterion, 2006).
96. Hechler, *The Fight for Coal Mine Health and Safety*, 269.
97. Jock Yablonski, statement, May 29, 1969, MFDR 23/32.
98. Richard J. Jensen, "Yablonski, Joseph A. 'Jock,'" in *Encyclopedia of U.S. Labor and Working-Class History*, ed. Eric Arnesen (New York: Routledge, 2006), 1:1555.
99. Lawrence D. Beck and Stuart Rawlings, "Coal—the Captive Giant: A Report on Coal Ownership in the United States," private report, 1971, MFDR 63/9.
100. *Proceedings of the Forty-Fifth Consecutive Constitutional Convention of the United Mine Workers of America* (Washington, DC: United Mine Workers of America, 1968), 5–6.
101. *Proceedings* (1968), 5–6.
102. *Proceedings* (1968), 78–85.
103. "His Kind of People: Backers Brave Cold for Yablonski Rites," *Daily News* (Lebanon, PA), January 10, 1970; "Yablonski of UMW Slain with Wife and Daughter," *NYT*, January 6, 1970.
104. Yablonski, statement, May 29, 1969.
105. Yablonski, statement, May 29, 1969.
106. Yablonski, statement, May 29, 1969.
107. James A. Wechsler, "Lonely Rebels," undated, MFDR, 23/25.
108. "Coal Mine Safety: 9 Comments."
109. Stanley Kaczmarczyk, letter to editor (newspaper unspecified), MFDR 83/10.
110. Ben A. Franklin, "Boyle Controversy Grips the Miners Union," *NYT*, August 31, 1969.
111. "The Time Has Come for a Major Change," *District 50 News*, MFDR 23/34.
112. Yablonski, statement, May 29, 1969; Michael K. Drapkin, "Coal Strikes Seen Being Settled Soon," *NYT*, March 4, 1969; "Coal Strike Hits 12 Mines," *Wall Street Journal*, August 19, 1969.
113. Yablonski, statement, May 29, 1969.
114. Yablonski, statement, May 29, 1969.

115. Yablonski, statement, May 29, 1969.
116. Annelise Orleck and Lisa Gayle Hazirjian, *The War on Poverty: A New Grassroots History, 1964–1980* (Athens: University of Georgia Press, 2011).
117. 83 Stat. 852 (1970); 42 U.S.C. § 7401; 86 Stat. 816 (1972); 88 Stat. 1660 (1974); U.S., Reorganization Plan No. 3 of 1970, *Federal Register*, 35 FR 15623, October 6, 1970.
118. ACLU, press release, November 19, 1969, MFDR 23/1.
119. Joseph A. "Chip" Yablonski, Election Day Violations, Appendix G, December 1969, MFDR 23/17.
120. Ben A. Franklin, "Boyle Declares Victory in Mine Union Race," *NYT*, December 11, 1969.
121. Franklin, "Boyle Declares Victory."
122. Jeanne Rasmussen, "Elmer Brown—in Memoriam," *Miner's Voice*, December 1971.
123. H. Elmer Brown to Harrison Williams, December 1969, MFDR 23/10.
124. Brown to Williams, December 1969.
125. *Monongahela Daily Republican*, December 29, 1969.
126. "Safety Walkout by Miners," *Pottsville Republican*, December 29, 1969.
127. Hechler, *The Fight for Coal Mine Health and Safety*, 276–77; Richard Nixon, Daily Diary, December 30, 1969, RC-11, White House Central Files, Staff Member and Office Files, Office of Presidential Papers and Archives, Richard Nixon Presidential Library and Museum, Yorba Linda, California.
128. Hechler, *The Fight for Coal Mine Health and Safety*, 276–77.
129. Ken Hechler, press release, January 5, 1970, in *The Fight for Coal Mine Health and Safety*, 274–78.
130. Clay County Poor Peoples Association, press release, November 13, 1970, MFDR 101/3.
131. Arthur H. Lewis, *Murder by Contract: The People vs. "Tough Tony" Boyle* (New York: Macmillan, 1975), 2–10; Brit Hume, *Death and the Mines: Rebellion and Murder in the United Mine Workers* (New York: Grossman, 1971), 245–59; Paul F. Clark, *The Miners' Fight for Democracy: Arnold Miller and the Reform of the United Mine Workers* (Ithaca, NY: ILR/Cornell, 1981), 26.
132. "Police Widen Yablonski Probe," *Pittsburgh Press*, January 11, 1970, 1.
133. Lewis, *Murder by Contract*, 2; Kopple, *Harlan County, U.S.A.*
134. Ben A. Franklin, "More Miners Protest Slayings," *NYT*, January 7, 1970; "Murder of a Miner May Bring Reforms," *NYT*, January 11, 1970.
135. "His Kind of People."
136. Kopple, *Harlan County, U.S.A.*
137. "Patrick Stresses Contract," *Miner's Voice*, June 1972; DOI, BM, Health and Safety District C, *Report of Fatal Machinery Accident, No. 44 Mine, Bethlehem Mines Corporation (Delaware), Idamay, Marion County, West Virginia, September 11,*

1964, by Joseph J. Dobis (Morgantown, WV: Bureau of Mines, 1964), MSHA-DL; Interview with Harry Patrick by George Hopkins, August 8, 1974, E-0022, in the SOHP, Series E: Labor (04007E), SHC.
138. Joseph L. Rauh, address to MFD Convention, Wheeling, West Virginia, May 27, 1972, JHP 11/20.
139. Franklin, "More Miners Protest Slayings."
140. 338 F. Supp. 924 *Barnes & Tucker Co. v. United Mine Workers of America, District No. 2, United Mine Workers of America, et al.* Civ. A. No. 71–1110. United States District Court, W. D. Pennsylvania. February 16, 1972, quote is William Shakespeare, *Macbeth*, Act V, sc. 3, lines 20–22.

Second Interlude: This Total-Energy Dream

1. "How Gulf Beats Industry Averages," *Business Week*, September 3, 1966; U.S. Congress, Senate, Select Committee on Small Business, Subcommittee on Monopoly, *The International Petroleum Cartel: Staff Report to the Federal Trade Commission*, 82nd Cong., 2nd sess., 1952, Committee Print No. 6, 25; David S. Painter, *Oil and the American Century: The Political Economy of U.S. Foreign Oil Policy, 1941–1954* (Baltimore, MD: Johns Hopkins University Press, 1986), 4–14.
2. Painter, *Oil and the American Century*, 205–7.
3. "How Gulf Beats Industry Averages."
4. Laurence D. Beck and Stuart Rawlings, *Coal: The Captive Giant—A Report on Coal Ownership in the United States*, 1971, 10–11, MFDR 63/9.
5. "TVA Pacts Let for Steam Coal," *Tennessean*, August 9, 1963; Arthur R. Friedman, "Gulf Offers $123 Million for Company," *Pittsburgh Post-Gazette*, September 11, 1963.
6. Corporate Information Center, *Gulf Oil: Portuguese Ally in Angola*, March 1972, 15, AAA 368; Rodney P. Carlisle and Joan M. Zenzen, *Supplying the Nuclear Arsenal: American Production Reactors, 1942–1992* (Baltimore, MD: Johns Hopkins University Press, 1996), 177n18.
7. Beck and Rawlings, *Coal*, 61.
8. "How Gulf Beats Industry Averages."
9. "Bolivia: Legislation Concerning Nationalization of Bolivian Gulf Oil Properties," *International Legal Materials* 10, no. 6 (1971): 1202–23.
10. U.S. Congress, House of Representatives, Committee on Foreign Affairs, Subcommittee on Africa, *U.S. Business Involvement in Southern Africa: Hearings Before the Subcommittee on Africa, Part 3*, 93rd Cong., 1st sess., 1973, 388.

11. AEC, Division of Technical Information, Office of the Assistant General Manager for Reactors, *Nuclear Reactors Built, Being Built, or Planned in the United States as of June 30, 1970*, TID-8200 (22nd Rev.), 8–9; *International Union, United Mine Workers of America v. Public Utilities Com. et al.*, 170 Colo. 556 (1970).

12. *Proceedings of the Forty-Fifth Consecutive Constitutional Convention of the United Mine Workers of America* (Washington, DC: United Mine Workers of America, 1968), 4–13; *International Union, United Mine Workers of America v. Public Utilities Com. et al.*, 170 Colo. 556 (1970); A. F. Grospiron to W. A. Boyle, July 22, 1968, W. A. Boyle to A. F. Grospiron, July 24, 1968, UMWPO 40/16.

13. NRC, Energy Resources Committee, *Energy Resources and National Policy* (Washington, DC: Gov't. Print. Off., 1939).

14. Neil Fligstein, *The Transformation of Corporate Control* (Cambridge, MA: Harvard University Press, 1990), 260.

15. Robert D. Lifset, "A New Understanding of the American Energy Crisis of the 1970s," *Historical Social Research* 39, no. 4 (2014): 25–27; Richard H. K. Vietor, *Energy Policy in America Since 1945: A Study of Business-Government Relations* (New York: Cambridge University Press, 1984), 193–202.

16. Giuliano Garavini, *The Rise and Fall of OPEC in the Twentieth Century* (New York: Oxford University Press, 2019), 190–209.

17. Christopher R. W. Dietrich, *Oil Revolution: Anticolonial Elites, Sovereign Rights, and the Economic Culture of Decolonization* (New York: Cambridge University Press, 2017), 190–93; Anthony Sampson, *The Seven Sisters: The Great Oil Companies and the World They Made* (New York: Viking, 1975), 230–43.

18. Richard H. K. Vietor, *Environmental Politics and the Coal Coalition* (College Station: Texas A&M University Press), 18–20.

19. Norm Weintraub to A. F. Grospiron, June 10, 1968, UMWPO 40/16.

20. Beck and Rawlings, *Coal*, 10–12.

21. A. F. Grospiron to Edward V. Long, July 19, 1968, UMWPO 40/16.

22. "PP&L's 'Fleet' Trains: Now There Are Five," *Railway Age*, June 14, 1971, 5; P. W. Seikman, "The Story of a Train," 1965 PP&L annual meeting, Harrisburg, PA, April 10, 1965, PPLR 49/9.

23. Richard Hirsh, *Technology and Transformation in the American Electric Power Industry* (New York: Cambridge University Press, 2002), 111–12.

24. Quoted in Beck and Rawlings, *Coal*, 97.

25. U.S. Congress, Senate, Committee on Government Operations, Subcommittee on Intergovernmental Relations, *Intergovernmental Coordination of Power Development and Environmental Protection Act: Hearings Before*

the Subcommittee on Intergovernmental Relations, Part 1, 91st Cong., 2nd sess., February 3, 1970, 4–29.
26. Lifset, "A New Understanding of the American Energy Crisis."
27. Carl E. Bagge, remarks at Colby College, Waterville, Maine, March 2, 1972, UMWDO 3/88.
28. Elburt F. Osborn, remarks, University of Utah, Salt Lake City, October 15, 1971, MFDR 45/20.
29. U.S. Congress, Senate, Committee on Government Operations, Subcommittee on Intergovernmental Relations, *Intergovernmental Coordination of Power Development and Environmental Protection Act*, 41.
30. U.S. Congress, Senate, Committee on Government Operations, Subcommittee on Intergovernmental Relations, *Intergovernmental Coordination of Power Development and Environmental Protection Act*, 39; FPC, *1970 National Power Survey: Part I* (Washington, DC: GPO, 1971), I-1-4-5.
31. U.S. Congress, Senate, Committee on Government Operations, Subcommittee on Intergovernmental Relations, *Intergovernmental Coordination of Power Development and Environmental Protection Act*, 1–4, 30–37.
32. U.S. Congress, Senate, Committee on Government Operations, Subcommittee on Intergovernmental Relations, *Intergovernmental Coordination of Power Development and Environmental Protection Act*, 30.
33. "Will America's Lights Go Out?," *MV*, June 1970.
34. "Energy Workers Must Organize!," *MV*, December 1969.
35. "Energy Workers Must Organize!"
36. On the invisibility of oil workers, see Kaveh Ehsani, "Disappearing the Workers: How Labor in the Oil Complex Has Been Made Invisible," in *Working for Oil: Comparative Social Histories of Labor in the Global Oil Industry*, ed. Touraj Atabaki, Elisabetta Bini, and Kaveh Ehsani (Cham: Springer, 2018), 11–34; on uranium workers, see Gabrielle Hecht, "Africa and the Nuclear World: Labor, Occupational Health, and the Transnational Production of Uranium," *Comparative Studies in Society and History* 51, no. 4 (2009): 896–926.
37. U.S. Congress, Senate, Committee on Government Operations, Subcommittee on Intergovernmental Relations, *Intergovernmental Coordination of Power Development and Environmental Protection Act*, appendix 3, 397–423.
38. "High Finance: Anatomy of a Big Deal," *Time*, October 22, 1965.
39. "High Finance."
40. William Bellano to Henry Jackson, circa 1970, in Beck and Rawlings, *Coal*, 36–37.
41. Beck and Rawlings, *Coal*, 22.
42. Kennecott Copper Company, "Kennecott: Its Men and Its Minerals," 1968, 20–21, in Beck and Rawlings, *Coal*, 31, emphasis added.

43. Beck and Rawlings, *Coal*, 24–25.
44. Quoted in Beck and Rawlings, *Coal*, 16.
45. EIA, "Coal Production, 1949–2011," *Annual Energy Review*, 2012.
46. "Back to Good Ole Coal," *Southern Exposure* 2, no. 2/3 (Fall 1974): 164–65, JDC 1/4.
47. U.S. Congress, Senate, Committee on Government Operations, Subcommittee on Intergovernmental Relations, *Intergovernmental Coordination of Power Development and Environmental Protection Act*, 660.
48. Beck and Rawlings, *Coal*, 125.
49. U.S. Congress, Senate, Select Committee on Small Business, Subcommittee on Financing and Investment, *SBA's Financial Assistance Programs: Hearings*, April 6, 1967, 766–68; Donald Turner, "The Scope of Antitrust and Other Economic Regulatory Policies," *Harvard Law Review* 82 (1969): 1207, 1230–31; Victor H. Kramer, "Commentary: Economic Concentration and the Antitrust Laws," *Washington University Law Review*, 1975, 165.
50. Beck and Rawlings, *Coal*, 166.
51. See Cara New Daggett, *The Birth of Energy: Fossil Fuels, Thermodynamics, and the Politics of Work* (Durham, NC: Duke University Press, 2019); Ann Norton Greene, *Horses at Work: Harnessing Power in Industrial America* (Cambridge, MA: Harvard University Press, 2008).
52. Based on a survey of government reports from 1840 through 1980. Before 1950, mentions of energy largely refer to things like "electrical energy" or "tidal energy" but distinguish these from "fuels."
53. David E. Nye, *Electrifying America: Social Meanings of a New Technology* (Cambridge, MA: MIT Press, 1992), 138–84, 238–86.
54. Kristen Moana Thompson, "Live Electrically with Reddy Kilowatt, Your Electric Servant," in *Animation and Advertising*, ed. Malcolm Cook and Kristen Moana Thompson (Cham: Springer, 2019), 127–44.
55. Reddy Kilowatt correspondence from 1970, PPLR 50/19.
56. "Coal Is Now Power," *Panorama*, August 16, 1970, MFDR 102/10.
57. David E. Nye, *Consuming Power: A Social History of American Energies* (Cambridge, MA: MIT Press, 1999), 187–215.
58. Natasha Zaretsky, *No Direction Home: The American Family and the Fear of National Decline, 1968–1980* (Chapel Hill: University of North Carolina Press, 2007), 1–3.
59. Elizabeth Hinton, *America on Fire: The Untold History of Police Violence and Black Rebellion Since the 1960s* (New York: Liveright, 2021), 10; Robert O. Self, *All in the Family: The Realignment of American Democracy Since the 1960s* (New York: Hill & Wang, 2012), 17–45; Judith Stein, *Pivotal Decade: How the United States Traded Factories for Finance in the Seventies* (New Haven, CT: Yale University Press, 2010), 26–28.

60. Timothy Mitchell, *Carbon Democracy: Political Power in the Age of Oil* (New York: Verso, 2011), 178.

VI. Walk Out—Before They Carry You Out

1. DOI, BM, *Report of Fatal Coal Mine Roof-Fall Accident, No. 51 Mine, Bethlehem Mines Corporation, Ellsworth, Washington County, Pennsylvania, April 8, 1970*, by Paul E. Margocee and Henry Zavora (Pittsburgh: BM, 1970), MSHA-DL; "Miner Killed in Roof Fall," *Monongahela Republican*, April 9, 1970.
2. DOI, BM, *Report of Fatal Coal Mine Roof-Fall . . . April 8, 1970.*
3. Holmes Safety Association, "How About You?," January 1967, UMWPO 11/23.
4. 1930 U.S. Census, Washington, Pennsylvania, populations schedule, Bentleyville, ED 6, sheet 10B, 197, 209, Joe Stanish, NARA microfilm publication T626, roll 2160; Commonwealth of Pennsylvania, Department of Health, Bureau of Vital Statistics, Death Certificate, Joseph Stanis, June 27, 1934, File 59461.
5. PDER, *Annual Report, 1970: Anthracite, Bituminous Coal and Oil and Gas Divisions* (Harrisburg: PDER, 1971), 131; "Miner Killed in Roof Fall at Ellsworth," *Uniontown Evening Standard*, April 9, 1920; DMMR, *Anthracite and Bituminous Division, Annual Report, 1969* (Harrisburg: DMMR, 1970), 115; DOI, BM, *Report of Fatal Coal Mine Roof-Fall Accident, No. 51 Mine, Bethlehem Mines Corporation, Ellsworth, Washington County, Pennsylvania, February 15, 1965*, by R. J. Kirk (Pittsburgh: BM, 1965), MSHA-DL; DOI, BM, *Report of Fatal Coal Mine Roof-Fall Accident, No. 51 Mine, Bethlehem Mines Corporation, Ellsworth, Washington County, Pennsylvania, Injured: May 12, 1965, Died: May 14, 1965*, by R. J. Kirk and E. M. Rudolph (Pittsburgh: BM, 1965), MSHA-DL.
6. DMMR, *Anthracite and Bituminous Division, Annual Report, 1969*, 115; "Miner Killed in Rock Fall," *Clearfield Progress*, March 14, 1969; *Monongahela Daily Republican*, July 25, 1969; "Miner Killed at Marianna," *Canonsburg Daily Notes*, September 18, 1969.
7. *Report of Fatal Coal Mine Roof-Fall . . . April 8, 1970.*
8. Clarice R. Feldman Aff. Appendix C, June 25, 1970, MFDR 45/32.
9. "Death Toll Up—Inspections Down," *BLB*, September 1970, MFDR 44/35.
10. Also see Richard Fry, "Dissent in the Coalfields: Miners, Federal Politics, and Union Reform in the United States," *Labor History* 55, no. 2 (2014): 173–88.

11. Paul Sabin, *Public Citizens: The Attack on Big Government and the Remaking of American Liberalism* (New York: Norton, 2021), xvii; Richard. A Harris and Sidney M. Milkis, *The Politics of Regulatory Change: A Tale of Two Agencies*, 2nd ed. (New York: Oxford University Press, 1996), 53–55; Richard A. Harris, *Coal Firms Under the New Social Regulation* (Durham, NC: Duke University Press, 1985), 2; Nancy Frank, "Maiming and Killing: Occupational Health Crimes," *Annals of the American Academy of Political and Social Science* 525 (January 1993): 112.

12. Joseph L. Rauh Jr., interviewed by Robert S. Peck, January 10, 16, 17, 23, February 7, 21, 28, July 3, 1992, Oral History Project, Historical Society of the District of Columbia Circuit; Michael E. Parrish, *Citizen Rauh: An American Liberal's Life in Law and Politics* (Ann Arbor: University of Michigan Press, 2010), 195–210.

13. Thomas Kiffmeyer, *Reformers to Radicals: The Appalachian Volunteers and the War on Poverty* (Lexington: University Press of Kentucky, 2008); Ronald Eller, *Uneven Ground: Appalachia Since 1945* (Lexington: University Press of Kentucky, 2008), 131–63.

14. 1950 U.S. Census, Essex, Massachusetts, population schedule, Essex, ED 5-92, sheet 9, 83, John W. Bethell and Thomas N. Bethell, NARA digital publication T628; interview with Ann C. Pollard by Margaret Brown, November 30, 1990, 1991OH003 App 291, Appalachia: War on Poverty Oral History Project, NCOH; Interview with Tom Bethell by George Hopkins, August 6, 1974, E-0019, SOHP Series E: Labor (04007E), SHC.

15. Kiffmeyer, *Reformers to Radicals*, 188–94.

16. "Walk Out . . . Before They Carry You Out!" *MV*, June 1972, MFDR 31/29.

17. Feldman Aff.; Nick DeVince, Aff. ¶3 October 16, 1970, MFDR 60/26; Mike Trbovich Aff. ¶5 October 14, 1970, MFDR 60/26; Brief for Appellant, *U.S. Steel Corp. v. United Mine Workers of America et al., Local Union No. 1248*, Appellant, Civil Action No. 71–1975, 3rd Cir., MFDR 61/6.

18. Edward Verlich, "Pickets Shut 28 District Mines," *Pittsburgh Press*, June 22, 1970; Transcript of Record, June 23, 1970 at 17, *U.S. Steel Corp. v. United Mine Workers of America* 320 F. Supp. 743 (W.D. Pa. 1970).

19. Chuck Washlack Aff. ¶3, undated copy, circa October 1970, MFDR 60/26.

20. Trbovich Aff. ¶3–4; Transcript, June 23, 1970, 70.

21. Charles J. Krewetz Aff. ¶2, circa October 1970, MFDR 60/26; PDER, *Annual Report, 1970*, 131.

22. Memorandum of points and authorities of defendants Edward F. Monborne and Charles Krawetz, *Bethlehem Mines Corporation v. United Mine Workers of America District 2, et al.*, 320 F. Supp. 743 (W.D. Pa. 1970), MFDR 59/11.

23. Complaint, *U.S. Steel v. United Mine Workers of America et al.*, Civil Action 70-724, June 22, 1970, MFDR 58/23; Complaint, *Jones & Laughlin v. United Mine Workers of America et al.*, Civil Action 70-7025, June 22, 1970, MFDR 59/1; Complaint, *Bethlehem Mines Corp. v. United Mine Workers of America, et al.*, Civil Action 70-727, June 22, 1970, MFDR 59/7; Complaint, *Republic Steel Corp. v. United Mine Workers of America et al.*, Civil Action 70-728, June 22, 1970, MFDR 59/12.

24. *Boys Market, Inc. v. Retail Clerks Union, Local 770*, 398 U.S. 235 (1970); Jefferson Cowie, *Stayin' Alive: The 1970s and the Last Days of the Working Class* (New York: Basic Books, 2010), 257.

25. 1910 U.S. Census, Columbiana, Ohio, population schedule, Wellsville, ED 62, sheet 2B, 44, 44, Wallace Gourley, NARA microfilm publication T624, roll 1162; "Gourley Named Assistant D.A.," *Monongahela Daily Republican*, April 30, 1936; "Endorsed by Labor: Wallace S. Gourley," *Canonsburg Daily Notes*, September 8, 1939; "Gourley Goes Into Federal Judge's Robe," *Canonsburg Daily Notes*, December 17, 1945.

26. Transcript, June 23, 1970, 9.

27. In addition to the UMW Counsel's arguments, District 5 kept files on dissident locals. UMW District 5 Records, 25/14.

28. Transcript, June 23, 1970, 15.

29. Amended Supplemental Complaint, *Burton v. Hickel*, Civil Action No. 861-70, June 25, 1970, MFDR 45/31; Ben A. Franklin, "3 in House to Sue to Speed U.S. Mine Regulations," *NYT*, March 24, 1970.

30. Ben A. Franklin, "Nixon Ousts Head of Mines Bureau," *NYT*, March 1, 1970; "Gain for Mine Safety," *NYT*, October 8, 1970.

31. Franklin, "Nixon Ousts Head of Mines Bureau"; Ben A. Franklin, "Geologist Considered for Mines Post," *NYT*, September 19, 1970.

32. Tom Bethell, *The Hurricane Creek Massacre: A Report on the Circumstances Surrounding the Deaths of 38 Men in a Coal Mine Explosion in Eastern Kentucky, December 30, 1970*, January 26, 1971, 50–51, MFDR 46/15.

33. Bethell, *The Hurricane Creek Massacre*, 50–51.

34. Memorandum of points and authorities of defendants Monborne and Krawetz.

35. Transcript, June 23, 1970, 38; 83 Stat. 742 §307–8.

36. Transcript, June 23, 1970, 38; DOI, BM, *Report of Fatal Coal Mine (Haulage) Accident, Maple Creek Mine, United States Steel Corporation, Coal Operations-Raw Materials, Frick District, New Eagle, Washington County, Pennsylvania, April 30, 1970*, by John A. Noon and James B. Shannon (Pittsburgh: BM, 1970), MSHA-DL.

37. Transcript of Testimony, July 14, 1971 at 18–22, *U.S. Steel v. United Mine Workers of America, et al.*, Civil Action 71-561, (W.D. Pa. 1971), MFDR 61/1;

Kenneth Warren, *Wealth, Waste, and Alienation: Growth and Decline in the Connellsville Coke Industry* (Pittsburgh, PA: University of Pittsburgh Press, 2019), 236–58.
38. Transcript, June 23, 1970, 46.
39. Transcript, June 23, 1970, 46.
40. Transcript, June 23, 1970, 39.
41. Transcript, June 23, 1970, 41, 48.
42. Transcript, June 23, 1970, 103–21.
43. Transcript of Record, June 24, 1970 at 131, *U.S. Steel Corp. v. UMW* 320 F. Supp. 743 (W.D. Pa. 1970), MFDR 59/16.
44. Thomas Robert Mulroy, "The Taft-Hartley Act in Action," *University of Chicago Law Review* 15, no. 3 (1948): 601.
45. P.L. 80-101, 61 Stat. 136 §502.
46. Bert Michael Whorton, "Labor Law-Safety Disputes-Walkouts Under Section 502 of the Taft-Hartley Act," *West Virginia Law Review* 76, no. 1 (November 1973): 58–62; *NLRB v. Knight Morley Corp.*, 251 F.2d 753 (6th Cir. 1957); *NLRB v. Fruin-Colnon Construction Co.*, 330 F.2d 885 (8th Cir. 1964); *Philadelphia Marine Trade Assoc. v. NLRB*, 330 F.2d 492 (3rd Cir. 1964).
47. Transcript, June 24, 1970, 131,
48. Transcript, June 24, 1970, 128–30.
49. Transcript, June 24, 1970, 129.
50. *U.S. Steel Corp. v. UMW*, No. 19,308–19,041 (3rd Cir. 1970), order for *de novo* hearing, June 30, 1970, MFDR 60/2.
51. Transcript, June 24, 1970, 133–34.
52. Transcript, June 24, 1970, 167.
53. Paul J. Nyden, "Rank-and-File Rebellions in the Coalfields, 1964–80," *Monthly Review* 58, no. 10 (2007); *Consolidation Coal Co. v. Disabled Miners of Southern West Virginia*, 442 F.2d 1261, MFDR 58/2-13.
54. Memorandum of Appellants in Support of Reversal, *U.S. Steel Corp. v. UMW*, No. 19,308–19,041 (3rd Cir. 1970), MFDR 60/5.
55. Memorandum of Appellants in Support of Reversal.
56. *U.S. Steel Corp. v. UMW*, order for *de novo* hearing.
57. Joseph A. Yablonski to Members of UMW Local Unions 1248, 1197, 762, and Mike Trbovich, July 2, 1970, MFDR 60/3.
58. Robert Walker, "Warnings on Coal Shortage Reach Crescendo," *NYT*, September 6, 1970.
59. Bethell, *The Hurricane Creek Massacre*, i.
60. "Coal Miner, 68, Crushed, Dies," *Somerset Daily American*, July 3, 1970; "Prospect Man Killed Near Portersville," *New Castle News*, October 21, 1970; PDER, *Annual Report, 1970*, 131.

61. "Death Tolls Up—Inspections Down," *BLB*.
62. Bethell, *The Hurricane Creek Massacre*, i.
63. U.S. Congress, House, Committee on Education and Labor, General Subcommittee on Labor, *Investigation of the Hyden, Kentucky, Coal Mine Disaster of December 30, 1970: The Official Report, Minority and Additional Views*, 92nd Congress, 1st Session, July 1971, v.
64. Bethell, *The Hurricane Creek Massacre*, 15–16.
65. Bethell, *The Hurricane Creek Massacre*, 15–16.
66. Bethell, *The Hurricane Creek Massacre*, 16.
67. Bethell, *The Hurricane Creek Massacre*, 17.
68. "Rescuers Dig for Bodies in Mine Where 39 Died," *Tallahassee Democrat*, December 31, 1970.
69. Chris Kenning, "39 Miners Went In, Only 1 Came Out: 50 Years of Pain from a Kentucky Coal Mine Disaster," *Louisville Courier-Journal*, December 23, 2020.
70. "Friends Dig Graves for 38 Mine Victims," *Pittsburgh Post-Gazette*, January 2, 1971; Bethell, *The Hurricane Creek Massacre*, 17–18.
71. Bethell, *The Hurricane Creek Massacre*, 17–18.
72. U.S. Congress, House, Committee on Education and Labor, General Subcommittee on Labor, *Investigation of the Hyden, Kentucky, Coal Mine Disaster*, 26.
73. Bethell, *The Hurricane Creek Massacre*, 17–18.
74. Bethell, *The Hurricane Creek Massacre*, 18.
75. James D. Ausenbaugh, *At Sixth and Broadway: Tales from the Glory Days of a Great Newspaper* (Scottsville, KY: Mews, 1998), 132–33.
76. "Friends Dig Graves for 38 Mine Victims," *Pittsburgh Post-Gazette*, January 2, 1971; Bethell, *The Hurricane Creek Massacre*, 23–24.
77. "His Life Spared: I Will Never Go Into Another Mine Again," *York Dispatch*, January 2, 1971.
78. Bethell, *The Hurricane Creek Massacre*, 24.
79. Bethell, *The Hurricane Creek Massacre*, 17–18; U.S. Congress, House, Committee on Education and Labor, General Subcommittee on Labor, *Investigation of the Hyden, Kentucky, Coal Mine Disaster*, ix. Kentucky did not have a state black lung bill like West Virginia that might have assumed disability based on the number of years worked rather than on X-ray or autopsy evidence.
80. U.S. Congress, House, Committee on Education and Labor, General Subcommittee on Labor, *Investigation of the Hyden, Kentucky, Coal Mine Disaster*, 7–9, 11.
81. Bethell, *The Hurricane Creek Massacre*, 10–12.

82. U.S. Congress, House, Committee on Education and Labor, General Subcommittee on Labor, *Investigation of the Hyden, Kentucky, Coal Mine Disaster,* 15.
83. U.S. Congress, House, Committee on Education and Labor, General Subcommittee on Labor, *Investigation of the Hyden, Kentucky, Coal Mine Disaster,* 14.
84. U.S. Congress, House, Committee on Education and Labor, General Subcommittee on Labor, *Investigation of the Hyden, Kentucky, Coal Mine Disaster,* xiii.
85. U.S. Congress, House, Committee on Education and Labor, General Subcommittee on Labor, *Investigation of the Hyden, Kentucky, Coal Mine Disaster,* 15, 17.
86. U.S. Congress, House, Committee on Education and Labor, General Subcommittee on Labor, *Investigation of the Hyden, Kentucky, Coal Mine Disaster,* xi.
87. U.S. Congress, House, Committee on Education and Labor, General Subcommittee on Labor, *Investigation of the Hyden, Kentucky, Coal Mine Disaster,* 7–10.
88. U.S. Congress, House, Committee on Education and Labor, General Subcommittee on Labor, *Investigation of the Hyden, Kentucky, Coal Mine Disaster,* xiii.
89. Quoted in Bethell, *The Hurricane Creek Massacre,* 26.
90. Bethell, *The Hurricane Creek Massacre,* 26.
91. Bethell, *The Hurricane Creek Massacre,* 22.
92. U.S. Congress, House, Committee on Education and Labor, General Subcommittee on Labor, *Investigation of the Hyden, Kentucky, Coal Mine Disaster,* xiii.
93. Bethell, *The Hurricane Creek Massacre,* 51.
94. Bethell, *The Hurricane Creek Massacre,* 51.
95. Thomas Bethell to Elburt Osborn, January 26, 1971, MFDR 46/15.
96. U.S. Congress, House, Committee on Education and Labor, General Subcommittee on Labor, *Investigation of the Hyden, Kentucky, Coal Mine Disaster,* iv.
97. U.S. Congress, House, Committee on Education and Labor, General Subcommittee on Labor, *Investigation of the Hyden, Kentucky, Coal Mine Disaster,* iv.
98. James Gilliam, statement, circa November 1970, MFDR 101/3. I have retained Gilliam's spelling, only adding insertions for clarity.
99. U.S. Congress, House, Committee on Education and Labor, General Subcommittee on Labor, *Investigation of the Hyden, Kentucky, Coal Mine Disaster,* vii.

100. Bethell, *The Hurricane Creek Massacre*, 35.
101. U.S. Congress, House, Committee on Education and Labor, General Subcommittee on Labor, *Investigation of the Hyden, Kentucky, Coal Mine Disaster*, iii.
102. Ana Honig, "Electric Utilities Are Seeking a Long-Range Solution to the Energy Crisis," *Muncie Star*, May 21, 1971; "20,000 Coal Miners Walk Off Jobs," *Raleigh Register*, June 14, 1971; "TVA Coal Stockpile Lowered by Holiday," *Johnson City Press*, July 16, 1971; "Coal Operators Ask Government Intervention in Railway Strikes," *Raleigh Register*, July 28, 1971.
103. "The Cherokee Shaft: The Story of Mines and Men," ABC Broadcast, May 22, 1971, 8:30–9:30 PM EDT, MFDR 63/1.
104. Holmes Safety Council, "Injury Rates in 1968," 1969, UMWPO 11/24.
105. "The Cherokee Shaft."
106. "The Cherokee Shaft."
107. DOI, BM, *Report of Fatal Coal Mine Haulage Accident, Maple Creek Mine, United States Steel Corporation, Coal Operations-Raw Materials, Frick District, New Eagle, Washington County, Pennsylvania, June 1, 1971*, by Charles Battistoni (Pittsburgh, PA: BM, 1971), MSHA-DL.
108. DOI, BM, *Report of Fatal Coal Mine Haulage Accident . . . June 1, 1971*.
109. DOI, BM, *Report of Fatal Coal Mine Haulage Accident . . . June 1, 1971*.
110. "Card of Thanks," *Uniontown Evening Standard*, June 9, 1971.
111. *U.S. Steel Corp. v. United Mine Workers of America* Civil Action No. 71-561, transcript, July 16, 1971, 288–290, Smorada-Direct (W.D. Pa. 1971), MFDR 61/1.
112. "Fatal Mishap at Maple Creek Mine," *Uniontown Morning Herald*, June 2, 1971; "Card of Thanks."
113. Brief for Appellant, *United States Steel v. United Mine Workers of America et al.*, No. 71-1975, 3rd Cir. 1971, MFDR 61/6.
114. *U.S. Steel Corp. v. United Mine Workers of America* Civil Action No. 71-561, transcript, July 14, 1971, 65 (W.D. Pa. 1971), MFDR 61/1.
115. *U.S. Steel Corp. v. United Mine Workers of America* Civil Action No. 71-561, Transcript, July 16, 1971, 250.
116. *U.S. Steel Corp. v. United Mine Workers of America* Civil Action No. 71-561, Transcript, July 14–15, 1971, 92, 96, 135–37, 156, 205–10.
117. *U.S. Steel Corp. v. United Mine Workers of America* Civil Action No. 71-561, Transcript, July 14, 1971, 117.
118. *U.S. Steel Corp. v. United Mine Workers of America* Civil Action No. 71-561, Transcript, July 15, 1971, 205.
119. "The Cherokee Shaft."
120. *U.S. Steel Corp. v. United Mine Workers of America* Civil Action No. 71-561, Transcript, 15, 1971, 206.

VII. If Letcher County Was a Pie . . .

1. Jerry DeMuth interview notes, July 1971, JDC 1/3.
2. DeMuth interview notes.
3. Statistics from Bureau of Disability Insurance, Social Security Administration, November 6, 1970, MFDR 101/3.
4. DeMuth interview notes.
5. DeMuth interview notes.
6. 1930 U.S. Census, Knott, Kentucky, populations schedule, Magisterial District 2, ED 60-4, Sheet 11B, 186, 189, Henry H. and Bert Caudill; NARA Microfilm Publication T626, roll 760; 1920 U.S. Census, Knot, Kentucky, populations schedule, Magisterial District 4, ED 51, Sheet 11B, 158, 164, Henry H. and Bert Caudill; NARA microfilm publication T625, roll 577.
7. 1940 U.S. Census, Letcher, Kentucky, populations schedule, Magisterial District 4, ED 67-24, Sheet 3B, 39, Henry H. Caudill; NARA Microfilm Publication T627, roll 1330; Henry H. Caudill, d. June 10, 1941, Registration district 880, Primary District Registration Number 6671, State File Number 15570, Office of Vital Statistics, Frankfort, Kentucky.
8. Steven Stoll, *Ramp Hollow: The Ordeal of Appalachia* (New York: Hill and Wang, 2018); Chad Montrie, *To Save the Land and People: A History of Opposition to Surface Mining in Appalachia* (Chapel Hill: University of North Carolina Press, 2003), 14–17.
9. DeMuth interview notes; Skip Rozin suggested that the Caudills sold the stripping rights, but this "sale" was usually a way for strippers to ease the process of beginning the mining process, rather than a legally required sale. Skip Rozin, "People of the Ruined Hills," *Audubon*, November 1972.
10. Yablonski campaign strategy papers, undated, MFDR 23/37.
11. James Parton, "Pittsburg," *Atlantic Monthly* 21 (January 1868): 21.
12. Winthrop Lane, *Civil War in West Virginia* (New York: B. W. Huebsch, 1921), 36–41; Ronald Eller, *Miners, Millhands, and Mountaineers: Industrialization of the Appalachian South, 1880–1930* (Knoxville: University of Tennessee Press, 1982), 162.
13. Montrie, *To Save the Land and People*, 21–22.
14. Richard Cartwright Austin and Peter Borrelli, eds., *The Strip Mining of America: An Analysis of Surface Coal Mining and the Environment* (New York: Sierra Club, 1971), 13.
15. Jeanne Rasmussen, "Stripping Means Fast Profit, Ruined Land," *Miner's Voice*, February/March 1971.
16. People's Hearing on Strip Mining, December 4, 1971, transcribed in *People Speak Out on Strip Mining*, undated, MFDR 105/12.

17. Jean Ritchie, "Black Waters," 1968, JDC, 1/3.
18. Harry Caudill, "Introduction," in *The Strip Mining of America*, 5; DeMuth interview notes; "Coal's Hollow Prosperity," *Newsweek*, January 1971; Richard Cartwright Austin, Citizens to Abolish Strip Mining news release, January 28, 1971, MFDR 105/7.
19. Wendell Berry, *A Continuous Harmony: Essays Cultural and Agricultural* (Berkeley: Counterpoint, 2012), 169.
20. Austin, news release, January 28, 1971, MFDR 105/7.
21. Rasmussen, "Strip Mining Means Fast Profit, Ruined Land."
22. Richard Cartwright Austin, untitled draft, 1971, MFDR 105/7.
23. DeMuth interview notes.
24. Richard Nixon, State of the Union Address, January 22, 1970, APP.
25. Everett Tharp, report on strip mining, April 31, 1971, MFDR 105/12; Bill Bishop, "Political Culture Stunts Region," *Lexington Herald-Leader*, July 4, 1999.
26. DeMuth interview notes.
27. T. N. Bethell, "Hot Time Ahead," in *Appalachia in the Sixties: Decade of Reawakening*, ed. David S. Walls and John B. Stephenson (Lexington: University Press of Kentucky, 1972), 118; Montrie, *To Save the Land and People*, 66–70.
28. Ritchie, "Black Waters."
29. People's Hearing, December 4, 1971.
30. People's Hearing, December 4, 1971.
31. People's Hearing, December 4, 1971.
32. People's Hearing, December 4, 1971, emphasis in original.
33. People's Hearing, December 4, 1971.
34. People's Hearing, December 4, 1971.
35. Rasmussen, "Strip Mining Means Fast Profit, Ruined Land."
36. DeMuth interview notes.
37. DeMuth interview notes.
38. Rozin, "People of the Ruined Hills."
39. Michael Kline and Todd Bethell, "Strip Away," in *Voices from the Mountains: The People of Appalachia, Their Words, Their Faces, Their Songs*, ed. Guy Carawan and Candie Carawan (Athens: University of Georgia Press, 1996), 36.
40. People's Hearing, December 4, 1971; Richard Carelli, "'It's Gotten So We Don't Know When to Go to Bed Near This Thing,'" *Beckley Post-Herald and Raleigh Register*, October 24, 1971.
41. Brian J. McCabe, *No Place Like Home: Wealth, Community, and the Politics of Homeownership* (New York: Oxford University Press, 2016), 47.
42. McCabe, *No Place Like Home*, 21–43.
43. Clifton E. Bryant to Don Stillman, January 28, 1971, MFDR 83/27.

44. People's Hearing, December 4, 1971.
45. Austin, news release, January 28, 1971.
46. Robb Burlage, "Toward a People's ARC," in *Appalachia in the Sixties*, 246–57; West Virginia, Governor's Task Force on Housing, *Homes for Mountaineers: A Challenge to Meet the Total Housing Needs of West Virginia* (Charleston, WV: n.p., 1967); Justin Gray Associates, "New Towns for Coal Miners: An Evaluation of Housing Developments Under Construction at Fairdale and Wadestown, West Virginia," report for Eastern Associated Coal Company, undated, c. 1970, MFDR 104/16.
47. DeMuth interview notes.
48. Yablonski campaign strategy papers.
49. Montrie, *To Save the Land and People*, 140.
50. UMW News Release, January 14, 1971, MFDR 105/11.
51. U.S. Congress, House of Representatives, Committee on Interior and Insular Affairs, Subcommittee on Mines and Mining, *Regulation of Strip Mining: Hearings*, 92nd Cong., 1st sess., 348.
52. Rasmussen, "Strip Mining Means Fast Profit, Ruined Land."
53. DeMuth interview notes.
54. DeMuth interview notes.
55. Rasmussen, "Strip Mining Means Fast Profit, Ruined Land."
56. Appalachian Strip-Mining Information Service leaflets, circa 1971, MFDR 105/5.
57. Montrie, *To Save the Land and People*, 61–105.
58. Samuel P. Hays, *Beauty, Health, and Permanence: Environmental Politics in the United States, 1955–1985* (New York: Cambridge University Press, 1987); J. R. McNeill, *Something New Under the Sun: An Environmental History of the Twentieth-Century World* (New York: Norton, 2001), 325–54.
59. Matthew T. Huber, *Lifeblood: Oil, Freedom, and the Forces of Capital* (Minneapolis: University of Minnesota Press, 2013).
60. BM Press Release, September 13, 1971, MFDR 45/20.
61. "U.S. Bureau of Mines Director cites . . .," MFDR 45/20.
62. Conservation Foundation of Washington, DC, *Mid-Appalachian Environmental Service Newsletter*, December 1972, UMWJR 3/4.
63. Austin, news release, January 28, 1971, MFDR 105/7.
64. Adapted from Bethany Moreton, *To Serve God and Wal-Mart: The Making of Christian Free Enterprise* (Cambridge, MA: Harvard University Press, 2010), 265; also see Montrie, *To Save the Land and People*, 142–43.
65. Austin, untitled draft, 1971, MFDR 105/7.
66. Iain McLean and Martin Johnes, *Aberfan: Government and Disaster* (Cardiff: Welsh Academic Press, 2019).

67. Citizens' Commission, inventory of coal mine refuse banks in West Virginia, reviewed through December 1972, MFDR 101/18.
68. Citizens' Commission to Investigate the Buffalo Creek Disaster, *Disaster on Buffalo Creek: A Citizens' Report on Criminal Negligence in a West Virginia Mining Community* (Citizens' Commission to Investigate the Buffalo Creek Disaster, 1972), 24, MFDR 101/18.
69. Citizens' Commission, *Disaster on Buffalo Creek*, 24.
70. Testimony of Denny Gibson in *The Buffalo Creek Disaster: Official Report from the Governor's Ad Hoc Commission of Inquiry* (Charleston, WV, 1973).
71. Mary Walton, "Every Time It Rains, It Scares Everyone to Death," *Charleston Gazette*, July 3, 1972.
72. The actual number of deaths is disputed. Steinberg says the flood killed 139 people; most accounts list 124 or 125 as the final number of dead. Ted Steinberg, *Acts of God: The Unnatural History of Natural Disaster in America* (New York: Oxford University Press, 2000), 74.
73. U.S. Congress, Senate, Committee on Labor and Public Welfare, Subcommittee on Labor, *Buffalo Creek (W.Va.) Disaster, 1972: Hearings Before the Subcommittee on Labor, Part 1, Appendix A*, 92nd Cong., 2nd sess., 305.
74. U.S. Congress, Senate, Committee on Labor and Public Welfare, Subcommittee on Labor, *Buffalo Creek (W.Va.) Disaster*, 227.
75. Plaintiff's summaries, undated, UMWJR, 3/3.
76. Plaintiff's summaries, undated, UMWJR 3/3.
77. Plaintiff's summaries, undated, UMWJR 3/2.
78. Citizens' Commission, *Disaster on Buffalo Creek*, 22.
79. Plaintiff's summaries, undated, UMWJR 3/2.
80. *Late News* transcript, WTTG Television, February 28, 1972, UMWPC, 80/11; *NBC Nightly News* transcript, February 28, 1972, UMWPC 80/11.
81. George Vecsey, "West Virginia Flood Toll at 60 with Hundreds Lost," *NYT*, February 28, 1972, 1.
82. *NBC Nightly News* transcript, February 28, 1972. UMWPC, 80/11.
83. "Rattlesnakes Hamper Flood Cleanup Operations; Death Toll Reaches 71," *Piqua Daily Call*, March 1, 1972, 14.
84. Citizens' Commission, *Disaster on Buffalo Creek*, 6.
85. *ABC Evening News* transcript, February 28, 1972, UMWPC, 80/11.
86. *ABC Evening News* transcript, February 28, 1972.
87. "Retired Miner Wants to Say Goodbye to Buffalo Creek," *Piqua Daily Call*, March 7, 1972, 13.
88. Citizens' Commission, *Disaster on Buffalo Creek*, 5.
89. S U.S. Congress, Senate, Committee on Labor and Public Welfare, Subcommittee on Labor, *Buffalo Creek (W.Va.) Disaster, 1972: Hearings*, 236–230.

90. Mimi Pickering, dir., *Buffalo Creek Flood: Act of Man* (Whitesburg, KY: Appalshop, 1975); Citizens' Commission, *Disaster on Buffalo Creek*, 10.
91. Jim Kincaid, "Possibility of Dynamite Blast Causing Dam Flood in W.Va.," *ABC Evening News*, March 7, 1972, UMWJR 4/4.
92. Citizens' Commission, *Disaster on Buffalo Creek*, 19.
93. *Late News* transcript, WTTG Television, February 28, 1972, UMWPC 80/11.
94. Mary-Lynn Evans and Jordan Freeman, *Blood on the Mountain* (New York: Virgil Films, 2016).
95. "Welcome to the Wall of Ignorance," *Buffalo Spokesman*, April 4, 1971, New Left Pamphlet Collection, Eberly Family Special Collections, Penn State University, 1/5.
96. *Buffalo Creek Flood: An Act of Man*.
97. David E. Nye, *American Technological Sublime* (Cambridge, MA: MIT Press, 1996), 23.
98. Doug and Ruth Yarrow, "The Buffalo Creek Flood," performed by Jack White, in *Buffalo Creek Flood: An Act of Man*.
99. *Late News* transcript, WTTG Television, February 28, 1972, UMWPC 80/11.
100. Tom Flannery, "Oh Well, They Were Only Coal Miners," *Baltimore Sun*, March 6, 1972.
101. Barbara Kopple, *Harlan County, USA* (New York: Criterion, 2006).
102. Plaintiff's summaries, UMWJR 3/3.
103. Citizens' Commission, *Disaster on Buffalo Creek*, 5, 22.
104. Citizens' Commission, *Disaster on Buffalo Creek*, 5.
105. Citizens' Commission, *Disaster on Buffalo Creek*, 31; Pickering, *Buffalo Creek Flood*.
106. *Late News* transcript, WTTG Television, February 28, 1972, UMWPC 80/11.
107. U.S. Congress, Senate, Committee on Labor and Public Welfare, Subcommittee on Labor, *Buffalo Creek (W.Va.) Disaster*, 15; Pickering, *Buffalo Creek Flood*; Ben A. Franklin, "U.S. Warned West Virginia in 1967 That 30 Coal-Waste Piles Were Unstable," *NYT*, March 1, 1972, 22; Ben A. Franklin, "From God, No Comment," *NYT*, March 5, 1972, E3.
108. Pickering, *Buffalo Creek Flood*; Thomas N. Bethell and Davitt McAteer, *The Pittston Mentality: Manslaughter on Buffalo Creek* (Huntington, WV: Appalachian Movement Press, 1972).
109. Citizens' Commission, *Disaster on Buffalo Creek*, 27.
110. Citizens' Commission, *Disaster on Buffalo Creek*, 10.
111. Citizens' Commission, *Disaster on Buffalo Creek*, 15.
112. Pickering, *Buffalo Creek Flood: An Act of Man*.

113. Citizens' Commission, *Disaster on Buffalo Creek*, 6.
114. Citizens' Commission, *Disaster on Buffalo Creek*, 6.
115. Pickering, *Buffalo Creek Flood*.
116. Pickering, *Buffalo Creek Flood*; Kai T. Erikson, *Everything in Its Path: Destruction of Community in the Buffalo Creek Flood* (New York: Simon and Schuster, 1978), 156–244.
117. Gerald M. Stern, *The Buffalo Creek Disaster: How the Survivors of One of the Worst Disasters in Coal Mining History Brought Suit Against the Coal Company—and Won* (New York: Vintage, 2008), 6–11.
118. "Buffalo Creek Flood Suit Is Settled Out of Court," *Beckley Post-Herald and Raleigh Register*, July 6, 1974, 1.
119. Stern, *The Buffalo Creek Disaster*, 269–71.
120. Pickering, *Buffalo Creek Flood: Act of Man*.

VIII. Jobs, Lives, and Land

1. Kenneth and Joseph Yablonski Jr., press statement, March 6, 1970, JHP 11/18.
2. David Witwer, "The Landrum-Griffin Act: A Case Study in the Possibilities and Problems in Anti-Union Corruption Law," *Criminal Justice Review* 27 (2002): 301–21; George W. Hopkins, "Union Reform and Labor Law: Miners for Democracy and the Use of the Landrum-Griffin Act," *Journal of Labor Research* 31 (2010): 348–64.
3. *Hodgson v. United Mine Workers* 34 F.Supp. 17 (1972).
4. Aaron Brenner, Robert Brenner, and Cal Winslow, *Rebel Rank and File: Labor Militancy and Revolt from Below in the Long 1970s* (New York: Verso, 2010); Jefferson Cowie, *Stayin' Alive: The 1970s and the Last Days of the Working Class* (New York: New Press, 2010), 23–38.
5. Philip F. Rubio, *Undelivered: From the Great Postal Strike of 1970 to the Manufactured Crisis of the U.S. Postal Service* (Chapel Hill: University of North Carolina Press, 2020), 119–46.
6. Cowie, *Stayin' Alive*, 38–74.
7. Radio spot, audio cassette recording, UMWAV 1/91.
8. Fred Scott, "Miners Reprieve," September 16, 1970, MFDR 83/13.
9. Staughton Lynd, "Government Without Rights: The Labor Law Vision of Archibald Cox," *Industrial Relations Law Journal* 4 (1981): 483–95; Michael K. Brown, "Bargaining for Social Rights: Unions and the Reemergence of Welfare Capitalism, 1945–1952," *Political Science Quarterly* 112, no. 4 (1997): 645–74; William J. Novak, Stephen W. Sawyer, and James T. Sparrow,

"Toward a History of the Democratic State," *Tocqueville Review* 33, no. 2 (2012): 7–18.
10. Samuel Walker, *The Rights Revolution: Rights and Community in Modern America* (New York: Oxford University Press, 1998), 60–64.
11. MFD Pamphlet, 1972, JHP 11/20; Neil Boggs, "United Mine Workers President Found Guilty," WRC News 4, March 31, 1972, MFDR 89/7; Chris Kelly, "Finger of Implication Pointed at Others," CBS News, April 13, 1972, MFDR 89/7.
12. Laurence Learner, "The United Mine Workers Holds an Election," *NYT*, November 26, 1972; David Witwer, *Corruption and Reform in the Teamsters Union* (Urbana: University of Illinois Press, 2003), 2; *Proceedings of the Forty-Fifth Consecutive Constitutional Convention of the United Mine Workers of America* (Washington, DC: UMW, 1968), 245–49.
13. Harry Huge, interview, June 26, 1999, NCOH; *Blankenship v. Boyle* 329 F.Supp. 1089 (D.D.C. 1971); Robert H. Zieger, *John L. Lewis: Labor Leader* (Boston: Twayne, 1988), 182.
14. MFD Fundraising Pamphlet, c. 1972, JHP 11/20.
15. Leamer, "The UMW Holds an Election."
16. "Patrick Presses Dist. 31 Reforms," *MV*, February–March 1972.
17. "Patrick Presses Dist. 31 Reforms."
18. Robert Engler, "Oil, Politics, and Power," *BLB*, May 1971, 44/8.
19. Interview with Harry Patrick by George Hopkins, August 8, 1974, SHC.
20. Interview with Harry Patrick.
21. Ben A. Franklin, "Arnold R. Miller Is Dead at 62," *NYT*, July 13, 1985; Ginny Savage Ayers and Lon Kelly Savage, *Never Justice, Never Peace: Mother Jones and the Miner Rebellion at Paint and Cabin Creeks* (Morgantown: West Virginia University Press, 2018), 276.
22. Interview with Arnold Miller by George Hopkins, October 22, 1974, E-0021, in SOHP, Series E: Labor (04007E), SHC; Strat Douthat, "Former UMW President Dies," AP, July 12, 1985.
23. Franklin, "Arnold R. Miller Is Dead"; Douthat, "Former UMW President Dies."
24. Leamer, "The United Mine Workers Holds an Election."
25. Arnold Miller, "The Energy Crisis as a Coal Miner Sees It," *Center*, November/December 1973.
26. Interview with Arnold Miller.
27. "Miller to Build Union," *MV*, June 1972.
28. Interview with Arnold Miller; Thomas Kiffmeyer, *Reformers to Radicals: The Appalachian Volunteers and the War on Poverty* (Lexington: University Press of Kentucky), 201.
29. "Miners Speak Out," *MV*, June 1970.

30. "How Kanawha Voted," *Charleston Daily Mail*, May 13, 1970.
31. *BLB*, March 1971, MFDR 44/35.
32. "Run for Office," *BLB*, January 1972, MFDR 44/35.
33. "Candidates Seek Office on 'People's' Platform," *MV*, April 1972.
34. Interview with Arnold Miller.
35. John Dewey, *Freedom and Culture* (New York: G. P. Putnam's Sons, 1939), 162; William Novak, *New Democracy: The Creation of the Modern American State* (Cambridge, MA: Harvard University Press), 77–83.
36. John Hoerr, "Coal Miners' Revolt," January 26, 1972, MFDR 83/6.
37. Mike Trbovich, statement, 1970, MFDR 82/26.
38. Junior Hicks to *MV*, July 19, 1971, MFDR 83/11.
39. Harry Patrick, "Another Sellout Contract," *MV*, December 1971.
40. Mike Trbovich, statement, 1970, MFDR 82/26; Interview with Ed James by George Hopkins, October 23, 1974, E-0020, in the SOHP, Series E: Labor (04007E), SHC.
41. Interview with Harry Patrick; Interview with Ed James.
42. Quoted in Paul Nyden, *Black Coal Miners in the United States* (New York: American Institute for Marxist Studies, 1974), 57.
43. Christian Wright, *Carbon County USA: Miners for Democracy in Utah and the West* (Salt Lake City: University of Utah Press, 2020).
44. Interview with Rick Bank by George Hopkins, August 8, 1974, E-0018, in SOHP, Series E: Labor (04007E), SHC.
45. Memo from Ed James, undated, MFDR 92/13; Nyden, *Black Coal Miners*, 56.
46. Joe William Trotter Jr., *Workers on Arrival: Black Labor in the Making of America* (Berkeley: University of California Press, 2019), 110–39.
47. Nancy MacLean, *Freedom Is Not Enough: The Opening of the American Workplace* (Cambridge, MA: Harvard University Press, 2008); Lane Windham, *Knocking on Labor's Door: Union Organizing in the 1970s and the Roots of a New Economic Divide* (Chapel Hill: University of North Carolina Press, 2017).
48. Adom Getachew, *Worldmaking After Empire: The Rise and Fall of Self-Determination* (Princeton, NJ: Princeton University Press, 2019), 144–60; Marianne Maeckelbergh, "The Road to Democracy: The Political Legacy of '1968,'" *International Review of Social History* 56, no. 2 (2011): 303–4.
49. "The Miners' Bill of Rights," *MV*, June 1972; Robert H. Zieger, *The CIO: 1935–1955* (Chapel Hill: University of North Carolina Press, 1997), 253–93; Ellen Schrecker, *Many Are the Crimes: McCarthyism in America* (Boston: Little, Brown, 1998), 183–90.
50. "Miners' Bill of Rights."
51. "Trbovich Asks Safe Mines," *MV*, June 1, 1972; DOI, BM, *Report of Fatal Coal Mine Belt Accident, Gateway Mine, Gateway Coal Company, Clarksville,*

Greene County, Pennsylvania, May 23, 1972, by Henry Zavora and William Schlaupitz (Pittsburgh, PA: BM, 1972).
52. "Miners' Bill of Rights."
53. "Miners' Bill of Rights."
54. "Miners' Bill of Rights."
55. Harry M. Caudill, "Strip Mining Coast to Coast," *Nation*, April 19, 1971.
56. "Bulldozer Damage Probed," *Wheeling Intelligencer*, November 1, 1972; Chad Montrie, *To Save the Land and People: A History of Opposition to Surface Coal Mining in Appalachia* (Chapel Hill: University of North Carolina Press, 2003), 85–105.
57. "Miners Bill of Rights"; Arnold Miller to R. Norman, R. B. Padgett, and Clifton Gather, September 14, 1972, MFDR 92/4.
58. Samuel P. Hays, *Beauty, Health, and Permanence: Environmental Politics in the United States, 1955–1985* (New York: Cambridge University Press, 1989), 212; Adam Rome, *The Bulldozer in the Countryside: Suburban Sprawl and the Rise of American Environmentalism* (New York: Cambridge University Press, 2001), 221–53.
59. James Stenger, "Report on the Energy Crisis," undated, MFDR 104/20.
60. "Miller Means Jobs," 1972, JHP 11/20.
61. "Miller Means Jobs."
62. "Anti-Strip-Mining Groups Join," *Raleigh Register*, June 18, 1972.
63. See Joshua P. Howe, *Behind the Curve: Science and the Politics of Global Warming* (Seattle: University of Washington Press, 2014); Naomi Oreskes and Erik M. Conway, *Merchants of Doubt: How a Handful of Scientists Obscured the Truth on Issues from Tobacco Smoke to Global Warming* (New York: Bloomsbury, 2010); Benjamin Franta, "Early Oil Industry Disinformation on Global Warming," *Environmental Politics* 30, no. 4 (2021): 663–68.
64. Karl Boyd Brooks, *Before Earth Day: The Origin of American Environmental Law, 1945–1970* (Lawrence: University Press of Kansas, 2009).
65. Bill Singer to Arnold Miller, July 19, 1972, MFDR 91/17.
66. Campaign schedule, July 24–28, 1972, MFDR 92/12.
67. Interview with Harry Patrick.
68. Interview with Arnold Miller.
69. Mary McGrory, "Tony Boyle Faces New Challenges," *Boston Globe*, November 20, 1972.
70. Ed James to Fred Hutton, undated, MFDR 92/12; Alan Smith, "Miller Says He Has Comfortable Margin for Victory," WTTG-TV, *Ten O'clock News*, December 15, 1972, MFDR 89/6.
71. Bob Daniels, "Running Against Tony Boyle," *Boston Globe*, December 3, 1972.

72. Ed James to John, undated, MFDR 92/12; Ed James to Arnold Miller, undated, MFDR 92/12 and MFDR 92/13.
73. Interview with Arnold Miller.
74. Radio spot.
75. Fred Scott, "Miners for Democracy," undated, MFDR 83/13.
76. Bill Singer to Arnold Miller, July 19, 1972, MFDR 91/17.
77. Virgil G. Debaun to Arnold Miller, September 10, 1972, MFDR 99/15.
78. Victor Powers, letter to the editor, undated, MFDR 83/12.
79. John Tom Peace to *MV*, undated, MFDR 83/12.
80. Daniel Schorr, "UMW Election Most Honest in History, Says Labor Department," WTOP Television Eyewitness News, 1:00 PM EST, December 12, 1972, MFDR 89/6.
81. Alan Smith, "Boyle Leading in First Day's UMW Presidential Election," WTTG-TV, December 12, 1972, MFDR 89/6.
82. "Labor Department Officials Begin Counting UMW Ballots," *ABC Evening News*, December 12, 1972, MFDR 89/6; Election Summary, *MV*, Winter 1973, 9.
83. John Chancellor, "Miller Leads Boyle with 25% of Votes Counted," *NBC Evening News*, December 13, 1972, MFDR 89/6; Harry Reasoner, "Miller Supporters Claim Victory," *ABC Evening News*, December 13, 1972, MFDR 89/6; Paul Harvey, "Boyle Threatened in Pension Locals," ABC Radio, December 13, 1972, MFDR 89/6.
84. Walter Cronkite, "Miller Now Leading Boyle in UMW Election," *CBS Evening News*, December 14, 1972, MFDR 89/6.
85. "Christmas Party Turns to Vigil," *Beckley Post-Herald/Raleigh Register*, December 17, 1972; "Gas Buildup Blamed for Itmann Blast," *Raleigh Register*, December 18, 1972.
86. "Christmas Party Turns to Vigil"; Bernard Aronson, "Shriver Hears Miners," *Raleigh Register*, September 4, 1972.
87. DOI, BM, *Official Report of Major Mine Explosion Disaster, Itmann No. 3 Mine (ID 46–01576), Itmann Coal Company, Itmann, Wyoming County, West Virginia, December 16, 1972,* by W. R. Park, Sylvester E. Gaspersich, and Fred E. Ferguson (Washington, DC: BM, 1973), MSHA-DL; "Gas Buildup Blamed for Itmann Blast," *Raleigh Register*, December 18, 1972.
88. Maury Povich, "Miller Disgusted with Mine Safety Standards," WTTG-TV, *Ten O'clock News*, December 17, 1972, MFDR 89/6.
89. John Chancellor, "Tony Boyle Resigns as UMW President," *NBC Nightly News*, December 18, 1972, MFDR 89/6.
90. "Gas Buildup Blamed for Itmann Blast"; "5 Killed and 3 Hurt after Blast Strikes West Virginia Mine," *NYT*, December 17, 1972; "In Wake of West

Virginia Blast, UMW Pledges Safety Programs," *Uniontown Evening Standard*, December 20, 1972; Laurence D. Beck and Stuart Rawlings, *Coal: The Captive Giant—a Report on Coal Ownership in the United States*, 1971, 10–11, MFDR 63/9.
91. "Slate Fall Fatal to Wyoming Man," *Beckley Post-Herald*, January 11, 1972.
92. DOI, BM, *Report of Fatal Rib-Roll Accident, Itmann No. 4 Mine, Itmann Coal Company, Itmann, Wyoming County, West Virginia, March 21, 1972*, by Fred E. Ferguson, Jesse P. Cole, and Thomas E. Moore (Mount Hope, WV: BM, 1972), MSHA-DL.
93. DOI, BM, *Report of Fatal Track-Haulage Accident, Itmann No. 2 Mine, Itmann Coal Company, Itmann, Wyoming County, West Virginia, July 28, 1972*, by Morris E. Bragg, Fred E. Ferguson, Franklin M. Walls, and James E. Justice (Mount Hope, WV: BM, 1972), MSHA-DL; DOI, BM, *Report of Fatal Coal-Mine Haulage Accident, Itmann No. 4 Mine (ID No. 46–01577), Itmann Coal Company, Itmann, West Virginia, November 14, 1972*, by Sylvester Gaspersich, Fred E. Ferguson, and Jesse P. Cole (Mount Hope, WV: BM, 1972), MSHA-DL.
94. DOI, BM, *Official Report . . . December 16, 1972*.
95. J. Davitt McAteer, *Continental Oil Company/Consolidation Coal Company: A Citizens' Report, 1972*, 3–5, MFDR 64/37.
96. *Today Show*, NBC, December 18, 1972, MFDR 89/6.
97. Barbara Kopple, *Harlan County, USA* (New York: Criterion, 2006).
98. Election Results, *UMWJ*, December 1972.
99. James Ridgeway, "Irony in the Energy Crisis," *MV*, Winter 1973.

Third Interlude: East and West

1. Giuliano Garavini, *The Rise and Fall of OPEC in the Twentieth Century* (New York: Oxford University Press, 2019), 216–27.
2. "A Good Home for UMW," *Pittsburgh Post-Gazette*, December 3, 1973.
3. *Proceedings of the Forty-Sixth Consecutive Constitutional Convention of the United Mine Workers of America* (Washington, DC: United Mine Workers of America, 1973), 8–9.
4. Richard Nixon, Address to the Nation About National Energy Policy, November 25, 1973, APP.
5. *Proceedings* (1973), 13.
6. *Proceedings* (1973), 11.
7. *Proceedings* (1973), 11.
8. *Proceedings* (1973), 12.

9. *Proceedings* (1973), 74.
10. Natasha Zaretsky, *No Direction Home: The American Family and the Fear of National Decline, 1968–1980* (Chapel Hill: University of North Carolina Press, 2007), 71–103; for a fuller version of this argument, see Trish Kahle, "The Front Lines of Energy Policy: The Coal Mining Workplace and the Politics of Security in the American Century," *American Quarterly* 72, no. 3 (2020): 627–49.
11. Barry Commoner, *The Poverty of Power: Energy and the Economic Crisis* (New York: Bantam, 1976); Michael Egan, *Barry Commoner and the Science of Survival: The Remaking of American Environmentalism* (Cambridge, MA: MIT Press, 2009), 149–55.
12. *Proceedings* (1973), 254–56.
13. Christopher F. Jones, "Petromyopia: Oil and the Energy Humanities," *Humanities* 5, no. 2 (2016): 36.
14. Megan Black, *The Global Interior: Mineral Frontiers and American Power* (Cambridge, MA: Harvard University Press, 2018), 218; Judith Stein, *Running Steel, Running America: Race, Economic Policy, and the Decline of Liberalism* (Chapel Hill: University of North Carolina Press, 1998), 197–210.
15. Stein, *Running Steel, Running America*, 3–4.
16. Judith Stein, *Pivotal Decade: How the United States Traded Factories for Finance in the 1970s* (New Haven, CT: Yale University Press, 2011), 90–96.
17. George C. Wilson, "Deep-Mined Coal Termed Essential for Clean Energy," *Washington Post*, September 27, 1973.
18. Jimmy Carter, Louisville, Kentucky remarks, July 31, 1979, APP.
19. Talking Points, White House Conference on Coal Industry, March 21, 1975, MRDP, Box 5, Meeting with the President, Coal Industry, March 21, 1975.
20. Charles Halvorson, *Valuing Clean Air: The EPA and the Economics of Environmental Protection* (New York: Oxford University Press, 2021), 32.
21. Ryan Driskell Tate, "Coal Frontier: Corporate Power and the Making of the Powder River Basin, 1965–1985," PhD diss., Rutgers University, 2020.
22. Black, *The Global Interior*, 219; James Robert Allison, *Sovereignty for Survival: American Energy Development and Indian Self-Determination* (New Haven, CT: Yale University Press, 2015); Tate, "Coal Frontier"; Andrew Needham, *Power Lines: Phoenix and the Making of the Modern Southwest* (Princeton, NJ: Princeton University Press), 234.
23. Wallace Stegner and Page Stegner, "Rocky Mountain Country," *Atlantic*, April 1978.
24. Melani McAlister, *Epic Encounters: Culture, Media, and U.S. Interests in the Middle East Since 1945* (Berkeley: University of California Press, 2005), 135–36; Black, *The Global Interior*, 229; on the way race and empire made their

way from the United States to the Middle East, also see Vitalis, *America's Kingdom*, 38–61.

25. Tate, "Coal Frontier."
26. Christian Wright, *Carbon County, USA: Miners for Democracy in Utah and the West* (Salt Lake City: University of Utah Press, 2019), 213.
27. Arnold Miller, press release, c. spring 1974, AAA item 210-849-23327.
28. "Study of Pollution at Plants Underway," *Scott County Times* (Mississippi), January 24, 1973; ads reproduced in David Anderson, "Southern Company Knew: How a 'Clean' Coal Utility Was Warned About Climate Change Risks Years Before It Funded Climate Disinformation, 1964–2022," Energy and Policy Institute, June 2022, 12.
29. "Exec Denies Imported Coal Effort to Undermine Jobs," *Jackson Sun* (TN), August 22, 1974.
30. Don Stillman, "UMWA Launches Battle to Stop South African Coal Imports," *UMWJ*, June 1–15, 1974.
31. Stein, *Running Steel, Running America*, 225.
32. Peter Cole and Peter Limb, "Hooks Down! Anti-Apartheid Activism and Solidarity Among Maritime Unions in Australia and the United States," *Labor History* 58, no. 3 (2017): 312–20; also see Jessica Ann Levy, "Black Power in the Boardroom: Corporate America, the Sullivan Principles, and the Anti-Apartheid Struggle," *Enterprise & Society* 21, no. 1 (March 2020): 170–209.
33. Arnold Miller, press release.
34. "The Rank and File Speaks," *UMWJ*, June 1–15, 1974.
35. "South African Miners Live, Suffer, and Die in Slavery," *UMWJ*, June 1–15, 1974.
36. "Alabama Coal Miners Protest Slave Labor in South Africa," *Atlanta Voice*, July 27, 1974; "Miners Stage Walkout Over Coal Imports," *Birmingham Post-Herald*, May 23, 1974.
37. Arnold Miller, press release; Ernest B. Ferguson, "Looking at Coal, Blinders Off," *Baltimore Sun*, May 7, 1974, 22.
38. Arnold Miller, press release.
39. Arnold Miller, press release.
40. "The Rank and File Speaks," *UMWJ*, June 1–15, 1974.
41. Don Stillman, "UMWA Launches Battle to Stop South African Coal Imports," *UMWJ*, June 1–15, 1974.
42. "Exec Denies Imported Coal Effort to Undermine Jobs," *Jackson Sun*, August 22, 1974.
43. Solomon McIntyre, "Joseph Lowery of SCLC Blasts South African Connected Firm," *Atlanta Voice*, April 23, 1977; Richard Trumka, statement on

joining the "Free South Africa Movement," January 9, 1986, AAA item 210-849-26019.

IX. Rights and Obligations

1. UMW, *Proceedings of the Forty-Sixth Consecutive Constitutional Convention of the United Mine Workers of America* (Washington, DC: UMW, 1973), 40.
2. *Proceedings* (1973), 59.
3. *Proceedings* (1973), 59.
4. *Proceedings* (1973), 222.
5. Barbara Kopple, *Harlan County, USA* (New York: Criterion, 2006). On women in the Brookside strike, see Sally Ward Maggard, "Gender Contested: Women's Participation in the Brookside Coal Strike," in *Women and Social Protest*, ed. Guida West and Rhoda Blumberg (New York: Oxford University Press, 1990), 75–98; Jessica Wilkerson, *To Live Here, You Have to Fight: How Women Led Appalachian Movements for Social Justice* (Urbana: University of Illinois Press, 2019), 146–70.
6. *Proceedings* (1973), 78–79.
7. Norman Yarborough, interview with Kelly Motley, October 1, 1988, Accession 1988oh231_app195, NCOH.
8. Duke Power, *Annual Report*, 1972, 30–32.
9. Duke Power, *Annual Report*, 1974, 31.
10. Kopple, *Harlan County, USA*; Lois Scott, interview by Sally Ward Maggard, August 27, 1986, Women and Collective Protest Oral History Project, NCOH.
11. Kopple, *Harlan County, USA*.
12. Yarborough, interview, October 1, 1988.
13. Kopple, *Harlan County, USA*.
14. Scott, interview, August 27, 1986.
15. Kopple, *Harlan County, USA*.
16. Kopple, *Harlan County, USA*.
17. Nancy MacLean, *Democracy in Chains: The Deep History of the Radical Right's Stealth Plan for America* (New York: Viking, 2017), 45–60.
18. Kopple, *Harlan County, USA*.
19. Kopple, *Harlan County, USA*.
20. Kopple, *Harlan County, USA*.
21. Kopple, *Harlan County, USA*.
22. Cynthia L. Estlund, "The Ossification of American Labor Law," *Columbia Law Review* 102 (2002): 1527.

23. Kopple, *Harlan County, USA*.
24. Fred Harris, "Burning Up People to Make Electricity," *Atlantic*, July 1974.
25. Duke Power, *Annual Report*, 1975, 8–11.
26. Kopple, *Harlan County, USA*.
27. Kopple, *Harlan County, USA*.
28. "More Gasoline Needed in Greenbrier County," *Beckley Post-Herald*, February 27, 1974.
29. "Miller Urges Miner Relief," *Beckley Post-Herald*, February 27, 1974.
30. "Miners Without Gas to Decide Strike Fate," *Charleston Sunday Gazette Mail*, February 24, 1974.
31. "Temporary Injunction Issued by Federal Court," *Bluefield Daily Telegraph*, March 13, 1974, UMWPO, 203/15.
32. Danny Deskins to Arnold Miller, February 24, 1974, UMWPO 203/16.
33. Roger Petterson, "UMW Begins Five Day Shutdown," *Charleston Daily Mail*, August 19, 1974.
34. Arnold Miller to Danny Deskins, February 26, 1974, UMWPO 203/16.
35. *Dan Lucas Show*, transcripts, March 11–13, 1974, UMWPO 203/15; Tom Bethell to Rick Bank, March 11, 1974, UMWPO 203/16; UMW Press Release, March 11, 1974, UMWPO 203/16; *CBS Saturday Evening News*, March 9, 1974, transcript, UMWPO 203/16.
36. UMW Research Department, "West Virginia Gas Shortage," March 3, 1974, UMWPO 203/16.
37. UMW Research Department, "West Virginia Gas Shortage."
38. Survey of District 29 Gasoline Filling Stations, March 1, 1974, UMWPO 203/16; UMW Research Department, "West Virginia Gas Shortage," March 2, 1974, UMWPO 203/16.
39. UMW Research Department, "West Virginia Gas Shortage," March 3, 1974, UMWPO, 203/16.
40. UMW Statement, March 3, 1974, UMWPO, 203/16.
41. UMW Press Release, February 26, 1974, UMWPO, 203/16.
42. "Perkins Warns Kentucky Coal Miners Are on Verge of Strike," *Richmond Register*, February 27, 1974, UMWPO 203/15; "Miners Continue Protest," *Uniontown Standard*, February 28, 1974, UMWPO 203/17; Matt Witt, "Energy Report: Gas Shortage Closes W.Va. Mines," *UMWJ*, March 1–15, 1974; *Dan Lucas Show*, transcripts, March 11–13, 1974; Brief on Behalf of Appellants in Support of Their Motion for an Injunction Pending Appeal, *Armco Steel Corporation v. United Mine Workers of America*, Temporary Emergency Court of Appeals of the United States, March 12, 1974, UMWPO 203/15.
43. UMW Research Department, "Coal-Producing Counties Primarily Affected by Gas Shortage," March 2, 1974, UMWPO 203/16.

44. Arnold Miller, WLOG Announcement, aired March 7–8, 1974, UMWPO 203/15.
45. "West Virginia Miners Stay Out in Gas Protest," *Washington Star-News*, March 11, 1974.
46. UMW Press Release, March 11, 1974, UMWPO 203/16.
47. Edward Cowan, "Oil Allocation Act Signed as Nixon Ends Opposition," *NYT*, November 28, 1973.
48. Richard Nixon, Statement on the Economic Stability Act Amendments of 1971, December 22, 1971, APP.
49. Joseph A. Yablonski to William E. Simon, March 11, 1974, UMWPO 203/16.
50. *Dan Lucas Show*, transcript, March 11, 1974.
51. *Dan Lucas Show*, transcript, March 11, 1974.
52. *Dan Lucas Show*, transcript, March 11, 1974.
53. John Doe to Arnold Miller, March 26, 1974, UMWPO 203/15.
54. James T. Wooten, "West Virginia's Miners Conserving Their Own Energy in Gasoline Strike," *NYT*, March 12, 1974.
55. Joseph A. Yablonski, memo, April 23, 1974, UMWPO 203/15.
56. UMW Research Department, "West Virginia Gas Shortage."
57. UMW Research Department, "West Virginia Gas Shortage."
58. UMW Research Department, "West Virginia Gas Shortage."
59. Tom Bethell to Rick Bank, March 11, 1974, UMWPO 203/16.
60. UMW Research Department, "West Virginia Gas Shortage," March 2, 1974.
61. Bethell to Bank, March 11, 1974.
62. Bethell to Bank, March 11, 1974.
63. *Armco Steel Corporation v. United Mine Workers of America*, No. 74–8024, 4th Cir., March 12, 1974, UMWPO 203/16.
64. UMW Research Department, "Coal-Producing Counties Primarily Affected by Gas Shortage," March 2, 1974.
65. Joseph A. Yablonski to William E. Simon, March 11, 1974, UMWPO, 203/16.
66. Lewis W. Foy to Ken Hechler, March 11, 1974, UMWPO, 203/16.
67. Appellant's Brief, *Armco Steel Corporation v. United Mine Workers of America*, Temporary Emergency Court of Appeals of the United States, March 12, 1974, UMWPO 203/15.
68. *Armco Steel Corp, v. United Mine Workers of America*.
69. *Armco Steel Corp, v. United Mine Workers of America*.
70. *Armco Steel Corp, v. United Mine Workers of America*.
71. *Armco Steel Corp, v. United Mine Workers of America*.
72. Wayne Scarberry, "Two Mine Pickets and One Woman Shot at Keystone," *Welch Daily News*, March 13, 1974, UMWPO 203/15.

73. "10,000 Miners End West Virginia Strike, 15,000 Still Idle," *NYT*, March 15, 1974; UMWA Statement, March 13, 1974, UMWPO 203/15.
74. Yablonski to Simon, March 11, 1974, UMWPO 203/16; *Dan Lucas Show*, transcripts, March 11–13, 1974.
75. Sidney E. Rolfe, "Coal—The Great Black Hope of Energy," *Mountain Eagle*, December 27, 1973, JDC 1/4. This section of the chapter adapted, with permission, from Trish Kahle, "Accounting the Dead: The Moral Economy of the Coal-Fired Social Contract," in *New Energies: Energy Transitions in Europe and America During the Twentieth Century*, ed. Stephen Gross and Andrew Needham (Pittsburgh, PA: University of Pittsburgh Press, 2023), 62–75.
76. *Usery v. Turner Elkhorn Mining Co.* 428 U.S. 1 (1976).
77. GAO, *Report to the Congress: Achievements, Administrative Problems, and Costs in Paying Black Lung Benefits to Coal Miners and Their Widows*, B-164031(4), 1972, 1; on the coalfield SSA protests, see Richard Fry, "Making Amends: Coal Miners, the Black Lung Association, and Federal Compensation Reform, 1969–1972," *Federal History* 5 (2013): 35–56.
78. Black Lung Benefits Act, 30 U.S.C. 922 (1972).
79. U.S. Congress, House, General Subcommittee on Labor, *Black Lung Benefits: Hearings Before the General Subcommittee on Labor*, 92nd Cong., 1st sess., 1971, 42–44; GAO, *Achievements, Administrative Problems, and Costs in Paying Black Lung Benefits to Coal Miners and Their Widows*, 17–18, 66–67; U.S. Office of Management and Budget, *The Budget of the United States Government, Fiscal Year 1972* (Washington, DC: Government Printing Office, 1971), 234, 317; Robert D. Lifset, "A New Understanding of the American Energy Crisis of the 1970s," *Historical Social Research* 39, no. 4 (2014): 22–42.
80. Oral arguments, December 2, 1975, at 8:53, 33:32, 1:01:34, *Usery, Secretary of Labor, et al. v. Turner Elkhorn Mining Co.* 428 U.S. 1 (No. 74–1302), Oyez.
81. *Usery v. Turner Elkhorn Mining Co.* 428 U.S. 1 (1976).

X. Revolution of Declining Expectations

1. Jimmy Carter, West Frankfort, IL, remarks, October 13, 1980, APP.
2. "Ga. Power Says Economic Future Looks Disastrous," *Atlanta Daily World*, November 17, 1974; "Ga. Power Gets U.S. Loan of $513 Million," *Atlanta Daily World*, January 9, 1975; Casey Cater, *Regenerating Dixie: Electric Energy and the Making of the Modern South* (Pittsburgh, PA: University of Pittsburgh Press, 2019), 156–84.
3. Carter, West Frankfort remarks.

4. Carter, West Frankfort remarks.
5. Jimmy Carter, Address to the Nation on Energy, April 18, 1977, APP.
6. DOI, BM, "Trends in Productivity, Deep & Surface Mines, 1967–1976," October 6, 1977, MFDR 11/16.
7. GAO, *U.S. Coal Development—Promises, Uncertainties: Report to the Congress*, EMD-77-43, September 22, 1977, xii. Hereafter USCD.
8. Carter, Address, April 18, 1977.
9. Carter, Address, April 18, 1977.
10. Carter, Address, April 18, 1977.
11. USCD, vii.
12. USCD, 9.11.
13. Richard Nixon, Remarks on Signing a Bill Authorizing the Trans-Alaska Oil Pipeline, November 16, 1973, APP.
14. Carter, Address, April 18, 1977.
15. Judith Stein, *Pivotal Decade: How the United States Traded Factories for Finance in the Seventies* (New Haven, CT: Yale University Press, 2011), 205; Jefferson Cowie, *Stayin' Alive: The 1970s and the Last Days of the Working Class* (New York: New Press, 2010), 12.
16. Curtis Seltzer, *Fire in the Hole: Miners and Managers in the American Coal Industry* (Lexington: University Press of Kentucky, 1985), 158.
17. "Comparison of Idleness Rates Due to Strikes," 1977, MFDR 11/16.
18. "Coal Negotiations," *Editorial Research Reports* no. 2 (1974).
19. Walter Mossberg, "A Doubtful Ace in the Hole," *WSJ*, March 16, 1978.
20. *Proceedings of the Forty-Sixth Consecutive Constitutional Convention of the United Mine Workers of America* (Washington, DC: UMW, 1973), 9; William Cleaver, "Wildcats in the Appalachian Coalfields," in *Midnight Oil: Work, Energy, War, 1973–1992* (Jamaica Plain, MA: Autonomedia, 1992), 169–84.
21. Kim Moody, *Battle Line: The Coal Strike of '78* (N.p.: Sun, 1978).
22. BCOA, statement, October 6, 1977, MFDR 11/16; Peter Navarro, "Union Bargaining Power in the Coal Industry, 1945–1981," *ILR Review* 36, no. 2 (1983): 218.
23. Walter Mossberg, "Miner Problems," *WSJ*, February 15, 1978; Helen Dewar, "A Coal Walkout No Longer Poses an Instant Crisis," *Washington Post*, November 20, 1977.
24. Mossberg, "Miner Problems."
25. Mossberg, "Miner Problems."
26. "Entering the Doomsday Era," *Time*, February 27, 1978.
27. "Entering the Doomsday Era."
28. Art Pine, "Economy on Brink of Setback," *Washington Post*, March 6, 1978.
29. Pine, "Economy on Brink."

30. Seltzer, *Fire in the Hole*, 152–53.
31. PCC, *First Public Hearing of the President's Commission on Coal: Charleston, West Virginia, October 20, 1978* (Washington, DC: PCC, 1979), 57.
32. Mossberg, "Miner Problems."
33. Trish Kahle, "Electric Discipline: Gendering Power and Defining Work in Electric Power Systems," *Labor* 21, no. 1 (2024).
34. David E. Nye, *When the Lights Went Out: A History of Blackouts in America* (Cambridge, MA: MIT Press, 2010), 118.
35. Reginald Stuart, "Cities Turn Off the Lights as They Run Out of Coal," *NYT*, February 16, 1978.
36. Seltzer, *Fire in the Hole*, 159–62.
37. Stuart, "Cities Turn Off the Lights."
38. Seltzer, *Fire in the Hole*, 151–53.
39. Mossberg, "A Doubtful Ace in the Hole."
40. "Entering the Doomsday Era."
41. "Auger Dynamited in Coal Walkout," *Richmond Times-Dispatch*, December 10, 1977.
42. "Entering the Doomsday Era," 12; Seltzer, *Fire in the Hole*, 152–60.
43. Jimmy Carter, remarks, March 6, 1978, APP.
44. Carter, remarks, March 6, 1978.
45. Carter, remarks, March 6, 1978.
46. Helen Dewar and Edward Walsh, "President Invokes Taft-Hartley Act," *Washington Post*, March 7, 1978; Seltzer, *Fire in the Hole*, 153, 165.
47. Jane D. Poulsen, "The Feeble Strength of One? Interdependence, Strategic Interaction, and the Decentralization of Collective Bargaining," *Sociological Forum* 21, no. 1 (2006): 3–30.
48. Stuart, "Cities Turn Off the Lights"; Seltzer, *Fire in the Hole*, 148–69.
49. Navarro, "Union Bargaining Power in the Coal Industry," 224.
50. Seltzer, *Fire in the Hole*, 164.
51. PCC, "Recommendations and Summary Findings," 18, UMWPO 208/25.
52. John Corcoran, "Coal Commission—Take It Easy," *Coal Industry News*, January 22, 1979.
53. Jimmy Carter, Executive Order 12062, May 26, 1978, APP.
54. Jimmy Carter, remarks, Charleston, West Virginia, May 26, 1978, APP.
55. Carter, remarks, May 26, 1978.
56. *First Public Hearing of the President's Commission on Coal*, 71.
57. *First Public Hearing of the President's Commission on Coal*, 72–74.
58. Arnold Miller, statement, July 13, 1979, UMWPO 208/25.
59. Miller, statement, July 13, 1979.
60. Photos in UMWJR 55/9.
61. Carter, remarks, May 26, 1978.

62. Carter, remarks, May 26, 1978.
63. PCC, Summary Findings and Recommendations.
64. PCC, Summary Findings and Recommendations.
65. Carter, remarks, October 13, 1980.
66. BCOA opening bargaining statement, October 6, 1977, MFDR 11/16.
67. PCC, *Labor-Management Seminar I: Collective Bargaining in the Coal Industry* (Washington, DC: PCC, 1979), 28–29.
68. Walter Rosenbaum, *Coal and Crisis: The Political Dilemmas of Energy Management* (Westport, CT: Praeger, 1978), 1.
69. USCD, 1.4–1.5.
70. USCD, 9.11–9.12.
71. USCD, 9.12.
72. Carter, address, April 18, 1977.
73. Carter, remarks, October 13, 1980.
74. *Proceedings of the Forty-Eighth Consecutive Constitutional Convention of the United Mine Workers of America* (Washington, DC: UMW, 1979), 3.
75. Arnold Miller to John D. Rockefeller, IV, May 15, 1979, UMWPO 208/25.
76. Mossberg, "A Doubtful Ace in the Hole."
77. Kyle Harvey, *American Anti-Nuclear Activism, 1975–1990* (New York: Palgrave MacMillan, 2014), 12–41.
78. Ralph Nader and John Abbotts, *The Menace of Atomic Energy* (New York: Norton, 1977), 258.
79. Barry Commoner, *The Politics of Energy* (New York: Knopf, 1979).
80. PCC, Summary Findings and Recommendations; USCD, 6.51.
81. Paul F. Clark, *The Miners' Fight for Democracy: Arnold Miller and the Reform of the United Mine Workers* (Ithaca, NY: ILR Press, 1981), 136–37.
82. Sam Church Jr. to Jimmy Carter, February 12, 1980, UMWPO 208/26.
83. Nuclear Regulatory Commission, Special Inquiry Group, *Three Mile Island: A Report to the Commissioners and to the Public* (Washington, DC: NRC, 1980), 1.
84. Natasha Zaretsky, *Radiation Nation: Three Mile Island and the Political Transformation of the 1970s* (New York: Columbia University Press, 2018), 203–4.
85. PCTMI, *The Need for Change: The Legacy of TMI* (Washington, DC: PCTMI, 1979), 7.
86. Kate Brown, *Plutopia: Nuclear Families, Atomic Cities, and the Great Soviet and American Plutonium Disasters* (New York: Oxford University Press, 2015), 306–18.
87. Sam Church Jr. and Joseph P. Brennan to Jimmy Carter, March 12, 1980, UMWPO 208/25.
88. *Proceedings* (1979), 294.

89. *Proceedings* (1979), 294.
90. PCTMI, *The Need for Change*, 8.
91. Jimmy Carter, address, July 15, 1979, APP.
92. USCD, 9.1.
93. James Schlesinger, "Energy Risks and Energy Futures," *WSJ*, August 23, 1979.
94. Carter, address, July 15, 1979.
95. Michael S. Koleda, remarks, September 20, 1979, UMWPO 208/25.
96. Schlesinger, "Energy Risks and Energy Futures."
97. Ben A. Franklin, "Miners to Protest Plan on Black Lung," *NYT*, February 28, 1981.
98. Franklin, ""Miners to Protest Plan on Black Lung."
99. Allen R. Prunty and Mark E. Solomons, "The Federal Black Lung Program: Its Evolution and Its Current Issues," *West Virginia Law Review* 91, no. 3 (1989): 711.
100. Sam Church Jr., circular, February 24, 1981, LCSEFE, 1/1.
101. Paul LeBlanc to Mobilization for Survival, Pittsburgh chapter, January 5, 1981, LCSEFE 1/3.
102. March announcement, March 1981, LCSEFE 1/4.
103. Ben A. Franklin, "Labor Rift Accompanies Three Mile Island Protest," *NYT*, March 29, 1981.
104. Church Jr., February 24, 1981.
105. Ben A. Franklin, "Dig They Must, Agree UMW and Big Coal," *NYT*, March 8, 1981.
106. Pennsylvania COMPAC Newsletter, February 1981, LCSEFE 1/1.
107. Franklin, "Labor Rift Accompanies Three Mile Island Protest."
108. Church Jr., February 24, 1981.
109. Pennsylvania COMPAC Newsletter, February 1981.
110. Franklin, "Labor Rift Accompanies Three Mile Island Protest."
111. Church Jr., February 24, 1981.

Conclusion. Energy Citizenship in Transition

1. Julian Robinson, "Big Tech and the Return of Company Towns," *Bull and Bear*, April 7, 2021, https://bullandbearmcgill.com/big-tech-and-the-return-of-company-towns/.
2. For example, Gabriel Winant, *The Next Shift: The Fall of Industry and the Rise of Health Care in Rust Belt America* (Cambridge, MA: Harvard University Press, 2021); Elizabeth Hinton, *From the War on Poverty to the War on Crime:*

The Making of Mass Incarceration in America (Cambridge, MA: Harvard University Press, 2016).
3. Sylvia Ryerson, "Precarious Politics: Friends of Coal, the UMWA, and the Affective Terrain of Energy Identification," *American Quarterly* 72, no. 3 (2020): 719–47.
4. All fatal accident reports can be found at the MSHA-DL; specifically referenced are DOL, MSHA, *Report of Investigation, Underground Coal Mine, Fatal Powered Haulage Accident, April 19, 2001, Powhatan No. 6 Mine, Alledonia, Belmont County, Ohio*, by Daniel L. Stout and Charles J. Thomas (Morgantown, WV: MSHA District 3, 2001), MSHA-DL; DOL, MSHA, *Report of Investigation, Surface Coal Mine Fatal Machinery Accident, December 29, 2017, Black Jewel S-7 Surface Mine, Fayette County, West Virginia*, by Franklin E. Stover (Mount Hope, WV: MSHA, District 4, n.d.), MSHA-DL.
5. U.S. House of Representatives, Committee on Education and Labor, *The Upper Big Branch Mine Tragedy: Field Hearing*, 111th Cong., 2nd Sess., May 24, 2010, 24–25.
6. U.S. House of Representatives, Committee on Education and Labor, *Upper Big Branch Mine Tragedy*, 4.
7. U.S. House of Representatives, Committee on Education and Labor, *Upper Big Branch Mine Tragedy*, 63.
8. U.S. House of Representatives, Committee on Education and Labor, *Upper Big Branch Mine Tragedy*, 36.
9. EIA, *Annual Coal Report*, 2021, table ES.1; Leo Fishman and Betty G. Fishman, "Bituminous Coal Production During World War II," *Southern Economic Journal* 18, no. 3 (1952): 393.
10. Andrea Germanos, "'History Going the Wrong Direction' as Worst Form of Black Lung Disease Rises Again," *Common Dreams*, May 23, 2018, https://www.commondreams.org/news/2018/05/23/history-going-wrong-direction-worst-form-black-lung-disease-rises-again.
11. Chris Hamby, *Soul Full of Coal Dust: A Fight for Breath and Justice in Appalachia* (New York: Little, Brown, 2020).
12. Erica Peterson and Whitney Jones, "Kentucky Doesn't Have Any More Working Union Coal Miners," WFPL, February 26, 2015, https://wfpl.org/kentucky-doesnt-have-any-more-working-union-coal-miners/.
13. EIA, Form EIA-7A, "Annual Survey of Coal Production and Preparation," 2021; U.S. Department of Labor, Mine Safety and Health Administration, Form 7000-2, "Quarterly Mine Employment and Coal Production Report," 2021.
14. Justin Worland, "Coal's Last Kick," *Time*, 2017, https://time.com/coals-last-kick/; Wenonah Hauter, *Frackopoly: The Battle for the Future of Energy and the Environment* (New York: New Press, 2016).

15. Leah Stokes, "This Year Was the Beginning of a Green Transition," *NYT*, December 26, 2022.
16. Kayla Desroches, "U.S. Coal Production Is Up Sharply After Hitting a 50-Year Low Last Year," *NPR*, October 22, 2021, https://www.npr.org/2021/10/22/1048108267/u-s-coal-production-is-up-sharply-after-hitting-a-50-year-low-last-year.
17. UMW, "Preserving Coal Country: Keeping America's Coal Miners, Families, and Communities Whole in an Era of Global Energy Transition," 2021, https://umwa.org/wp-content/uploads/2021/04/UMWA-Preserving-Coal-Country-2021-1.pdf.
18. UMW, "Preserving Coal Country."
19. Matthew Daly, "Miners' Union Backs Shift from Coal in Exchange for Jobs," Associated Press, April 19, 2021.
20. Trish Kahle, "Challenging the Industrial Narrative," *Jacobin*, April 25, 2015; Trish Kahle, "The Seeds of an Alternative," *Jacobin*, February 29, 2015.
21. Tom Hansell, *After Coal: Stories of Survival in Appalachia and Wales* (Morgantown: West Virginia University Press, 2018), 161–201.
22. UMW, "Preserving Coal Country."
23. DOL, BLS, "Employment, Hours, and Earnings from the Current Employment Statistics Survey (National), Coal Mining, NAICS Code 2121," November 25, 2022.
24. Bonnie E. Stewart, *No. 9: The 1968 Farmington Mine Disaster* (Morgantown: West Virginia University Press, 2012), 210.
25. Stewart, *No. 9*, 209.
26. Simon Evans, "Analysis: Which Countries Are Historically Responsible for Climate Change?," *Carbon Brief*, October 5, 2021; Nadja Popovich and Brad Plumer, "Who Has the Most Historical Responsibility for Climate Change?," *NYT*, November 12, 2021.
27. "China Pledges to Cut Mining Deaths After Spate of Accidents," *Bloomberg News*, August 11, 2022.
28. Tom Bethell, *The Hurricane Creek Massacre*, January 26, 1971, i, MFDR 46/15.
29. Daniel Becerril, "La vida sigue en las minas de Sabinas," *El País*, October 15, 2022.
30. Andrés Manuel López Obrador, "Visita técnica a la Central Carboeléctrica 'José López Portillo,' en Nava, Coahuila," October 24, 2020, https://lopezobrador.org.mx/2020/10/24/version-estenografica-visita-tecnica-a-la-central-carboelectrica-jose-lopez-portillo-en-nava-coahuila/; Jackie Botts, "Mexico State Utility Bought Coal from Uninspected Mines, Including Fatal Site," Reuters, September 7, 2022; David Agren, "Mexico Was Once a Climate Leader—Now It's Betting Big on Coal," *Guardian*, February 15, 2021;

"Mexico to Buy 2 Million Tons of Coal for Power Plants," Associated Press, July 15, 2020.

31. Daniel Becerril, "Deep Underground: Mexican Coal Miners Remember Those Who Never Came Back," Reuters, October 1, 2022.

32. Noura Alkhalili, Muna Dajani, and Yahia Mahmoud, "The Enduring Coloniality of Ecological Modernization: Wind Energy Development in Occupied Western Sahara and the Occupied Golan Heights," *Political Geography* 103 (May 2023).

33. Thea Riofrancos, "What Green Costs," *Logic* 9 (December 7, 2019), https://logicmag.io/nature/what-green-costs/; Todd C. Frankel, "The Cobalt Pipeline," *Washington Post*, September 30, 2016.

Index

Akers, Nathan, 257
Akers, Larry, 257
Alabama, 278, 317; and Arnold
  Miller, 254; and Birmingham, 31;
  and bituminous coal, 305; and
  coalfields, 37, 270; and coal
  miners, 270–71; and coal
  operators, 259; and coal seams, 6;
  and convict leasing schemes, 25;
  and Harlan County War, 18; and
  Mobile, 269; and Sayreton Mine,
  85; and United Mine Workers
  (UMW), 270
Ambern, Ab, 88
American Federation of Labor (AFL),
  19, 50, 132
Americanness, 83, 106
anthracite, 37, 72, 77, 83, 91, 110, 268,
  305; and exports, 74; and markets,
  109; and miners, 38, 72–74, 76, 83
  and Pennsylvania, 48, 109, 259; and
  production, 74; and Three Mile
  Island, 318

antistripping activism, 216–18, 220–23,
  243–45, 247, 250, 253. *See also* strip
  mining
antiwar protestors, 185, 247
apartheid (South African), 270–71
Appalachia, 49, 76, 148, 211, 312, 326;
  and activists, 222; and Black political
  life, 9, 247; and Black workers, 21;
  and coal-fired social contract, 66,
  213; and coal industry, 8, 17, 19, 22,
  25, 27, 52–53, 145, 212–13, 218–20,
  244, 250, 252, 267–68, 281, 310, 326;
  and coal miners, 7–8, 259, 320; and
  coal wars, 18; and economic
  integration, 21; and energy
  citizenship, 311; and energy
  dependence, 19; and environmental
  destruction, 2, 211, 223, 252; and
  governance, 19; and Great
  Depression, 52; and Great Society,
  190; and health crisis, 132; and
  housing crisis, 209; and Miners for
  Democracy (MFD), 259; and

[415]

Appalachia (*continued*)
  National Recovery Administration (NRA), 48; and power cutbacks, 305; and role (in the U.S.), 8; and social welfare, 279; and surface mining, 114, 210, 213, 219, 222; and United Mine Workers (UMW), 48; and violence, 6, 145; and white poverty, 8; and wildcat strikes, 302
Appalachian Alliance, 310–11
Appalachian Electric Power Company, 111
Appalachian Volunteers, 190, 198, 216
Arab-Israeli War (1973), 263
"atomic age," 117, 120, 137
Atomic Energy Commission (AEC), 112, 118, 120–21, 130, 132; and Dow Chemical, 133; and Glenn Seaborg, 124–25; and Jock Yablonski, 161–62; and United Mine Workers (UMW), 123, 125; and W. A. "Tony" Boyle, 135–36, 162
atomic power, 177; and boosters, 117; civilian, 128; and coal industry, 118, 120, 137, 316; and coal miners, 122; commercial, 118; critics of, 117, 121, 126–29, 130–31, 133, 135–36, 164; development of, 102, 121, 130; and Dow Chemical, 133–34; and Glenn Seaborg, 125; and governmental oversight, 130; and government subsidy, 122; plants, 122, 128; technology, 124; and United Mine Workers (UMW), 130, 133–35, 137, 317; and W. A. "Tony" Boyle, 133, 164. *See also* nuclear power

bituminous coal, 59, 291, 305; and 1950 agreement, 117, 147, 155; and 1974 agreement, 302; and Consol No. 9, 139; distribution of, 54; and fuel shortages, 72; industry, 57, 75, 79, 268; and Kentucky, 285; and miners, 74, 198; and National Recovery Administration, 48; and output, 69, 174, 176; and Pennsylvania, 197; and steel firms, 289; and strikes, 78, 81, 83; supply of, 37; and sympathy strikes, 68; and United Mine Workers (UMW), 110, 276, 301, 303, 322; use of, 72; wage conference, 68
Bituminous Coal Agreement (1950), 89, 91–92, 117, 120, 147
Bituminous Coal Division, 61–63, 69
Bituminous Coal Operators Association (BCOA), 287, 303, 306–8, 322
black lung, 2, 158, 179, 203, 259, 328; activism, 144, 151–54, 221, 232, 235, 243, 274, 321; and Appalachian coalfields, 132, 145; and compensation, 133, 159–60, 167, 189, 201–2, 212, 219, 250, 253, 294–95, 321; and Consol No. 9 disaster, 143; effects of, 7, 146–47, 149, 152, 162, 166, 208, 214, 218, 239–40, 250, 321; and federal programs, 168, 201, 244, 276, 321; and mine disasters, 143, 214, 240; and Social Security Administration, 168, 189; strikes, 153–54, 157, 160, 162–63, 206, 244, 287, 318; and United Mine Workers, 147, 220
Black Lung Association (BLA), 144, 149–50, 188, 218, 232, 243–45, 247, 294
Black Lung Benefits Act (1972, BLBA), 5, 293–95
Black Lung Bulletin, 188, 198
Booz-Allen Hamilton, 112, 114
Boyle, Jack J., 123, 164
Boyle, W. A. "Tony," 135, 142, 241, 252, 254–59, 309, 317, 323; and antinuclear

[416] INDEX

politics, 119, 121, 126, 128–33, 137; and atomic energy, 126; and Atomic Energy Commission, 120, 136, 162; and Black Lung Association, 150; and boycotts, 131; and coalfield activism, 237–38; and coal production, 123, 180; and coal research, 125; and coal industry deaths, 155; and Consol No. 9, 140–41, 143, 145, 164; critics of, 154; and David E. Lilienthal, 121, 126; and Hanford nuclear site, 123; and Jack Boyle, 123–24; and Jock Yablonski, 160, 162–64, 168–69, 173, 238; and John L. Lewis, 102; and Miners for Democracy (MFD), 240; and nuclear industry, 118; and Rex Lauck, 127; and safety regulations, 159, 164; and strip mining, 220; as UMW president, 116, 118, 122, 133–34, 140, 144, 151, 163, 166, 169, 192; and unionism, 120

Boys Market, Inc v. Retail Clerks Union (1970), 191–92, 197, 290–91

Buffalo Creek, 224–25, 229, 232–34, 244

Buffalo Creek Disaster, 235, 247, 254

Bureau of Mines, 191–93, 195, 201–4, 210, 222, 257–58; accident reports, 186, 208; and Black Lung Association, 188; and mine safety, 9, 58, 67, 85, 164, 188–90, 275; and mine safety violations, 65, 159; statistics, 60; and United Mine Workers (UMW), 177

Cabinet Committee on Energy Supplies and Resources, 105

Campbell, Daniel, 198

carbon dioxide, 253, 299, 316

carbon emissions, 328, 330

carbon monoxide, 90, 199–201, 257

Carter, James Walter, 55

Carter, Jimmy, 184, 296–303, 306–7, 310, 312–17, 319–20

Carter v. Carter Coal Company, (1936), 55–58

Caserta, John, 155

Catawba nuclear power station, 281

Caudill, Bert, 220, 235

Caudill, Harry H., 212, 250

Caudill, Ruby, 211, 216, 235

central competitive field (CCF), 37–38

Childs, Richard, 198

Chileski, Henry, 198

Church, Sam, 317, 322–23

citizenship, 46, 107, 156, 206, 219, 295; coalfield, 29, 50; coal-fired, 166, 188; consumer, 108, 154, 177, 230, 302; and democracy, 143, 234, 239, 249, 325, 330; denial of, 37–38; energy, 6, 9, 13, 71, 106, 114, 119, 154, 165, 188, 233, 236–38, 274–76, 299, 304, 310–11, 324–26, 330; good, 40, 83–84; miners', 82–83, 221, 276, 280; national, 32; New Deal, 51; politics of, 10; rights of, 84, 152, 217, 238–39, 256, 275, 325–26, 329; social, 6, 51, 141, 143, 152, 240; unequal, 39, 216; United States, 2, 5, 9, 36, 39–40, 238, 324

"civil war," 17, 32–33, 43–44, 243

Clean Air Act (1970), 165, 268

Clean Water Act (1972), 165

coalfield wars, *See* mine wars

Coal Creek War, 18, 32

coal-fired social contract, 4, 10, 106, 143, 153, 236, 266, 271, 309–10, 321–22; and 1950 bituminous coal agreement, 117; and 1969 coalfield revolt, 145; and black lung, 167; and Consol No. 9, 148; and consumers, 157; and defense production, 58; and democracy, 51; and energy

INDEX [417]

coal-fired social contract (*continued*)
citizenship, 13; enforcement of, 275; failures of, 234, 254; fragility of, 143; and inequality, 213, 235, 325; and Jock Yablonski, 163, 165; and Krug-Lewis Agreement, 89; legitimacy of, 119, 176–77, 179, 220–21; and mechanization, 151; and miners, 12, 89, 154, 239, 326; and Miners for Democracy, 169, 239, 252; and miners' health, 151, 155; and mining deaths, 141, 156; and New Deal, 5, 47, 51, 54, 75, 162, 275, 296; and nuclear power, 135; postwar, 136, 143; and renegotiation, 12, 89, 92, 11, 154, 180, 185, 189–90, 204, 237, 239, 252, 259, 263, 274, 300; and safety crisis, 160; and security politics, 103; structure of, 233; sustainability of, 12; and Tennessee Valley Authority (TVA), 122; and United Mine Workers (UMW), 95, 122, 165, 265, 275–76, 292, 295; unraveling of, 137, 238; and violence, 6; and wage agreements, 66; and W. A. "Tony" Boyle, 116, 120, 131, 133, 136, 163

Coal Miners' Political Action Committee (COMPAC), 265, 318, 323

coal operators, 5, 10 17, 20, 73, 86, 216, 21; and 1950 bituminous agreement, 155; and antiunionism, 17, 43; and antiunion violence, 31; Appalachian, 48, 76; and Bituminous Coal Operators Association (BCOA), 303, 306; and Chip Yablonski, 192; and Clear Creek, 217; and Coal Conservation Act, 56; and coal miners, 17, 20, 32, 41, 136, 192, 204; and coal prices, 69: and collective bargaining, 55; and company towns, 23, 29; demands of, 89; and energy consumers, 63, 136; and energy security, 322; and energy system, 27; and export markets, 259; and Federal Coal Mine Health and Safety Act, 217; and Frances Perkins, 66; and Guffey-Vinson Coal Act, 77; and Gulf Oil, 284; and Harlan County, 50; and Harry Bandholtz, 35; and Jock Yablonski, 162; and John L. Lewis, 42, 53, 66, 76; and Kentucky, 217; and labor contracts, 64, 66; and labor organizing, 181, 322; and local elections, 29; and Logan County, 32; and machinery manufacturers, 151; and Miners for Democracy (MFD), 250–51, 253; and miners' subjugation, 11, 24; and mining disasters, 26–27, 230; and National Recovery Administration (NRA), 48, 54–55; and negotiations, 89; and New Deal, 55; and noncompliance permits, 167; and Ohio, 38; and penalties, 203; and Pennsylvania, 38; and portal-to-portal pay, 78; and productivity, 314; and profits, 166, 251, 295; and property rights, 234; and safety strikes, 206; and safety violations, 65; and strip mining, 220; and Supreme Court, 295; and surface mining, 213; and United Mine Workers (UMW), 54, 91–92, 95, 97, 251; and Walter Hickel, 193; and National War Labor Board, 77; and W. A. "Tony" Boyle, 166; and West Virginia, 24, 31, 36; and working conditions, 60, 63–64

Cold War, 111, 131; and coal industry, 97, 101–2; and decolonization, 247; and energy consumption, 100; global, 102; liberalism, 1;

militarization, 100; and national security, 107, 266; and nuclear age, 95; preparedness, 106; and security politics, 103, 106–7; and U.S. power, 101, 120

collective bargaining, 10; and 1968 agreement, 194–96; and *Boys Market, Inc v. Retail Clerks Union* (1970), 290; and coal-fired social contract, 292; and coal industry, 48, 54, 65, 194–96; and excluded parties, 308; and grievance procedures, 191; and John L. Lewis, 48; and National Labor Relations Act (NLRA), 56, 58; and National Recovery Administration (NRA), 69; process of, 65, 287, 308; right to, 36, 54, 56, 58, 238; and unionism, 152; and United Mine Workers (UMW), 48; and United States' governance, 118; and wildcat strikes, 302; and working conditions, 64

Colorado Coalfield War, 18

company authoritarianism, 29, 43, 49

Compers, Paul, 90

Congressional Subcommittee on Labor, 158, 206

Congress of Industrial Organizations (CIO), 50, 132

Consol No. 9 disaster, 137–40, 145, 154–55, 159–60, 164, 169, 191, 198, 229, 245–46, 298, 330; and black lung strike, 162; and coal-fired social contract, 148; and miners' health, 143; and mine safety, 199; and nuclear power, 141; and safety records, 188; and widows, 166

Consolidation Coal, 140–41, 164, 166, 176, 179, 181–82, 256–58, 271, 283, 289

Continental Oil, 176, 179, 182, 257–58, 283, 289

Council of Energy Resource Tribes (CERT), 268–69

decarbonization, 332

democracy, 196, 207, 235, 244, 246–48, 255, 274–76, 279, 302, 311, 317–18, 330–31; "arsenal of," 2, 72; and authoritarianism, 25; and autocracy, 11; and capitalism, 123; and citizenship, 143, 234, 237, 239, 249, 256, 325, 330; and civil society, 10, 18–19, 45–46, 189, 207, 310; and coal dependence, 19, 146; and coalfields, 22, 44, 53; coal-fired, 2, 5–7, 10, 13, 72, 97, 179, 189, 210, 236, 258, 295, 299, 321, 329, 332; and coal miners, 4, 6, 11, 51, 81–82, 162–64, 166, 238–40, 246, 259, 302; and coal towns, 22, 326; and democratic growth, 2; and development, 52; and economy, 46; energy, 6, 12, 271, 274–75, 286–87, 291; and energy abundance, 120; energy-intensive, 46, 51, 100, 121, 331; and energy systems, 46, 179, 266, 286; fights for, 84, 177; and freedoms, 48; and free enterprise, 106; and governance, 25, 53, 280; industrial, 10, 275; and institutions, 37, 47, 67, 249; and labor organizing, 44; and law, 146; liberal, 40, 123, 326; limits of, 6–7, 166, 325; and New Deal, 69; paradoxes of, 9, 13, 312; and politics, 119–20, 157, 243, 248; and rights, 32, 145, 157, 306–7; and United Mine Workers, 40–41, 120, 154, 163, 241, 263, 292, 307, 309; United States, 1, 4, 12–13, 274, 292, 297–98; workplace, 163, 299

Democratic Party, 148, 158, 245, 281

Deverall, Richard, 81–82, 85–86

Dillon, Harvey, 35

Dillon, Van Crockett, 257
District 50 (UMW), 131, 133–36, 164
Duke Power, 276–82
Dunn, G. South, 111

Eastover Mining Company, 276–78
electricity, 1, 125, 136, 142–43, 181, 281–82, 331; and atomic reactors, 120, 135, 316; and bituminous coal, 72; coal-fired, 3, 12, 25, 51, 97–98, 100, 102, 104, 107, 111–12, 115, 137, 141–42, 146, 154–55, 157, 169, 182, 204–5, 207, 213, 220, 233, 239, 254, 258, 269, 271, 287, 297, 303–5, 323, 326; and conservation, 80; and consumption, 25, 121–22, 136–37, 143, 158, 178, 184, 214, 218, 266; and energy systems, 183–84, 271, 314; hydropower, 52; and modernization, 179; shortages, 246, 306; and sustainability, 106; and Tennessee Valley Authority (TVA), 51–53
energy crisis, 274, 276, 285, 320, 323–24; and coal demand, 288; and coal industry, 207, 233, 264, 293, 305, 313; and coal miners, 185, 275, 280, 292, 311; and coal strikes, 290; and death, 207; and democracy, 279; and employment law, 291; and energy citizenship, 275, 310; and energy regulation, 291; experiences of, 178, 185, 263, 303; and fuel sectors, 207; and governance crisis, 185; and Jimmy Carter, 296, 298–301, 304, 313, 315; and Miners for Democracy (MFD), 252, 259; and national security, 266; and natural gas shortages, 267; as political problem, 177; and Richard Nixon, 264; and South African coal, 271; and utility companies, 305 energy crisis, 274, 276, 285, 320, 323–24; and coal demand, 288; and coal industry, 207, 233, 264, 293, 305, 313; and coal miners, 185, 275, 280, 292, 311; and coal strikes, 290; and death, 207; and democracy, 279; and employment law, 291; and energy citizenship, 275, 310; and energy regulation, 291; experiences of, 178, 185, 263, 303; and fuel sectors, 207; and governance crisis, 185; and Jimmy Carter, 296, 298–301, 304, 313, 315; and Miners for Democracy (MFD), 252, 259; and national security, 266; and natural gas shortages, 267; as political problem, 177; and Richard Nixon, 264; and South African coal, 271; and utility companies, 305
energy dependence, 100, 137, 267–68, 300; on coal, 10, 44–45, 52, 58, 71, 111, 142, 265, 301–2, 327; on domestic oil, 104; on foreign oil, 4, 106, 301 315; on fossil fuels, 301
energy system, 76, 80, 145, 153, 155, 175, 190, 230, 258, 295, 321, 323; and Black Lung Benefits Act (BLBA), 294; and Brookside miners, 290, 282; and Buffalo Creek, 233–34; coal, 6, 54, 57–58, 62, 80, 91, 98, 116–17, 119, 141–42, 205, 218, 249, 276, 293, 310, 325, 327, 329; and coal dependence, 3, 7, 19, 158–59, 319–20; and coalfield authoritarianism, 43–44; and coal miners, 12, 23, 27, 50, 79, 107, 154, 162, 180, 217, 223, 237, 239–40, 246, 249–50, 275, 292; and coal prices, 69; and Cold War, 99; and Consol No. 9, 298; costs of, 2, 160, 318; democratization, 7, 52, 70, 73, 240, 244, 265–66, 309, 330; development of, 3; and Duke Power, 281; and

[420] INDEX

energy citizenship, 6, 13, 39, 71, 143; and energy consumption, 163; and environmental harms, 118; and Foreign Oil Policy Committee, 104; global, 267, 331; and governance, 4–5, 7, 10, 189; and Guffey system, 64; and Hyden disaster, 204; and independence, 267, 313; and industrial welfare regime, 136; and law, 189; and mass consumption, 152, 163, 314; multifuel, 57, 97–98, 314–15; and National War Labor Board (WLB), 79; and New Deal, 54; and political agency, 26; postwar, 120; and Price-Anderson Act, 127; and price mechanisms, 70; and Ray Zell, 108; and Richard M. Nixon, 263; and strikes, 79–80, 307; and surface mining, 221; and sustainability, 36; and Three Mile Island, 297; and transformation, 22, 98, 162–63, 173, 184, 210, 220, 296, 299; and United Mine Workers (UMW), 95, 97, 109, 116, 122, 177; viability of, 46; violence of, 25, 27–28, 143, 196, 283, 326, 332; and wages, 69; wartime, 74, 78

environment, 235, 266, 269, 314; and activism, 179, 312–13, 323; Appalachian, 211, 220, 223; conditions of, 162, 211; and degradation, 118–20, 162, 179, 213–15, 220–22, 239, 251–52, 299, 317–18, 326; and electric power, 179; and energy systems, 7; and environmental health, 156, 165, 223, 314; and environmental inequality, 221; and environmental justice movement, 13; and environmental and rights, 156, 216, 240; and regulations, 165, 168, 179, 252, 271, 328; and mining industry, 4, 203, 220, 223, 250, 252, 266, 299, 321, 330; and mine safety, 120, 127; and nuclear safety, 126, 128, 318; protection of, 6, 12, 165, 179, 222, 246, 251–53, 259, 265, 298, 300, 323, 325

environmentalism, 222–23, 232, 243, 251–53, 316, 329

Environmental Protection Agency (1970), 165, 266

Federal Coal Mine Health and Safety Act (1969), 5, 188–89, 195, 199, 206, 212, 217, 220, 250, 275, 293
Feldman, Clarice, 189, 197
Finley, Bill, 9, 247
Finley, Charles, 199, 201–5
Finley Coal Company, 199, 232
Foreign Oil Policy Committee (FOPC), 103–5, 108
Fort St. Vrain, 128–30, 173–74
fossil fuels, 1, 3–4, 183, 266, 296, 300–1, 316, 328–29
Foy, Lewis L., 289–90
Fuller, Luther E., 53

Gallo, Tony, 249
Gaudiano, Dan, 208–9
Gaydos, Mike, 194, 207–8
Gedraitis, Joseph, 198
Gompers, Samuel, 19, 35
Gourley, Wallace, 191–92, 194–97
governance, 56, 68; coalfield, 32, 36, 41, 43, 48, 50–51, 53, 65, 69–70, 97; company, 22, 34; crisis of, 185, 204; democratic, 25, 274; energy, 19, 44, 55, 63, 67, 70, 79, 266, 274, 288, 295, 308, 311; industrial, 48; national, 95; national security, 106; patterns of, 19; practices of, 4, 10, 12, 32; risk, 26; self, 10, 18; workplace, 302

Great War, 18, 31–34, 40–41
Guffey, Joseph, 54
Guffey-Snyder Coal Act (Bituminous Coal Conservation Act, 1935), 5, 54–56, 92
Guffey-Vinson Coal Act (Bituminous Coal Conservation Act, 1937), 56, 58–59, 61–62, 64–67, 70, 75–77, 88, 92
Gulf General Atomic, 174. *See also* Gulf Oil
Gulf Oil, 173–76, 284, 308

Hall, Elmer, 135
Hall, Herman, 35
Harding, Warren, 11, 33, 35
Harlan County (KY), 43, 48, 50, 276, 278–79, 282–82
Harlan County War ("Bloody Harlan"), 18, 43
Hatfield, Bill, 257
Hatfield, Wayne Brady, 227
Hickel, Walter, 158, 193
Hohman, Gus, 90
House Committee on Education and Labor, 327
House Subcommittee on Mines and Mining, 121, 126
House Ways and Means Committee, 54, 62–65
Hutchinson, Duane, 198
Hyden disaster (1970), 204–6, 228–29, 232, 254, 327

Ickes, Harold, 62–63, 65–66, 72–74, 77–79, 81, 85, 89
Illinois, 11, 36, 38, 90, 259, 296
immigration, 27, 40; and immigrant communities, 8, 40, 130; and immigrant miners, 9, 26, 38; and immigrants, 39, 130; and

Polish immigrants, 162, 187, 189
Indiana, 38, 238, 303
industrial relations, 12, 102, 116, 118, 185, 280, 287, 290, 307
inequality, 2, 331; and American liberalism, 137; coal-fired, 214, 218, 223, 229–30, 239, 332; economic, 326; energy system, 257, 265, 323
International Executive Board, 160
international markets, 3, 175, 235, 263, 268, 306, 314
international oil companies, 106, 123, 173, 315
Island Creek Coal Company, 176, 181
Island Creek Colliery Company, 31

Johnson, Lyndon B., 1–2, 10, 127, 285, 319
Josephson, Thomas E., 198

Kalanavich, Nick, 198
Kennedy, John F., 110
Kennedy, Robert, 282
Kennedy, Thomas, 65, 116
Kentucky, 43, 48, 213; and antistripping activism, 250; and Bert Caudill, 212; and Black Lung Association, 150; and black lung benefits, 212; and Clear Creek, 217; and coalfields, 37, 277; and coal miners, 50, 70, 328; and coal research, 112; and coal strikes, 285, 303; and Duke Power, 277; and Eastover Mining Company, 276–77; and environmental harm, 214–15; and Fort Thomas, 83; and Harlan County War, 18; and Harold Ickes, 66; and Hyden, 199–200; and Letcher County, 190, 211; and miners' deaths, 86; and Shawnee Steam Plant, 17; and strip mining,

[422] INDEX

216, 218; and Tennessee Valley Authority (TVA), 218; and union miners, 328; and United Mine Workers of America (UMW), 276; and violence, 66; and W. A. "Tony" Boyle, 259; Workmen's Compensation Fund, 201

Kmetz, Thomas, 198

Kovach, Stephen, 187

Krug-Lewis Agreement, 89–91

labor: activists, 11, 247; and arbitrated labor settlements, 36; and capital, 18; child, 48; and citizenship, 70; and coalfield labor conflicts, 72; of coal miners, 2, 47–48, 50, 70, 214; contract mechanisms, 64; contracts, 205, 287; convict, 32; disputes, 33, 35, 39, 70, 77, 79, 84, 117–18, 194, 196, 280, 289, 291; and economic administration, 75–76; and energy, 75–76; of extraction, 106, 253; forced, 25, 195; and industrial relations, 142; law, 12, 194, 196, 237, 280, 307; and militancy, 50; monopoly, 279; movement, 40, 116, 174, 241, 248, 264, 280, 302, 322–23, 329; and National Labor Relations Act (NLRA), 56, 58; and National Industrial Recovery Act (NIRA), 58; and organizations, 134; organizing, 4, 10, 124; politics, 40, 238; provisions, 56, 58; relations, 24, 48, 65, 102, 238, 297, 299, 301, 306–8, 310–11, 313, 315; rights, 6, 47, 148, 280, 302; shortages, 77–78; slave, 270; and Solid Fuels Administration for the War (SFAW), 77–78; unions, 6, 248; and United Mine Workers, 140; unrest, 56, 63, 181, 299; and Warren Harding, 35

Labor Committee for Safe Energy and Full Employment, 322

Labor Management Reporting and Disclosure Act, 130

Lake, Lewis, 138–39

Lane, Winthrop, 17–19, 24–25, 32, 33, 44

Lewis, John L., 17, 46, 74, 98; and American Federation of Labor, (AFL), 50; and coal operators, 42–43, 48, 53; and Congress of Industrial Organizations (CIO), 50; and contract negotiations, 76, 89; critics of, 83–84; death of, 283; and District 50, 134; and energy governance, 79; and energy system, 58; and Franklin D. Roosevelt, 75, 79; and Guffey-Vinson Coal Act, 66; and Harold L. Ickes, 79; and industrial unionism, 53; and International Executive Board, 160; and Krug-Lewis Agreement, 89–91; and National Coal Policy Conference, 116; and National Industrial Recovery Act, 49; and National War Labor Board (WLB), 70, 77; and politics, 41–42, 44; as Republican, 40; and safety practices, 64; and Thomas Kennedy, 65; and underground mechanization, 95; and United Mine Workers (UMW), 134; as United Mine Workers president, 38, 41, 47, 68; and W. A. "Tony" Boyle, 102, 116, 123; and Welfare and Retirement Fund, 241; and welfare systems, 147; and West Virginia, 81–82

liberalism, 1, 153, 326; breadwinner, 185; coal-fired, 145, 230, 298; energy-intensive, 267; and miners, 12; New Deal, 189, 275; postwar, 137; and U.S. inequality, 137

Link, Lavern, 198
Little Steel formula, 70, 75–76

Mandatory Oil Import Program (MOIP), 105, 109, 112, 176
Maple Creek Mine, 190, 193–94, 207–10
Martin, Buddy, 168
Martin, Marshall, 135
mass death, 90, 119, 154, 157
Maust Coal and Coke, 176
McFall, Robert, 198
McGee, Elmer, 59–60
McMillion, Teddy, 257
Meador, David, 257
Mendez, Johnny, 9, 192, 247
migration, 21, 26, 40, 80; and migrants, 21, 30, 40
Milton, Willie, 212
Miner's Bill of Rights, 248–51, 254
miners' deaths, 6, 27, 157, 164, 206, 249, 257, 327; "acceptable" level of, 141, 154; and black lung, 152–53, 212, 240; and Centralia No. 5 disaster, 90; costs of, 26; and culpability, 26, 31, 187–88, 204; and death benefits, 294; and energy crisis, 207; inevitability of, 198; and mine disasters, 139; and narratives, 156; and postwar energy system, 120, 141, 155, 325; premature, 295, 314; preventable, 60–61, 127, 331; rates of, 28, 43, 60–61, 70, 86–87, 145, 188; and regulations, 190; and respiratory conditions, 146–48; and safety laws, 177, 209; and underground mining, 223; and W. A. "Tony" Boyle, 144; and "way of death," 139, 145, 153, 169, 178, 195–96
Miners for Democracy (MFD), 197, 285; and Appalachia, 259; and Arnold Miller, 246, 253–54; and Bill Finley, 247; and Black supporters, 9, 247; and Chip Yablonski, 195; and coalfield activism, 238; and coal-fired social contract, 169; and corruption, 241; and democracy, 239–40, 248; and disabled miners, 196; and energy governance, 274; and environmentalism, 222, 232, 252; and Harry Patrick, 241–42, 246; and Maple Creek mine, 208; and miners, 188, 191, 238–39, 246, 252; and Miners' Bill of Rights, 248–50; and platform 249; and politics, 238, 253–55; and reclamation laws, 251; and reform, 188, 239; and St. Clairsville (Ohio), 191; and strip mining, 243, 253; and United Mine Workers, 258, 272; and W. A. "Tony" Boyle, 255–56; and West Virginia, 241, 243; and workplace governance, 302
miners' safety committees, 48, 67, 89–90, 193, 195, 208–10, 249
mine safety, 58, 85, 120, 132, 143–45, 160, 187, 204, 239, 266, 309, 323; activism, 189; and Centralia, 90; conditions, 125, 143–44, 166, 202, 283, 308; costs of, 62; and energy consumers, 63; enforcement of, 64, 146; and Krug-Lewis Agreement, 89; and legislation, 60, 62, 67, 91, 108, 148–49, 153–55, 157–58, 162, 167, 177, 188, 190, 194, 245; and Miners' Bill of Rights, 249; and Miners for Democracy, 249–50, 254, 257–58; records, 197, 209–10, 227–28, 258; regulations, 9–10, 196, 203, 205–6, 304, 325, 327; research, 140; and strikes, 89, 206–7, 287; and United Mine Workers, 87, 89–90, 135–36, 163–64, 168, 223, 258, 265, 279; violations, 64–65, 91, 119, 124, 140, 157, 159, 191, 193, 277, 284

[424] INDEX

mine wars, 18, 25–26, 28, 32–33, 35, 38, 42, 47, 85–86
Moore, Arch, 153, 227, 229, 232, 282, 285, 288, 292
Moore, George E., 198
Moore, J. Cordell, 140, 149
Morgan, Adam, 327
Morgan, Ephraim, 33, 35
Morgan, Steve, 327
Mullen, James, 193–94, 208–9
Murray, Phillip, 36–37, 42–43
Murray, Thomas E., 118

National Coal Association, 105, 175, 178, 320
National Coal Policy Conference (NCPC), 102, 113, 116, 140, 175
national defense, 110, 122, 128, 132, 196
National Defense Mediation Board, 66, 70
national energy policy, 251–52, 288, 302, 311, 316; and Franklin D. Roosevelt, 58; and Jimmy Carter, 296, 298–300, 312; and miners' safety, 163; multifuel, 177; unified, 177, 184, 321
National Environmental Policy Act (1970), 165
National Guard, 34, 43, 50, 308
National Industrial Recovery Act (NIRA), 5, 47–51, 54, 58
nationalism, 101, 173
nationalization, 3, 101, 174–75
National Labor Relations Act (NLRA), 56, 58
National Labor Relations Board (NLRB), 195
National Miners Union (NMU), 41
National Recovery Administration (NRA), 47–48, 51, 54–56, 69
National Resources Committee (NRC), 58

national security, 104, 107, 179, 266, 296, 302, 321; and coal industry, 97, 102–3; costs of, 109; and energy stockpile, 99; and Korean War, 100; state, 103, 105–6, 110
National War Labor Board (WLB), 66, 70, 76–79, 81, 86, 310
natural gas, 57, 113–14, 131, 136, 142, 267, 275, 294, 301, 313–14, 328
Navajo nation, 129, 132, 268
New Deal, 57, 192; and 1950 agreement, 92; citizenship, 51, 166; and coal-fired social contract, 5, 47, 54, 75, 296; and coal miners, 7, 12, 69, 255; and democracy, 69; and electrification, 51; and energy systems, 52, 54; and federal authority, 55; and federal legislation, 49, 54–55; liberalism, 189, 267, 326; and Miners for Democracy, 255; and miners' rights, 47; and National Recovery Administration (NRA), 51; opponents of, 53, 275; and politics of security, 107; and river systems, 52; and social contract, 162; and Supreme Court, 55; and Tennessee Valley Authority (TVA), 51, 53, 121; and United Mine Workers of America (UMW), 53, 121, 136; and W. A. "Tony" Boyle, 136
Nixon, Richard M., 215, 258, 280; and Arnold Miller, 265; and Clean Air Act, 156; and conservationism, 301; and Consol No. 9, 199; and Elburt Osborn, 222; and energy conservation, 300; and energy crisis, 264; and energy development, 301; and energy independence, 264; and energy system, 263; and Federal Coal Mine Health and Safety Act, 160, 188, 199, 267–68; and gold standard,

INDEX [425]

Nixon (continued)
  267; and Hiram Emory Widener Jr.,
  290; and John F. O'Leary, 193; and
  law and order, 185, 291; and Miners
  for Democracy (MFD), 191; and
  Organization of Petroleum
  Exporting Countries (OPEC), 267;
  and price stabilization, 286; and
  "Project Independence," 265; and
  Walter Hickel, 158
nuclear power: and accidents, 118–19,
  141, 316; alternatives to, 141; and
  antinuclear politics, 126, 128–31,
  135–36, 140, 161, 317–18, 323; and
  boosters, 118, 121–22, 125; civilian,
  112, 119; and coal, 120, 123–24, 136,
  316, 323; and coal miners, 118,
  120–21, 128; and Cold War, 95, 120;
  commercial, 117; and David E.
  Lilienthal, 121, 126; development of,
  3, 117, 121–22, 128, 130–31, 133–34,
  315–16, 319; and Duke Power,
  281–82; and environmental politics,
  127, 318; and Gulf Oil, 173–74; and
  industry, 118; and nuclear bomb, 117;
  and oil, 313, 316, 320; safety, 126;
  stations, 173, 281–82, 319; subsidy,
  123; technology, 117–18, 124; Three
  Mile Island, 297; United States, 112;
  and uranium mines, 163; and
  weapons, 316; and workers, 322

occupational health and safety, 10, 12,
  92, 120, 132, 136–37, 143, 154, 156,
  166, 323
Office of Coal Research (OCR),
  112–13, 121
Office of Price Administration (OPA),
  70, 74, 76–77, 79, 81
Office of War Information (OWI), 81,
  84–85

Office of War Utilities, 80, 89
Ohio, 29, 28, 61, 80, 123, 130, 176, 191,
  199, 206, 259, 303
oil, 53, 57, 72, 74, 114, 123, 177, 306,
  320; and antitrust cases, 103; Arab,
  263, 267–68; and atomic power, 136;
  and coal, 181, 183–84; companies,
  105–6, 162, 173–76, 182, 265, 286;
  consumption, 264, 294; and
  dependency, 100, 106, 301; and
  domestic producers, 97, 101–2, 104,
  328; and embargo, 263, 274, 282, 286;
  and energy conglomerates, 179; and
  energy crisis, 267; and energy
  insecurity, 316; flows of, 101, 267;
  foreign, 4, 97, 315–16; fuel, 118; and
  gas, 98; and horizontal integration,
  161; and imports, 102, 105, 108–10,
  122, 301; and multifuel energy
  system, 314; and oilfields, 98; panics
  (shocks), 275–76, 297, 299–300, 312;
  power of, 112, 268; prices, 297, 313,
  315; and producers, 3; and reserves,
  100–101, 104; and United Mine
  Workers, 120; Venezuelan, 104; and
  wartime, 80; and workers, 180
Oil, Chemical, and Atomic Workers
  Union (OCAW), 175, 177
Organization of Arab Petroleum
  Exporting Countries (OAPEC), 274
Organization of Petroleum Exporting
  Countries (OPEC), 175, 263, 267–69,
  313
Orsini, Philip, 198
Owens, Willard, 118–19

Patrick, Harry, 169, 241–42, 246, 254,
  256, 276
Pennsylvania, 83, 168, 186, 189, 192, 242,
  247; and anthracite fields, 48, 109,
  305; and Arnold Miller, 259; and

bituminous coal, 305; and Black Lung Association, 149–50; and Canonsburg, 68; and central competitive field, 37–38; and coal industry, 6, 29, 81; and coal miners, 40, 47; and Coal Miners' Political Action Committee (COMPAC), 323; and coal strikes, 33, 37–38, 68, 150, 191, 303; Department of Mines, 24, 39, 60; and Ebensburg, 256; and Erie, 74; and Exeter, 91; and Joseph Guffey, 54; and labor organizing, 47, 150; and Local 2026, 135; and mine disasters, 60, 206; and miners' deaths, 155, 188, 198, 206; and mine walkouts, 196; and natural gas, 131; northern, 6, 18; and Pittsburgh, 68; and safety strikes, 206, 291; and steel factories, 21; and Three Miles Island-II, 317; and United Mine Workers (UMW), 37, 135

Perkins, Carl, 112

Perkins, Frances, 66

Petrisek, Adam, 188

pollution, 165, 255; and acid runoff, 222; air, 115, 120, 128, 130, 179, 252 268, 312, 314; coal, 314; control of, 125, 300; land, 120; and mining, 125; and pollutants, 165, 268, 330; and public health crises, 253; and regulation, 268, 298, 300, 312; river, 220, 251, 312; water, 120, 128–29, 142, 220–21, 252

post-Civil War, 4, 20, 35, 213

postwar era, 3, 5, 175, 184, 187, 211, 248; and coal-fired social contract, 89, 92, 95, 117, 153, 254; and coal production, 98 108, 144; economy, 86, 107–8; and electricity, 141; and energy crisis, 266; and energy production, 99–100, 141; energy system, 118, 120, 184; and industrial democracy, 275; and industrial relations, 287; and industry collapse, 102; liberalism, 137; and mass consumption, 12, 136; and mine disasters, 143; and mine safety, 91; and nuclear industry, 122; and political order, 92; and surface mining, 213; and underground mining, 214; and unionism, 152; and United Mine Workers (UMA), 89; and violence, 11

public safety, 141

race, 9, 29; and racial injustice, 326; and racial others, 10, 83; and racial tensions, 31, 42

racism, 9, 11, 18, 31, 83, 185

Rahall, Nick, 315

rights, 197, 201, 238, 259, 266, 278, 295, 330; basic, 148, 205; citizenship, 5–6, 41, 49, 84, 152, 217, 234, 239, 255–56, 275–76, 325, 329; civil, 32, 50, 232, 247, 323; collective bargaining, 54, 56; constitutional, 36, 46, 219, 325, 352n19; democratic, 32, 145, 306–7; and energy citizenship, 71, 188, 299, 304; environmental, 216, 240; human, 232; labor, 6, 47, 148, 280, 302; and labor action, 78, 84; mineral, 213, 216, 222; miners', 4, 10, 19, 29, 36–38, 41, 43–44, 47, 53, 55, 69, 77, 112, 148, 152, 155, 157–58, 165–66, 190, 204–7, 244–45, 265, 276, 292, 307; natural, 156, 248; political, 2, 53, 145, 237, 248; property, 19, 82, 212, 216–17, 234; and "right to breathe," 156–57; of sovereign states, 175; state's, 160; of union membership, 256; violation of, 215, 217, 223, 240, 281; voting, 235

INDEX [427]

Roosevelt, Franklin D., 255; and coal industry policy, 47, 57, 77; and coal miners, 49, 74–75, 83; and electrification, 51; and Guffey-Vinson Coal Act, 66; and Harold Ickes, 72, 77–79; and National Industrial Recovery Act (NIRA), 48; and Smith-Connally Act, 79; and Supreme Court, 57; and United Mine Workers of America (UMW), 54, 68

Safe Drinking Water Act (1974), 165
safety equipment, 76, 319
Sayreton Mine, 85
Schechter Poultry Corporation v. United States (1935), 54–56
Schlesinger, James, 304–7, 320–21
Schokora, George, 198
Scott, Fred, 239, 255
Scott, Lois, 278–79
Senate Committee on Education and Labor, 36–39
Senate Subcommittee on Intergovernmental Relations, 182
Shawnee Steam Plant, 174
Sholtis, Thomas, 198
Shrewsbury Jr., Van, 257
Sizemore, Roger, 257
Smith Connally Act, 78–79, 90
Solid Fuels Administration for the War (SFAW), 77–78, 80, 110
Solis, Hilda, 327
South Africa, 269–71, 313
Southern Company, 269–71
Standard Oil, 176, 182
Stanish, Joseph (d. 1934), 187
Stanish, Joseph (d. 1970), 186–88, 191
steel industry, 3, 5, 199, 238, 279, 303; and Armco Steel, 290; and Bethlehem Steel, 176, 181, 191, 193, 289; and bituminous coal, 72; and captive coal mines, 50, 68, 207–9; and coal production, 11–12, 50, 58, 146, 267, 290, 326; and coal shortages, 80; and conglomerates, 296; and Congress of Industrial Organizations (CIO), 50; and consumer goods, 204, 218; dangers of, 6; decline of, 98; and demand, 198; and energy system, 58; and factories, 21; and iron ore, 270; Japanese, 235; and Jones & Laughlin, 191; and labor organizing, 50, 68; and labor strikes, 289; and Maple Creek Mine, 193–94, 207; and Newfield Mine, 198; and overseas steel production, 233, 267; and Pennsylvania, 21; and Republic Steel, 191, 198; and Robena mine, 163; and steel mills, 65; and steelworkers' union, 37; and supply chains, 176, 181; and United Mine Workers (UMW), 68; and United States global dominance, 22; and U.S. Steel, 68, 163, 176, 181, 191, 193–94, 207–9, 289; and Venezuela, 270
strikes, 18, 35, 69, 84, 91, 150, 195, 271, 278; and 1977–1978 national strike, 292, 296, 302–3, 305–6, 309; and anthracite workers, 74, 76; and antistrike legislation, 78, 289–90; bituminous, 78, 83; black lung, 153–54, 157, 160, 162–63, 206, 244, 287, 318; breaking of, 42; Brookside, 276, 280, 282, 285–86; and central competitive field (CCF), 37–38; coal, 53, 59, 79, 160, 167, 249, 305–9; and coal miners, 49, 73–75, 82, 166, 193; critiques of, 80; and deaths, 68; Eastover, 277; effects of, 80; and energy crisis, 280, 286, 303; and energy system, 59; gasoline, 292; and Guffey Coal Act, 66; and

[428] INDEX

Harry S. Truman, 89; and industrial relations, 118; and John L. Lewis, 38, 74–75, 77, 83–84; and labor rights, 78; and mine disasters, 145; and miners' citizenship, 82; nationwide, 17, 33, 160, 167; rail, 206; right to, 302–4; safety, 197, 206, 287, 291; and "no strike" clauses, 191; and strikers, 68, 74, 76, 282, 285–86; sympathy, 68; and union-organizing, 39; and United Mine Workers, 31, 321–23; and violence, 196; and West Virginia, 31; wildcat, 73–74, 144, 149, 154, 160, 164, 238, 292, 302, 311
strip mining, 225, 227, 253, 268, 305, 309, 328; and air pollution, 312; and Appalachia, 211, 213, 219; and black lung, 294; and efficiency, 114; and energy system, 221–22; and environmental degradation, 210–14, 216–19, 223–24, 239–40, 250, 252; expansion of, 251, 321; and labor organizing, 269; and mechanization, 218; and mine disasters, 247; and miners, 214, 216–17; and Miners for Democracy (MFD), 252–53; and mineral rights, 216; and mine waste, 2, 224; opposition to, 127, 216, 243; and permits, 213; supporters of, 221; and United Mine Workers (UMW), 220–21, 250–51; and W. A. "Tony" Boyle, 220
strip-mining abolitionists. *See* antistripping activism
Sunshine Anthracite Coal Co. v. Adkins (1940), 57
surface mining. *See* strip mining

Taft-Hartley Act (Labor Management Relations Act of 1947), 195, 197, 291, 306–8

Tennessee Valley Authority (TVA), 51–54, 121–22, 178, 218, 235
Three Mile Island, 297, 313, 317–18, 322–23
Triolo, Antonio, 27–28, 346n49

Udall, Stuart, 149, 155
unionism, 24, 40, 53, 120, 151–52, 180, 278
United Mine Workers of America (UMW), 52, 85, 103, 108, 114, 130, 168, 274, 278, 284; and antinuclear politics, 119, 126, 135; and Atomic Energy Commission (AEC), 120, 123, 125, 161; and BCOA, 306–8; and Brookside, 278–80; and captive mines, 208; and Cecil Roberts, 329; and Chip Yablonski, 166, 192, 290–91; and citizenship, 13, 40, 188; and coalfield authoritarianism, 43; and coal industry, 105–6, 110; and Coal Miners' Political Action Committee (COMPAC), 265; and coal research, 102; and coal supply, 37, 155, 286; and Cold War, 120; Constitutional Convention (1968), 160, 177; and contract negotiations, 48, 50, 91; and democratization efforts, 239, 292, 301; District 15, 129; District 50, 131, 133–34; and Duke Power, 276, 282; and Eastover Mining Company, 276; and electric power generation, 102; and energy democracy, 271, 295, 299, 328; and Federal Energy Office (FEO), 288–89; and Guffey-Vinson Coal Act, 66, 77; nd Gulf General Atomic, 174; and Hanford, 125; and Harlan operators, 50; and Harold Ickes, 89; and hydropower, 52–54; and Illinois, 90; and Jack J. Boyle,

INDEX [429]

United Mine Workers of America (*continued*) 123; and Jimmy Carter, 306–7, 312; and Jock Yablonski, 161, 163–66, 173, 177; and John L. Lewis, 38, 43, 50, 83, 98, 116; and leadership, 35–36, 109, 180, 280, 303, 324; membership, 41, 110, 113, 129; and mine deaths, 155; and mine inspectors, 87; and Miners for Democracy (MFD), 241, 246, 249, 251; and miners' rights, 197, 241; and miners' safety, 64–65, 67, 77, 164, 167, 223; and modernization, 113; and national health care, 92; and National Recovery Administration (NRA), 47–48; and National War Labor Board (WLB), 77–78; and New Deal, 52–54; and oil, 118–20, 122, 180; and oil companies, 175; and organizing, 5, 149, 263–64, 269–70, 272, 280; and Pennsylvania, 42; and pension system, 235, 235; and Phillip Murray, 42; and Pittsburgh Coal Company, 42; policy committee, 76; and press office, 305; and Price-Anderson, 127; and Price-Anderson Act, 119; and Research Department, 151, 288; and safety practices, 87; and Sam Church, 322–24; and "social contract," 95, 176, 263, 271; and Solid Duels Administration for the War (SFAW), 77–78; and South Africa, 270; and steel companies, 68; and strip mining, 220–21; and Tennessee Valley Authority (TVA), 53–54, 121–22; and trade liberalization, 105; and unionism, 40; and utility markets, 105; and U.S. energy system, 43, 97–98; and W. A. "Tony" Boyle, 118, 140, 150–51; and welfare system, 235; Welfare and Retirement Fund, 92, 141, 147, 196, 240, 308; and West Virginia, 35–36, 40, 126, 133; and workplace action, 275

United States Army, 33–34, 86, 304

United States Department of Labor, 117–18, 237, 256–57, 327

uranium, 179, 182, 184; miners, 126–27, 131–32, 134; mining, 129, 132–33, 163, 174, 180

Venezuela, 103–4, 270

Vietnam War, 185, 190, 227, 238, 247, 267, 301

Virginia, 110, 130, 289

War Department, 33

warfare state, 67, 69–70, 89

war mobilization, 69, 71–72, 74, 76, 80, 83–84, 92, 300

War on Poverty, 165, 244

War Production Board, 75

wartime production, 70, 85, 95, 97, 104, 116

Wagers, Charlie, 202–4

Watson, Clarence W., 187

West Virginia, 30, 52–53, 146, 168, 213, 227, 259, 282, 290; and anti-strip mining activism, 221, 223–24; and Arch Moore, 153, 229; and Beckley, 256; and black lung activism, 151, 153, 157, 166, 244; and Black Lung Association, 149, 218, 243; and Bluefield, 17; and central competitive field (CCF), 37–38; and coal industry, 20, 22, 29, 31, 37, 81, 87, 133, 150, 159, 191, 243–44, 315, 318, 321; and coalfield wars, 18, 33; and coal miners, 49, 246, 283, 307; and Consol No. 9, 229; Department of Mines, 88; and energy policy, 289,

292, 303; and Farmington, 84, 137–38; and Federal Energy Office (FEO), 284–85; and Hulett Smith, 140; and Jennings Randolph, 126, 158; and James Kee, 111, 130; and Jimmy Carter, 312; and House of Delegates, 245; and Ken Hechler, 139, 148; and Logan County, 24, 31, 78, 258; and Marshall College, 148; and Matewan, 33, 317; and McDowell County, 247; and Miners for Democracy, 232, 252; and Mingo County, 111, 166; and mine disasters, 86; and Powder River Basin, 319; and Raleigh County, 149; and reform groups, 9; southern, 20, 22, 33–36, 41–42, 81, 167, 192, 219; and state law, 153; and strikes, 196, 206, 286, 309; and strip mining, 221, 223; State Police, 34; and Tazewell County, 283; and United Mine Workers (UMW), 40, 47; and Upper Big Branch mine, 327; and Wheeling, 68, 241

Whitfield, Ed, 31

Whitney, Earl, 31
Willard, Lester, 138–39, 154
Wilson, Woodrow, 33, 138–39
Wirtz, Willard, 310
workplace death, 29, 70, 155, 163, 205, 239. *See also* miners' deaths
workplace safety, 6, 64, 119, 137, 163–64, 189, 206, 240, 259, 314, 318
World War II, 3, 28, 67–68, 70, 73, 88, 136, 140, 187, 192, 306, 310, 312; and energy system, 74, 78–79; and miners, 107

Yablonski, Chip, 166, 168, 192–97, 288, 290–91
Yablonski, Ken, 168, 237
Yablonski, Joseph A. "Jock," 173–74, 192, 244; and grievance procedures, 164; murder of, 168–69, 240; platform of, 161–65; and United Mine Workers' presidential election, 160–62, 165, 220; and W. A. "Tony" Boyle, 118, 166

Zell, Ray, 108–10, 114–16, 127, 131

Printed in the USA
CPSIA information can be obtained
at www.ICGtesting.com
JSHW021347120924
69788JS00004B/100